Angela Davis / *An Autobiography*

Photos
(courtesy Mr. & Mrs. B. Frank Davis):

1. Angela at fifteen months.
2. Visiting New York, July, 1951.
3. Angela left, Fania right, summer, 1952.
4. Junior year at Brandeis.

Angela Davis

AN AUTOBIOGRAPHY

International Publishers

New York

Reprint, 1988 by International Publishers, New York

Printed in the United States of America

this printing, 2020

LIBRARY OF CONGRESS
Library of Congress Cataloging-in-Publication Data

Davis, Angela Yvonne, 1944-
    Angela Davis--an autobiography.
        p.   cm.
    Reprint, with new introd. Originally published: New York : Random House, [1974].
    ISBN-13: 978-0-7178-0667-6 (pbk.)
    1. Davis, Angela Yvonne, 1944-   2. Afro-Americans--Biography.
I. Title.
E185.97.D23A3 1988
322.4'2'0924--dc19
    [B]   88-8232
                                                                CIP

For my family, my strength
For my comrades, my light.
For the sisters and brothers whose fighting spirit was my
*   liberator.*
For those whose humanity is too rare to be destroyed
*   by walls, bars, and death houses.*
And especially for those who are going to struggle until
*   racism and class injustice are forever banished*
*   from our history.*

Introduction

This new edition of my autobiography appears nearly fifteen years after its first publication. I now appreciate the prodding of those who persuaded me to write about my experiences at what I thought was far too young an age to produce a comprehensive autobiographical work of significant value to its audience. Were I to contemplate today the preceding forty-four years of my life, the book I would write would be entirely different in both form and content. But I am glad that I wrote this book at age twenty-eight because it is, I think, an important piece of historical description and analysis of the late 1960s and early 1970s. It is also my own personal history up to that time, comprehended and delineated from that particular vantage point.

During that period of my life when, like many others, every moment of the day was devoted to the quest for activist solutions to the immediate practical problems posed by the Black liberation movement and for appropriate responses to the repressions emanating from the adversarial forces in that drama, I did realize how important it was to preserve the history of those struggles for the benefit of our posterity. Nevertheless, for the participants in those movements, the frantic pace of events seemed to preclude the kind of contemplative attitude necessary to chronicle and interpret those struggles from the standpoint of history.

When I expressed my initial hesitancy to begin working on an autobiography, it was not because I did not wish to write about the events of that time and generally in my lifetime, but rather because I did not want to contribute to the already widespread tendency to personalize and individualize history. And to be perfectly candid, my own instinctive reserve made me feel rather embarrassed to be writing about myself. So I did not really write about myself. That is to say, I did not measure the events of my own life according to their possible personal importance. Rather I attempted to utilize the autobiographical genre to evaluate my life in accordance with what I considered to be the political significance of my experiences. The political manner of measurement emanated from my work as an activist in the Black movement and as a member of the Communist Party.

When I was writing this book, I was vehemently opposed to the notion, developed within the young women's liberation movement, which naively and uncritically equated things personal with things political. In my mind, this idea tended to render equivalent such vastly disparate phenomena as racist police murders of Black people and the sexist-inspired verbal abuse of white women by their husbands. Since I personally witnessed police violence on a number of occasions during that period, my negative response to the feminist slogan, "the personal is political," was quite understandable. While I continue to disagree with all easy attempts to define these two dimensions as equivalent, I do understand that there is a sense in which all efforts to draw definitive lines of demarcation between the personal and political inevitably misconstrue social reality. For example, domestic violence is no less an expression of the prevailing politics of gender because it occurs within the private sphere of a personal relationship. I therefore express my regrets that I was not able to also apply a measuring stick which manifested a more complex understanding of the dialectics of the personal and the political.

The real strength of my approach at that time resides, I think, in its honest emphasis on grassroots contributions and achievements, so as to demystify the usual notion that history is the product of unique individuals possessing inherent qualities of greatness. Many people unfortunately assumed that because my name and my case were so extensively publicized, the contest that unfolded during my incarceration and trial from 1970 to 1972 was one in which a single Black woman successfully fended off the repressive might of the state. Those of us with a history of active struggle against political repression understood, of course, that while one of the protagonists in this battle was indeed the state, the other was not a single individual, but rather the collective power of the thousands and thousands of people opposed to racism and political repression. As a matter of fact, the underlying reasons for the extensive publicity accorded my trial had less to do with the sensationalist coverage of the prisoner uprising at the Marin County Courthouse than with the work of untold numbers of anonymous individuals who were moved to action, not so much by my particular predicament as by the cumulative work of the progressive movements of that period. Certainly the victory we won when I was acquitted of all charges can still be claimed today as a milestone in the work of grassroots movements.

The political threads in my life have remained essentially continuous since the early 1970s. In 1988, I remain a member of the National Committee of the Communist Party and I continue to work with the National Alliance Against Racist and Political Repression. I have also become an active member of the executive board of the National Black Women's Health Project.

This is a time when increasing numbers of people find themselves attracted to progressive causes. During the past eight years of the Reagan Administration, even as conservative forces in power have brought about the erosion of some of our previous victories, we have also witnessed a powerful surge of mass activism within the labor movement, on the campuses, and in the communities. Extensive and influential movements against apartheid in South Africa, against domestic racism, against intervention in Central America and against plant closings at home have compelled the political establishment to seriously address these issues. As more labor activists and women of color have begun to give leadership to the women's movement, the campaign for women's equality has acquired a much-needed breadth and has accordingly matured. As a direct result of grassroots activism, there are more progressive Black elected officials than ever before. And even though he did not win the Democratic Party presidential nomination, Jesse Jackson conducted a truly triumphant campaign, one that confirmed and further nurtured progressive thought patterns among the people of our country.

As I write this introduction, I join many friends and comrades in mourning the untimely death of Aaron Boye. Aaron was the nephew of Charlene Mitchell, of Franklin and Kendra Alexander, and the cousin of Steven Mitchell—all of whom are frequently mentioned in the pages of this autobiography. When Aaron graduated from UCLA two years ago, he invited me to speak at the Black students' graduation ceremonies. In my remarks, I urged the students to remain cognizant of the struggles which had carved out a place for them at that institution and to be willing, in turn, to add their own contributions to the ongoing quest for justice and equality. Surrounded in his childhood by relatives and friends who had dedicated their lives to these causes, Aaron was keenly aware that he had reaped the fruit of their contributions. And he had begun long ago to sow the seed for future struggles.

As this autobiography was originally dedicated to comrades who gave their lives during an earlier period, I add Aaron Boye's name to the roster of those who, were they still among us, would be on the frontlines today.

Angela Davis / An Autobiography

Acknowledgments

Unfortunately, it is not possible to include here the names of all those who helped in some way with the preparation of this book. However, there are some people who deserve special mention.

The writing of this book allowed me to work with and get to know a person who is a magnificent writer and inspiring Black woman. As my editor, Toni Morrison not only gave me invaluable assistance, but she was patient and understanding when the work on the book had to be continually interrupted by my responsibility in the movement to free political prisoners.

I am deeply grateful to the Cuban Communist Party and its First Secretary Fidel Castro for having invited me to spend several months in Cuba to work full time on the manuscript.

Charlene Mitchell, Franklin Alexander, Victoria Mercado, Bettina Aptheker, Michael Meyerson, Curtis Stewart, and my attorney, Leo Branton, read the manuscript at various stages. Sandy Frankel and the sisters and brothers on the staff of the

National Alliance Against Racist and Political Repression always tried to effectively blend my work on the book with the urgent task I had to perform as the Co-Chairperson of the Alliance. I am in debt to all of them.

Preface

I was not anxious to write this book. Writing an autobiography at my age seemed presumptuous. Moreover, I felt that to write about my life, what I did, what I thought and what happened to me would require a posture of difference, an assumption that I was unlike other women—other Black women—and therefore needed to explain myself. I felt that such a book might end up obscuring the most essential fact: the forces that have made my life what it is are the very same forces that have shaped and misshaped the lives of millions of my people. Furthermore I am convinced that my response to these forces has been unexceptional as well, that my political involvement, ultimately as a member of the Communist Party, has been a natural, logical way to defend our embattled humanity.

The one extraordinary event of my life had nothing to do with me as an individual—with a little twist of history, another sister or brother could have easily become the political prisoner whom millions of people from throughout the world rescued from persecution and death. I was reluctant to write this book because concentration on my personal history might detract from the movement which brought my case to the people in the first place. I was also unwilling to render my life as a personal "adventure"—as though there were a "real" person separate and apart from the political person. My life would not lend itself to this anyway, but even if it did, such a book would be counterfeit, for it could not convey my overwhelming sense of belonging to a community of humans—a community of struggle against poverty and racism.

When I decided to write the book after all, it was because I had come to envision it as a *political* autobiography that emphasized the people, the events and the forces in my life that propelled me to my present commitment. Such a book might serve a very important and practical purpose. There was the possibility that, having read it, more people would understand why so many of us have no alternative but to offer our lives— our bodies, our knowledge, our will—to the cause of our oppressed people. In this period when the covers camouflaging the corruption and racism of the highest political offices are rapidly falling away, when the bankruptcy of the global system of capitalism is becoming apparent, there was the possibility that more people—Black, Brown, Red, Yellow and white —might be inspired to join our growing community of struggle. Only if this happens will I consider this project to have been worthwhile.

Contents

The net will be torn by
the horn of a leaping calf . . .

PART ONE

Nets

7 believe I thanked her but I am not sure. Perhaps I simply watched her dig into the shopping bag and accepted in silence the wig she held out to me. It lay like a small frightened animal in my hand. I was alone with Helen hiding from the police and grieving over the death of someone I loved. Two days earlier, in her house perched on a hill in Los Angeles' Echo Park, I learned of the Marin County Courthouse revolt and the death of my friend Jonathan Jackson. Two days earlier I had never heard of Ruchell Magee, James McClain or William Christmas—the three San Quentin prisoners who, along with Jonathan, had been involved in the revolt which left him, McClain and William Christmas dead. But on that evening, it seemed as though I had known them for a very long time.

I walked toward the bathroom and stood before the mirror trying to fit the ends of my hair under the tight elastic. Like broken wings my hands floundered about my head, my thoughts completely dissociated from their movement. When finally I glanced into the mirror to see whether there were still bits of my own hair unconcealed by the wig, I saw a face so filled with anguish, tension and uncertainty I did not recognize it as my own. With the false black curls falling over a wrinkled forehead into red swollen eyes, I looked absurd, grotesque. I snatched the wig off my head, threw it on the floor and hit the sink with my fist. It remained cold, white and impenetrable. I forced the wig back on my head. I had to look normal; I could not arouse the suspicion of the attendant in the station where we would have to gas up the car. I didn't want to attract the attention of someone who might drive up alongside us and look in our direction while we waited at an intersection for the light to turn green. I had to look as commonplace as a piece of everyday Los Angeles scenery.

I told Helen that we would leave as soon as it got dark. But night would not shake off the day that kept clinging to its edges. We waited. Silently. Hidden behind drawn curtains, we listened to the street noises coming through the slightly opened balcony window. Each time a car slowed down or stopped, each time footsteps tapped the pavement outside, I held my breath—wondering whether we might have waited too long.

Helen didn't talk very much. It was better that way. I was glad that she had been with me during these last days. She was calm and did not try to bury the gravity of the situation under a mound of aimless chatter.

I don't know how long we had been sitting in the dimly lit room when Helen broke the silence to say that it was probably not going to get any darker outside. It was time to leave. For the first time since we discovered that the police were after me, I stepped outside. It was much darker than I thought, but not dark enough to keep me from feeling vulnerable, defenseless.

Outside in the open, entangled in my grief and anger was also fear. A plain and simple fear so overwhelming, and so elemental that the only thing I could compare it to was that sense of engulfment I used to feel as a child when I was left alone in the dark. That indescribable, monstrous thing would be at my back, never quite touching me, but always there ready to attack. When my mother and father asked me what it was that made me so afraid, the words I used to describe this thing sounded ridiculous and stupid. Now with each step, I could feel a presence which I could describe easily. Images of attack kept flashing into my mind, but they were not abstract —they were clear pictures of machine guns breaking out of the darkness, surrounding Helen and me, unleashing fire . . .

Jonathan's body had lain on the hot asphalt of the parking lot outside the Marin County Civic Center. I saw them on the television screen dragging him from a van, a rope tied around his waist . . .

In Jon's seventeen years he had seen more brutality than most people can expect to see in a lifetime. From the time he was seven, he had been separated from his older brother George by prison bars and hostile guards. And I had once stupidly asked him why he smiled so seldom.

The route from Echo Park down to the Black neighborhood around West Adams was very familiar to me. I had driven it many times. But tonight the way seemed strange, full of the unknown perils of being a fugitive. And there was no getting around it—my life was now that of a fugitive, and fugitives are caressed every hour by paranoia. Every strange person I saw might be an agent in disguise, with bloodhounds waiting in the shrubbery for their master's command. Living as a fugitive means resisting hysteria, distinguishing between the creations of a frightened imagination and the real signs that the enemy is near. I had to learn how to elude him, outsmart him. It would be difficult, but not impossible.

Thousands of my ancestors had waited, as I had done, for nightfall to cover their steps, had leaned on one true friend to help them, had felt, as I did, the very teeth of the dogs at their heels.

It was simple. I had to be worthy of them.

The circumstances that created my hunted state were perhaps a bit more complicated, but not all that different. Two years before, SNCC had held a fund-raising cocktail party. After the party, the police had raided the Bronson Street apartment of Franklin and Kendra Alexander—who were members of the Communist Party, and two of my closest friends—where a few of the group had gathered. Money and guns were confiscated and everyone there was arrested on charges of armed robbery. As soon as they discovered that one of the weapons—a .380 automatic—was registered in my name, they called me in for questioning. The charges did not stand up in court and, after a few nights in jail, the sisters and brothers were released and the guns returned to their owners.

The same .380 which the Los Angeles Police had reluctantly returned to me then was now in the hands of the Marin County authorities, having been used during the courthouse revolt. The judge presiding over James McClain's trial had been killed and the district attorney prosecuting the case had been wounded. Even before Franklin told me about the police lurking around my house, I knew they would be after me. Over the last months I had been spending practically all my time helping to build a mass movement to free the Soledad Brothers—Jonathan's brother, George, John Clutchette and Fleeta Drumgo—who were facing a fraudulent murder charge inside Soledad Prison. I had just been fired from my teaching position at the University of California by Governor Ronald Reagan and the Regents because I was a member of the Communist Party. No one needed to tell me that they would exploit the fact that my guns had been used in Marin in order to strike out at me once more.

By August 9, agents (Los Angeles police? FBI?) were swarming like angry wasps around Kendra, Franklin and my roommate, Tamu. Other members of the Che-Lumumba Club —our Party collective—and the Soledad Brothers Defense

Committee had told Franklin they were also under surveillance. Coming up to Helen and Tim's apartment in Echo Park that day, it had taken Franklin several hours to shake off the police tail—several hours of dodging and hiding, of changing cars in vacant alleys and of going in front doors and leaving by the back. He was afraid to risk another trip to get in touch with me. It might not be as successful.

If a full-fledged search were initiated, Helen and Tim's place would not be safe. I had known them for a number of years, and although they were not members of any movement organization, they had a history of radical political activity. Sooner or later, their names would appear in some policeman's notebook. We had to make a quick, camouflaged move.

The address given to Helen and me was located on a quiet, well-kept street in the West Adams area. The house was an older duplex encircled by nicely shaped hedges and flowers in bloom. After saying an awkward good-bye to Helen, I left the car and timidly rang the doorbell. What if we had misunderstood the house number and this was the wrong place? Anxiously waiting for the door to open, I wondered what the people were like, how they looked, how they would react to me. All I knew was that the woman, Hattie, and her husband, John, were Black people sympathetic to the movement. They had no questions when I arrived, and they ignored the usual formalities. They simply took me in, accepted me—totally and with the affection and devotion ordinarily reserved for family. They allowed their lives to be disrupted by my presence. For my protection, they reorganized their routines in order that one of them would be in the house all the time. Excuses were made to their regular visiting friends so no one would know that I was there.

After a few days, I began to feel as settled and comfortable as I could in such circumstances. It seemed as though I might be able to learn how to close my eyes for a few hours at night without falling into some terrifying nightmare about what had happened in Marin. I was even beginning to get used to the old iron bed which folded down out of the dining room wall. I was almost able to concentrate on the anecdotes Hattie told me about her career as an entertainer and how she had plowed her way through all the discrimination to assert herself as the dancer she wanted to be.

I was ready to hole up there indefinitely; that is, until the times were more auspicious. But the search for me had intensified (conservative newscaster George Putnam had announced on his TV program in L.A. that it extended even to Canada). Clearly it was best to get out of the state for a while.

I hated what I was doing: the nighttime moves, the veiling of eyes, the whole atmosphere of stealth and secretness. Although it was true that, for a long time, I had been convinced that the day would come when many of us would have to go underground, the realization of my fears didn't stop me from hating this furtive, clandestine existence.

A friend, David Poindexter, was in Chicago. I had not seen him for a long while, but I was certain that he would drop everything to help. I was prepared to make the trip alone and did not expect Hattie to insist on staying with me until I found David. I wondered at the source of her strength. It was as if she had to do this thing, regardless of the jeopardy to her own life.

After the preparations were made, we drove all night to Las Vegas. My friends had asked an older Black man—whom I met for the first time that night—to accompany us on that leg of the journey.

All dressed up, Hattie looked very much like the dancer she had been in her younger years. With the grace and dignity of a Josephine Baker, she turned heads wherever she went. In the Vegas airport, for the first time since I had gone underground, I was walking among people, and each time a white man stared at us harder than I thought he should, my pounding heart identified him as an agent.

Everyone knew that O'Hare Airport in Chicago was a center of intrigue and heavy CIA-FBI surveillance. We slipped through the throngs of people, frantically searching for David, who had not been there to meet us at the gate. I was cursing him under my breath, although I knew he was probably not to blame. It turned out that the message sent to him had been too cryptic and he had thought I would come straight to his place. We ended up taking a taxi there.

Hattie left after seeing me safely into David's apartment overlooking the calm waters of Lake Michigan. Although I was glad to see him, I had grown so close to Hattie that it hurt to see her leave. When we embraced, I couldn't say thank you—those words were far too small for someone who had risked her life to help save mine.

David was in the middle of a remodeling job on his apartment, and practically everything was in disarray. Wallpaper half-pasted on the walls, furniture piled up in the middle of the living room, paintings, little sculptures and other objects spread randomly across the couch.

I had forgotten how much David liked to talk. Whether he was discussing a problem of politics or telling you about a spot you had on your blouse, he was always glib. In the first five minutes he hit me with so many things that I had to ask him to slow down and backtrack a bit.

After I put down my things and splashed some cold water on my face, we went into his study and sat down on the thick blue carpet amid the deshelved books strewn across the room. There we talked about the situation. He couldn't cancel his trip out West, which was scheduled for the next day, he said, but he would shorten it in order to be back in a few days.

The prospect of spending the next days alone was appealing. I could use the time to orient myself, to reflect on the coming weeks, to pull myself together. The solitude would be good.

Later, David introduced me to Robert Lohman, who lived in the same building. Robert Lohman was, at the moment of the introduction, David's "very close friend." Someone who could be trusted, who, over the next days, would be available any time I needed him to look in on me, see to it that food was in the refrigerator and, if I felt like company, be happy to come up.

It was afternoon when I met Robert. By evening, he and David had been drawn into a ferocious argument about their jointly owned automobile. (Suppose David were captured driving me in a car that was registered to Robert . . .) When the hurling of words had subsided, their friendship was in ruins and Robert was in our eyes a potential informer. This forced us to rethink all of our plans.

David and I drove another car through the heavy night rain to the house where he and his wife had lived before her death. He refused to listen when I tried to apologize for driving this wedge into his life, for wrecking his friendships, forcing him, ultimately, to cancel his important trip to the West. All these things were trivial, he said.

Before David fell asleep (I sat up all night) we decided that it would be best to leave the city the next day.

My disguise had been all right for the first leg of the trip. But it was not good enough for a situation that would grow increasingly more dangerous. The curly wig, too close to the shape of my natural, did not really change the appearance of my face. Before we left Chicago, a young Black woman, to whom I identified myself as David's cousin in trouble, gave me another wig that was straight and stiff, with long bangs and elaborate spitcurls. She pulled out half of my eyebrows, glued false eyelashes to my lids, covered my face with all sorts of creams and powders and put a little black dot just above the corner of my lip. I felt awkward and over-painted, but I doubted my own mother could have recognized me.

We had decided to head for Miami. Since airports were more closely watched than anyplace else, we plotted a ground route—by car to New York and by train to Miami. After the car was rented and David had packed his things, we set out on this wild odyssey, the details of which we had to improvise as we went along.

In a turnpike motel on the outskirts of Detroit, I turned on the television to watch the news. "Today, Angela Davis, wanted on charges of murder, kidnapping and conspiracy in connection with the Marin County Courthouse shootout, was seen leaving the home of her parents in Birmingham, Alabama. She is known to have attended a meeting of the local branch of the Black Panther Party. When Birmingham authorities finally caught up with her, she managed to outrun them, driving her 1959 blue Rambler . . ."

Was it my sister they were talking about? But she was supposed to be in Cuba. And the last time I had seen my car, it was parked outside Kendra and Franklin's on 50th Street in L.A.

I was afraid for my parents. The FBI and the local police force must have been hovering around the house like buzzards. Knowing that the lines were tapped, I had not risked a phone call. All I could do was hope that Franklin had found some way to tell them that I was safe.

In the city of Detroit, we lost ourselves in the crowds as we searched for an optometrist who could quickly make me up a pair of glasses. I hadn't been home since the news of the rebellion, and had no luggage. I had to buy some clothes so I could get out of the things I had been wearing for the last few days.

From Detroit, we drove on to New York, where we boarded a train that took almost two days to arrive in Miami. There, under the blinding late summer sun, I barricaded myself inside an unfurnished apartment David rented, waiting for the times to change. I felt almost as much a prisoner as if I had been locked up in a jail and often felt jealous because David could go out when he wished—he even traveled back to Chicago. I stayed in, read and watched television news: draconic repression of the Palestinian movement by King Hussein of Jordan; the first of the major prison rebellions at the Tombs in New York.

There was never any news of George. Of George, John, Fleeta, Ruchell, San Quentin . . .

❋   ❋   ❋

Toward the end of September, signs pointed to a hot and deadly pursuit. David's mother, who lived near Miami, told him that two men had come to her house inquiring as to his whereabouts. The old fears erupted again, and I began to seriously doubt that it would be possible to elude the police without leaving the country altogether. But each time I considered going abroad, the thought of being indefinitely exiled in some other country was even more horrible than the idea of being locked up in jail. At least in jail I would be closer to my people, closer to the movement.

No. I would not leave the country, but I thought that I could lead the FBI to believe that I had managed to get out. The last thing I did in that bare Miami apartment was to draw up a statement to be delivered to someone who could release it to the press. I wrote about Jonathan's youthful, even romantic, determination to challenge the injustices of the prison system and about the tremendous loss we had experienced when he was killed on August 7 in Marin County. I affirmed my innocence and, implying that I was already out of the country, promised that when the political climate in California became less hysterical, I would return to clear myself through the courts. Meanwhile, I wrote, the struggle would go on.

OCTOBER 13, 1970

We were back in New York. I had been underground about two months. With the familiar tightness in my stomach, the now habitual knot in my throat, I woke up, got dressed, and struggled with my disguise. Another tedious twenty minutes trying to get the eye make-up to look presentable. More impatient pulls at the wig, trying to lessen the discomfort of the tight-fitting elastic. I tried to forget that today, perhaps tomorrow, perhaps any of a long string of days to come, might be the day of my capture.

When David Poindexter and I left the Howard Johnson Motor Lodge late that morning in October, the situation had become desperate. We were rapidly running out of money and everyone we knew was under surveillance. Wandering through the surrounding Manhattan neighborhood, we thought about our next move. Strolling down Eighth Avenue, lost in crowds of New Yorkers oblivious to everything going on around them, I felt better than I had in the motel. Hoping to calm our nerves, we decided to spend the afternoon at the movies. To this day I do not remember what movie we saw. I was hopelessly preoccupied with problems of eluding the police, wondering how much longer I could tolerate isolation, knowing that to contact anyone would be suicide.

The movie was over shortly before six. David and I talked very little as we headed in the direction of the motel. We passed the broken-down shops on Eighth Avenue and were crossing over to the motel side of the street when suddenly I seemed to see police agents all around me. Surely this was just another one of my recurring fits of paranoia. Yet as we walked through the glass doors of the motel, I had a sudden impulse to turn around and race back into the anonymous crowds I had just left. But if my instincts were correct, if all these nondescript white men were in fact policemen surrounding us, then the slightest abrupt move on my part would give them the excuse they needed to shoot us down on the spot. I remembered how they had murdered li'l Bobby Hutton, how they shot him in the back after telling him to run. If, on the other hand, my instincts were groundless, my running would only arouse suspicion. I had no choice but to keep on walking.

Inside the lobby, my fears seemed to be confirmed in every straight-looking white man standing around. I was positive that all these men were agents standing in a formation previously agreed upon, preparing themselves for attack. But nothing happened. As nothing had happened in the motel in Detroit, when I had also been certain that we were about to be captured. As nothing had happened on the countless other occasions when my unnaturally high level of tension had transformed perfectly ordinary events into scenes of impending capture.

I wondered what David was thinking. It seemed like a long time since we had said anything to each other. He could conceal his nervousness in tight situations and, besides, we rarely talked about those moments when we must both have suspected that the police were about to pounce upon us. When we made it past the front desk, I breathed a sigh of relief. Nothing had broken. This was probably just another normal day in the life of this typical New York motel.

I was just beginning to recuperate when a plump, red-faced white man, wearing what could have been the short, regulation haircut of a policeman, got into the elevator with us. My fears were rekindled. I again held my ritual soliloquy: He was probably an executive; after all, if you're being pursued, all white men with short hair and plain suits look like police agents. Besides, if they had really caught up with us, wouldn't it have been more logical for them to make the arrest downstairs?

During the interminable elevator ride to the seventh floor, I convinced myself that my overactive imagination had created this aura of danger, and that we would probably make it safely through that day. One more day.

Out of the habit of living in clandestinity, I lingered behind several yards while David went ahead to check out the room. While he was turning the key in the lock, which appeared to present more difficulties than usual, someone opened a door on the other side of the corridor. A frail figure peered through and, although he didn't look like a policeman, his sudden appearance sent me tumbling back into my terrifying fantasies. Of course, this pale little man could have simply been a motel guest on his way to dinner. But something told me that the scenario of the arrest had begun and that this man was number one in the cast. I thought I felt someone behind me. The man in the elevator. Now there was not the slightest trace of uncertainty in my mind. This was the real thing.

Precisely at the moment when all panic should have broken loose inside me, I felt calmer and more composed than I had in a long time. I lifted my head higher and began to stride confidently toward my room. As I passed the open door facing my room, the frail man reached out and grabbed my arm. He said nothing. More agents were pouring out behind him and others were streaming out of a room across the hall. "Angela Davis?" "Are you Angela Davis?" The questions were coming from all directions. I glared at them.

During the ten or twelve seconds between the elevator and the point of confrontation, all kinds of thoughts tore through my mind. I remembered the television program I had watched in the Miami apartment: *The FBI*—a typical, inane TV melodrama of agents pursuing fugitives, complete with the final violent encounter which left the pursued with bullets in their skulls and the FBI agents shown as heroes. Just as I moved to turn off the set, a photograph of me flashed on the screen as if it were a part of the fictionalized FBI pursuit. "Angela Davis," a deep voice said, "is one of the FBI's ten most wanted criminals. She is wanted for the crimes of murder, kidnapping and conspiracy. She is very likely armed, so if you see her, do not try to do anything. Contact your local FBI immediately." In other words, let your "very likely armed" FBI have the honor of shooting her down.

David and I were unarmed. If they pulled out their weapons we wouldn't have a chance. As the frail man reached for me, I saw the guns coming out. I imagined the deafening noise of gunshots and our bodies lying in pools of blood in the corridor of the Howard Johnson motel.

They forced David into a room on the right side of the corridor and shoved me into one on the left. There they ripped the wig off my head, cuffed my hands behind me and fingerprinted me on the spot. All the while pelting me with the same question: "Are you Angela Davis?" "Angela Davis?" "Angela Davis?" I said nothing. Obviously they had gone through similar scenes many times before. They had rehearsed this moment with the false arrests of scores, perhaps hundreds of tall, light-skinned Black women with large naturals. Only the fingerprints would tell them whether they had caught the real one this time. The prints were compared. The panic on the chief's face was replaced by relief. His underlings were ransacking my purse like bandits. As I stood there, determined to preserve my dignity, elaborate preparations were being made to get me out. I could hear them alerting other agents who must have been stationed at various points in and outside of the motel. All these "precautions," all these dozens of agents fit in perfectly with the image they had constructed of me as one of the country's ten most wanted criminals: the big bad Black Communist enemy.

About ten agents shoved me through the crowd that had already gathered in the downstairs lobby and on the sidewalk. A long caravan of unmarked cars was waiting. Speeding through the streets, I caught a glimpse of another caravan taking David to some unknown destination.

My hands were so tightly cuffed behind me that if I had not balanced my body on the very edge of the back seat, the circulation in my arms would have stopped. The agent in the front seat turned around and, smiling, said, "Miss Davis, would you like a cigarette?"

I spoke for the first time since the capture. "Not from you."

Inside the FBI headquarters, where the caravan came to a halt, I was met by a woman with bleached-out hair who looked more like a truck-stop waitress than the police matron she was. She searched me in a little room that looked like a gynecologist's office, although my short knit skirt and thin cotton blouse couldn't have concealed a weapon of any description.

Later, in a room with fluorescent lights flooding bright-red vinyl couches, some agents strode in with stacks of papers in their hands. They took seats directly opposite me and spread out their papers, confident that they were about to get into a long, involved interrogation. Before they formulated their first question, I told them I had nothing to say to the FBI.

I knew that they could not legally hold me for any period of time without allowing me to contact a lawyer. Nevertheless, each time I demanded access to a telephone, they ignored me.

Finally, they said that an attorney, Gerald Lefcourt, was on the telephone and that I could speak to him. I had never met Lefcourt before, but his name was familiar to me in connection with his work for the twenty-one members of the Black Panther Party on trial in New York.

In a gigantic room, a telephone with its receiver off the hook sat on one of the scores of desks. But Lefcourt was not on the other end, only silence. Looking around the room, I noticed my belongings spread out on some of the desks a few yards away from where I was sitting. David's possessions were scattered on another series of desks. Agents were hovering over our things, going through them meticulously.

The bearers of the handcuffs, who had removed them for the search and the mug shots and fingerprints, reappeared to fasten them on my wrists once more. I wondered why they cuffed my hands in front this time.

Going down in the elevator, my thoughts were far away. I was trying to figure out how to reach a comrade or a friend. When the doors slid open, furious flashes of light jolted me out of my reflections. That's why they had cuffed my hands in front. As far as I could see, reporters and photographers were crowded into the lobby.

Trying hard not to look surprised, I lifted my head, straightened my back and, between the two agents, made the long walk through the light flashes and staccato questions toward the caravan waiting outside.

When the wailing of the sirens tapered off and the caravan began to slow down, I realized that I was somewhere in Greenwich Village. As the car turned into a dark driveway, a corrugated aluminum door began to rise and once again, crowds of photographers with flashing lights jumped out of the shadows. The red brick wall surrounding this tall archaic structure looked very familiar, but it took me a few moments to locate it in my memory. Of course; it was the mysterious place I had seen so often during the years I attended Elisabeth Irwin High School, not too far from there. It was the New York Women's House of Detention, which stood there at the main intersection in the Village, at Greenwich and Sixth avenues.

While the car was rolling into the prisoners' entrance, a flock of memories fought for my attention. Walking to the subway station after school, I used to look up at this building almost every day, trying not to listen to the terrible noises spilling from the windows. They were coming from the women locked behind bars, looking down on the people passing in the streets, and screaming incomprehensible words.

At age fifteen I accepted some of the myths surrounding prisoners. I did not see them as quite the criminals society said they were, but they did seem aliens in the world I inhabited. I never knew what to do when I saw the outlines of women's heads through the almost opaque windows of the jail. I could never understand what they were saying—whether they were crying out for help, whether they were calling for someone in particular, or whether they simply wanted to talk to anyone who was "free." My mind was now filled with the specters of those faceless women whom I had not answered. Would I scream out at the people passing in the streets, only to have them pretend not to hear me as I once pretended not to hear those women?

The inside of this jail stood in stark contrast to the building I had just left. The FBI headquarters was modern, antiseptically clean, its plastic texture illuminated by fluorescent lights. The Women's House of Detention was old, musty, dreary and dim. The floor of the receiving room was unpainted cement, dirt from the shoes of thousands of prisoners, policemen and matrons etched into its surface. There was a single desk where all the paperwork seemed to be done, and rows of long benches which looked as though they had once been pews in a storefront church.

I was told to sit on the front bench in the right-hand row. A few other women were scattered unsystematically throughout the benches. Some, I learned, had just been booked; others had come in from a day in court. Food was brought in to us, but I had no appetite for the wrinkled hot dogs and cold potatoes.

Suddenly there was a loud rumble outside the gate. Scores of women were walking up to the entrance, waiting for the iron gate to be opened. I wondered what could have led to such a massive bust, but one of the sisters inside told me that these were the women returning from court on the last bus.

All the women I could see were either Black or Puerto Rican. There were no white prisoners in the group. One of the Puerto Rican sisters called out, "Are you Spanish?" At first I didn't think she could mean me, but then I remembered how I must have looked with my hair straight and flat after the agents had snatched the wig away. I said "no" with as warm a tone as I could manage, trying to convey that it did not really matter: the same jailers would be holding the same hammer over our heads. While the women who had returned from court were still standing outside the iron gates, I was led out of the room. I thought that I was on my way to the cells, but instead I found myself in a large windowless room, a dim light bulb barely illuminating the center of the ceiling. There were the same filthy cement floors, drab yellow tile walls and two very old office desks.

A robust white matron was in charge. When I discovered, amid the papers taped to the wall, my picture and description on an FBI Wanted poster, she snatched it down. My eyes shifted to the next poster. To my surprise it bore the photograph and description of a woman whom I had known in high school. Kathy Boudin had been in my eleventh- and twelfth-grade classes at Elisabeth Irwin High School. Now she was on the FBI's Wanted list.

When the work shift changed, I was still waiting in that dingy room. A new officer was sent to guard me. She was black, she was young—younger than I—she wore a natural, and as she approached, she showed none of the belligerence and arrogance I had learned to associate with jail matrons.

It was a disarming experience. Yet it was not the fact that

she was Black that threw me. I had encountered Black matrons before—in jails in San Diego and Los Angeles—but it was her manner: unaggressive and apparently sympathetic.

At first she was taciturn. But after a few minutes, in a quiet voice, she told me, "A lot of officers here—the Black officers—have been pulling for you. We've been hoping all along that you would get to someplace that was safe."

I wanted to talk to her, but I felt it was best to be wary of any involved conversation. For all I knew, she might have been instructed to assume this sympathetic posture. If I appeared to be deluded by her sympathy, if I appeared to become familiar with her, it would lend credibility should she decide to lie about the content of our conversations. I would be safer if I maintained the distance, the formality.

Thinking that I might be able to pry some information out of her about my predicament, I asked her why the delay was so long. She didn't know all the details, she said, but she thought that they were trying to decide how they could keep me away from the main jail population. The problem was the lack of facilities for isolation. It was her feeling that they would put me in 4b, the area of the jail reserved for women with psychological problems.

I looked at her in disbelief. If they locked me up in a tank for mental patients, their next step might be to declare me insane. Perhaps they would try to say that communism is a psychological illness—something akin to masochism, exhibitionism or sadism.

Surprised at my reaction, she tried to console me by saying that I'd probably be happier there—sometimes the women would ask to be moved to the "mental" cellblock because they couldn't tolerate the noise in the main population. But to me, jail was jail—there were no degrees of better or worse. And nothing could detract from the thought that they wanted to isolate me because they feared the impact the mere presence of a political prisoner would have on the other women.

I reminded the officer that I had not yet made the two

telephone calls due me. I needed a lawyer, and I knew I had the right to contact one.

"A lawyer by the name of John Abt has been trying to get in to see you," she said. "But visiting hours for attorneys are over at five o'clock. I'm sorry I can't do anything."

"If I can't see him, at least I ought to be able to call him."

"These people," she said, "haven't decided how to deal with you. They say you're a federal prisoner, under the jurisdiction of the federal marshals. We have federal prisoners all the time. The marshals are the ones who should have let you make the two phone calls. At least, that's what the captain said."

"For five hours," I insisted, "I have been trying to make a phone call, and everybody I ask gives me the run-around."

"You know, no prisoners here are actually allowed to use the phone. You have to write out your number and your message on a form and a special officer does the calling."

I started to protest, but soon realized that nothing I said would make them give me access to a telephone that evening. The only thing they relinquished was a card John Abt had left at the front gate.

The crowd of women just back from court had apparently been "processed," and I could now return to the receiving room to await my turn for this mysterious "process." As I entered the room, I saw a figure lying on a hospital cart, almost completely covered with a sheet. I didn't know whether it was living or dead. It was simply there, unattended, in the least conspicuous corner of the receiving room. When I tried to inspect it as carefully as I could from a distance, I noticed an elevation in the middle that seemed to be moving. It was a pregnant prisoner about to deliver—and soon. Wasn't anybody going to *do* anything? Were they going to let her have the baby right here in this dump? Even if they did take her to a halfway decent hospital, what would happen to the infant once it was born? Would it be placed in an orphanage while she did her time? I felt angry but helpless as I watched the sister go further and further into labor. Soon the iron gates opened, and the attendants of a police ambulance came to take her away. I watched them carry the stretcher into the night.

At last it was my turn. The print of my forefinger was stamped on an orange card, which, they informed me, was the jail identification that every prisoner had to keep with her at all times. Then came another body search. I vigorously protested this second search—the FBI had already done it once. The officer assigned to search me was ambivalent about the procedure. While I undressed in the shower room, she discreetly pretended to be looking for something. She gave me a hospital dressing gown and directed me to sit on a bench outside a closed door. From the women already waiting there, I learned that we were about to be searched internally. Each time prisoners left the jail for a court appearance, and upon their return, they had to submit to a vaginal and rectal examination.

It was one A.M. before they actually booked me into the jail. There were only three women left in the receiving room. One of them stared at me for a long time and finally asked whether I was Angela Davis. When I smiled and nodded, she said that coming in from court she had seen crowds outside demonstrating for me. All kinds of people—young, old, Black, white.

"What? Where?" I was tremendously excited by the possibility that people in the movement were near.

The sister told us to be quiet for a moment. If we listened especially hard, we might be able to hear some of the chants. Sure enough, muffled rhythms were penetrating these massive walls. Just outside the building, the sister said, they were chanting, "Free Angela Davis." The sister describing the scene was in jail for possession of heroin. (The first thing she was going to do when she got out, she said, was to look up her connection.) With an expression of triumph on her face, she assured me that I was going to win. She said this knowing that according to jail standards, I was facing very heavy charges.

The entire jail was shrouded in darkness when I finally reached the cell in 4b. It was no more than four and a half feet wide. The only furnishings were an iron cot bolted to the floor and a seatless toilet at the foot of the bed. Some minutes after they had locked me in, the officer in charge of that unit—another young Black woman—came to the iron door. She whispered through the grating that she was shoving a piece of candy under the door. She sounded sincere enough, but I couldn't take any chances. I didn't want to be paranoid, but it was better to be too distrustful than not cautious enough. I was familiar with jailhouse "suicides" in California. For all I knew, there might be poison in the candy.

The first night in jail, I had no desire to sleep. I thought about George and his brothers in San Quentin. I thought about Jonathan. I thought about my mother and father and hoped that they would make it through this ordeal. And then I thought about the demonstration outside, about all the people who had dropped everything to fight for my freedom.

I had just been captured; a trial awaited me in California on the charges of murder, kidnapping and conspiracy. A conviction on any one of these charges could mean death in the gas chamber. One would have thought that this was an enormous defeat. Yet, at that moment, I was feeling better than I had felt in a long time. The struggle would be difficult, but there was already a hint of victory. In the heavy silence of the jail, I discovered that if I concentrated hard enough, I could hear echoes of slogans being chanted on the other side of the walls. "Free Angela Davis." "Free All Political Prisoners."

The key rattling in the cell-gate lock startled me. A guard was opening the gate for a plump young Black woman wearing a faded blue prisoner's uniform and holding a big tray in her hands.

Smiling, she said in a very soft voice, "Here's your breakfast. Do you want some coffee?"

Her gentle manner was comforting and made me feel like I was among human beings again. I sat up on the cot, thanked her and told her that I would very much like a cup of coffee.

Looking around, I realized that there was no place to put the food—the bed and the toilet were the only furnishings in the tiny cell. But the sister, obviously having gone through this many times before, had already stooped down to a squatting position and was placing the food on the floor: a small box of cornflakes, a paper cup filled with watery milk, two pieces of plain white bread and a paper cup into which she began to pour the coffee.

"Is there any black coffee?" I asked her, partly because I didn't drink coffee with milk and partly because I wanted an excuse to exchange a few more words with her.

"When they give it to us, it's already like this," she answered, "but I'll see what I can do about getting you some black coffee tomorrow."

The guard told me I had to get ready for my court appearance. Then she slammed the gate on the young woman's exit. While she was unlocking the next cell, the sister whispered through the bars, "Don't worry about a thing. We're all on your side." And she disappeared down the corridor.

I looked down at my breakfast, and saw that a roach had already discovered it. I left it all spread out on the bare floor untouched.

After I had gone through the elaborate steps involved in getting dressed for court, a matron led me downstairs. A crowd of white men was milling around the receiving room. Seeing me, they swept toward me like vultures and clamped handcuffs around my wrists, which still ached from the previous day. Outside, shiny tan cars crowded into the cobblestone courtyard. It was still dark when the caravan reached the federal courthouse. A glimpse of the morning paper's bold-lettered headlines, peeping out from under some man's arm, stunned me: ANGELA DAVIS CAPTURED IN NEW YORK. It suddenly struck me that the huge crowd of press people summoned by the FBI the evening before had probably written similar headline stories throughout the country. Knowing that my name was now familiar to millions of people, I felt overwhelmed. Yet I knew that all this publicity was not really aimed at me as an individual. Using me as an example, they wanted to discredit the Black Liberation Movement, the Left in general and obviously also the Communist Party. I was only the occasion for their manipulations.

The holding cell where I spent the next several hours was cleaner than the jail cell I had just left and looked like a giant, unfinished bathroom. It had sparkling white tile walls and a light-colored linoleum floor. A seatless toilet stood in one of the corners. Long metal benches lined the three walls.

One of the federal bureaucrats came into the cell.

"I have nothing to say," I told him, "until I see my lawyer."

"Your father's lawyer is waiting outside," he said.

My father's lawyer? Perhaps it was a friend posing as my "father's lawyer" in order to get permission to see me.

In a large hall filled with rows of desks, John Abt was waiting to see me. Although I had never met him before I knew about the trials in which he had successfully defended members of our Party. With a great feeling of relief, I sat down to talk with him.

"I waited for hours last night at the jail, but they refused to let me in," John said. "I had to get your father to call them before they would let me see you this morning."

He went on to explain that I was about to be arraigned on the federal charges—interstate flight to avoid prosecution. Before he had gotten very far in his discussion of the legal proceedings before us, a group of people pressed through a door at the other end of the room. Without my glasses, which the FBI had not bothered to return, the people's faces were blurred. Noticing a young Black woman involved in a heated exchange with the marshals, I squinted in order to see her more clearly.

"That's Margaret!" I shouted.

Margaret Burnham was a very old friend of mine. During

my youngest years, her family and mine had lived in the same housing project in Birmingham. When the Burnhams moved to New York, we visited them every summer for four years, then we alternated the visits—sometimes they would come to Birmingham and we would go to New York. Our families had been so close that I had always considered Margaret, her sisters Claudia and Linda, and her brother Charles more family than friends. I had not seen her for several years. She had been in Mississippi, gotten married and given birth to a child. I knew that she had recently graduated from law school and I assumed she was now practicing in New York.

"Margaret," I called, as loudly as I could, "come on over." Apparently this was enough to settle the argument she was having with the marshal, for he did nothing to prevent her from walking over to the desk where John and I were. It felt so good to embrace her.

"Margaret," I said to her, "I'm so glad you came. You don't know how glad I am to see you." As we started talking about personal things, I almost forgot that there was business to be taken care of.

"Can you work on the case?" I asked her finally, desperately hoping she would say yes.

"You know I will, Angela," she answered, "if that's what you think I should do."

It was as if half the battle had already been won.

John Abt went on to explain the legal situation.

Back in August, Marin County had charged me with murder, kidnapping and conspiracy to commit murder and rescue prisoners. On the basis of an FBI agent's affidavit declaring that I had been seen by "reliable sources" in Birmingham, a federal judge had issued a warrant charging me with "interstate flight to avoid prosecution."

It was possible, John said, that I might be "removed" to California, which meant that without further litigation I would simply be transferred from the New York Federal District to the California Federal District. But more than likely, he surmised, I would be "turned over" to the State of New

York for extradition to California, and we would be able to challenge California in the New York courts.

As we were winding up this conference, David walked into the room, encircled by guards. I hadn't seen him since our arrest. He looked as if he hadn't slept either.

In a cool, crisp tone, he called out to me, "Remember now, no matter what, we're going to beat this thing."

"No talking between the prisoners," a voice announced. It could have come from any one of the marshals standing around.

"O.K., David," I said, ignoring the command. "You be sure to keep strong yourself."

I had never seen a courtroom so small. With its marred walls of blond wood, it had the worn-out elegance of an old mansion. There was just enough room for the bench and a single row of chairs lining the back wall. The smallness of the courtroom exaggerated the height of the judge's bench. The judge himself was little, like his courtroom. He was wearing old-fashioned plastic-rimmed glasses, and his white hair was spread sparsely over his head. I thought about Soledad guard O. G. Miller perched in his gun tower, aiming his carbine at the three brothers he killed in the yard in January.

There were no spectators. The only non-official people were reporters—and there were not very many of them. As I entered, a sister sitting in the seat closest to the door held up a copy of the hardcover edition of George's *Soledad Brother.* This was the first time I had seen the book, which I had read in manuscript.

The arraignment on the federal charges was short and to the point. All the prosecutor was required to do was to prove, for the record, that I was the Angela Davis named in the warrant. The bail figure was a farce. Who could even contemplate raising $250,000 to get me out of jail?

It was still early—late morning or early afternoon—when I returned to the holding cell. The last time I had been in the cell, my thoughts had been monopolized by the problem of finding a lawyer. Now that I had two fine lawyers whom I trusted and loved, I could no longer ward off thoughts of my imprisonment. I was alone with the shiny tile walls and the gray steel bars. Walls and bars, nothing more. I wished I had a book or, if not something to read, at least a pencil and a sheet of paper.

I fought the tendency to individualize my predicament. Pacing from one end of this cell to the other, from a bench along one wall to a bench along the other, I kept telling myself that I didn't have the right to get upset about a few hours of being alone in a holding cell. What about the brother— Charles Jordon was his name—who had spent, not hours, but days and weeks in a pitch-dark strip cell in Soledad Prison, hardly large enough for him to stretch out on the cold cement, reeking of urine and human excrement because the only available toilet was a hole in the floor which could hardly be seen in the dark.

I thought about the scene George had described in the manuscript of his book—the brother who had painted a night sky on the ceiling of his cell, because it had been years since he had seen the moon and stars. (When it was discovered, the guards painted over it in gray.) And there was Ericka Huggins at Niantic State Farm for Women in Connecticut. Ericka, Bobby, the Soledad Brothers, the Soledad 7, the Tombs Rebels and all the countless others whose identities were hidden behind so much concrete and steel, so many locks and chains. How could I indulge even the faintest inclination toward self-pity? Yet I paced faster across the holding cell. I walked with the determination of someone who has someplace very important to go. At the same time, I was trying not to let the jailers see my agitation.

When someone finally opened the gate, it was late in the evening. Margaret and John were waiting to accompany me to a court appearance in the same courtroom we had appeared in that morning. Aside from us, there were no "civilians" in the courtroom, not even the reporters from the morning session. I wondered what kind of secret appearance this was going to be.

The elderly judge announced that he was rescinding the

bail and releasing me on my own recognizance. I was sure I had misheard his words. But already, the Feds were approaching me to unlock the handcuffs. The judge said something else, which I hardly heard, and then suddenly several New York policemen moved in to replace the federal handcuffs with their own manacles.

With the New York handcuffs binding my wrists, there was a trip to a musty police precinct office, where I was officially booked as a prisoner of the State of New York. Forms, fingerprints, mug shots—the same routine. The New York police seemed to be as confused as their surroundings. Amid all the papers haphazardly strewn on desks and counters, they were running around like novices. Their incompetence calmed me. It must have been around ten in the evening when one of them announced that there would be yet another court appearance. (Did Margaret and John know about this third court session?)

The courtroom in the New York County Courthouse was larger than any I had ever seen. Its high ceilings and interminable rows of benches made it look like a church from another era. Most courtrooms are windowless, but this one seemed especially isolated from the outside world. It was so dimly lit, with hardly anyone but policemen sitting randomly on the benches, that I had the impression that what was about to happen was supposed to be hidden from the people outside. Neither Margaret nor John was there. When they told me that I had to be arraigned before a New York judge, I said that I wasn't budging from my seat until they contacted my lawyers. I was prepared to wait the whole night.

When John finally arrived, he said that the police had directed him to the wrong courtroom. He had been running all over New York trying to find me. After hours of waiting, the court appearance lasted all of two minutes.

Back at the jail, I was so physically and emotionally exhausted that I only wanted to sleep. Even the hard cell cot in the "mental" ward felt comfortable. But as soon as I closed my eyes, I was jolted out of my exhaustion by piercing screams in a language which sounded Slavic. They came from a cell at the other end of the corridor. Footsteps approached the cell in the darkness. Voices tried to calm the woman in English but could not assuage her terror. I listened to her all night—until they took her away in the morning.

The same unpalatable breakfast—cornflakes, powdered milk and stale white bread—was placed on the unswept floor of my cell the next morning. As she had promised, Shirley, who had brought my breakfast the morning before, had found me a cup of black coffee. Accompanying her this time was a tall, slim Puerto Rican woman wearing a very short natural. She introduced herself as "just Tex" and went on to say that when the sisters in her corridor learned that I was in 4b, they wanted me to know that they were convinced we would win.

After Shirley and Tex had gone, I called through the bars, telling the officer to bring me my cigarettes—they had kept them when I came from court the night before.

"You can't have a cigarette now," she called from the day room. "You'll have to wait till cigarette time, like the rest of the inmates." She spoke as if it were against the regulations not to understand that smoking took place only at "cigarette time." When she came around a half-hour later, she gave me a single cigarette and insisted on lighting it herself through the grating of the cell door. "Sorry, these are the rules. We have to follow the rules."

The corridor was quiet that morning. When I had finished my cigarette, I called to the guard once more.

"I'm ready to take my shower and get dressed."

She came back to my cell. "I can't let you out right now."

"I want to brush my teeth, take a shower and put on something other than this gown."

"I can't let you out. Hasn't anyone explained the rules of 4b? The 'girls' can only come out of their cells when *two* officers are on duty." (All prisoners—whether they were sixteen or sixty—were referred to as "girls.")

Nothing, I later discovered, absolutely nothing was allowed inside the cells—not only were cigarettes and matches banned, but also books, writing materials, toothbrushes, soap, washcloths, clothes and shoes. Before being locked into her cell, each prisoner was always checked to make sure she had removed her underwear and was wearing nothing except the flimsy, light-green nightgown she was given. A book or a magazine? How could they be used to inflict injury on oneself? And toilet paper? We could not even keep a roll of toilet paper in the cell. Like dependent infants, each time we wanted to use the toilet, we had to call the officer to bring us paper.

Shortly before lunch, the second officer arrived and the cell doors were unlocked. A strange mélange of women emerged from the cells: one very young Black woman, short and heavyset, with her natural thinning out on one side. Something seemed to be churning her up inside. Another Black woman with straight hair, and an incredibly serene expression. She was far away from this jail in her thoughts. A white woman with dyed red hair, looking young one moment and very old the next, who began to pace frantically around the day room, mumbling incomprehensibly under her breath. And a young white woman, small, frail, with short blond hair, who seemed on the verge of panic, but didn't know how to express it.

The women did not even notice that a new prisoner had been thrown in with them. Except for the woman who continued to pace, they each found places at the table in the day room and sat separate from one another, as if there were a mutual agreement that they would all refrain from invading the others' turf. After they took their seats, they became completely absorbed in themselves, blank stares telling me that no matter how much I wanted to talk, it would be futile to approach any of them.

Later I learned that these women received Thorazine with their meals each day and, even if they were completely sane, the tranquilizers would always make them uncommunicative and detached from their surroundings. After a few hours of watching them gaze silently into space, I felt as though I had been thrown into a nightmare.

Even there in the day room where the eyes of the officers were constantly following our most subtle gestures, we were not allowed to hold a pack of cigarettes or matches. If you wanted a cigarette, you approached the officer sitting at the desk, and she handed you one from your pack and lit it for you. If you were a chain smoker, as I was at the time, and especially if you had kept your sanity and your sobriety, this little ceremony was itself maddening.

I had loudly protested being kept in 4b from the very first day. I didn't belong there—or *had* I been judged a mental case? The officer said I had been placed in 4b not because I was psychologically unsound, but for my own safety and to keep me from disrupting the life of the jail. I was not persuaded.

I began to make as many requests as I could think of. I knew that there must be some kind of library in the building, so I asked to visit it, certain that if I read only the piles of *Reader's Digests* lying around, I too would be a candidate for Thorazine. The message which came back was that I could order books from the library, and they would be brought up to me. The same rule applied to the commissary—I could order whatever I needed, and it would be delivered to me. I had never seen the library or the commissary, but when virtually nothing came back in response to my lists, I realized that I had terribly overestimated both of these jail institutions. Even items like a ball-point pen or a natural comb were not sold in commissary and were therefore considered "contraband."

The day was dragging, and I was beginning to wonder whether they were planning to deny me contact with my attorneys. Either Margaret or John should have certainly come to see me by now. When I made inquiries about my attorneys' visits, the officer said that they had received instructions that although I was allowed to have counsel visits, I was to go nowhere without an "escort." (The jail euphemism for a guard.) Normally all a prisoner needed was a pass. At last the call came announcing the arrival of the lawyers. Going to meet them was my first opportunity to walk through any part of the jail at a normal hour—when the prisoners were not locked in or sleeping.

Women awaiting trial were always allowed to wear their own clothes. The women in 4b, however, the "mental cases," wore the uniforms of sentenced women, so I had to go down to the ground floor for my first visit in a dung-colored, un-hemmed cotton dress, at least two sizes too large and about five inches above my ankles. I had washed my hair that morn-ing and had my natural back for the first time in almost two months—but since we weren't allowed to use natural combs, my hair was in hopeless disarray. Yet excitement about my trip to the main floor totally annihilated any worry about my appearance.

When the iron door was opened, sounds peculiar to jails and prisons poured into my ears—the screams, the metal-lic clanging, officers' keys clinking. Some of the woman noticed me and smiled warmly or threw up their fists in gestures of solidarity. The elevator stopped on the third floor, where the commissary was located. The women who were waiting for the elevator recognized me and told me in a cordial, sisterly way, their words sometimes reinforced with their fists, that they were on my side. These were the "dangerous women" who might attack me because they didn't like "Communists," had I not been hidden away in 4b. This and subsequent trips to the main floor were further evidence of what I already knew: that the administration's allegations that the prison population might harm me were nonsense.

On the first floor I was directed to a booth which became a regular hangout over the next weeks. The first problem I discussed with Margaret and John was what we could do to get me out of 4b and into the main population. As we talked we noticed that the guard stationed at the table outside the booths was trying her best to listen to our conversation.

In the days that followed, familiarity with the routine in

4b did not diminish the horror of living behind bars. I not only pressed harder for my own release, but I was becoming increasingly persuaded that something had to be done about this maximum security arrangement camouflaged as a therapeutic cellblock. Regardless of why the women in 4b had been placed there, they were all being horribly damaged. Whatever problems they had had initially were not solved, but rather systematically aggravated. I could see the erosion of their will taking place even during the short time I spent there.

In the cell next to me lived a white woman somewhere between thirty and forty-five years old who had lost all contact with reality. Each night before she fell asleep the cellblock shook with her screams. Sometimes her rantings and ravings filled the air long after midnight. Her vile language, her weird imagery bespeckled with the most vulgar kind of racial epithets made me so angry that it was all I could do to prevent myself from trying to break through the steel and concrete that separated her cell from mine. I was convinced that she had been placed there intentionally as a part of the jailers' efforts to break me.

When I saw this pitiful figure the next morning, it was clear that her sickness was so far advanced—some stage of schizophrenia—that she was beyond the reach of argument. Her illness had become a convenient vehicle for the expression of the racism which had grown like maggots in her unconscious. Each night, and every morning before breakfast came, she went through a prolonged ritual which took the form of a violent argument with some invisible figure in her cell. More often than not, this figure would be a Black man, and he would be attacking her with a kind of sexual perversity which would have been inconceivable had not her own verbal imagery been so vivid. She would purge this figure from her cell with a series of incantations. When her imagined attacker assumed some other position, it brought about a corresponding change in her incantations.

One morning in the day room, Barbara, the young Black

woman from the cell directly across from mine, broke her habitual silence to tell me she had refused her daily dose of Thorazine. It was very simple: she was tired of feeling like a vegetable all the time. She was going to resist the Thorazine and was going to get out of 4b. She knew about my own attempts to get out, and if we were both transferred she said she would like very much to be my "cellie" in the main population.

In the cell next to Barbara's was a very young white woman who appeared to receive larger doses of Thorazine than any of the others. One day when she was not so spaced out, she wanted to know if I could help her with her case. (She was back from court and evidently had not been drugged so she would look more or less normal for the judge.) When I asked her about her charges, tears streamed down her face as she said repeatedly, "I could never do anything like that. I couldn't kill my own baby."

She didn't understand where she was and had no comprehension whatever of the judicial system. Who were her friends, she wanted me to tell her, and who were the ones who wanted to put her away? She had been afraid to talk to her lawyer, for fear he would tell the judge. Now she was thoroughly crushed because a doctor who had sworn himself to secrecy had just taken the stand and divulged everything she had told him. All she wanted now was just a little Thorazine. She wanted to get away, forget, get high.

Perhaps the most tragic of them all was Sandra—the teenager charged with arson. She was one of the women who had been in the receiving room the night I was arrested. I had noticed then that her hair was coming out in patches and had assumed that she had ringworm. My first day in 4b, she came out of the cell for meals. The second day, she ignored the key unlocking her cell gate at mealtimes. She silently and systematically pulled her hair out by the roots. From that day on, whenever I saw her, she was sitting quietly on her bed, yanking out hair by the handful. By the time I left, she was as thin as a wishbone, and all that was left of her natural was a few clumps of hair on one side of her pitiful hairless head.

Of all the officers who were sent to do duty in 4b—and there were different ones almost every day—no one cared about this young woman, no one except a sweet, motherly Black woman officer, who seemed quite out of character in her guard's uniform. The few times she was on duty, she would tenderly coax the poor girl out of her depression, draw words from her tortured soul, bring her out of her cell into the day room and persuade her to eat a little. But this officer was rarely there, and she was only one person poised against an entire system in which there was nothing to encourage concern for a prisoner who was being slowly, hopelessly engulfed by her desperation.

The week I spent in 4b was far worse than my worst fantasies of solitary confinement. It was torture to be surrounded by these women who urgently needed professional help. It was all the more torturous because each time I tried to help one of them out of her misery, I would discover that a wall—far more impervious than the walls of our cells—stood between us. I could not keep from becoming depressed myself when their "doctor" came to examine them—he simply prescribed larger doses of Thorazine, chloral hydrate, or other tranquilizers.

Even if prisoners with severe psychological problems were given more attention, I wonder whether the approach would be fundamentally different from what I witnessed in 4b. Psychology as it is generally practiced is not geared to cure. Often it does not reach the root of the problem because it does not recognize the social origin of many forms of mental illness.

How could the woman next door to me even begin to be cured if the psychologist treating her was not aware of the way in which racism, like an ancient plague, infects every joint, muscle and tissue of social life in this country? This woman was rotting in a snake pit of racism, flagellating herself daily with her obscene and graphic imagination. In order to understand her illness, it would be necessary to start with the illness of the society—for it was from the society that she had so perfectly learned how to hate Black people.

Trapped in this wasteland inhabited by the sick, the drugged, and their indifferent keepers, my life revolved around Margaret's daily visits. They were oases, refreshing reentries into humanity. Our conversations—about the little world of our childhood, our families, and the larger world of global politics, the movement, the case—sustained me more than anything else during this period. She brought messages from my parents, and continually assured my mother that my health was good and my spirits were high. Margaret was my only link to my comrades, my friends, and she kept me from being totally swallowed up by the madness of that dungeon.

She had grown very strong. Coupled with the responsibilities of her full-time job at the NAACP Legal Defense Fund and her total devotion to her six-year-old son, she was doing a full-time job on the case. And knowing how much I looked forward to her visits, she rarely missed a day.

She came into the case fighting and kept it up for the entire twenty months. That first morning in the Federal Building she had reached me only after fighting her way through an assemblage of marshals. When she came to visit me in jail, the jailers said she didn't look like a lawyer: she seemed too young to have passed the bar in New York. And besides, she was Black and, to complete the unpopular combination, she was a woman. When she had established her right to visit me as my lawyer, she launched into an interminable battle with the jail administration over my rights.

The first skirmish was fought in order to get me out of 4b. Margaret submitted request upon request to the administration, demanding that I be placed in some more normal section of the jail. She went from one officer to another, up the hierarchy from lieutenant to captain to deputy superintendent to the superintendent herself. Margaret insisted that she could not carry on a sensible conversation with this warden. (My own encounters with the woman confirmed everything I had heard about her from lawyers and prisoners alike. Unfortunately, she was Black. She was probably chosen for that reason—she had proved to be a convenient tool for the higher-ups in the New York Department of Corrections.)

Nowhere along the hierarchy could any reason for my incarceration in 4b be given, aside from the ridiculous notion that the other women might attack me if I were not kept in a safely guarded place. By now we had accumulated enough evidence through my trips from the cellblock to the main floor for lawyers' visits to demonstrate the affection which the vast majority of the women felt for me.

A little more than a week had passed when the warden informed Margaret that I was to be moved to the main population. I was extremely excited, but did not want to make it appear to the officers that this move was anything more than what I was due and had expected all along. Shortly before dinner, a young, emaciated-looking Puerto Rican officer came to fetch me from 4b. I gathered up my belongings—jail-issued dresses and underwear and the magazines I had managed to have brought in, said my good-byes to the women (even though most were irretrievably spaced out on drugs), and followed the officer through the iron door. I called to the women who were in the dining room across from the elevator and asked them to say good-bye to Shirley and Tex, who had brought our meals in 4b. When they heard I was leaving they both came running out, asking me to try to get back down that way to see them if I could.

The bed assigned me in the tenth-floor dormitory, where at least a hundred women were sleeping, was in the very front of the hall, only a few yards away from the officer's desk. After a tasteless dinner in the dining-recreation room next door, I struck up conversations with a number of women. Many of the women were recuperating and were assigned to the dormitory because they needed to be near the hospital across the hall in case some problem arose. Some had just had babies.

Others were elderly women who might not have survived the regular jail routine.

One woman looked familiar. I soon realized that she was the pregnant woman I had seen the night I was arrested. When I asked her how her baby was, she was surprised that I knew about it. After I explained, she said that she had been in so much pain then that she had no memory of what had happened. We had a lively conversation about the jail, her case, her personal problems. Finally she got up enough nerve to ask me to explain what communism was. Some of the other women began to listen. We were in the back of the hall; there were no officers around, yet I knew they would find out that we were holding political talks. Most of the women seemed honestly interested and I snatched the opportunity to tell them that most of what they had heard about communism was a carefully woven network of lies.

While I was arranging my personal effects in the small cabinet at the side of my bed, a young white woman came up to me and in an almost inaudible voice whispered, "I am a political prisoner also." She explained that a friend of her husband's had been arrested for possession of explosives in Oakland. They had apparently been tied into this affair by the police and were later arrested in New York. Their case was still in the extradition stages. She had given birth to a baby and was waiting here in almost total ignorance of developments in the lawsuit against them. (Later I learned that the officers had given her the name "Weatherman" although she didn't seem to have anything to do with that organization.)

That evening I received my introduction to a well-known institution in any prison—the grapevine. Several of the women told me that they had just heard "through the grapevine" that I had been transferred from 4b to the tenth floor for security reasons. The administration was afraid, so they said, that with the help of outside friends, I might attempt to escape from the fourth floor. Apparently it had been done before. There were even rumors that they had already uncovered some plot to rescue me. I don't know whether these were fantasies of the prisoners or of the jailers; in any event, I didn't completely dismiss the possibility that the administration was impelled by fear to transfer me to the tenth floor. It was amusing but also frightening, for if they had already acted on such irrational grounds, there was no telling what else they might try.

Sure enough, the very next day I was told that I was about to be transferred to another part of the jail. I protested being bounced back and forth like a Ping-Pong ball, but actually I didn't mind the move, thinking that I was going into the regular population. I hated the lack of privacy in the dormitory. If I decided to do some reading or writing, it was impossible to retreat, except perhaps into a bathroom stall. At least in the cellblocks, the cell would provide a hint of privacy. I had no idea that my longing for some degree of seclusion was about to be overfulfilled. The main population I thought I was about to enter turned out to be a hurriedly improvised special isolation room separated from all of the corridors on the sixth floor.

Outraged, I demanded to know what was going on, but of course there was no explanation from the officer who had silently led me away. After all, she said, she was only following the instructions of her supervisor. It was not hard to see the probable connection between the harmless discussion with the sisters upstairs about communism and this abrupt and unexplained move into solitary confinement.

I looked around the cell in angry disbelief. It seemed especially illogical that after they had transferred me from the psychiatric cellblock to the dormitory, they would now isolate me altogether. Even as these thoughts sifted through my head, I realized that it was futile to try to understand the perverted logic of jailers.

I learned later that this room was ordinarily used by the doctor, ostensibly for medical examinations. The isolation units which had existed in the past had been dismantled years ago, in an effort to remove from view the most blatant instances of inhumanity. Needless to say, they had not succeeded; inhumanity seethed from all the cracks and crevices of that place.

As the work shifts changed—first at midnight, then early the next morning, there was a noticeable changing of the guard in front of the door. I began to realize that they had assigned someone to watch me twenty-four hours a day. Not only had they isolated me, they had placed me under maximum security.

Later that night I looked out the window at the "free" people passing down Greenwich Avenue. I listened to the night sounds of the Village and paced back and forth in the room. When I finally got into bed, I kept my eyes open: I didn't want to be caught off guard in the middle of the night.

The next morning it struck me that there was no shower in this cell. I began to wonder quite seriously whether they would construct a "special facility" for me. When I announced to the officer outside the door that I was ready for my daily shower, she said I would have to wait. It took over an hour to arrange for my shower because all the women had to be cleared from the corridor and locked into their cells before I was let out of mine. The officer unlocked the door and directed me through an iron gate into a long corridor of cells.

This was the first time I had a chance to get a closer look at a corridor in the main jail population. When they weren't locked in their cells, I later discovered, the prisoners spent most of their time in corridors like these, sitting on cold, filthy cement floors. Apparently none of the cells had waste baskets, because paper and dirt were strewn along the entire length of the corridor—as if it had been casually thrown through the bars.

The shower was no more sanitary—a dead mouse huddled under the bench as if to be a little less obtrusive. When I emerged, I did not feel any cleaner than before, but I had gained a little satisfaction from the fact that my demand for this shower had forced the jailers to submit in a small way.

When Margaret and John came in, I gave them a detailed

account of the most recent offensive launched by the jail administration. We began to map out plans for our counteroffensive. Our response had to be both political and legal. There would be a federal lawsuit filed on the grounds that I was the victim of undue discrimination. The political campaign would have to reveal the precedent the jail administration and government were trying to set in the treatment of political prisoners.

At that time, the Department of Corrections must have felt it was extremely important to establish methods of quarantining resistance and radicalism in order to prevent their large-scale diffusion. In September, a month before, the Tombs had erupted in massive collective protests. Obviously, every prison in New York was searching for new ways of preventing these explosions. If we did not publicly contest the efforts to segregate me from the rest of the women, this apparatus would be ready and waiting for anyone deemed a political threat.

I decided to dramatize the situation by declaring myself on a hunger strike for as long as I was kept in isolation—I would hold my own on this side of the walls while things got rolling on the other side. It was not difficult to go on a hunger strike. If the food had looked palatable, it would have been hard; but the unsavory dishes they placed before me actually facilitated the strike. After taking a look at the food, I felt more like vomiting than eating.

Of the many officers assigned to guard me during those weeks, there were a few who were unmistakably sympathetic. I learned from them that the warden had instructed them to prevent any exchange of words between me and the other women—not even a greeting was allowed. The friendly officers ignored this order, in spite of the fact that if their superiors had become aware of the understanding they had reached with me, they could have been brought up on charges of insubordination.

I also learned from one of these officers that when they

came on duty, they took charge of a log entitled "Angela Davis' Daily Activities." Every hour on the hour, they were supposed to make an entry describing my activities of the previous hour—whether I had been reading (if so, what), writing, exercising—that exhausted the extent of the activities I could pursue in such confined quarters.

Some of them also told me that they had been instructed to conduct a thorough search of my quarters each time there was a changing of the guard. The friendlier ones didn't bother with the search. But those who took this duty seriously announced their presence at the post by entering the cell, intently looking around at the barren walls as if they might conceal a weapon, and finally by going through the drawers of the bed table. One eye always following my movements.

Unfortunately, I cannot describe the sympathetic officers or refer to them by name. My words might mean the loss of their jobs. They were an interesting conglomeration of Black women, both young and old, whose political sentiments ranged from "liberal" to straight-out sympathy with the most militant wings of the Black Liberation Movement.

They all explained that they had been driven by necessity to apply for this kind of job. Apparently it was one of the highest-paying jobs in New York that did not require a college education. In a way, these officers were prisoners themselves, and some of them were keenly aware that they were treading ambiguous waters. Like their predecessors, the Black overseers, they were guarding their sisters in exchange for a few bits of bread. And like the overseers, they too would discover that part of the payment for their work was their own oppression. For example, overtime was compulsory. And because of the military discipline to which they were forced to submit, failure to work overtime was punishable as insubordination. Sixteen-hour workdays, a few times a week, were never out of the ordinary for the young officers who held no seniority, and for the older ones who weren't well-liked in the top echelons of the jail hierarchy.

Still, even though their own grievances were reason enough to become involved in protest, whatever positive role they could play inside the jail was limited—they certainly could not revolutionize the penal system. But within these limitations there were a number of important things they did do. For instance, they communicated messages from prisoners to the outside, when it was not possible to send them through normal channels. They brought in "contraband" articles, such as natural combs. They got literature to the prisoners—particularly political literature that was banned from the library. If serious study groups were formed by women who wanted to learn more about the Black or Puerto Rican Liberation movements, sometimes these officers served as a shield between them and the administration.

All these things imply risks. These officers repeatedly pointed out that when two of their colleagues had been discovered to have ties with the Black Panther Party, they were swiftly discharged. While they were willing to risk losing their jobs, they thought it was more beneficial to the prisoners to do whatever they could manage within the jail system itself, than to become martyrs without reason. Yet a few of them said that if things reached a crisis, they would shed the uniform and join the army of the prisoners.

Of course, it was difficult to judge the seriousness and depth of their commitment, but it cheered me to see one of them coming to assume the guard post. Then I could talk with some of the sisters from the floor. One afternoon, the sisters from the two corridors nearest my cell marched single-file past my door chanting, "Free Angela. Free our sister."

Through the grapevine I learned that there were women all over the jail who were carrying out a hunger strike in sympathy with mine. I was especially moved when I heard that Shirley was organizing a hunger strike on the fourth floor. Since she worked in the kitchen, it must have required an unusually big effort on her part. As for myself, I had a glass of juice three times a day at meal times, lots of water and exercise. That, along with the *New York Times*, which now came daily, the one or two books I had, and the visits from Margaret and John, were enough to keep me going.

While I was in solitary, I finally began to receive regular evening visits from several friends. An officer would stand just close enough to hear my side of the conversation. (I assumed that they summarized it in the log book.) I was not a stranger to visiting arrangements in jails, for I had visited friends and comrades in prison on many occasions. But this visiting room was by far the worst I had seen. It is not unusual to have to speak to a visitor through a glass pane, but the panes in the House of Detention were less than a square foot in size, and the rust-colored dirt that covered them made it impossible to get a clear look at the person who had come to see you. The prisoners had to stand up during these twenty-minute visits and shout into telephones which inevitably seemed to stop functioning just when the most important part of the conversation had gotten under way.

One evening while I was still in solitary, I received a visit from Kendra Alexander, who had been subpoenaed to New York along with her husband Franklin to testify before the Grand Jury in the case against David Poindexter. She informed me that the demonstration protesting my solitary confinement was about to begin. They knew more or less where my room was located—I had carefully detailed the areas of Greenwich Avenue I could see from my window. The demonstrators were to gather on the corner of Greenwich and West Tenth.

I ran back upstairs. The officer guarding me was one of the friendlier ones, and turned her head and closed her ears while I spread the news. On five or six floors, the women who lived in the corridors with windows looking out on Greenwich Avenue would be able to see and hear the demonstration.

It was an enthusiastic crowd. Their shouts "Free Angela!

Free all our sisters!" rang through the night. Looking down from my cell window, I became altogether engrossed in the speeches, sometimes losing the sensation of captivity, feeling myself down there on the street with them. My mind flashed back to past demonstrations—"Free the Soledad Brothers," "Free Bobby and Ericka," "Free Huey," "End the war in Vietnam," "Stop police killings in our community now . . ."

Jose Stevens, a Communist leader from Harlem, had wound up his speech. Franklin was addressing his words, full of passion, to all the prisoners locked up in the Women's House of Detention. Then my sister, Fania, took the megaphone. The sound of her voice shocked me back into the reality of my situation, for I momentarily had forgotten that this demonstration was centered around me. I had been so absorbed in the rally that I had actually felt as if I were down there in the streets with them. Reflecting upon the impenetrability of this fortress, on all the things that kept me separated from my comrades barely a few hundred yards away, and reflecting on my solitary confinement—this prison within a prison that kept me separated from my sisters in captivity—I felt the weight of imprisonment perhaps more at that moment than at any time before.

My frustration was immense. But before my thoughts led me further in the direction of self-pity, I brought them to a halt, reminding myself that this was precisely what solitary confinement was supposed to evoke. In such a state the keepers could control their victim. I would not let them conquer me. I transformed my frustration into raging energy for the fight.

Against the background of the chants ringing up from the demonstration below, I took myself to task for having indulged in self-pity. What about George, John and Fleeta, and my codefendant, Ruchell Magee, who had endured far worse than I could ever expect to grapple with? What about Charles Jordan and his bout with that medieval strip-cell in Soledad Prison? What about those who had given their lives—Jonathan, McClain and Christmas?

The experience of the demonstration had worked up so much tension in me that I felt none of the debilitating effects of the fast. I did an extra heavy set of exercises to sufficiently lower my energy level so I could lie in bed in relative calm. There was no question of getting a full night's sleep. On this evening, I had to be especially vigilant. All was quiet in the jail, but I was convinced that the demonstration had aroused the jailers, and I had to hold myself in readiness in case they decided to strike sometime during the night.

On the tenth day of the hunger strike, at a time when I had persuaded myself that I could continue indefinitely without eating, the Federal Court handed down a ruling enjoining the jail administration from holding me any longer in isolation and under maximum security conditions. They had decided—under pressure, of course—that this unwarranted punishment was meted out to me because of my political beliefs and affiliation. The court was all but saying that Commissioner of Corrections George McGrath and Jessie Behagan, the superintendent of the Women's House of D., were so fearful of letting the women in the jail discover what communism was that they preferred to violate my most basic constitutional rights.

This ruling came as a surprise. I hadn't expected it to be so swift and to the point. It was an important victory, for we had firmly established that those in the Department of Corrections in New York would not have a clear course before them when they attempted to persecute the next political prisoner delivered into their hands. At the same time, however, I did not put it past the jail administration to concoct another situation which might not be solitary confinement, but which would give me an equally bad time. This thought subdued my delight at the news of the injunction.

Next destination: seventh floor, C corridor. When I arrived, there was a big shake-up going on. Women were being moved out, others were coming in. For a moment the thought struck me that they were preparing a special corridor for informers, jailer's confidantes—and me. But as it turned out, the lawsuit had forced the administration to get on its toes—so-called "first offenders" were supposed to be jailed separately from those who had already spent time in the House of Detention. Apparently the necessary shifts were being made.

There was little time to learn my way about before all the cell gates were locked, but some of my neighbors gave me a guided tour of my 8′ × 5′ cell. Because mine was the corner cell—the one which could be easily spied on from the officer's desk in the main hallway—it was also the smallest one on the corridor; the double bunk made it appear even smaller. The fixtures—the bed, the tiny sink, the toilet—were all arranged in a straight line, leaving no more than a width of two feet of floor at any point in the cell.

The sisters helped me improvise a curtain in front of the toilet and sink so they could not be seen from the corridor. They showed me how to use newspaper wrapped in scrap cloth to make a seat cover so the toilet could be turned into a chair to be used at the iron table that folded down from the wall in front of it. I laughed out loud at the thought of doing all my writing while sitting on the toilet stool.

Lock-in time was approaching; a sister remembered that she had forgotten to warn me about one of the dangers of night life in the House of D. " 'Mickey' will be trying to get into your cell tonight," she said, and I would have to take precautionary steps to "keep him out."

"Mickey?" Was there some maniac the jailers let loose at night to pester the women?

The sister laughingly told me she was referring to the mice which scampered about in the darkness of the corridors looking for cell doors not securely stuffed with newspapers.

It became a nightly ritual: placing meticulously folded newspapers in the little space between the gate and the floor and halfway up the gate along the wall. Despite the preventive measures we took, Mickey could always chew through the barricade in at least one cell, and we were often awakened by the shouts of a woman calling the officer to get the mouse out. One night Mickey joined me in the top bunk. When I felt him crawling around my neck, I brushed him away thinking that it was roaches. When I finally realized what it was, I called for the broom—our only weapon against him. Apparently mousetraps were too expensive, and they were not going to exterminate.

There was one good thing about Mickey. His presence reassured us that there were no rats in the vicinity. The two never share the same turf.

In a sense our daily struggles with Mickey—with all the various makeshift means devised to get the better of him—were symbolic of a larger struggle with the system. Indulging in a flight of fancy, I would sometimes imagine that all the preparations that were made at night to ward off those creatures were the barricades being erected against that larger enemy. That hundreds of women, all over the jail, politically conscious, politically committed, were acting in revolutionary unison.

That first evening, shortly after the sister had helped me stuff the gate with newspapers, an officer called out, "Lock-in time, girls. Into your cells." As the women slid their heavy iron gates closed, loud metallic crashing noises thundered from all four corridors of the seventh floor. I could hear the same sounds at a distance echoing from throughout the jail. (In 4b, I had never been able to figure out what all this commotion was about. The first time I heard it, I thought a rebellion had been unleashed.)

The officer came around to count each prisoner, and at 9 P.M. all lights in the corridor and cells were turned off by a master switch. In the darkness, a good night ritual was acted out. One sister shouted good night to another, calling her by name. The latter, catching the identity of the voice, would shout good night, also calling the first sister by name. Early on, someone from my corridor called out warmly, "Good night, Angela!" But having learned hardly anyone's name, much less to recognize their voices, I was an·outsider to this ritual and could only respond with a lonesome, unsupported, though no less vigorous, "good night." My call sparked off good night shouts to me, which came not only from my own corridor but from the others as well. I am sure that there had never been such a prolonged "saying of good nights." The officers did not interrupt, though silence should have prevailed long before.

Life in jail was arranged and controlled from above in accordance with pragmatic principles of the worst order. Just enough activities were provided to distract the prisoners from any prolonged reflection upon their wretched condition. The point was to fill up the day with meaningless activities, empty diversions.

As a result, a whole network of institutions was there to absorb the energies of the prisoners. Commissary, needless to say, was an important aspect of survival in captivity. Three days out of the week women awaiting trial visited this small store to purchase the little things that made life slightly less intolerable. Mondays and Wednesdays, there was a three-dollar limit on what we could buy; on Fridays we could spend one dollar more. The coveted articles on sale were such things as cigarettes, cosmetics, primitive writing materials—pencils (but no pens) and lined pads, and stamps; knitting and crocheting paraphernalia; and foodstuffs such as cookies, candies, sugar, instant coffee and hot chocolate. Unless you were pregnant, the only available source of real milk was the commissary.

The centrality of commissary emerges from the deprivation which is such an important element of official control and authority. In jail, you learn that nothing can be taken for granted; the normal need-fulfillment process is shattered. You cannot assume that even your most basic needs will be satisfied. There are always strings attached. If you conduct yourself in such a way as to provoke an officer to place you in lockup, you lose your commissary privileges. If you happen not to have cigarettes, you must simply do without. The threat of withdrawing commissary privileges is a powerful negative stimulus.

Another method used to fill time was the church services each Sunday morning. Out of curiosity, I went down to the chapel on the first Sunday I spent in the main population. I was surprised at the number of prisoners in attendance. But soon I realized that many of the women had ulterior motives unrelated to any serious religious feelings. It was one of the two consistent meeting places where women from one part of the jail could see and converse with their friends from other floors.

The other weekly meeting place was the movies—that is, if the projector was not broken. Not even the curiosity that attracted me to the church services could make me attend one of these insipid Hollywood movies. Needless to say, it was a favorite trysting place of homosexual couples.

For those who enjoyed reading, the library would have been a saving grace had it not been for the fact that the vast majority of the books were mysteries, romances and just plain bad literature whose sole function was to create emotional paths of escape. During my days of solitary confinement, after Margaret had persuaded the warden that I should have access to reading material, I spent a few sessions alone in the library. Within a short time I had combed the entire place, turning up only a few books which held the slightest interest: A book on the Chinese Revolution by Edgar Snow, the autobiography of W. E. B. DuBois and a book on communism written by an astonishingly objective little-known author.

After my discovery of these books, my thoughts kept wandering back to their enigmatic presence. And suddenly it hit me: they had probably been read by Elizabeth Gurley Flynn, Claudia Jones or one of the other Communist leaders who had been persecuted under the Smith Act during the McCarthy era. I myself had been told that if I received any books during my time there, I would have to donate them to the library—which was a pleasure, considering the state of that so-called place of learning. As I turned the pages of those books, I felt honored to be following in the tradition of some of this country's most outstanding heroines: Communist women leaders, especially the Black Communist Claudia Jones.

If you wanted books which were not in the library, they had to be mailed directly from the publisher. I decided to have as many books sent to me as possible, so as to provide, for succeeding prisoners, literature that was more interesting, more relevant, more serious than the trash on the shelves of the library. Apparently, the jailers saw through my scheme, especially when ten copies of George Jackson's *Soledad Brother* came in, for they harshly informed me that none of my books were to leave my hands. They would follow me to whichever jail I went.

The few remaining jail institutions were even more limited. There were short exercise periods on the roof of the building. This, I admit, was my favorite activity, and as long as the weather permitted, I looked forward with great pleasure to our volleyball games atop the jail. On the roof, in enclosed rooms, there were also arts and crafts, dancing, and games such as cards and Scrabble. With this, the range of activities behind the walls was practically complete. It was amazing, however, how much time could be consumed in these things, most of which contributed not in the least to the educational, cultural or social development of the prisoners. The main purpose of these pastimes was to encourage, in a subtle way, obedience and submissiveness.

Jails and prisons are designed to break human beings, to convert the population into specimens in a zoo—obedient to our keepers, but dangerous to each other. In response, imprisoned men and women will invent and continually invoke various and sundry defenses. Consequently, two layers of existence can be encountered within almost every jail or prison. The first layer consists of the routines and behavior prescribed by the governing penal hierarchy. The second layer is the prisoner culture itself: the rules and standards of behavior that come from and are defined by the captives in order to shield themselves from the open or covert terror designed to break their spirits.

In an elemental way, this culture is one of resistance, but a resistance of desperation. It is, therefore, incapable of striking a significant blow against the system. All its elements are based on an assumption that the prison system will continue to survive. Precisely for this reason, the system does not move to crush it. (In fact, it sometimes happens that there is an under-the-table encouragement of the prisoners' subculture.) I was continually astonished by the infinite details of the social regions which the women in the House of Detention considered their exclusive domain. This culture was contemptuously closed to the keepers. I sometimes wandered innocently through the doors and found myself thoroughly disoriented. A telling example happened on my second day in population. A sister asked me, "What did you think of my grandfather? He said he saw you this morning." I was sure I had misheard her question, but when she repeated it, I told her she must be mistaken, because I had no idea who her grandfather was. Besides, I hadn't had any visitors that day. But the joke was on me. I was in a foreign country and hadn't learned the language. I discovered from her that a woman prisoner who had come by my cell earlier in the day was the "grandfather" to whom she was referring. Because she didn't seem eager to answer any questions, I contained my curiosity until I found someone who could explain to me what the hell was going on.

A woman a few cells down gave me a fascinating description of a whole system through which the women could adopt their jail friends as relatives. I was bewildered and awed by the way in which the vast majority of the jail population had neatly organized itself into generations of families: mothers/wives, fathers/husbands, sons and daughters, even aunts, uncles, grandmothers and grandfathers. The family system served as a defense against the fact of being no more than a number. It humanized the environment and allowed an identification with others within a familiar framework.

In spite of its strong element of escapism and fantasy, the family system could solve certain immediate problems. Family duties and responsibilities were a way in which sharing was institutionalized. Parents were expected to provide for their children, particularly the young ones, if they could not afford "luxury items" from commissary.

Like filial relationships outside, some sons and daughters had, or developed, ulterior motives. Quite a few of them joined certain families because the material benefits were greater there.

What struck me most about this family system was the homosexuality at its core. But while there was certainly an overabundance of homosexual relationships within this improvised kinship structure, it was nevertheless not closed to "straight" women. There were straight daughters and husbandless, i.e., straight, mothers.

I recall with fondness a young woman of sixteen, with a very intense beauty, who told me plainly and simply one day that she was going to consider me her mother. Although I shared my commissary with her (and others as well) when she didn't have enough money in her account, she never once asked me for anything. She was quiet, serious and very curious about the Black Liberation movement. My obligations to her seemed to consist primarily of carrying on discussions with her about the movement. Housed with the "adolescents" in another corridor on my floor, she always managed with a calm firmness to persuade the officers to let her into my corridor.

Since the majority of the prisoners seemed to be at least casually involved in the family structure, there had to be a great number of lesbians throughout the jail. Homosexuality is bound to occur on a relatively large scale in any place of sexually segregated confinement. I knew this before I was arrested. I was not prepared, however, for the shock of seeing it so thoroughly entrenched in jail life. There were the masculine and feminine role-playing women; the former, the butches, were called "he." During the entire six weeks I spent on the seventh floor, I could not bring myself to refer to any woman with a masculine pronoun, although some of them, if they hadn't been wearing the mandatory dresses, would never have been taken for women.

Many of them—both the butches and the femmes—had

obviously decided to take up homosexuality during their jail terms in order to make that time a little more exciting, in order to forget the squalor and degradation around them. When they returned to the streets they would rejoin their men and quickly forget their jail husbands and wives.

An important part of the family system was the marriages. Some of them were extremely elaborate—with invitations, a formal ceremony, and some third person acting as the "minister." The "bride" would prepare for the occasion as if for a real wedding.

With all the marriages, the seeking of trysting places, the scheming which went on by one woman to catch another, the conflicts and jealousies—with all this—homosexuality emerged as one of the centers around which life in the House of Detention revolved. Certainly, it was a way to counteract some of the pain of jail life; but objectively, it served to perpetuate all the bad things about the House of Detention. "The Gay Life" was all-consuming; it prevented many of the women from developing their personal dissatisfaction with the conditions around them into a political dissatisfaction, because the homosexual fantasy life provided an easy and attractive channel for escape.

One of the corridors on the fourth floor, where the psychiatric bloc was located, was reserved for women with heavy heroin habits. When I caught glimpses of them during my trips to the elevator, I was struck by their physical deterioration. Their bodies were marred with leprous-like sores. These were the abscesses caused by dirty needles. Others had needle tracks all over their legs and arms and, because these veins had collapsed, they had begun to inject the drug into the veins in their necks.

The most tragic sight of all was the very young addicts, many of whom could have been no more than fourteen, despite the age they had given the police. Most of them had absolutely no intention of staying off the drug once they returned to the streets. To me, it was beyond comprehension that they could witness the most sordid effects of heroin while they were in jail and not be provoked to reconsider their own flirtations with the drug—flirtations that frequently became full-scale addiction.

Sometimes women with very heavy habits were brought in and left to kick alone in their cells. They would scream in agony all night long and not a single officer would help them. One evening an emaciated young woman was placed in the cell across from mine. By the time we were supposed to lock in for the night, she was doubled over, her whole face distorted in anguish. She needed medical help fast, but no doctor was forthcoming. Sisters in my corridor began to tell stories of women who had been in similar conditions and, left alone in their cells to kick, had died during the night. We decided that we would refuse to lock in unless she received medical attention immediately. Only after we took this stand did a doctor come to examine her and take her to the hospital.

There were many other occasions when we were forced to intervene in order to ensure medical help for one of our ill sisters. The most horrifying case of all was that of a woman on our corridor who began to complain one weekend about severe pains in her chest. On Monday morning at sick call, she saw one of the elderly white doctors, who told her that her problem was psychosomatic—the result of sitting around all day doing nothing. The doctor's advice to her was to "get a job." (If you were awaiting trial, as this sister was, you didn't even get the five or ten cents an hour that the sentenced prisoners received.)

The sister's pains grew worse over the next days, and finally we decided that we would have to issue a collective threat in order to force the jailers to get her the medical attention she needed. We refused to lock in until a competent doctor examined her. That day she didn't return to the cell; we later discovered that they had found tumors in her breasts and had rushed her to a hospital for tests and a possible mastectomy, if the tumors were found to be malignant.

The negligence toward the prisoners' health was also reflected in the daily routine of the jail. If pregnant women could not afford to buy a carton of milk on the three days we went to commissary, the only way they could supplement the three skimpy glasses of milk they received at mealtimes would be through our scheming. After I began to have problems with my eyes (a court injunction had allowed an outside doctor to examine me), a special diet, including milk, was prescribed for me. On numerous occasions, I smuggled my milk to a pregnant sister.

The first two weeks went by torturously slowly. I had the feeling that I had been in jail for a very long time. However, as soon as the jail routine began to inexorably impose itself, the days flowed imperceptibly into one another, and there seemed to be little difference between three days and three weeks.

At six o'clock each morning, the dim lights went on and the gates were unlocked for breakfast. Eight o'clock was the first lock-in of the day, and it lasted as long as it took to count prisoners and silverware to make sure a person or a spoon was not missing. Cleaning, doctor's rounds, mail time and commissary on Monday, Wednesday and Friday. Then lunch and silver count, followed by the 3 P.M. lock-in and count. Depending on the day of the week, afternoons were for roof exercises, the library or, once in a while, a movie. Dinner, silver count, visits, 8 P.M. lock-in and count and all lights out at nine.

I was fortunate to have Margaret's almost daily visits. John came as often as he could, and I received frequent visits from the lawyers working with Margaret on the suits around the jail conditions. They were Haywood Burns, the Director of the National Conference of Black Lawyers, and two members of the organization, Harold Washington and Napoleon Williams. We discussed the progress of the jail suit and the legal fight to prevent my extradition. John and Margaret were prepared to appeal the New York decision to return me to California all the way up through the appellate courts to the U.S. Supreme Court.

Those who had family or friends eagerly awaited the

moment, after dinner, when the officer distributed the visit slips to the small crowd gathered behind the bars at the end of each corridor. Evening visits never lasted longer than twenty minutes; nevertheless they broke up the monotony of the days.

Once my lawyers had pressured the jail bureaucracy to let me have the regular evening visits—shortly after I was released from solitary—I had visitors practically every night. Whenever my sister Fania, Franklin and Kendra Alexander, Bettina Aptheker and other friends and comrades were in town, they came in to see me. Exactly twenty minutes after the beginning of a visit, I could expect to hear the loud announcement that time was up; it usually took just about that long to get into a serious conversation.

I·always looked forward to Charlene Mitchell's visits. She was a close friend and member of the Political Committee (the leadership body) of the Communist Party. In the 1968 Presidential elections, she was our Party's candidate for President. Charlene had had a lot to do with my decision to join the Party, and over the last years my friendship with her had taught me a great deal about what it means to be a Communist. When the FBI pursuit began, without a hint of hesitation, she had placed herself in jeopardy in order to save my life. It was always frustrating to talk to her through the faulty telephones, and I was always painfully aware of the glass and wall which separated us. It would have meant so much to have simply been able to embrace her—or even to squeeze her hand.

One evening, I had an exciting visit with Henry Winston, the chairman of the Communist Party. Winnie, as our comrades affectionately called him, was born in Mississippi and, being both Black and a Communist, he had been an important target of the raging anti-communism of the forties and fifties. Close to ten years of prison, during which a brain tumor remained untreated, had left him almost totally blind. I had never seen him in person before his visit to the House of D. From the other side of the clouded pane, he greeted me with a very gentle voice, and I felt he could see me with far greater perceptiveness than someone with perfect eyesight. He wanted to know about my health, the jail food, and how I was being treated by the officers. He assured me that the Party was totally committed to the fight for my freedom and that he, personally, would do whatever was necessary to ensure victory.

I thought about my family all the time. Not a day passed when I did not worry about how my mother, who was still in Birmingham, was standing up to the whole ordeal. Despite my desire to see her, I told Margaret not to encourage her to make the trip to New York. She is such a sensitive person that I was afraid that she might not be able to bear the strain of seeing her daughter behind bars in a filthy, mouse-ridden jail. I was very reluctant to subject her to the frustration of a twenty-minute visit through telephones, concrete and the tiny, dirty window.

Mother was determined to see me, regardless of the conditions. When she told us she was coming to New York, Margaret worked for days to arrange for a "special visit"—in the social worker's office. Finally, when Margaret told the jailers that my mother had broken her foot and would find it difficult to stand during the visit, they agreed to the special visit.

Experience had taught me to be skeptical about everything. I didn't really believe that Mother would be allowed in the interior of the jail until the moment she actually arrived. She came walking in on crutches that morning, her foot still in a cast. When she put her arms around me, I could feel the tension throughout her body. For her benefit, I tried to appear especially cheerful. In an effort to conceal my thinness, I had worn the largest of the four jail-issued dresses. Even under normal circumstances, she gets upset when I lose a couple of pounds; during my fast I had lost fifteen pounds. Though she tried to appear in high spirits, I could tell from the deep furrows in her forehead that she was deeply disturbed. We talked about the family—Daddy, who was still at home;

Benny, whose wife, Sylvia, and child I had not yet seen, and Fania, who was now a few months pregnant. Although she did not say it, I felt that my father was taking the whole thing rather hard, and I told her to tell him there was nothing to worry about—it was just a matter of time. Whenever I said something as optimistic as this, I am sure she must have been thinking about the gas chamber in California. So I kept telling her that there wasn't a doubt in my mind that I would soon be free—out there with her.

It was good that the New York Committee to Free Angela Davis had organized several events in which they invited Mother to participate. I knew it would hearten her to see that there were many people concerned about my fate. Several of the sympathetic officers attended a reception in her honor. This was particularly important, for she could see that even among those who were supposed to be my jailers there were women who wanted to join the mass movement against repression.

In addition to these officially sanctioned visits, I received numerous "street visits." Though illegal, this was a well-established custom among the prisoners. Friends would simply shout up to the jail windows from the street below. One evening after lock-in, several women from the Harlem Black Women to Free Angela Davis gathered on Greenwich Avenue to inform me about the activities they had planned on my behalf. I saw a policeman walk over to one of them and obviously issue a warning; when she continued to call up to me, he grabbed her and dragged her away.

Once I felt settled in the main population, my thoughts naturally turned toward the possibility of collective political activity in jail. Many people are unaware of the fact that jail and prison are two entirely different institutions. People in prison have already been convicted. Jails are primarily for pretrial confinement, holding places until prisoners are either convicted or found innocent. More than half of the jail population have never been convicted of anything, yet they languish in these cells. Because the bail system is inherently biased in the favor of the relatively well-off, jails are disproportionately inhabited by the poor, who cannot afford the fee. The O.R. program—which allows one to be released without posting bond, on one's own recognizance—is heavily tainted with racism. At least ninety-five percent of the women in the House of D. were either Black or Puerto Rican.

The biggest problem jail prisoners face is how to get out on bail. The political issue, therefore, is how accused men and women can benefit equally from the so-called presumption of innocence by being free until proven guilty. I assumed that this was the issue around which we could most effectively organize sisters in the House of D.—and, in fact, this is what we later did.

Originally the jailers had insisted that I had been placed in solitary confinement for my own protection—the women on the corridor would be hostile toward me, they said, because of my Communist politics. It was all a lie. The women were hospitable from the first moment, and they were loving and protective. Nothing illustrated this more clearly than the demonstration staged by the sixth-floor women in front of my solitary cell and the hunger strike which began to spread throughout the jail in solidarity with my action. Throughout my stay I received numerous written messages of support from the sisters. (Any written communication between prisoners is illegal; these notes are called "kites" because of the shape they are folded in for easy concealment.)

On the seventh floor, only a few days had gone by when the sisters wanted to talk about the movement—and this was on their own initiative, without the least prodding from me. We talked about racism and how it is not just the attitude that Black people are inferior. Racism, in the first place, is a weapon used by the wealthy to increase the profits they bring in—by paying Black workers less for their work. We talked about the way racism confuses white workers, who often forget that they are being exploited by a boss and instead vent their frustrations on people of color. On the corridor and in the recreation room, we had numerous discussions on the meaning of communism; the sisters were especially interested in hearing about my experiences in Cuba in 1969—a trip which had proved to me what socialism can do to eradicate racism.

One evening, after lock-up, a loud question broke the silence. It came from a sister who was reading a book I had lent her.

"Angela, what does 'imperialism' mean?"

I called out, "The ruling class of one country conquers the people of another in order to rob them of their land, their resources, and to exploit their labor."

Another voice shouted, "You mean treating people in other countries the way Black people are treated here?"

This prompted an intense discussion that bounced through the cells, from my corridor to the one across the hall and back again.

Although I had ten copies of *Soledad Brother*, George's letters from prison, in my box in the library, not a single one was allowed on the corridor. Some of the friendly officers, however, smuggled a number of copies in from the outside. These became the most valuable pieces of contraband in the jail. They were always in demand and were widely read. When I wrote George of the enthusiastic reception of his book among the sisters there, it gave him pleasure to know that they were learning to relate to the movement through studying his individual political evolution. But there was one question that disturbed him: how were the sisters responding to the attitude toward Black women manifested in some of his early letters? In the past he had seen Black women as often acting as a deterrent to the involvement of Black men in the struggle. He had since discovered that this generalization was wrong, and was deeply concerned that the other women in the jail be informed of this.

Needless to say, there were reprisals for our activities. One sister was especially hard hit. Harriet had been in the

House of D. many times before and knew her way through the crevices of this jail far better than many of the officers. I had first met her during my stint in solitary. Her job in the laundry room allowed her to travel throughout the jail, and she was the only prisoner permitted to enter my cell. When she came, she always brought something with her—when I told her my pencil would not stay sharp, she brought me a contraband ballpoint pen.

Harriet had known Joan Bird and Afeni Shakur of the New York Panther 21 while they were in the House of D. She was intensely interested in becoming a part of the movement for the liberation of her people. Later, when I was moved to the seventh floor, she came each day on her laundry missions and brought "kites" and news from the other floors.

As the weeks passed, the jailers began to grow wary of the solidarity welding us all together, and security became visibly tighter. Harriet was ordered to keep away from my cell and from the other women in that corridor. They assigned another woman to bring the laundry to the floor.

Until this moment, Harriet had had relatively decent relationships with the officers, even with the higher-ups. She had one of the most enviable jobs, for it meant she could go anywhere in the eleven-floor jail without explicit permission. After she was prohibited from being on our floor, she proudly threw this "privilege" right back into the jailers' faces. She quit her job and refused to talk, except with hostility, to the officers who were responsible for the order. Many did not understand why Harriet took such a drastic way out—and, considering the structures of imprisonment, this was unequivocally drastic. She got the word to me that this incident involved fundamental and principled issues, on which she would never accept a compromise.

A real togetherness was developing. I was anxious to strengthen this sense of community, and I knew it needed more than books and discussions to thrive. In order to keep it alive, I invited the sisters to join me in exercising in the corridors. Exercising was an indispensable requirement for my own survival in jail. Often I could not fall asleep unless I exercised to the point of exhaustion.

After a few days of doing calisthenics together, we added some simple karate movements. One of the women who also knew a little karate helped out with the instruction. It was not long before rumors were flying through official jail circles that I was teaching karate to the women in preparation for a confrontation with the jailers. They ordered it stopped, but we found a way to do it anyhow. Once the calisthenic phase of the exercises was over, a woman kept watch at the gate while we punched and kicked our way down the length of the corridor.

As my stay in the House of Detention was drawing to a close, a number of women's groups in New York began to organize a bail fund for the women inside the House of Detention. There were women who spent months in jail simply because they didn't have fifty dollars to make their bail. As this work was being accomplished outside, there was organizing going on within. The problem was to prevent the bail fund from becoming just another service organization to provide bail for women inside, much the same way as lawyers are provided by Legal Aid. We came up with an ideal solution: the women who would receive funds from the organization outside were to be elected collectively by the women in each corridor. When a woman was elected to be a beneficiary, she would not only have her bail paid, but would have responsibilities to the bail fund as well. Once out on the streets, she would have to work with the fund, helping to raise money; making whatever political contributions she could to the development of the organization.

DECEMBER 21, 1970

On a cold Sunday afternoon a massive demonstration took place down on Greenwich Avenue. It was spearheaded by the bail fund coalition and the New York Committee to Free Angela Davis. So enthusiastic was the crowd that we felt compelled to organize some kind of reciprocal display of strength. We got together in our corridor, deciding on the slogans we would shout and how to make them come out in unison—even though we were going to be spread down the corridor in different cells, screaming from different windows. I had never dreamed that such powerful feelings of pride and confidence could develop among the sisters in this jail.

Chants thundered on the outside: "One, two, three, four, the House of D. has got to go!" "Free our Sisters, Free Ourselves," and other political chants that were popular at the time. After a while, we decided to try out our chants. It was far easier for us to be heard through the windows by the people outside than it was for us to be heard by ourselves, separated as we were by the thick concrete walls dividing the cells. Although our slogans may not have been transmitted in the most harmonious style, we managed to get our message across: "Free the Soledad Brothers," "Free Erika," "Free Bobby," "Long Live Jonathan Jackson."

While the chants of "Free Angela" filled me with excitement, I was concerned that an overabundance of such chants might set me apart from the rest of my sisters. I shouted one by one the names of all the sisters on the floor participating in the demonstration. "Free Vernell! Free Helen! Free Amy! Free Joann! Free Laura! Free Minnie!" I was hoarse for the next week.

As the demonstration moved into full swing, an officer unlocked the gate to our corridor and shouted to us to stop all the noise. We refused. They sent a captain to try to halt the demonstration. She approached me in my cell to say there would be sanctions for all of us if we did not calm down. Our exchange was heated. Within a matter of minutes, a confrontation had brewed. Shouts began to come from across the hall—the sisters in the next corridor had decided to join. There was nothing this captain could do to make us acquiesce; every word she uttered kindled our combativeness. The more militant we became, the less confident she became, and finally she left the corridor in defeat.

As long as there were demonstrators outside, we continued our chants. Even after they left, the floor was throbbing with excitement. We were proud of the staunch position we had taken vis-à-vis the bureaucracy. In this atmosphere of triumph, it was a cruel letdown for us to discover that the Supreme Court in Washington had just denied our appeal, and that I would soon be extradited to California. It was a Sunday; I assumed I would be taken back to the West Coast on Monday or Tuesday.

That night, still hot with the ardor of the demonstration, locked up in the darkness of their cells, the women staged a spontaneous demonstration of support. "One, two, three, four. We won't let Angela go!" "Five, six, seven, eight. We won't let them through the gate!" Shoes were banging on the cell bars; chants grew louder. An officer tried meekly to calm them down but had no success. A very vocal sister who was in one of the adolescent corridors was told to keep it quiet, but when she refused and all the sisters came vociferously to her aid, the officers hit her, knowing that all we could do was scream. They dragged her away to 4a—the punitive isolation unit. Frustrated by our inability to help her, we called out threats and beat even more loudly on the bars of our cells.

Someone noticed a sympathetic-looking white couple on Greenwich Avenue staring up in wonderment at the building, which was shaking with the clamor of protests from our floor. We called down to them that a sister had just been beaten and was probably being put through the third degree down in the hole. We were bold that evening. We shouted out loud and clear the names and ranks of the officers who had pulled her from her cell. We asked the couple to call the underground press and as many Left organizations as they could to let them know that we were expecting an even more severe crackdown. (I later discovered that they had spent the evening contacting everyone they felt could help us.)

A few hours passed and nothing unusual happened. The pace of our activity gradually eased off until the floor was silent. As I was dozing off to sleep, I was jolted into wakefulness by a bright light shining in my face. One of the "friendly" officers was aiming a flashlight at me. My lawyer was downstairs, she said. They were going to permit me to have a special visit with him so that he could inform me about my rights with respect to the forthcoming extradition. It was indeed strange to have an attorney's visit at three in the morning, but on the other hand, John had been in Washington all day for the Supreme Court extradition hearing. He had probably returned late and now expected me to be extradited before the night was over.

As soon as the elevator came to a stop on the main floor, I realized that they had just successfully played a confidence game on me. There were white police-types in civilian clothes casually standing around in the area outside the receiving room. The white assistant warden, dressed in her Sunday best, was conferring with some of them. A deputy warden, who at times had tried to wear a human mask, had been waiting for the elevator doors to open. She appeared to be in charge of the operation.

She bluntly informed me that I should prepare for a strip search. I angrily refused. Sarcastically, reminding them that they had told me that my lawyer was waiting for me, I walked over to the bench where prisoners waited to be called for visits and took a seat.

All around me was an acceleration of activity, which I pretended not to notice. The deputy warden approached me once more, this time accompanied by the woman second in command only to the warden. Again she told me to prepare for the strip search. Again I refused. Whether I agreed or not, she said, the search would take place, implying that if necessary they would use force. The two then left the area, apparently to confer about the situation with the police-types. They returned several times, sometimes bringing an officer who had hitherto been relatively nice to me. While they played the role of the stick, they wanted her to be the carrot.

As this confrontation was growing more heated, two familiar officers dressed in civilian clothes quietly crept into the room. When I saw them I was puzzled. Of all the officers in the House of Detention, they had been among the few for whom I had had a certain amount of respect. One was the librarian; the other worked at the front desk, checking in the attorneys when they came for visits.

For the moment, they were totally passive, bystanders as it were. Just as I was about to ask them what they were doing in the jail at that time of night, out of the corner of my eye I caught a glimpse of two men in guard's uniforms approaching me from behind. This was the first time I had seen male guards in the House of D. My mind flashed back to what the sisters had said about these "last resort" guards—the jail's riot squad—who were always on call for situations where force was deemed necessary. Realizing why they were there, I jumped up, took a battle stance and prepared to defend myself. One of them grabbed my arm. I kicked him. When the other man came to his aid, they both knocked me to the floor. By the time I could get up, the deputy warden and some of her female helpers were in on the action—as if two male prison guards weren't capable of subduing me.

At this moment, the two officers standing on the sidelines could no longer bear their position of neutrality. They both threw themselves into the fight. Their entrance into the battle was a shock—were they too willing to go to bat for the enemy? But it was even more of a shock to discover that they were not trying to subdue me but rather were beating the men who, by now, were really roughing me up.

The fight turned into a free-for-all. No one really knew who was on who's side. In all the confusion, both men managed to grab me, each one seizing an arm. They bent each arm upward behind my back in a hold that was impossible to break.

Bruised and breathless, there was nothing I could do to prevent them from locking the handcuffs. I knew that my rights had been violated; they were abducting me before I had even had the opportunity to learn the results of the Supreme Court decision from my lawyer. But for the time being, there was little I could do, except wait until I reestablished contact with my comrades outside.

My hands bound behind me, I was shoved, protesting, into a side room. Seeing that I was wearing the sleeveless cotton jail dress and canvas sneakers without socks, the librarian warned me it was very cold outside. I told her that my "court clothes" were at the booking desk.

The receptionist got my two civilian outfits: the navy-blue skirt and the blouse I had been wearing the day of my arrest, and a pair of wool pants and lightweight suede jacket. But I could not put them on because my hands were locked behind my back. The two women helped me slide my legs into the pants, which I wore under the dress, and wrapped the jacket around my shoulders.

I tried to concentrate on the concrete. Was I heading for the airport or would the extradition be carried out by train— or by car, as had been the case with Bobby Seale some months ago? The uncertainty was nerve-rending.

With the receptionist on one side and the librarian on the other, I walked slowly through the prisoners' gate onto the cold cobblestones of the courtyard. My anger gave way to pangs of regret at having to leave behind all my friends locked up in that filth. Vernell . . . Would they drop that phony murder charge? Helen . . . Would she go home? Amy . . . so old, so warm . . . What would happen to her? Pat . . . Would she write her book exposing the House of D.? And the organizing for the bail fund . . . Would it continue? Harriet . . . So committed to the struggle—would they continue to try to break her will?

The police van was waiting in the courtyard, the same van they had used to take me to court. Through the heavy grill on the windows, I could see nothing in the darkness. But suddenly, as the van rolled through the courtyard gates, I heard a thunderous burst of shouts of support. I could not figure out how so many people had learned I was being taken away that night. Later I found out they had come in response to the calls made by the white couple on Greenwich Avenue.

Not a single light illuminated the gigantic courtyard of the Tombs. All I could see was the outline of a collection of cars parked in the center, and the shadows of human figures moving back and forth between the vehicles. The atmosphere was reminiscent of postwar spy movies. A dozen white men swarming around their unmarked police cars, nervously awaiting the end of this transaction, this histrionic ceremony of repression unfolding under the dim glow of flashlights.

New York removed its handcuffs. California produced theirs and locked them around my wrists.

New York turned over documents. California aimed its flashlights on the papers before accepting them with approval.

New York handed over my clothes and a gray denim bag of shoes. California received them, as if by accepting my possessions, it was asserting control over my life.

The librarian and the receptionist, who had accompanied me this far, stood silently by. It was as if their individual identities were fading away. They appeared disturbed by their powerlessness. "I hope things turn out all right," one of them said. In spite of herself, she sounded like someone who must say something cheerful to a terminally ill patient.

The scene had a choreographed air about it. In the same silent rhythm, New York moved toward the van and California trudged toward the extradition vehicle. Something about the undisturbed perfection of this operation was far more terrifying than the extradition itself. I had to do something, anything, to disrupt their performance. Impulsively, I stopped short. Hands automatically tightened around weapons in answer to my little gesture of refusal.

"These handcuffs are too tight—and there's no reason why my hands need to be locked behind my back. If you're thinking about getting me into this car, you can think about changing these handcuffs."

At least I had smashed their rhythm of inevitability. At least I had taken them by surprise, and with no one to give them cues, they were momentarily at a loss. Still startled, and as if he were following the orders of a superior, the cop in charge instructed one of the others to unlock the cuffs and redo them with my hands in front.

This caravan without beginning and without end was the epitome of the insane violence of the state. It would speed through the city, then abruptly stop. Anonymous policemen would jump out of cars, whisper to one another, then some of the cars would head in one direction and others would go in the opposite direction. When we reached a tunnel, the cars came to a halt while the roadblock they were setting up for us was secured.

I had not realized how cold it was until I felt my body shivering and heard my teeth chattering. The man to my right was holding my wool skirt and blouse. Perhaps if I wrapped the skirt around my feet and used the blouse to cover my hands, I might be warmer.

At first he didn't object to my request for the skirt, but while I was awkwardly trying to wrap it around my feet with my manacled hands, he lunged toward me as if he expected me to aim a gun at him. For a moment I thought he had gone berserk. Only a madman could think that I might have concealed a weapon in those flimsy clothes, which moreover had already been searched by the FBI and the jailers at the House of D. Then it occurred to me that anyone in his place would have done the same thing—it was the madness of the institution he served that was driving him to hysterically search the hem of my skirt and the seams of my blouse.

We had been driving so long I was beginning to wonder whether they were planning to go the whole stretch across country this way. But when I ventured a question about our destination, the man to my right, after a bit of hesitation, said that it was McGuire Air Force Base in New Jersey. So in addition to armed agents, police, the attorney general's offices of two states, even the military had been brought in.

We drove onto the base and then shot diagonally across an airfield submerged in the darkness of the early winter morning. The plane was not yet visible, only the light shining through its windows. Did they expect an airborne battle? Is that why they called on the Air Force? It would hardly have surprised me if someone told me fighter planes were going to escort me to California.

As we got closer to the aircraft, I saw little clusters of people lined up in a U-formation around the stairway descending from the tail of the old freight plane. Agents with weapons in their hands. Shot guns. Rifles. Machine guns.

What if I tripped while I was walking toward the plane? Their attack reflexes would be set off. And my body would be riddled with bullets. Since this operation was being conducted in secrecy, away from the eyes of the press, there would be no one to contradict them if they said I was trying to escape.

With slow determination, despite my locked wrists, I managed a smooth descent from the automobile. Moving toward the plane, each step was full of effort. The gun barrels were tracing my path.

Flanked by plainclothes and uniformed men, two women were stationed at the top of the movable stairs. One was short and thin, with drab brown hair. Her keen-featured pale face betrayed the uncertainty of the novice. The older woman was tall and heavy-featured. Her hair had the look of a recent trip to the beauty parlor. I could tell immediately that she was strongly committed to her job; a policewoman par excellence. She seemed to enjoy being in charge of me, surrounded by those armed men who, in the event of an incident, would have to take instructions from her.

Throughout the trip, she was the one who most conspicuously imposed herself on me. Each time I shifted position, even slightly, she got up from her seat to inspect the small area surrounding me. And when I had to use the toilet, she insisted on stuffing herself inside the tiny booth. As she intently watched me urinate, I couldn't resist asking, "Do you think I'm going to flush myself down the toilet?"

She seemed a fitting representative of the government of California. That state held the dubious distinction of being one of the most advanced in the country when it came to quelling resistance. California could already claim more than its share of victims. I could trace the history of my political involvement there by the number of funerals I had attended.

During this interminable flight I wondered whether I too would become one of its victims. My confidence in the movement was invaded by the terrible specter of San Quentin, that fortress of horrors hanging over the San Francisco Bay as though it were clinging to the fringes of civilization. I thought about Aaron Henry, the last victim to be strangled by gas in San Quentin's death chamber. On the date of his execution, his mother begged for an audience with the governor. Ronald Reagan felt no compassion for her. He never even bothered to acknowledge her presence. Sitting on that plane, I thought of her and every Black mother like her.

It took twelve hours to fly from one end of the country to the other. Twelve hours for my thoughts to roam from one end of my life to the other. I thought of my family. What would happen to my mother, my father, Reggie, Benny, Fania? It had been so long since the days when we were all together—at home, secure, sheltered.

But had there ever really been such a time? Hadn't the people on that airplane always been there, holding us with hatred in their eyes, preying upon our lives?

I have a home in that rock,
don't you see? . . .

PART TWO

Rocks

*T*he big white house on top of the hill was not far from our old neighborhood, but the distance could not be measured in blocks. The government housing project on Eighth Avenue where we lived before was a crowded street of little red brick structures—no one of which was different from the other. Only rarely did the cement surrounding these brick huts break open and show patches of green. Without space or earth, nothing could be planted to bear fruit or blossoms. But friends were there—and friendliness.

In 1948 we moved out of the projects in Birmingham, Alabama, to the large wooden house on Center Street. My parents still live there. Because of its steeples and gables and peeling paint, the house was said to be haunted. There were wild woods in back with fig trees, blackberry patches and great wild cherry trees. On one side of the house was a huge Cigar tree. There was space here and no cement. The street itself was a strip of orange-red Alabama clay. It was the most conspicuous house in the neighborhood—not only because of its curious architecture but because, for blocks around, it was the only house not teeming inside with white hostility. We were the first black family to move into that area, and the white people believed that we were in the vanguard of a mass invasion.

At the age of four I was aware that the people across the street were different—without yet being able to trace their alien nature to the color of their skin. What made them different from our neighbors in the projects was the frown on their faces, the way they stood a hundred feet away and glared at us, their refusal to speak when we said "Good afternoon." An elderly couple across the street, the Montees, sat on their porch all the time, their eyes heavy with belligerence.

Almost immediately after we moved there the white people got together and decided on a border line between them and us. Center Street became the line of demarcation. Provided that we stayed on "our" side of the line (the east side) they let it be known we would be left in peace. If we ever crossed over to their side, war would be declared. Guns were hidden in our house and vigilance was constant.

Fifty or so yards from this hatred, we went about our daily lives. My mother, on leave from her teaching job, took care of my younger brother Benny, while waiting to give birth to another child, my sister Fania. My father drove his old orange van to the service station each morning after dropping me off at nursery school. It was next door to the Children's Home Hospital—an old wooden building where I was born and where, at two, I had my tonsils removed. I was fascinated by the people dressed in white and tried to spend more time at the hospital than at the nursery. I had made up my mind that I was going to be a doctor—a children's doctor.

Shortly after we moved to the hill, white people began moving out of the neighborhood and Black families were moving in, buying old houses and building new ones. A Black minister and his wife, the Deyaberts, crossed into white territory, buying the house right next to the Montees, the people with the hateful eyes.

It was evening in the spring of 1949. I was in the bathroom washing my white shoelaces for Sunday School the next morning when an explosion a hundred times louder than the loudest, most frightening thunderclap I had ever heard shook our house. Medicine bottles fell off the shelves, shattering all around me. The floor seemed to slip away from my feet as I raced into the kitchen and my frightened mother's arms.

Crowds of angry Black people came up the hill and stood on "our" side, staring at the bombed-out ruins of the Deyaberts' house. Far into the night they spoke of death, of white hatred, death, white people, and more death. But of their own fear they said nothing. Apparently it did not exist, for Black families continued to move in. The bombings were such a constant response that soon our neighborhood became known as Dynamite Hill.

The more steeped in violence our environment became, the more determined my father and mother were that I, the first-born, learn that the battle of white against Black was not written into the nature of things. On the contrary, my mother always said, love had been ordained by God. White people's hatred of us was neither natural nor eternal. She knew that whenever I answered the telephone and called to her, "Mommy, a white lady wants to talk to you," I was doing more than describing the curious drawl. Every time I said "white lady" or "white man" anger clung to my words. My mother tried to erase the anger with reasonableness. Her experiences had included contacts with white people seriously committed to improving race relations. Though she had grown up in rural Alabama, she had become involved, as a college student, in anti-racist movements. She had worked to free the Scottsboro Boys and there had been whites—some of them Communists—in that struggle. Through her own political work, she had learned that it was possible for white people to walk out of their skin and respond with the integrity of human beings. She tried hard to make her little girl—so full of hatred and confusion—see white people not so much as what they were as in terms of their potential. She did not want me to think of the guns hidden in drawers or the weeping black woman who had come screaming to our door for help, but of a future world of harmony and equality. I didn't know what she was talking about.

When Black families had moved up on the hill in sufficient numbers for me to have a group of friends, we developed our own means of defending our egos. Our weapon was the word. We would gather on my front lawn, wait for a car of white people to pass by and shout the worst epithets for white people we knew: Cracker. Redneck. Then we would laugh hysterically at the startled expressions on their faces. I hid this pastime from my parents. They could not know how important it was for me, and for all of us who had just discovered racism, to find ways of maintaining our dignity.

From the time we were young, we children would go to the old family farm in Marengo County. Our paternal grandmother and my Uncle Henry's family lived on the same land and in an ancient, unpainted weatherbeaten cabin similar to the one in which my father and all his sisters and brothers had been born. A visit to the country was like a journey backward into history; it was a return to our origins.

If there had been a mansion nearby, their cabin could have easily been the slave quarters of a century ago. The little house had two small bedrooms, a kitchen in the back and a common room where we children slept on pallets spread out on the floor. Instead of electricity, there were kerosene lanterns for the few hours of darkness before we went to bed. Instead of plumbing, there was a well outside where we drew water to drink and to heat over an open fire in the yard for our weekly baths in huge metal tubs. The outhouse frightened me when I was very young, so I urinated in a white enamel pot and would go into the brush to have a bowel movement rather than enter the putrid-smelling little house with the hole in the wooden plank where you could look down and see all the excrement floating around.

The family ate well; I did not realize then that this was probably one of the few pleasures that was available in a life which was work from sunup to sundown, when you were so exhausted that you could only think about recuperating for the next day's work. As a child on the farm, I did not distinguish work from play because the work there was novel to me and because I was not forced to do it all the time. When I fed the chickens, I would laugh at the way they all raced for the feed and gulped it down. When I gathered the eggs and fed the slop to the hogs, milked the cows and led the workhorses to the watering trough, I was enjoying myself.

Going to the country, to the green open spaces of the cotton and tobacco fields, was going to my own vision of paradise. I loved to chase the chickens barefoot, ride the work horses bareback, help take the few cows to pasture in the early hours of the morning. The only amusement available that was totally unrelated to the work of the farm was the refreshing swims in the nearby creek—"the crick," we called it—and the exciting trips into the swamps to explore this wonderful world inhabited by bizarre, crawling, slimy creatures.

Every Sunday after returning from the little wooden church a few miles down the road, there would be fried chicken and biscuits baked in the wood stove and spread with home-churned butter, greens and sweet potatoes from the fields, and fresh sweet milk from the cows in the barn.

Around the time I was twelve years old, my grandmother died. She had stayed with us in Birmingham for a while but had since moved to California to take turns living with my father's sisters and brothers who had trekked out to the West Coast in search of the mythical opportunities open to Black people there. Her body was brought back to Marengo County, Alabama, to be consecrated and buried in her little hometown of Linden. It was a tremendous blow to me, for she had always been a symbol of strength, of age, wisdom and suffering.

We had learned from her what slavery had been like. She was born only a few years after the Emancipation Proclamation, and her parents had been slaves themselves. She did not want us to forget that. When we were taught about Harriet Tubman and the Underground Railroad in school, it was my grandmother's image that always came to mind.

Not yet having accepted the finality of death, I still had a nebulous notion of an afterlife. Therefore amid all the desperate crying and shouting at the funeral, there were visions in my head of my grandmother going to join Harriet Tubman, where she would look down peacefully upon the happenings in this world. Wasn't she being lowered into the same soil where our ancestors had fought so passionately for freedom?

After her burial the old country lands took on for me an ineffable, awe-inspiring dimension: they became the stage on which the history of my people had been acted out. And my grandmother, in death, became more heroic. I felt a strange kind of unbreakable bond, vaguely religious, with her in that new world she had entered.

The summer before I went to school, I spent several months with Margaret Burnham's family in New York. Compared to Birmingham, New York was Camelot. I spent a rapt summer visiting zoos, parks, beaches, playing with Margaret, her older sister Claudia, and their friends, who were Black, Puerto Rican and white. With my Aunt Elizabeth, I rode buses and sat in the seat right behind the driver.

That summer in New York made me more more keenly sensitive to the segregation I had to face at home. Back home in Birmingham, on my first bus ride with my teen-aged cousin Snookie, I broke away from her and raced for my favorite place, directly behind the driver. At first, she tried to coax me out of the seat by cheerfully urging me to come with her to a seat in the back. But I knew where I wanted to sit. When she insisted I had to get up, I wanted to know why. She didn't know how to explain it. I imagine the whites were amused at her dilemma, and the Black people were perhaps just a little embarrassed about their own acquiescence. My cousin was distraught; she was the center of attention and had no notion of what to do. In desperation she whispered in my ear that there was a toilet in the back and if we didn't hurry she might have an accident. When we reached the back and I saw there was no toilet, I was angry not only because I had been tricked and lost my seat, but because I didn't know who or what to blame.

Near my father's service station downtown was a movie house called The Alabama. It reminded me of the ones in New York. Day and night the front of the building glittered with bright neon lights. A luxurious red carpet extended all the way to the sidewalk. On Saturdays and Sundays, the marquee always bore the titles of the latest children's movies. When we passed, blond-haired children with their mean-looking mothers were always crowded around the ticket booth. We weren't allowed in The Alabama—our theaters were the Carver and the Eighth Avenue, and the best we could expect in their roach-infested auditoriums was reruns of Tarzan. "If only we lived in New York . . ." I constantly thought. When we drove by the amusement park at the Birmingham Fairgrounds, where only white children were allowed, I thought about the fun we had at Coney Island in New York. Downtown at home, if we were hungry, we had to wait until we retreated back into a Black neighborhood, because the restaurants and food stands were reserved for whites only. In New York, we could buy a hot dog anywhere. In Birmingham, if we needed to go to the toilet or wanted a drink of water, we had to seek out a sign bearing the inscription "Colored." Most Southern Black children of my generation learned how to read the words "Colored" and "White" long before they learned "Look, Dick, look."

I had come to look upon New York as a fusion of the two

universes, a place where Black people were relatively free of the restraints of Southern racism. Yet during subsequent visits, several incidents sullied this image of racial harmony. Between the ages of six and ten, I spent a part of most summers in the city. My mother was working toward her master's degree in education, attending New York University during the summers. She always took her children along. In my mother's circle of friends, there was a couple whose futile efforts to find a place to live had brought them and their friends to despair. After listening to vague conversations on the subject, I managed to pry out of the adults the reason for their difficulty: she was Black and he was white.

Another situation in New York was in even sharper contradiction to the myth of Northern social harmony and justice. When I was around eight, the McCarthy period had reached a peak. Among the Communists forced underground was James Jackson, whom my parents knew from the time he and his family had lived in Birmingham. I did not really understand what was going on at the time; I only knew that the police were looking for my friend Harriet's father. Whenever I was with the Jackson children, they would point out the men following them who were always no more than half a block away. They were stern-looking white men dressed in suits, no matter how hot the weather got. They even started following our family, afterward questioning whomever we had visited during the day.

Why were they looking for my friend's father? He had done nothing wrong; he had committed no crime—but he was Black, and he was a Communist. Because I was too young to know what a Communist was, the meaning of the McCarthy witch hunts escaped me. As a result, I understood only what my eyes saw: evil white men out to get an innocent Black man. And this was happening not in the South, but in New York, the paragon of racial concord.

Like New York, California was thought to be far more advanced than the South. During my childhood, I heard numerous stories about the golden opportunities available to

Black people on the West Coast. Great westward pilgrimages were still being made by the poor and the jobless. One of my father's brothers and two of his sisters had joined the Black emigration to the West. We occasionally visited them in Los Angeles.

Some of the relatives had created comfortable circumstances for themselves—one of my aunts who had gone into real estate was even buying property in the hills of Hollywood. But another side of the family was in such difficult straits they were living off welfare. It depressed me to visit my cousins and discover that they did not have enough food in the house for a single decent meal—and that six or seven of them were living in a one-bedroom apartment. I recall their asking my father repeatedly if he would not give them some money so they could at least put some food in the refrigerator.

My childhood friends and I were bound to develop ambivalent attitudes toward the white world. On the one hand there was our instinctive aversion toward those who prevented us from realizing our grandest as well as our most trivial wishes. On the other, there was the equally instinctive jealousy which came from knowing that they had access to all the pleasurable things we wanted. Growing up, I could not help feeling a certain envy. And yet I have a very vivid recollection of deciding, very early, that I would never—and I was categorical about this—never harbor or express the desire to be white. This promise that I made to myself did nothing, however, to drive away the wishdreams that filled my head whenever my desires collided with a taboo. So, in order that my daydreams not contradict my principles, I constructed a fantasy in which I would slip on a white face and go unceremoniously into the theater or amusement park or wherever I wanted to go. After thoroughly enjoying the activity, I would make a dramatic, grandstand appearance before the white racists and with a sweeping gesture, rip off the white face, laugh wildly and call them all fools.

Years later, when I was in my teens, I recalled this child-ish daydream and decided, in a way, to act it out. My sister Fania and I were walking downtown in Birmingham when I spontaneously proposed a plan to her: We would pretend to be foreigners and, speaking French to each other, we would walk into the shoe store on 19th Street and ask, with a thick accent, to see a pair of shoes. At the sight of two young Black women speaking a foreign language, the clerks in the store raced to help us. Their delight with the exotic was enough to completely, if temporarily, dispel their normal disdain for Black people.

Therefore, Fania and I were not led to the back of the store where the one Black clerk would normally have waited on us out of the field of vision of the "respectable" white customers. We were invited to take seats in the very front of this Jim Crow shop. I pretended to know no English at all and Fania's broken English was extremely difficult to make out. The clerks strained to understand which shoes we wanted to try on.

Enthralled by the idea of talking to foreigners—even if they did happen to be Black—but frustrated about the com-munication failure, the clerks sent for the manager. The man-ager's posture was identical. With a giant smile he came in from his behind-the-scenes office saying, "Now, what can I do for you pretty young ladies?" But before he let my sister de-scribe the shoes we were looking for, he asked us about our background—where were we from, what were we doing in the States and what on earth had brought us to a place like Bir-mingham, Alabama? "It's very seldom that we get to meet people like you, you know." With my sister's less than ele-mentary knowledge of English, it required a great effort for her to relate our improvised story. After repeated attempts, however, the manager finally understood that we came from Martinique and were in Birmingham as part of a tour of the United States.

Each time this man finally understood something, his eyes lit up, his mouth opened in a broad "Oh!" He was utterly fascinated when she turned to me and translated his words. The white people in the store were at first confused when they saw two Black people sitting in the "whites only" section, but when they heard our accents and conversations in French, they too seemed to be pleased and excited by seeing Black people from so far away they could not possibly be a threat.

Eventually I signaled to Fania that it was time to wind up the game. We looked at him: his foolish face and obsequious grin one eye-blink away from the scorn he would have registered as automatically as a trained hamster had he known we were local residents. We burst out laughing. He started to laugh with us, hesitantly, the way people laugh when they suspect themselves to be the butt of the joke.

"Is something funny?" he whispered.

Suddenly I knew English, and told him that he was what was so funny. "All Black people have to do is pretend they come from another country, and you treat us like dignitaries." My sister and I got up, still laughing, and left the store.

I had followed almost to the *t* the scenario of my childhood daydream.

In September 1949, Fania had just turned one, and my brother Benny was about to turn four. Having spent three years playing the same games in nursery school and visiting the hospital next door, I was ready for something different and had pleaded to go early to elementary school. On the Monday after Labor Day, wearing my stiff new red plaid dress, I jumped into my father's truck, eager to begin my first day at "big" school.

The road to school took us down Eleventh Court across the overpass above the railroad tracks, through the street dividing the Jewish Cemetery in half and three blocks up the last hill. Carrie A. Tuggle School was a cluster of old wooden frame houses, so dilapidated that they would have been instantly condemned had they not been located in a Black neighborhood. One would have thought that this was merely a shoddy collection of houses built on the side of a grassless hill if it had not been for the children milling around or the fenced-in grave out front, bearing a sign indicating that Carrie A. Tuggle, founder of the school, was buried there.

Some of the houses were a motley whitewashed color. Others were covered with ugly brownish-black asphalt siding. That they were spread throughout an area of about three square blocks seemed to be proof of the way the white bureaucracy had gone about establishing a "school" for Black children. Evidently, they had selected a group of rundown houses and, after evicting the inhabitants, had declared them to be the school. These houses stood all along a steep incline; at the bottom of the hill, there was a large bowl-shaped formation in the earth, covered with the red clay that is peculiar to Alabama. This empty bowl had been designated the playground. Houses similar to the school buildings were located around the other sides of the bowl, houses whose outsides and insides were falling to pieces.

My mother, a primary school teacher herself, had already taught me how to read, write and do simple arithmetic. The things I learned in the first grade were far more fundamental than school learning. I learned that just because one is hungry, one does not have the right to a good meal; or when one is cold, to warm clothing, or when one is sick, to medical care. Many of the children could not even afford to buy a bag of potato chips for lunch. It was agonizing for me to see some of my closest friends waiting outside the lunchroom silently watching the other children eating.

For a long time, I thought about those who ate and those who watched. Finally I decided to do something about it. Knowing that my father returned from his service station each evening with a bag of coins, which he left overnight in a kitchen cabinet, one night I stayed awake until the whole house was sleeping. Then, trying to overcome my deep fear of the dark, I slipped into the kitchen and stole some of the coins. The next day I gave the money to my hungry friends. Their hunger pangs were more compelling than my pangs of conscience. I would just have to suffer the knowledge that I had stolen my father's money. My feelings of guilt were further appeased by reminding myself that my mother was always taking things to children in her class. She took our clothes and shoes—sometimes even before we had outgrown them—and gave them to those who needed them. Like my mother, what I did, I did quietly, without any fanfare. It seemed to me that if there were hungry children, something was wrong and if I did nothing about it, I would be wrong too.

This was my first introduction to class differences among my own people. We were the not-so-poor. Until my experiences at school, I believed that everyone else lived the way we did. We always had three good meals a day. I had summer clothes and winter clothes, everyday dresses and a few "Sunday" dresses. When holes began to wear through the soles of my shoes, although I may have worn them with pasteboard for a short time, we eventually went downtown to select a new pair.

The family income was earned by both my mother and father. Before I was born, my father had taken advantage of his hard-earned college degree, from St. Augustine's in Raleigh, North Carolina, to secure a position teaching history at Parker High School. But life was especially difficult during those years; his salary was as close to nothing as money could be. So with his meager savings he began to buy a service station in the Black section of downtown Birmingham.

My mother who, like my father, came from a very humble background, also worked her way through college and got a job teaching in the Birmingham elementary school system. The combined salaries were nothing to boast about, yet enough to survive on, and much more than was earned by the typical Southern Black family. They had managed to save enough to buy the old house on the hill, but they had to rent out the upstairs for years to make the mortgage payments. Until I went to school I did not know that this was a stunning accomplishment.

The prevailing myth then as now is that poverty is a

punishment for idleness and indolence. If you had nothing to show for yourself, it meant that you hadn't worked hard enough. I knew that my mother and father had worked hard —my father told us stories of walking ten miles to school each day, and my mother had her collection of anecdotes about the difficult life she had led as a child in the little town of Sylacauga. But I also knew that they had had breaks.

My preoccupation with the poverty and wretchedness I saw around me would not have been so deep if I had not been able to contrast it with the relative affluence of the white world. Tuggle was all the shabbier when we compared it to the white school nearby. From the top of the hill we could see an elementary school for white children. Solidly built of red brick, the building was surrounded by a deep-green lawn. In our school, we depended on potbellied coal stoves in winter, and when it rained outside, it rained inside. By the time a new building was constructed to replace the broken-down old one, I was too old to spend more than a year or so in its classrooms, which were reserved for the lower grades.

There were never enough textbooks to go around, and the ones that were available were old and torn, often with the most important pages missing. There was no gym for sports periods—only the "bowl." On rainy days when the bowl's red clay was a muddy mess, we were cooped up somewhere in one of the shacks.

Tuggle was administered and controlled as a section of the "Birmingham Negro Schools" by an all-white Board of Education. Only on special occasions did we see their representatives face to face—during inspections or when they were showing off their "Negro schools" to some visitor from out of town. Insofar as the day-to-day activities were concerned, it was Black people who ran the school.

Perhaps it was precisely these conditions that gave us a strong positive identification with our people and our history. We learned from some of our teachers all the traditional ingredients of "Negro History." From the first grade on, we all sang the "Negro National Anthem" by James Weldon Johnson when assemblies were convened—either along with or sometimes instead of "The Star Spangled Banner" or "My Country, 'Tis of Thee." I recall being very impressed with the difference between the official anthems, which insisted that freedom was a fact for everybody in the country, and the "Negro National Anthem," whose words were of resistance. And although my singing voice was nothing I wanted to call attention to, I always sang the last phrases full blast: "Facing the rising sun, till a new day is born, let us march on till victory is won!"

As we learned about George Washington, Thomas Jefferson and Abraham Lincoln, we also became acquainted with Black historical figures. Granted, the Board of Education would not permit the teachers to reveal to us the exploits of Nat Turner and Denmark Vesey. But we were introduced to Frederick Douglass, Sojourner Truth and Harriet Tubman.

One of the most important events each year at Tuggle was Negro History Week. Special events were planned for assembly, and in all grades each child would be responsible for a project about a Black historical or contemporary figure. Throughout those years, I learned something about every Black person "respectable" enough to be allotted a place in the history books—or, as far as contemporary people were concerned, who made their way into "Who's Who in Negro America" or *Ebony* magazine. The weekend before Negro History Week each year, I was always hard at work—creating my poster, calling on the assistance of my parents, clipping pictures, writing captions and descriptions.

Without a doubt, the children who attended the de jure segregated schools of the South had an advantage over those who attended the de facto segregated schools of the North. During my summer trips to New York, I found that many of the Black children there had never heard of Frederick Douglass or Harriet Tubman. At Carrie A. Tuggle Elementary School, Black identity was thrust upon us by the circumstances of oppression. We had been pushed into a totally Black universe; we were compelled to look to ourselves for spiritual nourishment. Yet while there were those clearly supportive aspects of the Black Southern school, it should not be idealized. As I look back, I recall the pervasive ambivalence at school, an ambivalence which I confronted in virtually every classroom, and every school-related event. On the one hand, there was a strong tendency affirming our identity as Black people that ran through all the school activities. But on the other hand, many teachers tended to inculcate in us the official, racist explanation for our misery. And they encouraged an individualistic, competitive way out of this torment. We were told that the ultimate purpose of our education was to provide us with the skills and knowledge to lift ourselves singly and separately out of the muck and slime of poverty by "our own bootstraps." This child would become a doctor, this one a lawyer; there would be the teachers, the engineers, the contractors, the accountants, the businessmen—and if you struggled extraordinarily hard, you might be able to approach the achievements of A. G. Gaston, our local Black millionaire.

This Booker T. Washington syndrome permeated every aspect of the education I received in Birmingham. Work hard and you will be rewarded. A corollary of this principle was that the road would be harder and rockier for Black people than for their white counterparts. Our teachers warned us that we would have to steel ourselves for hard labor and more hard labor, sacrifices and more sacrifices. Only this would prove that we were serious about overcoming all the obstacles before us. It often struck me they were speaking of these obstacles as if they would always be there, part of the natural order of things, rather than the product of a system of racism, which we could eventually overturn.

I continued to have my doubts about this "work and ye shall be rewarded" notion. But, I admit, my reaction was not exactly straightforward. On the one hand, I did not entirely believe it. It didn't make sense to me that all those who had not "made it" were suffering for their lack of desire and the defectiveness of their will to achieve a better life for themselves. If this were true, then, great numbers of our people—

perhaps the majority—had really been lazy and shiftless, as white people were always saying.

But on the other hand, it seemed that I was modeling my own aspirations after precisely that "work and be rewarded" principle. I had made up my mind that I was going to prove to the world that I was just as good, just as intelligent, just as capable of achieving as any white person. At that time—and until my high school years in New York—I wanted to become a pediatrician. Never once did I doubt that I would be able to execute my plans—after elementary school, high school, then college and medical school. But I had a definite advantage: my parents would see to it that I attended college, and would help me survive until I could make it on my own. This was not something that could be said for the vast majority of my schoolmates.

The work-and-be-rewarded syndrome was not the only thing which seemed to fly in the face of the positive sense of ourselves. We knew, for example, that whenever the white folks visited the school we were expected to "be on our P's and Q's," as our teachers put it. I could not understand why we had to behave better for them than we behaved for ourselves, unless we really did think they were superior. The visitors from the Board of Education always came in groups—groups of three or four white men who acted like they owned the place. Overseers. Sometimes if the leader of the group wanted to flaunt his authority he looked us over like a herd of cattle and said to the teacher, "Susie, this is a nice class you have here." We all knew that when a white person called a Black adult by his or her first name it was a euphemism for "Nigger, stay in your place." When this white assault was staged, I tried to decipher the emotions on the teacher's face: acquiesence, obsequiousness, defiance, or the pain of realizing that if she did fight back, she would surely lose her job.

Once a Black teacher did fight back. When the white men called him "Jesse" in front of his class, he replied in a deep but cold voice, "In case you have forgotten, my name is Mr.

Champion." He knew, as the words left his lips, that he had just given up his job. Jesse Champion was a personal friend of my parents, and I was appalled by the silence that reigned among the Black community following his act. It probably stemmed from a collective sense of guilt that his defiance was the exception and not the norm.

Nothing in the world made me angrier than inaction, than silence. The refusal or inability to do something, say something when a thing needed doing or saying, was unbearable. The watchers, the head shakers, the back turners made my skin prickle. I remember once when I was seven or eight, I went along with my friend Annie Laurie and her family on a trip to the country. At the house we visited, a dog was running around in the yard. Soon another dog appeared. Without any warning the two animals were tearing at each other's throats. Saliva was flying and blood gushed from the wounds. Everyone was just standing, looking, doing nothing. It seemed we would stand there all day watching the hot Alabama sun beat down on the stupid, pointless fight of two dogs gnawing out each other's guts and eyes. I couldn't stand it any longer; I rushed in and tried to pull the dogs apart. It wasn't until after the screaming adults had dragged me away that I thought about the danger. But then it didn't matter; the fight had been stopped.

The impulse I felt then was with me at other fights. Fights not between animals but between people, but equally futile and meaningless. All through school there were absurd battles—some brief, but many sustained and deadly. I frequently could not keep from stepping in.

The children fought over nothing—over being bumped, over having toes stepped on, over being called a name, over being the target of real or imagined gossip. They fought over everything—split shoes, and cement yards, thin coats and mealless days. They fought the meanness of Birmingham while they sliced the air with knives and punched Black faces because they could not reach white ones.

It hurt me. The fight in which my girl friend Olivia got stabbed with a knife. It hurt to see another friend, Chaney—furious when a teacher criticized her in front of the class—stand up, grab the nearest chair and fly into the teacher with it. The whole class turned into one great melee, some assisting Chaney, others trying to rescue the teacher, and the rest of us trying to break up the skirmish.

It hurt to see us folding in on ourselves, using ourselves as whipping posts because we did not yet know how to struggle against the real cause of our misery.

Time did not cool the anger of the white people who still lived on the hill. They refused to adapt their lives to our presence. Every so often a courageous Black family moved or built on the white side of Center Street, and the simmering resentment erupted in explosions and fires. On a few such occasions, Police Chief Bull Conner would announce on the radio that a "nigger family" had moved in on the white side of the street. His prediction "There will be bloodshed tonight" would be followed by a bombing. So common were the bombings on Dynamite Hill that the horror of them diminished.

On our side, old houses abandoned by their white inhabitants were gradually bought up, and the woods where we picked blackberries were giving way to new brick houses. By the time I was eight or nine, we had a whole neighborhood of Black people. When the weather was warm, all the children came out after dark to play hide and go seek. There were many hiding places within our boundaries, which were not less than one or two square blocks. The night made the game more exciting, and we could pretend we were outsmarting the white folks.

Sometimes we actually dared to penetrate their turf. "I dare you to go up on the Montees' porch," one of us would say. Whoever took him up would leave us on our side of the street as he hesitantly crossed over into enemy territory, tiptoed up the Montees' cement steps, touched the wooden porch with one shoe as if he were testing a hot stove, then raced back to us. When it was my turn, I could virtually hear the bombs going off as I ran up the steps and touched the Montee porch for the first time in my life. When this game began to lose its aura of danger, we made it more challenging. Instead of just touching the porch, we had to run to the door, ring the bell and hide in the bushes around their house, while the old woman or old man came out, trying to figure out what was going on. When they finally caught on to our game, even though they could seldom find us, they stood on the porch screaming, "You little niggers better leave us alone!"

In the meantime my playmates and school friends were learning how to call each other "nigger," or what, unfortunately, was just as bad in those days, "black" or "African," both of which were considered synonymous with "savage." My mother never allowed anyone to say the word "nigger" in the house. (For that matter, no "bad words"—"shit," "damn," not even "hell" could be uttered in her presence.) If we wanted to describe an argument we had had with someone, we had to say, "Bill called me that bad word that starts with an *n*." Eventually, my mouth simply refused to pronounce those words for me, regardless of how hard I might want to say them.

If, in the course of an argument with one of my friends, I was called "nigger" or "black," it didn't bother me nearly so much as when somebody said, "Just because you're bright and got good hair, you think you can act like you're white." It was a typical charge laid against light-skinned children.

Sometimes I used to secretly resent my parents for giving me light skin instead of dark, and wavy instead of kinky hair. I pleaded with my mother to let me get it straightened, like my friends. But she continued to brush it with water and rub vaseline in it to make it lie down so she could fix the two big wavy plaits which always hung down my back. On special occasions, she rolled it up in curlers made out of brown paper to make my Shirley Temple Curls.

One summer when our Brownie troop was at Camp Blossom Hill, it started to rain as we were walking from the mess hall to our cabins, and the girls' hands immediately went for their heads. The water was no threat to my unstraightened hair, so I paid no attention to the rain. One of the girls switched out and said, "Angela's got good hair. She can stroll in the rain from now to doomsday." I know she wasn't intentionally trying to hurt me, but I felt crushed. I ran back to my cabin, threw myself on the bunk sobbing.

My cousins Snookie, Betty Jean and their mother, Doll, lived in Ketona, Alabama. I always loved to spend the weekend with them, because I knew they would put the hot comb over the wood fire and run it through my hair until it was straight as a pin. If I begged my mother long enough, she would let me wear it to school for a few days before she made me wash it out.

Downtown near the post office was the Birmingham Public Library. It was open only to white people, but in a hidden room in the building, accessible only through a secret back entrance, a Black librarian had her headquarters. Black people could pass lists of books to her, which she would try to secure from the library.

As a result of my mother's encouragement and prodding, books became a gratifying diversion for me. Mother taught me how to read when I had hardly reached my fourth year and eventually, when I was a little older, we both established a quota system for the number of books I should be reading per week. My mother or father picked up my books downtown, or else the Black librarian, Miss Bell, would bring them by the house.

Later a new Black library was built down the hill, on the corner of Center Street and Eighth Avenue. The new red brick library, with its shiny linoleum floors and varnished tables, became one of my favorite hangouts. For hours at a time, I read avidly there—everything from *Heidi* to Victor Hugo's *Les Misérables*, from Booker T. Washington's *Up From Slavery* to Frank Yerby's lurid novels.

Reading was far more satisfying than my weekly piano lessons and Saturday morning dance classes. For my fifth Christmas, my mother and father had gotten enough money together to buy me a full-sized piano. Once a week I trudged over to Mrs. Chambliss' house, dutifully played my scales and compositions, suffering the humiliation of being screamed at if I made a mistake. When the lesson was over, I paid her seventy-five cents and, if it was dark, waited for Mother or Daddy to pick me up so I wouldn't have to walk by the cemetery alone. On the other six days, I had to practice before I went out in the neighborhood with my friends. Around the end of May each year, Mrs. Chambliss' recital took place either at St. Paul's Methodist Church or the 16th Street Baptist Church two blocks away from my father's service station. With my hair in curls, wearing a ruffled organdy dress, rigid with nervousness, I tapped out the piece I had been practicing for months. The reward for the ordeal was three whole months without the pressure of piano lessons.

Saturday mornings I joined scores of leotard-clad girls at the Smithfield Community Center in the projects where we used to live. There Mrs. Woods and her helpers made sure we did our pliés and arabesques. Ballet during the first part of the class, then tap, soft shoe. My natural clumsiness defied the delicate ballet steps, so I always tried to find a place to hide in one of the back rows. For a while, my little brother, Benny, was coming along, so I had the added responsibility of taking care of him. One morning as we were walking down Center Street, he ran out in front of me—straight across Ninth Avenue. A bus came screeching to a stop, practically knocking him down. Trembling violently, I ran to rescue him. He was totally oblivious to the fact that he had almost been killed. During the warm-up exercises, I was still shaking. Suddenly I felt something warm streaming down my legs. I dropped to the floor, into the puddle of my urine, so humiliated I couldn't bear to look up at the staring faces of the other pupils. A girl named Emma came over and put her arms around my shoulder. Saying, "Angela, don't worry. Let's go outside," she led me away. She never knew how much her gesture meant to me. Still, having to face this same crowd every Saturday filled me with shame.

Some years back, Black visitors to Birmingham had all of three post cards from which to choose if they wanted a souvenir of the Black section of the city. Sixteenth Street Baptist Church. Parker High School. A. G. Gaston's Funeral Home. Perhaps the white people who made the photographs and retouched them in bright reds and yellows had decided that our lives could be summarized by church, school and funerals. Once we were born, we got religion and a sprinkling of learning; then there was nothing left to do but die.

They tried to make this sprinkling of learning appear to come from the most impressive institution of education around. On the picture post card, Parker looked brand new, whiter than if it had been whitewashed the day before, and had bright-green grass painted in front, where the dry dust refused to yield even a weed. Above the picture, stamped in bold black print, were the words: "A. H. Parker High School, Largest in the World for Colored Pupils"—as if there should have been tourists from every region of the globe coming to get a glimpse of this wonder.

Perhaps, on its face, the statement was true—I don't think anyone ever did the research to confirm or contradict it. But whatever truth it contained rested squarely on the miserable conditions of Black people. If Parker was the "largest high school for colored pupils," it was for the same reason that there was not a single public high school in Harlem and the same reason that the education of Black youth in South Africa doesn't merit a grain of consideration. When my mother was high school age, the "world's largest" had been called Industrial High School, and it was the only Black high school for hundreds of miles around. She lived in the small town of Sylacauga, at least seventy-five miles from the city. The only way she could hope to get an education beyond the eighth grade was to leave her family and move to Birmingham. My friends and I were not overly eager to enter high school. When we graduated from Carrie A. Tuggle Elementary School, we had to enter Parker Annex, several blocks away from the main building. This was a cluster of beaten-up wooden huts not much different from what we had just left.

When we arrived on the first day we discovered that the inside of these structures was even more dilapidated than the outside. Unpainted wooden floors, ancient walls covered with graffiti no one ever bothered to remove. We realized that when the season began to turn, we would have to depend on the archaic potbellied stove in the corner of each house—we called them Shack I, Shack II, etc.

Very few of my classes were stimulating—biology, chemistry, mathematics were the subjects that interested me most. My history classes were a farce. Farcical not so much because of the teachers' deficiency as the deficiency of the textbooks assigned by the Board of Education. In our American History book I discovered that the Civil War was the "War for Southern Independence" and that Black people much preferred to be slaves than to be free. After all, the books pointed out, the evidence of our ancestors' cheerful acceptance of their plight was the weekly Saturday night singing and dancing sessions. In elementary school, we had already been taught that many of the songs by slaves had a meaning understood only by them. "Swing Low, Sweet Chariot" for instance also referred to the journey toward freedom in *this* life. But there was nothing about this in our high school textbooks. The teachers either had too much on their hands keeping the classes orderly or else they were not as concerned as our elementary-school teachers were about presenting us with an accurate picture of Black history.

The inner-directed violence which was so much a part of our school lives at Tuggle accelerated at Parker to the point where it verged on fratricide. Hardly a day would pass without a fight—in class or outside. And on one warm and wind-swept day—right there in the schoolyard—one of my school-mates actually succeeded in knifing all life from another.

We seemed to be caught in a whirlpool of violence and blood from which none of us could swim away.

About the time I entered high school, the civil rights movement was beginning to awaken some Black Alabamians from their deep but fretful sleep. But judging from the general inactivity at Parker High School, you never would have known that Rosa Parks had refused to move to the back of the bus in Montgomery on December 4, 1955, or that Martin Luther King was leading a full-scale bus boycott there, just a hundred miles away, or that, in fact, there was supposed to be a budding bus movement in Birmingham.

Some of us were affected by the boycott, however. On a few occasions, a small group of my schoolmates and I spontaneously decided to sit in the front of the bus to show our support of our sisters and brothers. Inevitably, a shouting match ensued between us and the bus driver. The Black people on the bus were forced to take sides. Because there was no extensive organized movement at that time in Birmingham, some of them were afraid of our audacity and implored us to do what the white man said.

Around this time, the NAACP was declared illegal in Alabama, and its members were threatened with imprisonment. My parents were both members and determined not to allow Bull Conner and company to scare them into submission. Like others who related to the movement, my parents received bomb threats, but they continued to pay their dues until the NAACP was officially dissolved and replaced by the Alabama Christian Movement for Human Rights, headed by Reverend Fred Shuttlesworth.

On the day after Christmas in 1956, the bus protest in Birmingham was scheduled to be launched by the ACMHR. Having decided to crush it before it had a chance to gather momentum, the racists, encouraged by Bull Conner, pulled out of the closet their old trusty weapons: the sticks of dynamite we had come to know so well. Christmas night, a roaring explosion ripped through the home of Reverend Shuttlesworth. They had planted the bomb beneath the house, directly under the bed where the minister was sleeping. People said that it was a miracle of God that everything around him was blown to pieces, yet the minister escaped without a scratch. We learned the next day that he had taken a neighbor who had been hurt during the explosion to the hospital and had returned home by bus, riding in the front. Later that day quite a number of people followed Reverend Shuttlesworth's example and were subsequently arrested.

I was very agitated during those days. Something was happening which could change our lives. But I was too young, so I was told (I was twelve), and a girl at that, to be exposed to the billy clubs and violence of the police. As the years passed, however, and the needs of the movement increased, it became necessary to incorporate every man, woman and child who was willing into all levels of protest activity. In fact, shortly thereafter, the Shuttlesworth children began to play leading roles in ACMHR's work.

While these upheavals were exploding in the streets of Birmingham, little of it penetrated Parker's campus. Over the next three years, the movement reached high points and then lulled. The daily schedule of classes, complemented by football and basketball games went on. The off-campus social life of the Black middle class continued undisturbed—except for the usual, routine racist incidents.

For instance, one Sunday some friends and I were driving home from the movies. Among those in the car was Peggy, a girl who lived down the street. She was very light-skinned, with blond hair and green eyes. Her presence usually provoked puzzled and hostile stares because white people were always misidentifying her as white. This time it was a policeman who mistook her for a white person surrounded by Black people. And just as my friends were about to drop me off in front of the house, he forced us over to the side, demanding to know what we niggers were doing with a white girl. He ordered us out of the car and searched all of us, except Peggy, whom he separated from the group. In Alabama at that time, there was a state statute which prohibited all except economic intercourse between Blacks and whites. The cop threatened to throw all of us in jail, including Peggy, whom he called a "nigger lover."

When Peggy angrily explained that she was Black like all the rest of us, the cop was obviously embarrassed. He worked off his embarrassment by harassing us with foul language, hitting some of the boys and searching every inch of the car for some excuse to take us to jail. This was a routine incident, perhaps even milder than most, but no less enraging because it was typical.

At fourteen, in my junior year, I felt restless and exceedingly limited. The provincialism of Birmingham bothered me, and I had not yet been swept up into the Civil Rights Movement to the extent that it could forge for me a solid raison d'être. I could not define or articulate the dissatisfaction I felt. I simply had the sensation of things closing in on me—and I wanted to get out. The time was fast approaching when, in order not to be outcasts, girls my age in middle-class circles had to play an active role in the established social life of the Black community. I hated the big formal dances and felt very awkward and out of place at the one or two such events I attended. I had to get away. One way or another, I was going to leave Birmingham.

I discovered two avenues of escape: the early entrance program at Fisk University in Nashville and an experimental program developed by the American Friends Service Committee, through which Black students from the South could attend integrated high schools in the North. I applied for both and, after some months, learned that I had been accepted by both.

With medical school in mind, at first I had a strong inclination toward the Fisk alternative. Fisk would not only be an escape from the provincialism I detested, it would also mean that I could more easily pursue my plans to become a pediatrician; Meharry Medical School was right on its campus. And Fisk was among the most academically prestigious Black universities in the country. It was the Fisk of W. E. B. DuBois. But it was also the University of the Black Bourgeoisie par excellence, and I could predict that my disinclination to become involved in purely social affairs would create enormous personal problems. Probably if I did not pledge a sorority, I would remain an outsider.

As far as the American Friends' program was concerned, I had been able to gather only the most rudimentary information. I knew that the school I would attend, Elisabeth Irwin High School, was in New York and that I would live with a white family in Brooklyn. Though I knew nothing about the school, New York still fascinated me. I thought of all the things I had not been able to do for the first fifteen years of my life. I could do them in New York. I had a very undeveloped appreciation of music or the theater; I could look forward to exploring a whole new cultural universe.

Ready and willing to accept the challenge of the unknown, I was only a little frightened. My mother thought more about the dangers I might confront, and though she wanted me to receive a fuller education, she was distressed about my having to leave home. I was only fifteen and she feared that a year on a university campus, surrounded by men and women much older than I, would rob me of the rest of my childhood and make me mature before my time. I don't think she quite realized that any Black child growing up in the South is forced to mature "before her time" anyway. But when she considered New York, all she could see was a gigantic house of horrors. Elisabeth Irwin was located in Greenwich Village, which, to her, was the haven of weird beatniks.

My own preference was Elisabeth Irwin High School, New York City, where I would live in the home of W. H. Melish. But because of Mother's misgivings, I was willing to content myself with Fisk. We telephoned the Melishes in New

York and informed them with regret of our decision. I tried to think about the positive side of Fisk: In four years, I would be nineteen and could attend Meharry Medical School; a few years later I would be curing children.

With my suitcases packed and my mind snapped shut, I was ready to go (even if I had not bought all the suggested clothes on the list, such as formals for various occasions). One or two days before I was to leave, my father, my dear father, broke out of his normal reticence and asked me to tell him frankly what I wished to do. But before I could answer, he said he wanted to tell me about some of his own experiences during his brief stay at Fisk. (He had graduated from St. Augustine College in Raleigh, North Carolina, but had done some graduate work at Fisk.) It was a very good school, he said. But to accomplish anything there you had to enter the place with an unwavering conception of what you were going to do. I had to see both sides of Fisk, he said, its historical significance to Black people—and its problems as well.

By the time we wound up the conversation, I knew that I would not be attending Fisk University, at least not that year. I would just have to persuade my mother that I was capable of defending myself against whatever dangers might be lurking in the streets of New York.

For better or for worse, I boarded the train for New York. The trip itself was symbolic. Getting on in the Black section of the train, I was surrounded by friends and acquaintances from Birmingham who were on their way to schools located along the route to New York. As the Jim Crow train moved through Alabama, Georgia, and up through Washington, my friends left the train in small groups. Some were going to Morehouse, Spellman, or Clark, in Atlanta, and the final group got off in Washington to attend Howard University. At each major train stop, the familiarity of the surroundings eroded a little more. By the time the train slid out of Washington, I had been abandoned to the company of strangers and to the strangeness of white people entering the car and taking seats which had been "For Colored" throughout the Southern states.

The prospects both excited and worried me. I had already assumed an obligation to live and study with white people over the next two years, but could I accustom myself to being around them all the time? In spite of the fact that, theoretically at least, the white people I was going to relate to at home and at school were committed, on some level, to fight for the equality of my people, the impact of racism upon me had been so tremendous that I knew I would have to exercise great effort to fit into a predominantly white world. I would have to be open and guarded at the same time. I would be watchful—prepared for any early sign of slight or hostility. (I did not yet know that what I would also encounter was white liberals' tendency to be oversolicitous of their few Black acquaintances.) But I would try hard to be at ease, to be accessible to whatever humaneness and kindness they might show me. I felt an almost unbearable tension—it was as if I were two persons, two faces of a Janus head. One profile stared disconsolately into the past—the fretful, violent, confining past broken only by occasional splotches of meaning, and by the love I had for my family. The other gazed with longing and apprehension into the future—a future glowing with challenge, but also harboring the possibility of defeat.

Reverend and Mrs. Melish were waiting for me in Pennsylvania Station when the train arrived. From the first moment I had heard about them, and the sacrifices they had made for the progressive movement, I had a great respect for both of them. At the height of the McCarthy period, Reverend Melish (who, together with his father, was the pastor of the largest Episcopal church in Brooklyn) had used his pulpit to defend the victims of McCarthy's witch-hunting insanity. He had preached about the need for true Christians to fight all forms of injustice and repression. Moreover, he was at that time a member of the Soviet-American Friendship Organization, and in those days, McCarthy and company didn't distinguish between defending the right of a people to be Communist and being a Communist oneself.

The Melishes had gone through a period of fierce and turbulent struggle with the hierarchy of the Episcopal Church; there had been the calumny of the public media, the ecclesiastical trial and finally the loss of the church. But their suffering had simply made them stronger and more determined.

There were three sons in the Melish family: two older and one younger than me. One was in the twelfth grade and another in the seventh grade at Elisabeth Irwin. I felt a little more comfortable knowing that someone would be helping me orient myself in this school which was, from all accounts, unlike any I had ever heard of.

I got settled at the house, and tried to explore the neighborhood. It was a relief to learn that the house was located in the heart of the Black community—in Bedford Stuyvesant on the corner of Kingston and St. Marks. It took me a while to realize that Black people too were affected by the character of New York. You did not go out on the street—especially if you were a woman—and strike up a conversation with a passing brother. In Birmingham, it would be considered the height of arrogance to pass one of your people on the street without a greeting like "Good evening." But here, they looked at you as though you were deranged if you spoke to a stranger on the street.

Before the official opening of the semester, I went with Mrs. Melish to visit the school and meet some of the teachers. Elisabeth Irwin High School, on the edge of Greenwich Village, was such a small brick building in the middle of a block of two-story apartment buildings, that you would have never noticed that it was a school unless you happened to pass by in the morning when school was about to begin or in the evening when it was letting out.

The history of the school impressed me. It had been conceived some decades before as an experiment within the public education system in progressive education. When the New York Board of Education decided to drop the experi-

ment, the teachers themselves resolved to take over the school
and guarantee its continued existence. They transformed it
into a private school, asking tuition fees of those who attended, and made themselves collective owners of the institution.

Aside from the high school there was an elementary
school and kindergarten as well, located in a red brick building on Bleecker Street, appropriately called The Little Red
School House. In each grade, from four years old through the
twelfth grade, there was a single class, consisting of from
twenty-five to thirty students.

The preview trip to the school completely shattered my
ideas of what schools were supposed to be like. All the teachers I had ever known had been conservative in appearance:
the men had worn suits and ties, the women simple but dressy
clothes. One of the first teachers I was introduced to was
wearing a pair of beat-up jeans, a wild-colored short-sleeved
shirt, and tennis shoes, and much of his face was hidden by a
beard. I was further stunned by the fact that I was introduced
to them by their first names. Even the director of the school, a
sympathetic, white-haired, dignified New England gentleman
—even he was presented by his first name.

Because it was a small school and because a sizeable
number of students had entered it at age four and stayed until
they graduated from high school, there was an inevitable tendency toward clannishness. I sensed this family-like atmosphere immediately and was not completely sure whether I
was going to be capable of integrating myself into it.

In trying to get a more complete picture of this school,
talking to the Melishes and others who knew something about
it, I learned that many of the present teachers had been
placed on the blacklist (whitelist?) by the Board of Education
and were therefore not permitted to teach in any public
school. Their politics ranged from liberal to radical, including
leanings toward communism, or so I thought.

Trying to put all this together, I felt as if I were swimming alone in unexplored waters. I did not know the undercurrents, I could never tell whether I was in deep or shallow waters or maybe a swamp or quicksand. And I had no guide who understood my strengths, my weaknesses—the strengths and handicaps of a young Black woman from the racist South.

As I leaped over the hurdles presented by my new environment, I began to feel more comfortable at home and at school. When I learned about socialism in my history classes, a whole new world opened up before my eyes. For the first time, I became acquainted with the notion that there could be an ideal socioeconomic arrangement; that every person could give to the society according to his ability and his talents, and that in turn he could receive material and spiritual aid in accordance with his needs.

I did not yet understand *scientific* socialism, but I tried to comprehend the utopian socialist experiments we discussed in our history classes. I was fascinated by these groups of people who resolved to isolate themselves entirely in order to build a new miniature socialist, human society. I did not stop with the material we read about in our history books. I went to the library and read whatever I could find about Robert Owens and the other leaders of that movement.

Perhaps it was the romantic strain in me which attracted me to the Utopian socialists. Because when I began to consider the real possibility of solving the problems of my people, and the problems of exploited white people as well, I could not find the transition from the real world of oppression and racism and injustice and the ideal world of communism. Perhaps a few people here and there might save their souls from the corruption of capitalism, but small collective, communist agricultural societies were definitely no way to liberate millions and millions of people.

The *Communist Manifesto* hit me like a bolt of lightning. I read it avidly, finding in it answers to many of the seemingly unanswerable dilemmas which had plagued me. I read it over and over again, not completely understanding every passage or every idea, but enthralled nevertheless by the possibility of a communist revolution here. I began to see the problems of Black people within the context of a large working-class movement. My ideas about Black liberation were imprecise, and I could not find the right concepts to articulate them; still, I was acquiring some understanding about how capitalism could be abolished.

I was particularly impressed by a passage in the *Manifesto* which portrayed the proletariat as the savior of all oppressed people: "All previous historical movements were movements of minorities, or in the interests of minorities. The proletarian movement is the self-conscious, independent movement of the immense majority, in the interest of the immense majority. The proletariat, the lowest stratum of our present society, cannot stir, cannot raise itself up, without the whole super-incumbent strata of official society being sprung into the air."

What struck me so emphatically was the idea that once the emancipation of the proletariat became a reality, the foundation was laid for the emancipation of all oppressed groups in the society. Images surged up in my mind of Black workers in Birmingham trekking every morning to the steel mills or descending into the mines. Like an expert surgeon, this document cut away cataracts from my eyes. The eyes heavy with hatred on Dynamite Hill; the roar of explosives, the fear, the hidden guns, the weeping Black woman at our door, the children without lunches, the schoolyard bloodshed, the social games of the Black middle class, Shack I/Shack II, the back of the bus, police searches—it all fell into place. What had seemed a personal hatred of me, an inexplicable refusal of Southern whites to confront their own emotions, and a stubborn willingness of Blacks to acquiesce, became the inevitable consequence of a ruthless system which kept itself alive and well by encouraging spite, competition and the oppression of one group by another. Profit was the word: the cold and constant motive for the behavior, the contempt and the despair I had seen.

Now I sensed a need to change some of my ideas about liberation. I realized then that despite my superficial aversion for some of the social activities of the Black middle class, I had been depending on it to guide the workers, the jobless and the poor among us to freedom.

Of course, the most powerful impact the *Manifesto* had on me—what moved me most—was the vision of a new society, without exploiters and exploited, a society without classes, a society where no one would be permitted to own so much that he could use his possessions to exploit other human beings. After the communist revolution "we shall have an association, in which the free development of each is the condition for the free development of all."

The final words of the *Manifesto* moved me to an overwhelming desire to throw myself into the communist movement:

> The Communists disdain to conceal their views and aims. They openly declare that their ends can be attained only by the forcible overthrow of all existing social conditions. Let the ruling classes tremble at a Communist revolution. The proletarians have nothing to lose but their chains. They have a world to win.
>
> WORKERS OF ALL COUNTRIES, UNITE!

Quite coincidentally, around the same time that I read the *Communist Manifesto*, I was invited by a friend to attend meetings of a youth organization called Advance. She was a daughter of a member of the Communist Party, and Advance was a Marxist-Leninist youth organization with fraternal ties with the Party. Many of the meetings were held in the house of Herbert Aptheker—the much-respected Communist historian—with his daughter Bettina Aptheker playing a major leadership role in the organization.

Eugene Dennis, the son of the Communist leader of the same name, was also a part of the group, as was Mary Lou Patterson, the daughter of the formidable Black Communist lawyer William Patterson. It was Patterson who carried the petition protesting the genocide of Black people to the United Nations in 1954. James Jackson's daughter Harriet, Mary Lou, and Margaret and Claudia Burnham, were already close friends of mine; now through our activities in Advance we became truly "comrades in arms."

Herbert Aptheker was teaching a course on the fundamentals of Marxism at the American Institute for Marxist Studies. Along with other members of Advance, I attended his lectures, which helped me to penetrate the mysteries in the *Manifesto*.

Advance participated in all the peace demonstrations that were being organized at the time by SANE (the Committee for a Sane Nuclear Policy) and the civil rights demonstrations in solidarity with the movement in the South. The first sit-ins had been launched on February 1, 1960, in Greensboro, North Carolina, and had spread throughout the South. After the demand for employment of Black clerks in F. W. Woolworth variety store was introduced, every Saturday morning we lugged our picket signs and literature down to the Woolworth's on Forty-Second Street, set up the line and tried to persuade New Yorkers not to patronize the store until it agreed to hire black clerks in the South.

Although I was involved in the movement in that way I felt cheated: precisely at the moment I had decided to leave the South a movement was mushrooming at home. In 1961, when the bus carrying the freedom riders arrived at the Greyhound Depot in Birmingham, I called my parents to tell them that I wanted to come home—and to please send me the money for the trip. When they told me it was best that I stay in New York and finish out my last year of studies there, I was too distressed and frustrated to keep my mind on my schoolwork. Each time I saw photographs or television coverage of the police aiming high-power hoses at demonstrators, sicking dogs on little children, I closed the door to my room so the Melishes would not see me cry.

They were exciting years—and I have never regretted my

decision to spend them in New York. But they were years of tension. The Janus head was still fixed—one eye full of longing to be in the fray in Birmingham, the other contemplating my own future. It would be a long time before the two profiles came together and I would know the direction to both the past and the future.

I go into genesis' landscape
of rumblings, collisions, and waters ...

FEDERICO GARCIA LORCA

PART THREE

Waters

*P*erched on an enormous boulder protruding from a grassy knoll on the outskirts of Waltham, Massachusetts, is a brass sculpture of Justice Louis Brandeis, his arms outstretched, winglike, as if he were about to take flight—as if there were nowhere else to go.

I had come to assume that in order to safeguard its unorthodoxy, Elisabeth Irwin had spun a cocoon around itself. During those two years in New York I never quite overcame the sense of being out of place, of being an outsider who had penetrated that cocoon by accident. Nevertheless, I confronted it head on. And when the atmosphere became too close, too oppressive, I could always tear away a piece of the wall and slip out to other worlds—my childhood friends, Margaret and Claudia, Mary Lou Patterson, Phyllis Strong; political work in Advance; my Black and Puerto Rican friends at the Youth Center run by Mrs. Melish in Brooklyn.

Brandeis University was different. There were no roads leading outside.

Its physical and spiritual isolation were mutually reinforcing. There was nothing in Waltham but a clock factory, and Cambridge and Boston were unreachable for those of us who couldn't afford a car.

I searched the crowds of freshmen for others who were Black. Just knowing they were there would have made me feel a little more comfortable. But the full scholarship Brandeis had bestowed upon me was apparently a guilt-motivated attempt to increase their Black freshman population of two. We three were all female. I was glad that one of them, Alice, lived on the same floor as I.

Although Alice and I struck up a friendship immediately, it did not essentially alter my attitude toward the college. I felt alienated, angry, alone and would have left the campus if I had had the courage and had known where to go. Since I was there—to stay, it seemed—I lived with this alienation and began to cultivate it in a romantic sort of way. If I felt alone, I refused to feel sorry for myself and refused to fight it by actively seeking friends; I would *be* alone, aloof, and would appear to enjoy it. It didn't help the situation that I had gotten very much involved in the writings of the so-called Existentialists. Camus. Sartre. I retreated into myself and rejected practically everything outside.

Only in the artificial surroundings of an isolated, virtually all-white college campus could I have allowed myself to cultivate this nihilistic attitude. It was as if in order to fight off the unreal quality of my environment, I leaped desperately into another equally unreal mode of living.

During that first semester, I didn't study very much. I told myself that the courses I was compelled to take were irrelevant anyway. I stayed out of the social life of the school, or would wander into a formal dance in the blue jeans I wore all the time—just for the sake of making a point. I called myself a communist, but refused to be drawn into the small campus movement because I felt that the politicos had approached me in an obviously patronizing manner. It seemed as if they were determined to help the "poor, wretched Negroes" become equal to them, and I simply didn't think they were worth becoming equal to.

The one thing that did excite me during that freshman year was the news that James Baldwin was scheduled to deliver a series of lectures on literature. Since I had first discovered *Go Tell It on the Mountain*, I read all of Baldwin's writings I could find. When he came to Brandeis, I made sure I captured a front seat. But he had hardly gotten into his lecturing when the news broke that the world was teetering on the edge of the abyss of World War III. The Cuban Missile Crisis had erupted.

James Baldwin announced that he could not continue his lectures without contradicting his moral conscience and abdicating his political responsibilities. In the meantime, a campus-wide rally was being pulled together, while students roamed the campus, either in a silent daze or else screaming out their fear that the world was about to be consumed in a nuclear holocaust.

Some of them got into cars and took off in a panic, saying they were on their way to Canada. What was so striking about the students' response to the crisis was its strongly selfish quality. They were not interested in the fact that the people of Cuba were in terrible jeopardy—or even that millions of innocent people elsewhere might be destroyed if a nuclear conflict broke out. They were interested in themselves, in saving their own lives. Girl friends and boyfriends went off together to get in their last little bit of love.

By the time the rally took place, large numbers of students had gone off by themselves and they were not able to hear the powerful speeches given by James Baldwin, Herbert Marcuse (this was the first time I heard him) and several other professors and graduate students. The point of their speeches was not to be frightened, not to despair, but to put pressure on the government to withdraw its threat.

It was good to feel part of a movement and once again be participating in rallies, teach-ins, demonstrations. But when the crisis was over, things settled back into their old grooves. During the brief period of protest, I was drawn toward the people with whom I felt I had most in common—the foreign students. I became friends with an Indian man, who was very gentle and had a keen sense of what was happening around us. It was my friendship with Lalit more than anything else, I suppose, that helped me understand concretely the interconnectedness of the freedom struggles of peoples throughout the world. I was profoundly moved when he talked about the incredible misery of his people in India. As he spoke I found myself constantly thinking about my people in Birmingham, my people in Harlem.

I also became friends with Melanie, a young woman from the Philippines, and Mac, a South Vietnamese woman about to be deported because she was opposed to Diem. Around the same time, I entered into a close friendship with Lani, probably because we both felt so outside things at Brandeis.

Flo Mason, one of my friends from Elisabeth Irwin, and I corresponded regularly. I don't remember who initially conceived the idea, but we both decided to attend the Eighth World Festival for Youth and Students in Helsinki, Finland, the following summer. I was eager to meet revolutionary youth from other parts of the world, but my decision to make this trip was also motivated by a simple desire to leave the country in order to get a better perspective on things. It seemed that the farther I became removed from my home, my roots, the more restricted I felt and the farther I wanted to go.

The rest of the year I worked to earn money for the trip. I refiled books in the library stacks, filed cards in the Biology Department, and worked in Chomondeleys, the campus coffee shop. And I found a job in a two-bit soda parlor in Waltham. Having gotten back into the habit of studying, between my jobs and my books I didn't have very much time to do anything else. Even my social life—I was seeing a German student, Manfred Clemenz, around this time—consisted mostly of coffee in the cafeteria after an evening of studying. Then it was June. My festival scholarship called for doing some volunteer work at the Festival Committee Headquarters in New York: typing, mimeographing, mailings. The Brandeis charter plane took us to London, where I wandered alone about the city for a day or two before my train left for Paris. My friend Harriet Jackson was going to meet me at the Gare du Nord, but a strike threw all the schedules awry, and there I was in Paris alone, knowing no one and without the slightest idea of how to find Harriet.

After a few days in a dirty hotel in the Latin Quarter exploring the city, and reading with horror the racist slogans scratched on walls throughout the city threatening death to the Algerians, I finally made contact with my friend. She had left a note at American Express in hopes that I would think of going there. By the time Flo arrived, we had moved into a tiny room on the top floor of an apartment building in the Sixteenth Arrondissement so close to the Eiffel Tower that from the one-foot-square window pane, you could see the elevator rising and falling. The *chambre de bonne* had been rented by one of Harriet's friends who was studying in Paris and had agreed to let us use it while she was away.

One of ten such rooms, it could only be reached by climbing six flights of a rusty fire-escape type stairway. Like all the others, it had no plumbing, only a filthy toilet bowl and a cold-water hydrant at the end of the corridor. There was just enough space for a bed, a small closet, a table, and floor room for an air mattress and a pallet. Flo, Harriet and I took turns sleeping on the bed, the air mattress and the floor. We thought it was crowded in our room until we became acquainted with the people across the hall—a frail woman from Martinique trying to live in the same amount of space with her four robust daughters, ranging in age from about fourteen to twenty. Having just arrived from the Caribbean, they all left each day in search of work. Each evening they returned with nothing to show for their day but tired bodies, a little less money and, frequently, horror stories of being mistaken for Algerian women.

The three of us rushed around Paris being tourists, doing the things that cost the least and gave discounts to students: the Louvre, the Rodin Museum, Molière at La Comédie Française (which cost one franc for students). Hanging around the crowded cafés along the Boulevard St. Michel, we met people with interesting and exciting stories to tell—especially when it came to their distaste for the French. They were Africans, Haitians, other Antillais and Algerians. We were introduced to working-class Algerian eating places, hidden in the network of back streets in the Latin Quarter.

To be an Algerian living in Paris in 1962 was to be a hunted human being. While the Algerians were fighting the French army in their mountains and in the Europeanized cities of Algiers and Oran, paramilitary terrorist groups were falling indiscriminately upon men and women in the colonialist capital because they were, or looked like, Algerians.

In Paris, bombs were exploding in cafés frequented by North Africans, bloody bodies were discovered in dark side streets and anti-Algerian graffiti marred the sides of buildings and the walls of métro stations. One afternoon I attended a demonstration for the Algerian people in the square in front of the Sorbonne. When the *flics* broke it up with their high-power water hoses, they were as vicious as the redneck cops in Birmingham who met the Freedom Riders with their dogs and hoses.

The new places, the new experiences I had expected to discover through travel turned out to be the same old places, the same old experiences with a common message of struggle.

After Harriet left for the Soviet Union, Flo and I decided spontaneously to board a train for Geneva, but ended up trying to hitch-hike with a Swiss student just back from the University of Wisconsin. It was typical of our luck that it happened to be July 14—anniversary of the storming of the

Bastille—and thus virtually impossible to catch a ride. We got as far as Orly Airport, just on the outskirts of the city, pitched the Swiss student's tent in a field, ate dinner at the airport and bedded down for the night, with him outside guarding the tent. Not doing very much better the next morning, we caught buses and trains till we reached Lausanne, where the student's mother put us up for a few days.

With its quaint little houses built on ascending levels on the slopes of hills, Lausanne was the cleanest, most beautiful city I had seen. Now I understood why the wealthy sent their children to Switzerland.

From Lausanne, it was Geneva, back to Paris and on to Finland for the festival. The drab, monotonous postwar architecture of Helsinki concealed the tremendous vibrancy of the youth who were gathering there from all over the world.

In the brief two weeks of the festival, there were spectacular cultural programs, mass political rallies and countless seminars on the struggle in Africa, Latin America, Asia, the Middle East. The most exciting dimension of the festival, in my own opinion, came from the bilateral delegation meetings, because they were occasions for more intimate contact with the youth of other lands.

The cultural presentation given by the Cuban delegation was the most impressive event of the festival. Not that they performed in the most polished, sophisticated manner, but because their performance conveyed a fiercely compelling spirit of revolution. They were the youth of a revolution that was not yet three years old. With the U.S. delegation as audience, the Cubans satirized the way wealthy American capitalists had invaded their country and robbed them of all traces of sovereignty. They presented their attack on the invaders in plays, songs and dances. During those days, long before women's liberation had been placed on the agenda, we watched the Cuban militia women zealously defending their people's victory.

It is not easy to describe the strength and enthusiasm of the Cubans. One event however illustrates their infectious dynamism and the impact they had on us all. At the end of their show, the Cubans did not simply let the curtain fall. Their "performance," after all, had been much more than a mere show. It had been life and reality. Had they drawn the curtain and bowed to applause, it would have been as if their commitment was simply "art." The Cubans continued their dancing, doing a spirited conga right off the stage and into the audience. Those of us openly enthralled by the Cubans, their revolution and the triumphant beat of the drums rose spontaneously to join their conga line. And the rest—the timid ones, perhaps even the agents—were pulled bodily by the Cubans into the dance. Before we knew it we were doing this dance—a dance brought into Cuban culture by slaves dancing in a line of chains—all through the building and on into the streets. Puzzled Finns looked on in disbelief at hundreds of young people of all colors, oblivious to traffic, flowing down the streets of Helsinki.

Though it was the dominant theme, camaraderie was not the whole story of the festival. In keeping with the dictates of the Cold War, the CIA had planted its agents and informers in all the strategic areas of the festival, including the delegation from the United States. (A fact later admitted by the Agency). Provocations were frequent and assumed varied forms. Members of the delegation from the German Democratic Republic were kidnapped, for example, tear-gas bombs were set off in crowds during mass events and Hell's-Angels types picked fistfights with delegates in the streets of downtown Helsinki.

After saying good-bye to my new friends, and spending some time visiting my German friend, Manfred, I returned to the States to find an FBI investigator awaiting me.

"What were you doing at that Communist Youth Festival this summer?" the agent wanted to know. "Don't you know how we feel about Communists? Don't you know what we do to Communists?"

      ❈   ❈   ❈

The experiences of the summer still very much alive, I felt older and more confident as I entered my second year at Brandeis. Meeting people from all over the world had taught me how important it was to be able to tear down the superficial barriers which separated us. Language was one of those barriers which could be removed easily. I decided to major in French. That year I immersed myself totally in my work: Flaubert, Balzac, Baudelaire, Rimbaud and the thousands of pages of Proust's *A La Recherche du Temps Perdu*. My interest in Sartre was still quite keen—every spare moment I could find, I worked my way through his writings: *La Nausée, Les Mains Sales, Les Séquestres d'Altona*, and the rest of the earlier and later plays, and the novels comprising the sequence *Les Chemins de la Liberté*. I read some of his philosophical and political essays and even tried my hand at *L'Etre et le Néant*. Since I had to contend with the isolation of the campus in one way or another, I decided to make constructive use of it by spending most of my waking hours in the library or in some hidden place with my books.

At first I roomed with Lani, but since we both preferred to live alone, she moved into a single when one became available. Tina, a Swedish friend, who wanted to live off-campus with a friend, pretended to move into my room, thus leaving me with the privacy I desired.

Gwen and Woody, graduate students at the university, were in charge of the Ridgewood men's dormitories. The fact that we were Black and had common friends in Birmingham made us feel close even before we got to know each other. If they wanted to go out on evenings and weekends, they could always count on me to stay with their baby boy while I studied. And whenever I felt like talking, they were ready to listen and give advice.

It was a quiet, subdued year on the campus—until the smug sense of comfort which reigned over this white liberal college was abruptly shattered by the appearance of Malcolm X. In the largest auditorium on campus, Gwen, Woody and I sat one-third of the way back, engulfed, it seemed, by the white crowd waiting breathlessly to hear this man who was the spokesman for the prophet Elijah Mohammed. Elijah Mohammed called himself the messenger of the Islamic God, Allah, chosen to reveal Allah's message to Black people in the United States.

Years before, at Parker High School, one of our classmates had been arrested for selling a "Black Muslim" newspaper. He was a gentle-looking, soft-spoken boy who kept to himself. Several times I had tried unsuccessfully to talk to him. On the day following his arrest, I learned for the first time that there was a nationwide organization of "Black Muslims" and, not questioning the prevailing propaganda, I thought they were a strange sect of people ranting and raving about Allah's future destruction of all white people—a group essentially unable to help solve the problem of racism. For a long time it bothered me that this classmate of mine was a member of the Muslims. I could not reconcile my own stereotyped notion of the Muslims with his sensitivity. I waited for him to get out of jail and return to school so I could ask him who the Muslims really were. But I never saw him again.

Finally Malcolm strode in, immaculately dressed, encircled by conservatively dressed, clean-shaven men, and women in long flowing robes. From their manner of carrying themselves I could feel the pride emanating from them. Quietly they took their seats in the first three rows. Malcolm, accompanied by several of the men, walked onstage.

Malcolm X began his speech with a subdued eloquence, telling about the religion of Islam and its relevance to Black people in the United States. I was fascinated by his description of the way Black people had internalized the racial inferiority thrust upon us by a white supremacist society. Mesmerized by his words, I was shocked to hear him say, speaking directly to his audience, "I'm talking about you! You!! You and your ancestors, for centuries, have raped and murdered my people!" He was addressing himself to an all-white crowd and I wondered whether Gwen, Woody and the four or five other Black people in the audience felt, from that moment on, as outrageously misplaced as I did. Malcolm was addressing himself to white people, chastising them, informing them of their sins, warning them of the Armageddon to come, in which they would all be destroyed. Although I experienced a kind of morbid satisfaction listening to Malcolm reduce white people to virtually nothing, not being a Muslim, it was impossible for me to identify with his religious perspective. I kept thinking that it must be a tremendous experience to hear him speaking to a Black audience. For the white people, listening to Malcolm had been disorienting and disturbing. It was interesting that most of them were so bent on defending themselves and on distinguishing themselves from the slave master and the Southern segregationist it never struck them that they themselves could begin to do something concrete to fight racism.

Earlier in the year I had applied for a place in the Hamilton College Junior Year in France Program. After receiving the news of my acceptance, I fought hard with the Brandeis scholarship office, until they finally agreed to do the unprecedented by extending my regular scholarship to cover my third-year studies in France.

By the time the two busloads of us arrived from Paris, the resort of Biarritz, on the Bay of Biscay, near the border of Spain, had already been abandoned by the wealthy tourists. This was where we were to have our preparatory language courses. Deserted, the gaudy beachside casinos seemed even more decadent than if they had been teeming with voracious vacationing gamblers. The countless trinket shops lining the arcade-covered streets had a ravaged appearance that was exaggerated by the absence of customers. The shopkeepers looked desperate, as if they were wondering how to survive the next months without the tourists' money, and at the same time relieved that they had managed to survive the summer onslaught.

Walking through the streets of Biarritz, I felt like someone wandering into a place where a long drunken party had just broken up. The last staggering guests had already gone home, but no one had gotten around to cleaning up the mess. The traces of the summer orgy were embarrassing—like dirty underwear inadvertently left behind—and at the same time infuriating. I could see them squandering enormous wealth without the vaguest feeling of compassion for those whose slavery had created that wealth.

Not long after our arrival, a curious thing happened in the abandoned city: there was a sudden, massive flea invasion, the likes of which the working people of Biarritz had never seen before. For days, it was impossible to find a single patch of land or air uninfested by fleas. In our classrooms, the teacher could hardly be heard over the constant scratching. People scratched in cafés, movie theaters, bookstores, and they scratched just walking down the street. People with sensitive skin were beginning to look like lepers, their arms and legs covered with infected bites. Like everyone else's, my sheet was covered with little spots of blood.

If Ingmar Bergman had done a movie on the oppressive, parasitical tourists who come to Biarritz, and had included the flea invasion in his script, critics would have written that his symbolism was too blatant. In this city in its odd position of trying to recuperate from tourists and fleas—in this group of typically American students which without my presence would have been lily-white—my old familiar feelings of disorientation were rekindled.

SEPTEMBER 16, 1963

After class I asked the three or four students with whom I was walking to wait a moment while I bought a *Herald Tribune*. My attention divided between walking and listening to the conversation, just skimming the paper, I saw a headline about four girls and a church bombing. At first I was only vaguely aware of the words. Then it hit me! It came crashing down all around me. Birmingham. 16th Street Baptist Church.

The names. I closed my eyes, squeezing my lids into wrinkles as if I could squeeze what I had just read out of my head. When I opened my eyes again, the words were still there, the names traced out in stark black print.

"Carole," I said, "Cynthia. They killed them."

My companions were looking at me with puzzled expressions. Unable to say anything more, I pointed to the article and gave the newspaper to an outstretched hand.

"I know them. They're my friends . . ." I was spluttering.

As if she were repeating lines she had rehearsed, one of them said, "I'm sorry. It's too bad that it had to happen."

Before she spoke I was on the verge of pouring out all the feelings that had been unleashed in me by the news of the bomb which had ripped through four young Black girls in my hometown. But the faces around me were closed. They knew nothing of racism and the only way they knew how to relate to me at that moment was to console me as if friends had just been killed in a plane crash.

"What a terrible thing," one of them said. I left them abruptly, unwilling to let them have anything to do with my grief.

I kept staring at the names. Carole Robertson. Cynthia Wesley. Addie Mae Collins. Denise McNair. Carole—her family and my family had been close as long as I could remember. Carole, plump, with long wavy braids and a sweet face, was one of my sister's best friends. She and Fania were about the same age. They had played together, gone to dancing lessons together, attended little parties together. Carole's older sister and I had constantly had to deal with our younger sisters' wanting to tag along when we went places with our friends. Mother told me later that when Mrs. Robertson heard that the church had been bombed, she called to ask Mother to drive her downtown to pick up Carole. She didn't find out, Mother said, until they saw pieces of her body scattered about.

The Wesleys had been among the Black people to move to the west side of Center Street. Our house was on Eleventh

Court; theirs was on Eleventh Avenue. From our back door to their back door was just a few hundred feet across a gravel driveway that cut the block in two. The Wesleys were childless, and from the way they played with us it was obvious that they loved children. I remembered when Cynthia, just a few years old, first came to stay with the Wesleys. Cynthia's own family was large and suffered from the worst poverty. Cynthia would stay with the Wesleys for a while, then return to her family— this went on until the stretches of time she spent with the Wesleys grew longer and her stays at home grew shorter. Finally, with the approval of her family, the Wesleys officially adopted her. She was always immaculate, her face had a freshly scrubbed look about it, her dresses were always starched and her little pocketbook always matched her newly shined shoes. When my sister Fania came into the house look-ing grubby and bedraggled, my mother would often ask her why she couldn't keep herself clean like Cynthia. She was a thin, very sensitive child and even though I was five years older, I thought she had an understanding of things that was far more mature than mine. When she came to the house, she seemed to enjoy talking to my mother more than playing with Fania.

Denise McNair. Addie Mae Collins. My mother had taught Denise when she was in first grade and Addie Mae, although we didn't know her personally, could have been any Black child in my neighborhood.

When the lives of these four girls were so ruthlessly wiped out, my pain was deeply personal. But when the initial hurt and rage had subsided enough for me to think a little more clearly, I was struck by the objective significance of these murders.

This act was not an aberration. It was not something sparked by a few extremists gone mad. On the contrary, it was logical, inevitable. The people who planted the bomb in the girls' restroom in the basement of 16th Street Baptist Church were not pathological, but rather the normal products of their surroundings. And it was this spectacular, violent event, the savage dismembering of four little girls, which had burst out of the daily, sometimes even dull, routine of racist oppression.

No matter how much I talked, the people around me were simply incapable of grasping it. They could not understand why the whole society was guilty of this murder—why their beloved Kennedy was also to blame, why the whole ruling stratum in their country, by being guilty of racism, was also guilty of this murder.

Those bomb-wielding racists, of course, did not plan specifically the deaths of Carole, Cynthia, Addie Mae and Denise. They may not have even consciously taken into account the possibility of someone's death. They wanted to terrorize Birmingham's Black population, which had been stirred out of its slumber into active involvement in the struggle for Black liberation. They wanted to destroy this movement before it became too deeply rooted in our minds and our lives. This is what they wanted to do and they didn't care if someone happened to get killed. It didn't matter to them one way or the other. The broken bodies of Cynthia, Carole, Addie Mae and Denise were incidental to the main thing—which was precisely why the murders were even more abominable than if they had been deliberately planned.

In November our group moved to Paris. I was assigned to the Lamotte family at 13 bis rue Duret, a little ways from the Arc de Triomphe. Two other women from the Hamilton program lived there too. Jane was on the third floor with M. and Mme. Lamotte and their three children. Christie and I shared one of the two bedrooms in the smaller second-floor apartment of M. Lamotte's mother. Each morning she brought us a big wooden tray with two large bowls of café au lait, pieces of a freshly baked *baguette*, and two hunks of butter. In the evening we had dinner with the family upstairs. We walked through the old cobblestone courtyard to the métro station around the corner, and traveled underground on the old red trains to the Latin Quarter to attend our classes. Most of mine were at the section of the Sorbonne called the Institut de Préparation et de Perfectionnement de Professeurs de Français à L'Etranger.

In the Sorbonne, I always felt as if I were in church—it was centuries old, with tremendous pillars holding up uncommonly high ceilings which displayed faded old paintings. The sacredness exuded by the place forced thousands of students inside to observe the silence. My business there seemed incongruous with the surroundings. My studies were devoted almost entirely to contemporary literature—one course on contemporary French novels, another on plays, one on poetry and one on Ideas. The only other course I took was organized by the Hamilton program itself and required attending the theater each week and discussing and writing about the plays we had seen. By the time the year was up, I had the feeling I had seen most of what was interesting on the stage in Paris—including the Peking Opera and the Ballet Africaine from Guinea.

When the news broke in Paris that Kennedy had been shot, everyone rushed down to the U.S. Embassy. Kennedy's assassination was certainly no source of joy to me. Though his hands were far from clean (I kept remembering the Bay of Pigs), killing him was not going to solve any problems. Besides, the Vice President from Texas and his cronies in the oil monopolies would probably only make things worse for my people. Nevertheless, I felt out of place at the Embassy, surrounded by crowds of "Americans in Paris" and it was difficult to identify with their weeping. I wondered how many of them had shed tears—or had truly felt saddened—when they read the *Herald Tribune* story about the murders of Carole, Cynthia, Addie Mae and Denise.

Later on in the year, I accompanied a friend who had been invited to attend the Vietnamese Tet celebration. That night, two New Year's programs were taking place—one organized and attended by the South Vietnamese who remained loyal to Diem and the other organized and attended by the North Vietnamese, together with the socialist and other opposition forces in the South. We attended the North Vietnamese celebration. Held in a gigantic stadium in a working-class district of Paris, it was a grand seven-hour spectacle consisting of songs, comedy acts, acrobatic numbers and skits, all full of the vigor of their struggle and conveying a message that did not require an understanding of Vietnamese. Like the thousands of Vietnamese sitting around the stadium, I was enchanted. But I was shocked back to the brutal realities of their experiences by the recurring satires directed against the U.S. government and its military. The longest and most vehement applause and laughter were always at the appearance of an actor dressed up like a U.S. GI, who was the butt of jokes or, in more serious episodes, fell in defeat.

Although I was on the verge of receiving a degree in French Literature, what I really wanted to study was philosophy. I was interested in Marx, his predecessors and his successors. Over the last years, whenever I could find the time, I read philosophy on the side. I didn't really know what I was doing, except that it gave me a feeling of security and comfort to read what people had to say about such formidable things as the universe, history, human beings, knowledge.

During my second year at Brandeis, I had picked up *Eros and Civilization* by Herbert Marcuse and had struggled with it from beginning to end. That year he was teaching at the Sorbonne. When I arrived in Paris the following year, he was already back at Brandeis, but people were still raving about his fantastic courses. When I returned to Brandeis, the first semester of my senior year was so crowded with required French courses that I could not officially enroll in Marcuse's lecture series on European political thought since the French Revolution. Nevertheless, I attended each session, rushing in to capture a seat in the front of the hall. Arranged around the room on progressively higher levels, the desks were in the style of the UN General Assembly room. When Marcuse walked onto the platform, situated at the lowest level of the hall, his presence dominated everything. There was something imposing about him which evoked total silence and attention when he appeared, without his having to pronounce a single word. The students had a rare respect for him. Their concentration was not only total during the entire hour as he paced back and forth while he lectured, but if at the sound of the bell Marcuse had not finished, the rattling of papers would not begin until he had formally closed the lecture.

One day, shortly after the semester began, I mustered up enough courage to put in a request for an interview with Marcuse. I had decided to ask him to help me draw up a bibliography on basic works in philosophy. Having assumed I would have to wait for weeks to see him, I was surprised when I was told he would be free that very afternoon.

From afar, Marcuse seemed unapproachable. I imagine the combination of his stature, his white hair, the heavy accent, his extraordinary air of confidence, and his wealth of knowledge made him seem ageless and the epitome of a philosopher. Up close, he was a man with inquisitive sparkling eyes and a fresh, very down-to-earth smile.

Trying to explain my reasons for the appointment, I told him that I intended to study philosophy in graduate school, perhaps at the university in Frankfurt, but that my independent reading in philosophy had been unsystematic—without regard for any national or historical relations. What I wanted from him—if it was not too much of an imposition—was a list of works in the sequence in which I ought to read them. And if he gave me permission, I wanted to enroll in his graduate seminar on Kant's *Critique of Pure Reason.*

"Do you really want to study philosophy?" Professor Marcuse asked, slowly and placing emphasis on each word. He made it sound so serious and so profound—like an initiation into some secret society which, once you join, you can never leave. I was afraid that a mere "yes" would ring hollow and inane.

"At least, I want to see if I am able," was about the only thing I could think of to answer.

"Then you should begin with the Pre-Socratics, then Plato and Aristotle. Come back again next week and we will discuss the Pre-Socratics."

I had no idea that my little request would develop into stimulating weekly discussions on the philosophers he suggested, discussions which gave me a far more exciting and vivid picture of the history of philosophy than would have emerged from a dry introduction-to-philosophy course.

Shortly after the Nazi seizure of power in Germany, Marcuse had emigrated to the United States, along with a group of intellectuals who had established the Institut für Sozialforschung. Among them were Theodor Adorno and Max Horkheimer. They had continued their work for a number of years in this country, but after the defeat of the fascists, they reestablished the Institute as a part of the regular university in Frankfurt. I had first become acquainted with the work of the Institute through Manfred Clemenz, the German student I had met my first year at Brandeis. During the summer after my studies in France, I had spent several weeks in Frankfurt attending a few of Adorno's lectures, and getting to know some of the students there. At that time, my knowledge of German was minimal, but the people around me translated the essential points of the lectures into English or French. Later I read all of Adorno's and Horkheimer's works that had been translated into English or French, in addition to Marcuse's writings. In this way I had acquainted myself with their thought, which was collectively known as Critical Theory.

During that last year at Brandeis, I made up my mind to apply for a scholarship to study philosophy at the university in Frankfurt. Marcuse confirmed my conviction that this was the best place to study, given my interest in Kant, Hegel and Marx. The remaining months of the school year were consumed by intensive preparation in philosophy, German language and the final requirements for my B.A. degree, including a year-long honors project on the Phenomenological Attitude, which I thought I had discovered in the works of the contemporary French novelist Robbe-Grillet. The most challenging and fulfilling course was the graduate seminar that Marcuse conducted on the *Critique of Pure Reason*. Poring over a seemingly incomprehensible passage for hours, then suddenly grasping its meaning gave me a sense of satisfaction I had never experienced before.

My parents were not overjoyed at the idea of my leaving the country again, particularly since I had not yet decided how long I wanted to remain in Germany. Nevertheless, they were extremely proud to attend the graduation ceremony, where they heard my name called among the Phi Beta Kappas and magna cum laudes. I gave my mother the diplomas, certificates and medals and we packed up the things I had accumulated over the last four years, dropped off my friend Celeste in Providence and headed down the highway for Birmingham.

Along the way, we stopped at a liquor store where my father bought several bottles of bourbon to take home with him—in Alabama's state-controlled liquor stores, the only brands available were the ones approved by the government. (We always thought that one of Wallace's relatives must be the owner of the factory producing all the off-the-wall brands of alcohol, which you never saw anyplace except in Alabama.) We crossed over into Tennessee very late that night, and because we knew that we'd never find a motel run by Black people where we could spend the night, we decided to drive straight through to Birmingham.

In one of those towns along the highway in Tennessee, around two in the morning, we heard a siren screaming behind us. The fat, tobacco-chewing cop, letting his white Tennessee drawl tumble out of a grotesque smile, said to my father, "Y'all know y'alls driving too fast. Git out of the car." All the time he was fingering the holster strapped to his waist. I thought about the stories I had heard about Black people or Northern whites disappearing for weeks, sometimes forever, in these small-town jails. The cop searched the front of the car and told my father to open the trunk. When he saw all the suitcases, he seemed startled and immediately asked where we were coming from. After my father said that he had just attended his daughter's college graduation, the cop assumed a less slovenly posture and became more official. But when he saw the bourbon, his eyes lit up.

"This is a dry county, y'all know. No liquor allowed nowhere in the jurisdiction."

"The bottles are unopened and we're only passing through," my father insisted.

"Don't make no difference. The county is dry and ain't no liquor allowed no kind of way. Y'all can do thirty days in jail for this. And the judge ain't even in town—won't be back till next week. Look like y'all gone have to stay in jail till he get back."

When my father talked about getting in touch with his lawyer, the cop said, "I tell you what. I'm gon do you a favor. Treat ya like I treat my boys around here. Git back in the car and follow me into town." He took the whiskey to the patrol car.

Thinking we were headed for the police station, and knowing that it would be fatal to try to get away, we followed the police car through the dark streets. When it came to a halt, there was nothing around which bore the faintest resemblance to a police station. We were in an unpaved alley and the cop was opening a garage door. Although this wasn't the first time we had been trapped into a situation like this, we were all silently nervous.

"Davis," my mother said, "I don't think you should go in there. There's no telling what he might try to do." But there wasn't the slightest trace of fear in my father—in fact, I have never seen him afraid of anything. He went on in while we waited on tenterhooks in the car. After what seemed like hours he came out with a wry smile on his face. Starting up the car, he told us, chuckling, "All the man wanted was the liquor and twenty dollars." It was a small-time racket which he probably pulled whenever he caught up with Black people driving through the town. The alternative to giving him the twenty dollars would probably have been much more terrible than the thirty days in jail.

When I boarded the boat sailing for Germany, Watts was burning. I felt again the tension of the Janus head—leaving the country at that time was hard for me. But in a little more than a week, I was on the other side of the ocean.

My stipend consisted of the boat fare and a hundred dollars a month—for rent, food, tram fare to and from the university, books, and whatever else I needed. As I searched the city for a room, the agencies kept telling me, *"Es tut uns leid, aber wir haben keine Zimmer für Ausländer."* "Sorry but we don't have rooms for foreigners," their attitude clearly implying, "Our rooms are only for good Aryans."

In historical time, twenty years is not very long—half the people I saw on the streets, and practically all the adults, had gone through the experience of Hitler. And in West Germany, unlike the German Democratic Republic, there had been no determined campaign to attack the fascist and racist attitudes which had become so deeply embedded.

Eventually, after days of reading the fine print of the *Frankfurter Allgemeiner*, I found a little room near the zoo, on the top floor of a postwar apartment building—like the *chambre de bonne* I had lived in in Paris. The family to whose apartment the room was attached seemed to be exceptional, as far as the masses of West Germans were concerned. They were curious and concerned about the condition of Black people in the United States and they never failed to draw the appropriate parallels between the Nazi oppression of the Jews in their country and the repression of my people in the United States. They repeatedly invited me to their apartment for dinner and discussions. In the beginning when my German was not very polished, these discussions helped me orient myself to the language.

During the first few weeks, I didn't understand a word of what Adorno was saying. Not only were the concepts difficult to grasp, but he spoke his own special aphoristic variety of German. It was a consolation to discover that most German students attending his lectures for the first time were having almost as much trouble understanding Adorno as I.

I saw old friends from previous trips to Europe, and entered into new friendships as well. It was a great relief to find that not too far from me lived a young Black man from Indiana who had been stationed in Frankfurt as a GI and had decided to stay on to pursue his studies in literature at the university. We were good friends throughout my stay in Germany. I was friendly with a group of Haitian students, a Black South African and two couples who, like myself, had come from the United States to study with Adorno.

I was paying eighty marks a month for my room—practically a quarter of the hundred dollars I had to live on. Almost inevitably, when the end of the month approached, I was eating nothing but *Quark* (something between yogurt and cottage cheese), and writing my parents for a few dollars to tide me over until the next check came in. I was very relieved to find a room on Adalbertstrasse, near the university, which cost only a few marks a month. It was in a massive old building of crumbling red brick, an abandoned factory which the owner rented out I imagine in order to avoid paying a watchman.

The three floors of one side were occupied by a sculptor who fashioned huge abstract metal forms which he kept in the courtyard. The side I moved into had been taken over by a group of students, all as poor as I. The entire place cost us seventy-five marks (less than twenty dollars) a month, and it could comfortably accommodate up to five people in the little nooks that had served as offices when the factory was in operation.

It was a dilapidated old abandoned building with dirty cement floors, no showers—not even hot water—and no central heating, only potbellied coal stoves. But paying only about five dollars a month for rent and a few more dollars for coal during the winter months, I could afford to eat a little better—even buying meat a couple of days a week—and was able to buy more books and a new blouse once in a while. As throughout Europe, cultural events could always be attended by students at a great discount, so for about fifty cents, I could see a movie or go to the theater, the opera, the ballet or a museum.

During the spring of my first year there, all the students who had received scholarships from the exchange program were given a trip to Berlin from whatever section of Germany they happened to be living in. Anxious to see Socialist Germany, I spent most of the time in Berlin, the capital of the German Democratic Republic. Each day, I walked across at Checkpoint Charlie—the border point for people with passports from capitalist countries. Crowds of white tourists from the United States would be standing in line, probably waiting to cross the border in order to tell people they had seen the other side of the "wall"—so they could say, in Kennedy's war-filled words, *"Ich bin ein Berliner,"* that is, I am ready to fight communism. The tourists were always complaining about the wait. But I never had any trouble—each time I went across, I would receive the signal to go on only a few moments after I had shown my passport. This was their way of showing their solidarity with Black people.

Claudia and Margaret Burnham's stepbrother Bob had recently come through Frankfurt, stayed a while at the "factory" and then gone on to study at the Brecht Theater in Berlin. Through him, I was introduced to several people in the GDR who showed me around the city. Living in Bob's apartment building was a group of Cubans—the national director of the ballet and several of his assistants. I was amazed at their youth—the director was in his early twenties and the rest around the same age. They talked about their efforts to more fully integrate the African element of Cuban culture into their classical dances and described the way in which they were developing the old Yoruba dances which, before the revolution, had been restricted to the remote areas of the country where Black people still retained African customs.

Esther and James Jackson, old friends of my parents from Birmingham, were in Berlin at the time. Jim, the International Affairs Director of the Communist Party, U.S.A., was representing the party at the May Day celebration. I spent an evening with them. We talked about the old days when Jim had been underground, and how puzzled I had been as a child, seeing those sinister white men following us all over New York looking for him; Jim was one of the lucky ones whom the FBI never succeeded in tracking down. We discussed the socialist transformation of the GDR and its active campaign against the remnants of fascism in the mentality of the people. The next day I watched the parade, participated in the May Day Festivities and then went on back through Checkpoint Charlie to catch my plane for Frankfurt.

When the West German police said they were going to detain me at the airport, I was certain they were going to accuse me of being too friendly with the people in the GDR— and, of course, they would have been correct. But, according to them, the reason they wouldn't let me board the plane had to do with my failure to check out with the Frankfurt police when I had moved, some months before, out of the room near the zoo, and had not registered with the police station near the factory. I could never get used to the incredible bureaucracy in which one must become embroiled merely as a prerequisite for living an ordinary life. Everyone, citizen or foreigner, not registered at the nearest police station—and there was no lack of them—was technically liable to arrest, including those visiting with friends for only a few days. Although I had registered when I moved into the first place (the process is called *Anmeldung*—announcing one's arrival), it had not crossed my mind to tell them I was leaving (called *Ausmeldung*) and to go through the *Anmeldung* at the Adalbertstrasse police station. The West Berlin police were serious: they were talking about deporting me. It took several hours before I could persuade them that my failure to register had been an innocent omission. After it was all over and they had left the threat of deportation hanging over me unless I cleared myself the next day with the Frankfurt police, I was still positive that the harassment was a little retaliatory action for my trip to the GDR.

Frankfurt was a very intensive learning experience. Stimulating lectures and seminars conducted by Theodor Adorno, Jürgen Habermass, Professor Haag, Alfred Schmidt, Oscar Negt. Tackling formidable works, such as all three of Kant's Critiques and the works of Hegel and Marx as well (in one seminar, we spent an entire semester analyzing about twenty pages of Hegel's *Logic*).

Most of the students living in the factory studied either philosophy or sociology. Many were members of S.D.S.— Sozialistischer Deutscher Studentenbund, the German Socialist Student League. And they were very seriously striving to arrive at some form of practical resistance capable of ultimately overturning the enemy system. Aside from the concern with the social contradictions inside their own country, they consistently tried to force an internationist awareness among their members. I participated in rallies and demonstrations directed against U.S. aggression in Vietnam. Those of us who were not citizens had to be especially careful because an arrest would mean a sure deportation. One demonstration, which took place outside the U.S. Embassy, was particularly dangerous. Chanting "*U.S. raus, U.S. raus, U.S. raus aus Vietnam!*" and "Ho, Ho, Ho Chi Minh!" the crowds of demonstrators were attacked almost immediately by mounted police. One young woman was trampled under the hooves of the horses. Since it had been decided beforehand that we would resist this expected attack, the agreed upon hit-and-run, disruptive tactics were put into operation. The idea was to move along the main street leading to the center of the city, disrupting the functioning of the tramway. As the crowds of demonstrators marched down the main street on the sidewalks on both sides of the street, some would periodically separate from the group and sit down on the tramway tracks. Watching the approach of the police, they waited until the very last moment to run into the refuge of the crowd. Not all of us made it. When it was my turn to do the sitting and running, I had to make sure I was fast enough to reach the safety of the crowd, not wanting to have a case foisted upon me by the West German courts. After several hours of sitting and running, and a sizeable number of arrests, we made it to the Hauptwache, the center of the city, and listened to an arousing speech by Rudi Dutsche, the Chairman of S.D.S., who was later shot in the head by a would-be assassin who said he was inspired by the assassination of Martin Luther King.

Toward the end of my second year, a mass student demonstration, organized by S.D.S. in Berlin protesting the visit by the Shah of Iran, was attacked by the Shah's security, aided by the West Berlin police, with such terrible force that it ended in the death of a student—Ben Ohnesorge, who was attending his first political protest. The response throughout West Germany was swift and intense. In Frankfurt, there were mass gatherings, demonstrations and teach-ins.

I was most impressed by the consciousness of the student movement when I heard about the Berlin campaign led by S.D.S. against the movie *Africa Adio*, directed by two Roman playboy-types, dealing with the ousting of the colonialists from Africa. Not only was this movie thoroughly racist in that it depicted the African Liberation Fighters as aggressors against the pure, educated, civilized whites, but the directors went so far as to stage actual killings in order to do on-the-spot documentary coverage of Africa. S.D.S. members in Berlin tore up a theater which refused to boycott the film.

Students and workers were being drawn en masse into the arena of political protest in Germany. At the same time, great upheavals were taking place in the States.

My decision to study in Frankfurt had been made in 1964, against the backdrop of relative political tranquillity. But by the time I left in the summer of 1965, thousands of sisters and brothers were screaming in the streets of Los Angeles that they had observed the rules of the game long enough, too long.

Watts was exploding; furiously burning. And out of the ashes of Watts, Phoenix-like, a new Black militancy was being born.

While I was hidden away in West Germany the Black Liberation Movement was undergoing decisive metamorphoses. The slogan "Black Power" sprang out of a march in Mississippi. Organizations were being transfigured— The Student Non-Violent Coordinating Committee, a leading civil rights organization, was becoming the foremost advocate of "Black Power." The Congress on Racial Equality was undergoing similar transformations. In Newark, a national Black Power Conference had been organized. In political groups, labor unions, churches and other organizations, Black caucuses were being formed to defend the special interests of Black people. Everywhere there were upheavals.

While I was reading philosophy in Frankfurt, and participating in the rearguard of S.D.S., there were young Black men in Oakland, California, who had decided that they had to wield arms in order to protect the residents of Oakland's Black community from the indiscriminate police brutality ravaging the area. Huey Newton, Bobby Seale, li'l Bobby Hutton— those were some of the names that reached me. One day in Frankfurt I read about their entrance into the California Legislature in Sacramento with their weapons in order to safeguard their right (a right given to all whites) to carry them as instruments of self-defense. The name of this organization was the Black Panther Party for Self-Defense.

The more the struggles at home accelerated, the more frustrated I felt at being forced to experience it all vicariously. I was advancing my studies, deepening my understanding of philosophy, but I felt more and more isolated. I was so far away from the terrain of the fight that I could not even analyze the episodes of the struggle. I did not even have the knowledge or understanding to judge which currents of the movement were progressive and genuine and which were not. It was a difficult balance I was trying to maintain, and it was increasingly hard to feel a part of the collective coming to consciousness of my people.

I am certain that what I was feeling was a variation and reflection of the same feelings that were overwhelming larger and larger numbers of Black people abroad. Many others of us must have felt pained, when reading about some new crisis in the struggle at home, to be hearing about it secondhand.

I had thought mine was the perfect dilemma: the struggle at home versus the need to remain in Frankfurt until the completion of my doctorate, for I was certain that Frankfurt was far more conducive to philosophical studies than any other place. But each day it was becoming clearer to me that my ability to accomplish anything was directly dependent on my ability to contribute something concrete to the struggle.

Adorno had readily agreed to direct my work on a doctoral dissertation. But now I felt it would be impossible for me to stay in Germany any longer. Two years was enough. I arranged for an appointment with Adorno at the Institute and explained to him that I had to go home. In my correspondence with Marcuse, he had already agreed to work with me at the University of California in San Diego, where he had accepted a position after having been practically pushed out of Brandeis for political reasons. I wanted to continue my academic work, but I knew I could not do it unless I was politically involved. The struggle was a life-nerve; our only hope for survival. I made up my mind. The journey was on.

fire eaters from the sun
we shall lay the high white dome to siege
cover screams with holy wings, in those days
we shall be terrible

HENRY DUMAS

PART FOUR

Flames

*I*t was the summer of 1967. On the way home I stopped off in London to attend a conference where Herbert Marcuse and Stokely Carmichael were among the main speakers. It was good to talk to Herbert and his wife Inge, whom I had not seen for quite some time, and I was looking forward to hearing Stokely's presentation. Convened around the theme "The Dialectics of Liberation," the conference was headquartered in a huge railroad turntable called the Roundhouse. The gathering was an unlikely conglomeration of Marxist theoreticians, philosophers, sociologists and psychologists, radical political activists, hippies and Black Power advocates. In the enormous barn-like structure, its floor covered with sawdust, the air reeked heavily of marijuana, and there were rumors that one speaker, a psychologist, was high on acid. Stokely Carmichael and Michael X, the militant West Indian leader of community struggles in London, were the two central figures of the small Black contingent in attendance.

My natural hair style, in those days still a rarity, identified me as a sympathizer with the Black Power Movement. Immediately I was approached by the group around Michael and Stokely.

Between conference sessions I spent my time with Stokely and Michael X's group, accompanied them to meetings in London ghettos, helping on occasion to pull the gatherings together. I was struck by the degree to which West Indian communities in London were mirror images of Black communities at home. These warm, receptive, fiery, enthusiastic people were also searching for some way to avenge themselves. As in the United States, there was a natural inclination to identify the enemy as the white man. Natural because the great majority of white people, both in the United States and England, have been carriers of the racism which, in reality, benefits only a small number of them—the capitalists. Because the masses of white people harbor racist attitudes, our people tended to see *them* as the villains and not the institutionalized forms of racism, which, though definitely reinforced by prejudiced attitudes, serve, fundamentally, only the interests of the rulers. When white people are indiscriminantly viewed as the enemy, it is virtually impossible to develop a political solution. Such were my thoughts as I moved through the conference. I learned more about the new movement there in London than from all the reading I had done. I was learning that as long as the Black response to racism remained purely emotional, we would go nowhere. Like the playground fights at Parker High, like the sporadic headless anger of those who fell under police clubs in Alabama—it would solve nothing in the long run.

As I listened to Stokely's words, cutting like a switchblade, accusing the enemy as I had never heard him accused before, I admit I felt the cathartic power of his speech. But I also wanted to know where to go from there. I was distressed to discover that among some of the Black leaders there was the tendency to completely dismiss Marxism as "the white man's thing." It had been clear to me for a long time that in order to achieve its ultimate goals, the Black Liberation struggle would have to become a part of a revolutionary movement, embracing all working people. It was also clear to me that this movement must push in the direction of socialism. And I knew that Black people—Black workers—had an important leadership role to play in the overall fight. Therefore I found it disappointing that the nationalist posture of the Black leaders in London involved a strong resistance to socialism. I was encouraged, however, to learn that Stokely was about to make a trip to Cuba. Once he saw Black, Brown, and white people constructing together their socialist society, he would be compelled, so I thought, to reexamine his own position. When I asked Stokely about movement contacts in Southern California, he told me about Tommy J., a community leader in Los Angeles. The address he gave me was in Watts.

When I arrived in Southern California a few weeks later, one of the first things I did was look up the address Stokely had given me. There was no such number. After desperately knocking on door after door, it was clear that no one in the neighborhood had ever heard of Tommy J. Because I was straining toward a permanent involvement, not being able to find this brother depressed me enormously. Reluctantly, I left for San Diego without any contacts in or concrete information about the movement in Southern California.

In San Diego, the only people I knew were graduate students in the philosophy department, primarily students who were there because of Marcuse. Ricky Sherover and Bill Leiss, for example, had been graduate students at Brandeis during my senior year and had accompanied Marcuse to UCSD. Nevertheless, I did manage to get the telephone numbers of two Black community leaders: the director of a youth organization in San Diego, and a man who I later discovered was a member of the Communist Party.

I telephoned the first brother.

"Hello, this is Angela Davis. I've just arrived in San Diego to study philosophy at the university. I've been abroad for the last two years, and I want to try to contribute whatever I can to the Black movement here. Someone gave me your name and number . . ."

At the end of my little speech there was only silence. I did not realize then how I must have sounded—like an effervescent adolescent, or like an agent trying to worm her way to the inside. The silence continued for a while, then he finally promised to call me soon and tell me about a meeting I could attend. I didn't detect very much enthusiasm in his voice and I didn't really expect to hear from him after I hung up. I was right.

The days clumped by, the chances of a speedy acceptance into the San Diego community becoming more and more remote. Sometimes I would get into my car and, out of sheer frustration, drive into San Diego and head toward Logan Heights, where the largest concentration of Black people lived, and drive around aimlessly, daydreaming, trying to devise some way of escaping this terrible isolation.

There was little more to do than wait for classes at the university to begin. And so I studied, socialized with the philosophy students and professors, and waited, waited. At last the dormitories came alive with students returning to campus. As the resident student body grew, so did my disappointment. Not everyone had arrived, but I was hard at work searching every corner and crevice for sisters and brothers. Each day brought on a more profound dejection, for there were still no Black people on campus.

I was like an explorer who returns to his homeland after many years, with precious bounty and no one to give it to. I believed my energy, my commitment, my convictions were the treasure I had accumulated, and I looked high and low for a way to spend it. I roamed the campus, examined the bulletin boards, read the newspapers, talked to everyone who might know: Where are my people? It was as if I would be churned up and destroyed inside by these irrepressible desires to become a part of a liberation movement if I did not soon discover an outlet for them. Therefore, I turned to the radical students' organization on campus, and participated in the planning of an action against the war in Vietnam.

In 1967 masses of people had not yet arrived at the conclusion that the war ought to come to an immediate halt. Consequently many of our efforts to talk to the people in the streets of San Diego were immediately and abruptly rebuffed. Many refused to even take our literature. But since this was my first demonstration in the United States, for a number of years, I was enthusiastic and excited. The hostile attitudes of the people in the streets gave me all the more reason to talk harder, longer and more persuasively.

As zealous as I felt, as clearly as I understood the political necessity for this demonstration, I still experienced a sense of alienation among these students. Emotionally I was a stranger —in a way that I had never been a stranger among white people before. It was not the feeling of my childhood in the South. It was not the alienation I experienced in New York upon realizing that many of the whites around me were going out of their way to make me feel that they were not racist. It was a new strangeness that I felt. But one I would have to deal with later.

Meanwhile, the contingent of police overseeing our demonstration grew larger. A police car was stationed on every corner now. Uniformed and plainclothes agents were all around. San Diego was not used to such demonstrations. That its defenses would be extreme could have been predicted beforehand.

When the atmosphere seemed to be reaching a boiling point, the decision was made to return to the campus and pick up reinforcements. Since my '58 Buick was one of the largest cars we had, I accepted the assignment of making the fifteen-mile trip back to La Jolla. But by the time we reached the university, a call had come in telling us that arrests had already been made.

The next step was to retrieve the prisoners. We mustered up enough for the bond. Three of us, a man, another woman and I, went down to the jail, posted the money and awaited the release of our companions. The charges that had been lodged against them were still an enigma to us. We inquired about the precise circumstances surrounding the arrest. Previously we had been told that the charge was "obstructing pedestrian traffic."

Since no one in the front office could satisfy us, we were directed to the chambers of the patrol captain. We entered into a dark room musty with the odor of San Diego justice. Again, we posed the question. Why the arrests? Again the answer was mechanically spouted out to us: "obstructing pedestrian traffic on the sidewalk." We were persistent. What does that mean? We ourselves were passing out literature as well; we knew we did not prevent anyone from passing.

"Well," said the patrol captain, "as long as you are standing on the sidewalk, you may be considered to be obstructing pedestrian traffic."

"Then how many times have you arrested Jehovah's Witnesses distributing their religious literature?"

Silence.

"Sir, could you be a little more explicit and a little clearer in your explanation of the reasons for the arrests of our friends?"

The captain began to say something, but became so completely tongue-tied he was not able to get the words out. Finally, out of sheer frustration and evidently disturbed by our logic, he blurted out—"It is not the police's job to understand the law; that is the job of the district attorney. If you want to understand the meaning of this law, go to the D.A.!"

Although we realized that we were in the chambers of our enemy, this remark was so stupid and so funny that all three of us roared with laughter.

"Get out of this place! Get out!" the captain, now out of control, screamed.

We were trying to regain our composure when we noticed him dialing a number on his telephone. In less than a minute, his office was full of policemen who came for a single purpose: to throw us into jail.

Our male companion was carted off; Anna and I were handcuffed and pushed into the back seat of a patrol car parked in the steaming hot courtyard of the city jail complex. The windows were closed, and we saw that police cars have no door handles on the inside. The police officer slammed the doors and walked away. Fifteen minutes passed, then twenty. The heat had become absolutely intolerable. Sweat was pouring down our faces and our clothes were drenched. We banged on the windows and screamed. No one came.

Just as our fear began to approach panic, the officer walked toward the car, got in and started up the motor.

"What do you girls do for a living?" he asked.

"We don't have jobs," we answered.

"If you don't have a job, then we can pin vagrancy on you."

"We have money in our purses; that proves we aren't vagrants."

"That's even better," he said. "If you have money, but no job, we can charge you with robbery—or better than that, armed robbery."

On the way to the jail, we looked at San Diego through the windows of the police car. The screeching of the siren attracted stares from the crowds of people in the downtown area. What were they thinking? Were we prostitutes, drug users, robbers, or had we gotten caught in a confidence game? I doubt if the idea crossed any of their minds that we might be revolutionaries.

In the woman's section of the county jail, we were directed to a room and instructed to remove all of our clothes in the presence of a matron. Anna and I protested this degradation long and hard before we were forced to acquiesce. The next stage was a hot shower in a room where a heavy iron door was locked behind us. After being left for an hour in the shower room, we were placed in separate silvery-colored, padded cells, where we had to suffer through another waiting period. Thinking I could use some of this time constructively, I scratched political slogans on the walls with a burnt match for the benefit of the sisters who would occupy this cell next.

Many hours passed before the mug shots and fingerprints were finally taken, our booking sheet written up. We made the telephone calls due us and, dressed in prisoner's uniforms, were taken to the jail population upstairs.

They put us in a large tank separated from the outside corridor by a double gate of electrically operated bars. The first gate slid open at the push of a button. Anna and I stepped inside between the two gates. It slid closed. Only when it was securely locked did the second gate leading into the tank open.

The tank itself was as depressingly sterile as jail tanks are meant to be. It was divided into two sections—one with the bunks for sleeping and the other for eating and game-playing. We explained to each sister who inquired what we had done to be arrested. Our explanation singled us out, in 1967, as curiosities. Many of the sisters, in jail on such charges as possession of drugs and prostitution, tried to comfort us. They felt that the charges against us were silly and would be dropped.

They were right. At long last we were released.

In the meantime other demonstrators had informed the news media that three people in San Diego had been arrested when they tried to inquire about the of a law. A rock station based in Los Angeles was running a spot every hour: "Have you heard about the people down south who got arrested because they wanted to know about the law?"

The university agreed to lodge an official protest, and within two days, the district attorney of San Diego dropped the charges and made a formal apology.

A few days later, during a meeting of the group that had organized the demonstration, I was excited to see a young Black couple sitting on the other side of the room. They were the first Black students I had seen on the campus—and their presence at the meeting meant they were interested in the movement. After the meeting, we introduced ourselves, and within a short time Liz and Ed and I decided to try to organize a Black Student Union. We began by systematically investigating the dormitories, asking whether there were any Black students on the floor. After we combed all the halls, we attacked the graduate departments, going into the main office of each one with pen and paper, requesting the names of all Black students and employees. We also involved Black workers; if we hadn't we would have been too small to get the attention we needed to function.

We made contact with some fifteen to twenty Black students and workers. About ten of them showed up at our meeting, leaving us quite proud of our first efforts at independent political organizing. One Black professor attended the meeting and agreed to act as the group's sponsor. Soon another professor, from Jamaica, became heavily involved in the work of the organization.

We realized that to be successful we would have to establish ties with similar groups. Otherwise, when making demands, it would be hard to convince the university administration of our strength. We decided therefore to affiliate, in a loose way, with the Black Students' Council at San Diego State College, and to seek community ties as well.

It struck me, about this time, that I was being looked upon as somewhat of a leader of the Black movement at the university. It was not that I had sought out this position; it simply emerged that, despite my two-year absence, I was one of the most experienced organizers on campus.

We discovered that the San Diego Black Conference—a coalition of community organizations spearheaded by Ron Karenga's US-Organization—was trying to build support for a Black seaman, Ed Lynn, who was challenging racial discrimination at Balboa Naval Base. Liz, Ed and I decided to attend the Thursday night meeting of the conference. The facts surrounding Ed Lynn's case were classic. It had created a huge stir at the base when Ed circulated a petition protesting race prejudice, asking both Black and white seamen to sign. In the course of this petition drive, Ed had charged that President Johnson condoned racism in the military. Within a short time he was told that he faced court-martial for having made "offensive" statements about the President of the United States. The small meeting was being held at a community center in Logan Heights. The participants stared at the three strangers who said they were representing Black students at the University of San Diego—no one had ever heard of our group. Some probably thought we were agents. We worked hard to persuade them that we were genuinely interested in the case of Ed Lynn. Ed himself was quite willing to let us help him in his defense. He readily accepted our invitation to speak about his case at the university and enthusiastically greeted our idea of setting up a permanent table on the campus plaza with literature on him and the battle at Balboa Naval Base. In this way, the Black Student Council entered into a close working relationship with Ed Lynn. In the course of these activities, Ed and I became good friends.

The Second Baptist Church in Watts glowed with colorful African patterns and fabrics—the women wore "traditional" long dresses of red, purple, orange and yellow; the men wore bubas that rivaled in every way the fiery beauty of the women's clothes. The walls of the registration room were alive with poster art that hailed Blackness as an ancient and peerless beauty.

It was November of 1967, and my exhilaration was as bright and intense as the colors that dappled the room. I was a stranger to this kind of gathering and found literally staggering the energy and resolve of the people attending the Black Youth Conference. London and San Diego had been sad miniatures compared to this massive display of strength. I walked around calling everyone sister and brother; smiling, elated, high on love.

I came down. Slowly, at first, but then with a jolt.

A gun battle broke out during the first hours between two organizations—The United Front and Ron Karenga's US-Organization. Beneath the façade of unity, under the wonderful colors of the bubas, lay strong ideological differences and explosive political conflicts, and perhaps even agents provocateurs. I knew it was as important to understand this side of the movement as the nicer side—but my idealism had received a strong, and probably necessary, kick in the teeth. I was expecting too much, needing too much, and my eagerness to learn and submerge myself in this movement made me giddy with excitement.

In the midst of the chaos which followed the shooting, I read the literature, sat in on some of the workshops, and discovered that about the only thing we really had in common was skin color. No wonder unity was fragile.

There were the cultural nationalist organizations, talking about a new culture, a new value system, a new life-style among Black people. There were the severely anti-white factions who felt that only the most drastic measure—elimination of all white people—would give Black people the opportunity to live unhampered by racism. Others simply wanted to separate and build a distinct Black nation within the United States. And some wanted to return to Africa, the land of our ancestors.

There were those who felt the most urgent task of the movement was to refine the spirit of confrontation among Black people. They wanted to spark mass uprisings, such as the Watts and Detroit rebellions. Related to them were those who called upon us all to "pick up the gun" as the major weapon of liberation and transformation—although they seldom seemed to know exactly what it was they wanted to usher in with the gun.

There were the pseudo-militant groups that insisted that the racist establishment should be challenged—but only in order to pressure the big foundations to finance service programs which they themselves would develop and, probably, profit from. Indicative of the confusion was the fact that one workshop went so far as to propose before the plenary session the use of drums as a new means of communication among Black people in the cities.

It seemed to me that two steady rays of lucidity shone

through the confusion—James Forman of SNCC (Student Non-Violent Coordinating Committee) and Franklin Alexander of the Communist Party. Forman spoke to the plenum of the conference and emphatically defended the proposition that we could not afford to make a *skin* analysis alone; we also needed a *class* analysis. I watched Franklin as he co-chaired a workshop on the subject of Black Politics and Economics. His presentation was clear and incisive: power relationships which placed Black people at the bottom stemmed from the use of racism as a tool of the economically ascendant class—the capitalists. Racism meant more profits and, insofar as white workers are concerned, division and confusion.

After the conference adjourned, I was invited, quite by happenstance, to attend a small house meeting where James Forman and Ralph Featherstone talked about their recent trip to Africa. They gave a fascinating, detailed account of what they had seen in Tanzania, and discussed plans to establish within SNCC a "skill bank" through which Black people here with special scientific and technical skills could commit themselves to spending certain periods of time in Africa.

Besides Franklin and Kendra Alexander, at this meeting there were representatives of an organization called the Black Panther Party. It was a small cadre group which felt its role was to develop theoretical analyses of the Black movement, as well as to build structures within the existing movement. It bore no relationship to Huey Newton and Bobby Seale's Black Panther Party for Self Defense, except that both had taken their names from the Lowndes County Black Panther Party in Alabama. In fact, to distinguish it from Huey and Bobby's party, it was called the Black Panther Political Party.

This meeting was the beginning of my long and deep relationship with many of the members of the BPPP. Their understanding of the Black Liberation Movement was far more sophisticated and more satisfying than what I had discovered in San Diego. Though I continued my commitment to both the university and the community in San Diego, I found real strength and vision in L.A.

One of my missions during this trip to Los Angeles was to contact speakers for a San Diego rally we were planning in support of Ed Lynn. Leaders of several groups agreed to come: John Floyd, the chairman of the Black Panther Political Party; Brother Crook, a leader of the Community Alert Patrol; Ron Karenga, whose US-Organization was popular in San Diego; and Walter Bremond, the chairman of the Black Congress, a working coalition of Black organizations in the area of Los Angeles.

In organizing for this rally back in San Diego, I ran headlong into a situation which was to become a constant problem in my political life. I was criticized very heavily, especially by male members of Karenga's organization, for doing "a man's job." Women should not play leadership roles, they insisted. A woman was supposed to "inspire" her man and educate his children. The irony of their complaint was that much of what I was doing had fallen to me by default. The arrangements for the publicity of the rally, for instance, had been in a man's hands, but because his work left much to be desired, I began to do it simply to make sure that it got done. It was also ironical that precisely those who criticized me most did the least to ensure the success of the rally.

I became acquainted very early with the widespread presence of an unfortunate syndrome among some Black male activists—namely to confuse their political activity with an assertion of their maleness. They saw—and some continue to see—Black manhood as something separate from Black womanhood. These men view Black women as a threat to their attainment of manhood—especially those Black women who take initiative and work to become leaders in their own right. The constant harangue by the US men was that I needed to redirect my energies and use them to give my man strength and inspiration so that he might more effectively contribute his talents to the struggle for Black liberation.

❖   ❖   ❖

For me revolution was never an interim "thing-to-do" before settling down; it was no fashionable club with newly minted jargon, or new kind of social life—made thrilling by risk and confrontation, made glamorous by costume. Revolution is a serious thing, the most serious thing about a revolutionary's life. When one commits oneself to the struggle, it must be for a lifetime.

As 1968 got under way I realized how much I needed to find a collective. Floating from activity to activity was no revolutionary anything. Individual activity—sporadic and disconnected—is not revolutionary work. Serious revolutionary work consists of persistent and methodical efforts through a collective of other revolutionaries to organize the masses for action. Since I had long considered myself a Marxist, the alternatives open to me were very limited.

I had already begun to consider the possibility of joining the Communist Party, and had been involved in numerous discussions about this with Kendra and Franklin Alexander. In January I was among those invited to attend an open meeting of the Che-Lumumba Club at Charlene Mitchell's house; she was the founding chairwoman of this Black collective of the Party. Charlene made a presentation on the relationship between reform and revolution. Her paper was brilliant. It was the most lucid analysis I had encountered of the way to organize people around their own daily problems and, through this, propel them in the direction of the revolutionary overthrow of the capitalist system.

But because there were too many unanswered questions in my own mind, I did not join the Party at that time. Since my high school days in New York, and since the summer of 1962 when I had attended the Eighth World Youth Festival in Helsinki, I had been more or less out of touch with members of the Communist Party. Instead, I had been relating to Marxist groups and theoreticians and activists who were often strongly critical of members of the traditional Communist parties. Later, looking back upon my European days, I realized how deeply I had been influenced by the anti-communism which permeated the European Left movement. I saw the Communist parties as being too conservative and behind the times in their uncritical attitude toward the working class. In this respect, I thought that there was no hope for white workers in the United States—they had been irreparably corrupted by racism on the one hand and concessions by the ruling class on the other.

Yet, even if these particular problems had not bothered me, I was ill-prepared to join the Party right then. Still, to become a Communist is to make a lifetime commitment that requires a great deal of serious thinking about whether one has the knowledge, the strength, the stamina and the discipline that a Communist must have. During the first months of 1968 I let joining the Party remain an open question.

The Black Panther Party, however, appeared flexible enough to accept Marxist ideas. It was a small collective of young Black people, the majority of whom came from the Black intelligentsia—students, teachers, and a professor or two.

I had become acquainted with some of the members of the BPPP after the Youth Conference in November, and had started to develop some friendships with a few of them. When they decided, early in January, to broaden their membership by three, they issued one invitation to a brother at California State who had a reputation as a very good writer. The second was extended to Franklin Alexander, and the third to myself. I accepted the invitation. Inviting Franklin was, I thought, a sign of their willingness to open up to Marxist ideas. I saw them as an interim political base from which I could think over and decide upon the ultimate political direction I was going to take. They, in turn, saw me as their representative down south in San Diego. The BPPP was a member organization of the Los Angeles Black Congress—a broad coalition of community groups in the area.

Around this time the Black Panther Party for Self Defense, whose highest leader, Minister of Defense Huey Newton, was in prison, decided to build a chapter in Los Angeles.

Unfortunately some of their new recruits moved into that territory with belligerent claims of the exclusivity of the name "Black Panther Party." One afternoon, when I was in the Black Congress Building, I caught the eye of a brother drinking a bottle of wine—something prohibited, as I recall, in the Congress building. I turned my eyes from him and began to walk down the corridor toward an office. As I passed him, he pulled a gun out of his pocket and, with lightning speed, grabbed me by the shoulder, pointed the piece toward my temple and pulled me into the nearest office.

He wanted to talk, he said. His words were slurred and his breath clotted with wine. He wanted to talk about the Black Panther Party and his Black Panther Party for Self Defense. The wine bottle, the slurred words, the fact that he had a gun and I had nothing told me that if I didn't want my head blown off, I had better remain as tight-lipped as possible. So I listened.

"The Black Panther Party for Self Defense," he screamed, "demands that your motherfuckin' party get rid of the name the Black Panther Party. In fact, you better change it to the motherfuckin' Pink Pussycat Party. And if you haven't changed your name by next Friday, we are going to off you all."

To make sure I knew that he was dead serious, he told me that he had found out that I lived in San Diego; that he had my address and that I could expect someone to knock on my door if we didn't do what they were demanding. (In all fairness to Huey's Black Panther Party, it is important to say that this screaming drunk with a gun was later expelled from the Panthers for being an agent provocateur.)

A crisis situation had erupted. Other members of our group were similarly threatened. Guns were the common persuaders; death was the consequence of disobedience. I could do one of two things—obey him or get my own protection. I chose the latter and, for a while, was fully armed at all times. I knew that if I were ever stopped by the police and searched, I could end up in jail, yet if I did not take that risk, I could very easily end up dumped in an alley somewhere with a bullet in my brain.

We held emergency meeting after emergency meeting, but during that brief period, were unable to resolve this crisis. Some members wanted an open confrontation with the Panthers for Self Defense, even if it meant coming to blows. Others simply wanted to ignore the threats, insisting that the Panthers were bluffing. And there were one or two who were willing to quit, bend under the Panthers' threats and disband the organization.

The final solution came about as a result of a fortuitous trip of James Forman to Los Angeles. He came to town to speak at a rally organized by the New Politics Convention. We seized the occasion to acquaint him with the strife between the two organizations and to get his ideas on how to prevent this conflict from erupting into open warfare. After giving our predicament some thought, he said he had a proposal.

He prefaced his proposal by telling us of recent efforts to strengthen relations between SNCC and the Panthers for Self Defense. They had both agreed to move toward a merger between the two organizations. Stokely Carmichael had already been appointed Prime Minister of the BPP, Rap Brown became Minister of Justice, and Forman himself became Minister of International Affairs.

One of the obstacles to the consolidation of the merger was the geographical separation of the headquarters of the organizations: SNCC was in New York; the BPP was in the San Francisco Bay area. Forman felt it was essential to build a strong SNCC chapter on the West Coast. If we would consider transforming ourselves into Los Angeles SNCC, Forman said, our problems as well as SNCC's might be solved. First of all, our name would no longer be an issue. We would also acquire new national dimensions for our own collective and overcome, thereby, some of the provincialism that plagued us. From Forman's standpoint we would be assisting SNCC— which then was considered by many to be the leading force in the Black Liberation Movement—to build a base on the West

Coast. Finally we would be able to cement the relationship between the BPP and SNCC. If a lasting coalition were to develop, it would be a tremendous advance.

At first there was opposition. Some called Forman's recommendation too superficial to provide a lasting solution to our problems. They said we would have to deal with the brothers like the one who put the gun to my head whether we remained in our old clothes or whether we put on the new clothes of SNCC.

I was in favor of joining SNCC—not because I thought that the merger was going to dispel the discord between us and the new L.A. Panthers, but rather because I respected the historical contributions SNCC had made to the movement. The peace talk, however, in no way encouraged me to relax my own vigilance. The trusty weapon was still within reach at all times. Most of the sisters and brothers on our side were equally wary and did not immediately disarm themselves.

With everyone still on pins and needles, a peace-making meeting was called. It was an impressive gathering. With the exception of two or three of our members who had dropped out, all of us were present. On the Panthers' side, the line-up was all the major leaders (except Huey, of course, who had been arrested in October). Eldridge Cleaver was present. Until that meeting, most of us knew very little about him except that he was the "Minister of Information" who was "underground," according to the designation that followed the title each week in their newspaper. Bobby Seale was there, Emory Douglas and li'l Bobby Hutton, as well as seven or eight others.

I was most impressed by li'l Bobby. He was human, natural, and so clearly unconcerned about fitting the image of a cold, calculating revolutionary. Li'l Bobby initiated a friendly conversation with me by asking some everyday, down-home questions: where I was from, what I did. He had a beautiful smile and an uncorrupted, youthful enthusiasm. After talking to him for a few mintues, I knew that he was serious about the struggle and that there was little, if any, egoism in his motives.

The light conversation with li'l Bobby was the only relief for me in a meeting that was otherwise shrouded in tension.

When, a few months later, I heard that li'l Bobby had been shot, I felt as if it were a brother of mine who had been murdered by the Oakland police.

For better or worse, it was decided by both groups that our first common effort would be the issuing of a call to the entire Black Liberation Movement on the West Coast for two mass meetings—one in Northern California, and the other in Southern California—to demand Huey Newton's freedom on the occasion of his birthday.

The most widely known political prisoner, Huey Newton was an important symbol of Black militancy. At a time when it was perfectly legal to carry unconcealed weapons in California, he and his comrades had armed themselves in order to protect the Black community in Oakland from the arbitrary brutality of the Oakland Police Department. Because he had posed a serious threat to their authority, they had cornered him in a situation which left him with a bullet in his stomach and one policeman dead. Huey was awaiting trial for murder. We turned our energies full force to organizing this rally and to making it a major event.

We enlisted the support of the Black Congress and, after a series of hassles, we secured the Sports Arena for the meeting. It was the largest indoor meeting place in Los Angeles at the time. We printed thousands of leaflets, bought advertisements or asked for free time on radio and television stations.

It was an exciting evening. Although the turnout was not what we had expected, practically the entire main floor of the arena was full. The list of speakers was impressive: Stokely Carmichael, Rap Brown, Bobby Seale, James Forman, Reis Tijerina, Ron Karenga.

The importance of the rally was obvious. I was, therefore, especially disturbed by the content of some of the speeches. Stokely, for example, spoke of socialism as "the white man's thing." Marx, he said, was a white man and therefore irrelevant to Black Liberation. "As Black people," Stokely shouted, "we have to forget about socialism, which is a European creation, and have to start thinking about African communalism."

His speech was all the more disturbing because I knew that he had been in Cuba the preceding summer and had been warmly received wherever he went. He had officially congratulated the Cuban people—Black, Brown and white—for their superb achievements in building socialism. Moreover, I knew for a fact that he had publicly stated that his trip to Cuba had unequivocally demonstrated to him that socialism alone could liberate Black people. In a socialist country, to people whose sisters and brothers, and mothers and fathers had given their lives in the defense of their socialist revolution, Stokely had said that he was convinced that socialism was the answer for his people as well. Now that he was back in the United States, where the official propaganda made socialism less popular, he was opportunistically reversing his position. Because he knew how to turn a phrase, he had the audience applauding, not so much what he said as his way of saying it. I was glad he was no longer the chairman of SNCC, because after hearing such a speech, I would have left the organization on the spot.

The speech of Rap Brown, who had replaced Stokely in the chairmanship of SNCC, was one of the best of the evening.

A serious problem permeated the entire rally. We were supposed to be calling for mass support for Huey Newton. However, no strategy followed, graced or even decorated this demand. There were no specific, concrete proposals placed before the people in attendance. In response to the appeal, the applause was ample enough, but where were we to go from there? The only answer to this question was the slogan "The sky is the limit." That is to say, if Huey Newton was convicted and sentenced to death, the ruling class could expect a hundred police stations to be attacked, fifty power plants to be bombed, etc., etc., etc. It wasn't even clear whether the speakers were saying that they themselves would carry out these demolitions, or whether they were appealing to the people in attendance to go out and respond in this way if Huey was convicted. The gaping void was a clear-cut line of action spelling out the way to organize masses of people in struggle in order to guarantee that Huey Newton would be set free.

At this time, Rap Brown faced several very serious charges—clearly fraudulent—stemming from his speeches and political activity. He had been released on bail with the proviso that he remain within the boundaries of Manhattan, New York, except for trips to confer with his attorney. He was on just such a trip then to meet with William Kuntsler—a convenient trip for us because he had been able to speak at the rallies celebrating Huey's birthday.

We did not know—Rap did not know—that he would not get very far when he left California. He was to be seized by the FBI, reimprisoned, this time with a bail of $100,000, plus an extra $25,000 for allegedly insulting the arresting officer.

Our first grass-roots organizing effort was, therefore, a bail campaign for the national chairman of our organization. We decided to circulate a petition demanding that the exorbitant sum be lowered. At the same time, we began to organize a door-to-door drive to raise money for Rap's bond. Sisters and brothers were recruited to go out on weekends, into the community—in houses, churches, community centers, shopping centers, we asked people to put their donations into our coin cans and sign the petition.

The modesty of this approach was surpassed only by its success. As a result of the all-day expeditions with the cans labeled "Let Rap rap," we attracted a sizeable number of sisters and brothers to our organization. Increasing SNCC's membership on the Coast was an important gain, over and above the money that was collected and the message that reached large numbers of Black people in Los Angeles.

Shortly after our campaign to support Rap had gotten off the ground, we opened up a headquarters on Jefferson Avenue near Arlington. When my university responsibilities for the week were fulfilled, I would jump into my beat-up 1958 Buick and race up the highway from La Jolla to Los Angeles, heading straight to SNCC headquarters to join the others in getting down to the real business of struggle.

We felt we had the energy of stallions and the confidence of eagles as we rushed into the neighborhoods of L.A.—on the streets, in houses, campuses, offices—driving, walking, meeting, greeting. We experienced the heights of brotherhood and sisterhood doing something openly, freely and above ground about our own people. This was no sly manipulation of the establishment, marked by compromise and gradualism. Nor was it the individual heroism of some one person whose outrage had reached the point of no return. Our stance was public and our commitment was to our people—and for some of us, to the class. The time was indeed ours to seize. In spite of the absence of a homogeneous ideology, in spite of the disparate ways in which problems were approached, we knew we could not retire to reflect, could not halt the tide until every detail was worked out to everyone's satisfaction. Like new alchemists we lit the fire and trusted the heat to refine our recipe for victory.

Those were exciting times. The potential we had for building a mass movement among Black people in L.A. was staggering, and we went to work straightaway, pounding out a more comprehensive program for our organizers to follow. We were on our own. Because of the origins of our membership, we were not under the direct authority of the national organization of SNCC. Moreover, the merger with the Panthers had all but dissolved. After a minor run-in with Eldridge and company over the money raised during the February 18 rally, whatever superficial agreement had initially prevailed withered away for want of a mutual desire to sustain it. Fortunately, overt hostilities had also withered.

Although we tried to learn from the organizing experiences of SNCC—particularly during the year of its greatest influence in the South—we did not feel committed to follow rigidly the same line or program which had been developed by SNCC. For all intents and purposes, we were an autonomous organization.

With all the gusto of the novice, I accepted the responsibility for drawing up plans for a "Liberation School" and for being its director once it was established.

It was during this period of work on the bail campaign for Rap that we learned about a brutal police murder committed on the very day of the February 18 rally. One evening while we were in the office—and, if I recall correctly, Franklin, Bobbie Hodges, John Floyd, myself and others were deeply embroiled in a fiery discussion about the significance of Marxism for the Black Liberation struggle—two brothers came in (one of whom was the author Earl Ofari). They gave us the gory details of the police slaying of eighteen-year-old Gregory Clark not too far from our office. The brothers appealed to us to immediately organize a movement of resistance.

The next day some of us went out to investigate the facts of the killing and to explore the sentiment of the community. According to Gregory's family and friends and witnesses to the act, these were the facts: On a warm afternoon in February, Gregory Clark and a friend were cruising down Washington Boulevard in a late-model Mustang. They were drinking soda pop, the cans covered by brown paper bags. When they reached Vineyard, they were motioned over to the curb by an LAPD cop who, according to the brother who survived, told them that they didn't look like they "fit" the car they were driving. Then, seeing the brown bags and without a shred of proof, he accused them of drinking beer while driving.

The two brothers protested, the witnesses said. They had the registration to prove that they hadn't stolen the car and the cans themselves were proof of what they had been drinking. But the cop, Warren B. Carleson, refused to hear their explanation. All he heard was niggers talking back to a white man in uniform. Ordering them out of their car, he prepared to handcuff them. Perhaps Gregory began to raise his voice in protest. Perhaps he snatched his hands away to prevent the cop from clamping on the handcuffs. Perhaps he did nothing. In any case, there was a brief scuffle before Carleson locked the manacles around his wrists. The victim was caught, but Carleson did not stop there. According to those watching the encounter, he knocked Gregory Clark to the sidewalk, and while he lay face down, his hands cuffed behind him, Carleson shot Gregory in the back of the head with a .38 revolver.

As I stood there on the corner of Washington and Vineyard, staring at the two-week-old bloodstains on the sidewalk, this scene unfolded before me in all its original horror. But the hurt and the rage meant nothing by themselves. What was needed was an organized struggle.

Over a hundred people showed up at the community meeting we called. They listened avidly as witnesses to the murder told what they had seen. The community people eagerly accepted our suggestion that we should mobilize people to attend the coroner's inquest which would determine, for the benefit of officialdom, whether charges should be pressed against the cop or whether the act was a legitimate expression of his duty as a "peace officer."

We did not feel that we were strong enough at that point to influence the outcome of the inquest simply by our presence. More than likely they would declare that the killing of Gregory Clark was a "justifiable homicide." But large numbers of people there would certainly alert the ruling cliques that we were preparing ourselves for battle.

The scenario unfolded as we knew it would: the panel accepted Carleson's version of the story: He had been frightened; thinking that Gregory Clark might be armed (prostrate with his hands cuffed behind him?), he shot him in self-defense. The verdict: justifiable homicide.

Still, there was partial victory: the leaflets we had sent out into the community; the vigilance at the inquest. Our promises to expose the Gregory Clark case put the LAPD on the spot. We had sent people to track Carleson down on his beat and photograph him for our literature, but the LAPD had secreted him somewhere. That evening Carleson was interviewed by a major television station and forced to justify his act before the eyes of thousands of people, and our photographer snapped a photograph of him which we used to announce a People's Tribunal. Carleson was going to be tried by the people he had offended. The sisters and brothers who had been attracted to SNCC by the protests we were spearheading constituted themselves into a People's Tribunal Committee. A date was set for the trial to be held in South Park. While some were selecting the "lawyers," "judges," those who would play significant roles in the trial, other SNCC and People's Tribunal Committee members composed and printed the literature. I was in the propaganda department. Of all the material we produced, I was most proud of the poster which carried the photograph of Carleson which had been shot from the television set. If we had been consciously seeking a picture of a typical "racist pig," we couldn't have made a better choice. Carleson's soul was fully revealed in his face. Printed across the poster in large, broad letters was the word "Wanted." Under the photograph was the description: "LAPD Cop for the Murder of Brother Gregory Clark."

These posters were put up all over the Black community —the area where the brother was killed was saturated with them. Fact sheets about the case and leaflets announcing the trial were distributed door-to-door, after work at factories, in churches, and wherever Black people were.

The fruits of our labors were a tremendous awareness in the community of the case of Gregory Clark and a very large turnout at the people's trial.

The prosecuting attorney was Ben Wyatt, a Black lawyer and community activist. No one wanted to accept the position of defense attorney, but finally Deacon Alexander—Franklin's brother—accepted this unenviable role. The panel of judges consisted of a variety of persons active in the Black community, all representative of organizations which counted themselves among the advocates of Black Liberation.

If someone accused us of being one-sided, we made no claims to impartiality. We were not trying to duplicate the bourgeois judicial system which tries to conceal its class and race bias behind meaningless procedures and empty platitudes about democracy. We were demanding justice—about which Black people needed to be defiant and passionate. After hundreds of years of suffering the most persistently one-sided bestiality and violence, how could we seriously assume a posture of unbiased observers?

The witnesses were called; they gave their testimony of events leading up to and following Gregory's death. Other witnesses were called to give "expert testimony" on the unchecked racism in the LAPD. Past police murders in the Black community were documented, stitch by stitch, and a tapestry of racist horrors was woven. At the center of this tapestry was Gregory Clark, whose killer was arrogantly screaming "self-defense." We tried and convicted Carleson—not for being the originator and sole perpetrator of the crime, but because he had been an all-too-willing accomplice in the routine business of a racist system. Warren B. Carleson had not acted alone; he had helped the system to add one more victim to its rolls. And it was for this that he deserved the maximum penalty.

"You have heard the evidence against the defendant and you have also heard his defense. Are the people ready to pronounce their verdict?"

"Guilty! Guilty! Guilty!" roared the audience, and their unanimous thunderous verdict tore through the park air like bullets.

It would have been anticlimactic for the process to end with the mere rendering of the verdict. Yet we could not carry out a penalty unless it involved the continuation of our collective struggle. Our proposal to the Tribunal was therefore that we pressure the city councilmen, particularly the Black representatives, to call for Carleson to be tried for murder. As a dramatization of the seriousness of our proposal, we wanted to bring hundreds of people, thousands if possible, to City Hall; people who would demand that the popular verdict of guilty be given its due consideration.

It was too little. Following all the excitement, the sensations of strength, the will to resist that had been aroused during the course of the trial itself, the proposal seemed too conservative.

"Death! Death!" screamed a group of people. Others voiced their agreement. "Death to the pig," brothers continued to shout. Appoint a commission to execute the sentence, they said. They were volunteering.

Rage had transported these brothers into a desperate fantasy world. I understood how they felt. When I saw Gregory Clark's blood on the sidewalk, rage had pulled my instincts in the very same direction. But understanding the real value of mass action, I therefore had something else to lean on, something which could absorb my anger and set it on the right track.

Chaos reigned in the crowd. The reactions were partly the product of pent-up frustrations which were seeking the easiest way out. They were partly the result of conscious encouragement of the "pick up the gun" movement, perhaps aided by agents provocateurs sent into our midst to disrupt.

It was Franklin who pulled things back together. He had done an irreproachable job of presiding over the tribunal and the confusion presented a supreme test of his ability to lead masses of people. It was awesome to see him almost effortlessly gather up all the pieces of the meeting and mold them back into something whole. He moved with the people, identified with their desire to see the swift execution of the justice they demanded. He explained the fact that though we were growing stronger, the balance of power was still overwhelmingly on the side of the enemy. It would not begin to shift until we could bring increasingly greater numbers of people into our movement. That was what would have the greatest impact upon those who pretended to rule us. Our strategy therefore had to be that of reaching out to more and more of our people, bringing them over to our side.

By the time Franklin was ready to close the Tribunal, people were eagerly agreeing with and applauding the proposal that we make a journey to City Hall to lodge our demands. His phenomenal capacity to reach out to people made a deep impression on me, not only as an individual, but also—even more so—as a Communist. The respect he had commanded, the clarity of his explanation and the forcefulness of his method of presenting it were rooted in years of experience he had accumulated as a member of the Communist Party.

APRIL 4, 1968

I spent the morning at the SNCC office. In the afternoon, I went down to the Los Angeles Committee to Defend the Bill of Rights to see about some material I wanted to have printed.

The normal course of that Thursday was shattered by a scream "Martin Luther King has been shot!" A stonelike incredulity locked my face. The wound was in the head, put there by a white assassin, and there was little hope that he would survive.

My disbelief gave way to a sadness which made me feel, for the time being, very helpless, like I was sinking. An amorphous sense of guilt fell upon me. We had severely criticized Martin Luther King for his rigid stance on nonviolence. Some of us, unfortunately, had assumed that his religion, his philosophical nonviolence and his concentration on "civil rights," as opposed to the larger liberation struggle, had rendered him an essentially harmless leader. Never would any of us have predicted that he would be struck down by an assassin's bullet. Never would any of us have predicted that he would have needed our protection. I don't think we had realized that his new notion of struggle—involving poor people of all colors, involving oppressed people throughout the world—could potentially present a great threat to our enemy. It was not coincidental, I thought, that on that day he had been marching in the streets with sanitation workers on strike.

Back at the SNCC office, my anger and sorrow over the death of Dr. King could find its proper expression—its collective expression. Together with my SNCC comrades, I discussed the way we were going to fight back.

Many people in the community would be looking to us, L.A. SNCC, for leadership. We were going to need all the mind and muscle we could find. The crisis of King's assassination had erupted at the precise moment when we were having some serious problems among our own cadre, some of whom preferred to be TV revolutionaries and to excite crowds with militant rhetoric—but they didn't like the unromantic day-to-day work of building an enduring organization. Since the People's Tribunal, Franklin had emerged as the most capable leader of all our cadres. His competence and magnetism provoked envy among the Hollywood revolutionaries and stimulated undercurrents of anti-communism which had further complicated our internal situation. Yet, if we did not act immediately, we would be abdicating our responsibility to the Black community. Franklin was not in town. He had taken advantage of the relative quiet around L.A. to visit Kendra, who was attending an Ideological School for Communist Party cadres in New York. At the time of the assassination, he was driving across country—he called us from Chicago to ask what we thought he should do. We wanted him to turn around and head back to L.A.

That night in New York, the streets of Harlem and Bedford-Stuyvesant were teeming with angry Black youth attacking white businesses with stones and bottles—and the police sent to repress them. Raleigh, North Carolina, was in rebellion and Jackson, Mississippi, and Nashville, Tennessee, were on the verge of exploding.

Ghettos all over Los Angeles could easily reach the boiling point and reenact August 1965 once more. We knew that some elements would encourage spontaneous outbursts of a collective frustration and desperation, playing right into the hands of the police, for we were certain that the LAPD would be only too happy to have the opportunity to test all their new "riot-equipment." Every Black person who appeared to be disturbed about the assassination of Martin Luther King would be a potential target of attack. Many of its members having been recruited from the Deep South, the LAPD was perhaps the most vicious in the country—and more important than its viciousness, it was also the best equipped.

A physical confrontation had to be avoided, for in it the Black community would be doomed. Nevertheless, the eagerness to fight back could not be permitted to wither away—it had to be channeled into a political direction. We needed a mass political event to put forth a call for a renewed, intensive struggle against racism: Racism was Martin Luther King's assassin, and it was racism that had to be attacked.

The Black Congress ratified that position. All the member organizations agreed to work toward a mass rally call for an escalation of the battle against racism. Meanwhile, we had to develop a crescendo of mass activities which would climax with the rally. The community had to be kept in movement without being pushed to the point of explosion. The day after the assassination, we asked high school students to participate in a campaign to explain the assassination to the community and to distribute literature asking our people to attend a meeting at the Second Baptist Church. Our three mimeograph machines were rolling twenty-four hours a day, printing the leaflets to be distributed by hundreds of high school students who waited in and outside the office at every moment of the day.

Some people accused us of trying to "calm down" the community and of assuming a conservative stance before the fact of the assassination. These accusations came from those who advocated immediate rebellion. Our strategy, however, was proven correct, for the day after the murder, the police were themselves ready to provoke a rebellion. The scouts we sent out to investigate the mood of the community returned with reports of police provocations all over the city. Machine guns had been mounted atop the major police stations in the ghetto; the operators were at their posts at all times. That evening, a younger brother, with blood streaming down his face, walked into the office and told us that he had been beaten up by the police on the other side of town and was dropped off in front of our office. We took care of his wounds and saw to it that he got home.

Tension was mounting; we felt as if we were on top of a simmering volcano which could explode at any moment. On April 5, the day following the assassination, Lyndon B. Johnson had issued orders to the Secretary of Defense to utilize all the force that was necessary to safeguard "law and order." By April 6, there were twenty people dead throughout the country: nine in Chicago, five in Washington, two in Detroit and one each in New York, Tallahassee, Minneapolis and Memphis, the place of the assassination. A thousand had been wounded and two thousand had been arrested. Twenty-three cities were in rebellion.

The night of the meeting at the Second Baptist Church, we left three brothers from our security force to keep watch over the office. The situation was very tense; anything might happen. The brothers stayed there as a safeguard against police frenzy.

The first sign of trouble was that no one answered our knocks when we returned to the office after the church meeting. Bobbie and I were about to get angry at the brothers for leaving their posts at such a critical moment. But we knew they were extremely trustworthy—it didn't seem likely that they would have left the office unguarded.

The front door was unlocked—something was wrong. Inside, chairs were turned over, literature had been snatched from the shelves and scattered all over the floor and our Rap Brown poster had been ripped to pieces. In the mimeograph room, the drums of our machines had been slashed with broken glass. Mimeo ink had been randomly squirted on the floor and the walls.

Within a few minutes the two women who ran the restaurant next door came rushing into the office. They told us that approximately ten to fifteen black-and-white police cars had pulled up in front of the office. Some police had gone around to the back door. We saw that it had been chopped down with an ax. According to the two sisters, about ten minutes later, the police had led our three security brothers out the front door, their wrists cuffed together. They had shoved them into a patrol car and sped away.

It was not coincidental that they had attacked our printing machines. The work of our organization was, in the first place, educational. We had just produced hundreds of thousands of leaflets protesting Dr. King's murder, explaining the racist forces behind his assassination and suggesting how we should manifest our resistance. Although they did not often admit it, the ruling circles feared this educational approach far more than they feared the rhetorical threats to "off the pigs." They knew that our strategy was to organize the masses and that increasing numbers of people were looking to us for knowledge and leadership.

We recuperated from the initial shock and set aside our rage long enough to inspect the mess more closely and to start the wheels moving to post bail for the brothers. Someone suggested we eat, and turned the fire on under the big pot of spaghetti which had been cooked earlier in the day. Bowls were passed out, and we were starting to eat, when someone shouted, "Hey, there's a nail in this spaghetti." It was true. Tacks were in his food and in the other bowls as well—they had been stirred into the pot by the police who had broken into our office.

We decided to leave the office as it was, including the pot of spaghetti on the stove and to call a press conference for the following morning. So that the press could see with their own eyes the malicious work of the "brave" police.

By the end of April 1968, L.A. SNCC was barely two months old. But it had developed into one of the most important organizations in the L.A. Black community. Our People's Tribunal Committee, still active around Gregory Clark's case, dealt with police brutality and repression. We had built a youth organization—SNCC Youth Corps—which had attracted over fifty active members, and the Liberation School, which was under my charge, drew scores of people each time it convened.

Our telephone rang constantly; people were continually reporting acts of discrimination and repression to us, asking for our leadership on how to counter them. The office was hardly ever empty: it was a place where people came to find out about the struggle, how they could participate in it.

As the organization grew stronger, the truly committed cadres were being separated from the staff members who wanted the credit but not the responsibility for building SNCC. On the original central staff there had been six men and three women. The three women on the staff—Bobbie, Rene and myself—always had a disproportionate share of the duties of keeping the office and the organization running. Now only two of the men were doing anything significant in the organization—Franklin, of course, and a brother by the name of Frank, who headed the security and SNCC Youth Corps. Bobbie, Rene and I worked full time.

Some of the brothers came around only for staff meetings (sometimes), and whenever we women were involved in something important, they began to talk about "women taking over the organization"—calling it a matriarchal coup d'état. All the myths about Black women surfaced. Bobbie, Rene and I were too domineering; we were trying to control everything, including the men—which meant by extension that we wanted to rob them of their manhood. By playing such a leading role in the organization, some of them insisted, we were aiding and abetting the enemy, who wanted to see Black men weak and unable to hold their own. This condemnation was especially bitter because we were one of the few organizations on the Black Liberation Front in Los Angeles, and probably in the country, where women did play a leading role. It was a period in which one of the unfortunate hallmarks of some nationalist groups was their determination to push women into the background. The brothers opposing us leaned heavily on the male supremacist trends which were winding their way through the movement, although I am sure that some of them were politically mature enough to understand the reactionary nature of these trends. After all, it had been a voice of the Johnson administration, Daniel Moynihan, who in 1966 had rekindled the theory of the slavery-induced Black matriarchate, maintaining that the dominant role of Black women within the family and, by extension, within the community was one of the central causes of the depressed state of the Black community.

The brothers knew this; they also knew that Bobbie, Rene and I, together with Franklin and Frank, had moved into leadership of SNCC because of their own defective commitments. Still, they were determined to have a fight. I knew things were bad; that we were on the verge of something serious, perhaps devastating. But I did not know that this skirmish was going to mushroom into open warfare.

Franklin and Frank, naturally, fought on our side. When the work of the organization slowed down, adversely affected by this internal struggle, we decided to call New York SNCC headquarters for help. Forman was out of the country; some other national staff person said he would come out. But when he arrived, he was not so much interested in the specific difficulties we had called him about as in the general quality of the work we were doing in L.A. He summarily dismissed our problem of male-female political relationships, saying that it was not important enough to merit a special discussion. They would be solved, he said, in the course of dealing with other problems. What this brother wanted to discuss was the great dissimilarity between our organization and the other SNCC chapters across the country, especially the national operation in New York. He was right, of course. We had formulated our own strategy and program without regard to the policies of New York SNCC. In fact, we received hardly any input from national SNCC, except permission to use the name and the initial advice we got from Forman.

The brother from New York complained that the office was not "businesslike"; there were too many people "hanging

around" who "were not sitting behind desks." We weren't fulfilling what should have been one of our major duties, i.e.,
fund-raising for the national organization. He admonished us
for not arranging enough cocktail parties up in the hills where
the more affluent of our people could be persuaded to share
their prosperity with SNCC.

I was personally criticized for the courses I had included
in the curriculum for the Liberation School. Whereas I saw
the school as being a consciousness-raising vehicle, as impart-
ing *political* education to the community, the brother from
New York thought it should be geared fundamentally toward
teaching skills to the community—skills such as radio and TV
repair and computer programming. The school, he said,
should become an instrument of survival; it should teach people the knowledge they required in order to get a job. While
the need for jobs and job skills was at a crisis level in Black
communities, it was not the role of the SNCC Liberation
School to be a job-training center. My overall vision of the
school I directed was of a place where political understanding
was forged and sharpened, where consciousness became explicit and was urged in a revolutionary direction. This is why I
taught and found others to teach courses on such topics as
Current Developments in the Black Movement, Liberation
Movements in the Third World, and Community Organizing
Skills.

The national representative also criticized my inclusion of
courses involving Marxist ideas. After all, Black people were
afraid of communism, he said; they would be alienated from
the organization if they thought communists were around.
This was the first signal that an all-out attack on Franklin was
brewing.

After a fund-raising event during the brother's stay in
L.A. (we did have fund-raising events in order to cover our
own local expenses), Franklin invited some of the brothers on
security to his apartment. They had the money which had
been collected as well as the weapons to protect it. Using the
pretext that there was noise coming from the apartment, the

police broke in, arrested all the brothers, confiscated the money and the weapons (all of which were legally owned) and charged them with armed robbery.

It was not difficult to discern the motive of this seemingly arbitrary attack. A rally was scheduled for the next morning in front of City Hall to climax the series of confrontations with the City Council on the Gregory Clark case. Franklin was the central figure of the rally. A large mobilization was expected, and the police hoped to cut the sting out of the rally by imprisoning Franklin. The arraignment was set at the same time as the rally, and there was no chance of getting him released on bail before the court appearance that Monday morning.

The police doubtless expected us to cancel the mobilization—or even if we didn't, they probably thought it would be a defeat for the People's Tribunal Committee to try to pull it off in the absence of their leader. That morning in front of City Hall, the people attending the mobilization decided, almost spontaneously, to take the demonstration to the courthouse across the street and demand Franklin's immediate release. The eager crowd streamed into the halls of the courthouse and filled to capacity the courtroom where the arraignment was taking place. Without an explanation, the judge suddenly announced that he was dropping all charges against Franklin and the other brothers.

Franklin was unwashed and unshaven, and it was easy to see that he had not slept that night in jail. Nevertheless, he led the rally with his usual vigor, and it seemed that the people were even more militant than if the police had not tried to intervene. Having witnessed the evidence of their collective power—the release of Franklin in response to their demands—they were raring to fight for more such victories.

The next day, the L.A. *Times* published an extensive article on the rally and the way Franklin's release was achieved. In the article, Franklin was called a "Maoist Communist." As a member of the Communist Party, U.S.A., Franklin was not, of course, a Maoist. Yet the brother from the New York office was mesmerized by this phrase, even though he knew it to be false. I imagine he didn't care what kind of communist Franklin was. It was the fact that he was a communist at all and that the news media had seized upon this that worried him so much.

The *Times* article prompted him to call a meeting of the staff and other SNCC workers. I discovered later that certain select staff members had been informed that the purpose of the meeting was to discuss the advisability of having a Communist play a leading role in the organization. I had not been informed, for they knew where my politics and my loyalties were.

The SNCC representative's presentation before the gathering was as simple as it was opportunistic. SNCC simply could not afford to be associated with Communists. It had been incorrect to permit Franklin to play such a "visible" role in the organization, particularly without consulting the New York office first. He was expelling Franklin, so he insisted, in line with the policy of the national organization, and was further decreeing that the office and the operation should be purged of all traces of communism and Marxism. Silence. Was this going to be a reenactment of the McCarthy purges? Franklin's brother Deacon and I were the only ones who resisted this move at all. And we were a tiny fraction of those present. Obviously, we had left a fatal defect in the organization we had built if a man from the New York office could come in and expel the leading figure from our midst without even a feeble effort at resistance. Or was it that the fear of communism was so powerful that it could engender compromises of principle and concessions of all the things we had fought so hard to attain?

It was a depressing time. I felt alienated from sisters and brothers whom I had not only considered my comrades in arms, but whom I had come to regard as close friends as well. Franklin had been unilaterally kicked out of the organization without having been given the opportunity to defend himself before the people who had looked upon him as their comrade and their leader. Franklin, Deacon and I caucused about our next moves. My first instinct was to resign. But after the discussion, we decided that Deacon and I should stick it out a while longer; perhaps we could help the others back to political sanity.

But it was too late. The first concession, the first endorsement of an irrational, anti-Communist policy, the first act of tolerance toward an autocratic, apolitical businessman-type who called himself a revolutionary was the beginning of the end of our organization. The national representative appointed a chairman who assumed the same dictatorial stance. And one by one, this chairman effectively isolated all the good people in SNCC. I was relieved of my position as director of the Liberation School, at which point I submitted my resignation and from the sidelines watched the rest first pushed around and then pushed out of the organization. Within a matter of weeks, only the shell of what we had created was left. Whereas we had had over two hundred workers whom we could count on and hundreds more who could be mobilized, by the beginning of the summer there were no more than ten people left.

L.A. SNCC was dead. The office closed down and people wondered what had happened to all of us. This was a victory for reactionary forces. The downfall of SNCC could not have been better planned if it had been the work of an agent of the government.

Hours, days were consumed by exhausting discussions about the destruction of L.A. SNCC. Could the final downfall have been avoided? What had we done wrong? Could we have brought the majority of the staff over to our side? Could we have convinced them to withdraw from the national organization? After all, we had built everything without assistance from New York.

Kendra, who had been attending a Party School during the crucial period, criticized Franklin, as well as Deacon and myself, for not having waged a more determined battle from the outset against the little signs of anti-communism. There had been signs—passive acquiescence in anti-communism as well as active encouragement of it—but these signs had been either subtle or sporadic and disconnected. I had not realized that they could be the germs of a collective attitude which could erupt so abruptly into a witch hunt.

I felt that I was not entirely without blame, for on occasion I had agreed to certain anti-Communist notions prevalent on the Left. I had not done this in any official capacity or in circumstances involving formal meetings. Yet, in casual conversations around the office, I had sometimes joined the others in putting Franklin on the spot. We had accused the Communist Party of not paying sufficient attention to the national and racial dimensions of the oppression of Black people, and therefore submerging the special characteristics of our oppression under the general exploitation of the working class. I had gone along with others in criticizing, from an ultra-left standpoint, the general "conservatism" of the Party.

It was not that I shouldn't have criticized the Communist Party at all. The point was that I had made these charges without having carefully investigated the Party's positions. Given the circumstances, my statements—especially coming, as they did, from someone who called herself a Marxist—may have encouraged in some way the widespread no-struggle attitude toward the anti-communism.

From this point forward I tried to acquire the information I needed in order to decide whether I wanted to become a member of the Communist Party. At this stage in my life and my political evolution—even more than during the San Diego days—I needed to become a part of a serious revolutionary *party*. I wanted an anchor, a base, a mooring. I needed comrades with whom I could share a common ideology. I was tired of ephemeral ad-hoc groups that fell apart when faced with the slightest difficulty; tired of men who measured their sexual height by women's intellectual genuflection. It wasn't that I was fearless, but I knew that to win, we had to fight and the fight that would win was the one collectively waged by the masses of our people and working people in general. I knew that this fight had to be led by a group, a party with more permanence in its membership and structure and more substance in its ideology. Confrontations were opportunities to be met; problems were entanglements to be sorted out with the right approach, the correct ideas. And I needed to know and respect what I was doing. Until now all our actions seemed to end, finally, in an ellipsis—three dots of irresolution, inconsistency and ineffectiveness.

During that depressing time, I reread Lenin's *What Is To Be Done*, and it helped me to clarify my own predicament. I read Du Bois again, particularly his statements around the time he decided to join the Communist Party.

Since Frankfurt, since London, since San Diego, I had been wanting to join a revolutionary party. Of all the parties that called themselves revolutionary or Marxist-Leninist, the Communist Party, in my opinion, alone did not overstate itself. Despite my criticisms of some aspects of the Party's policies, I had already reached the conclusion that it would be the Communist Party or, for the time being, nothing at all.

But before I could make my decision I had to examine it, study it. The Che-Lumumba Club, the Black cell of the Party in Los Angeles, was the section of the Party which interested me. I wanted to know what its role and responsibilities were within the Party and how it maintained its identity and consistency as its cadres involved themselves in the Black Liberation Movement. As with all the other Communist parties, the basic unit of the CPUSA was and remains the "club" (or cell, as it is called in other countries). In general, the club is composed of from five to twenty members. There are sections, districts, states, regions, and finally the national leadership, which carries out policy which is made by periodic national conventions. Insofar as the democratic centralist structure of the Party was concerned, the Che-Lumumba Club was just like any other club. Yet it did have a special role, originating from the fact that Black Communists in Los Angeles had fought within the Party for a club that would be all Black and whose primary responsibility would be to carry Marxist-

Leninist ideas to the Black Liberation struggle in L.A. and to provide leadership for the larger Party as far as the Black movement was concerned.

The club had been established in 1967—at a time when the Black movement was approaching its zenith. The Communist Party was bound to be affected by the stirrings in the ghettos from Harlem to Watts. Because L.A. was the scene of one of the first recent, full-scale Black uprisings, it seemed inevitable that the Che-Lumumba Club would come into existence in that city.

The knowledge I gained about the Che-Lumumba Club did not satisfy me completely, because I had little firsthand knowledge of the larger Party. Kendra and Franklin, therefore, introduced me to some of the white comrades. I began to pay visits to Dorothy Healey, who was then the District Organizer of Southern California. We had long, involved discussions—sometimes arguments—about the Party, its role within the movement, its potential as the vanguard party of the working class; its potential as the party that would lead the United States from its present, backward, historically exploitative stage to a new epoch of socialism. I immensely enjoyed these discussions with Dorothy and felt that I was learning a great deal from them, regardless of whether I ultimately decided to become a Communist myself.

In July 1968, I turned over my fifty-cents—the initial membership dues—to the chairman of the Che-Lumumba Club, and became a full-fledged member of the Communist Party, U.S.A. Shortly thereafter I had to retreat to La Jolla in order to do the last intensive preparations for my Ph.D. qualifier examinations. For weeks and weeks I only studied. Days, I studied in my office at the university. Evenings, I worked— often well into the night—in the isolated house in Del Mar which friends lent me for the last part of the summer. My thoughts became so thoroughly wedded to philosophical things that I even found myself dreaming sometimes about the ideas of Spinoza, Kant, Hegel. I had wanted to pass the exams at this time and not wait until after my second year of classes, as was the normal procedure. This meant that I had to study on my own works that I would have ordinarily read in connection with courses. I had to work, work and work—until the point of absolute saturation.

As exam week approached, the simmering desperation among graduate students preparing to take the test exploded into open panic. In the middle of a discussion, for example, someone might break into tears for no apparent reason. The fear of not passing was omnipresent. And there was something that was feared even more than flunking the exams: passing them with a terminal master's degree and thus being shut out of the Ph.D. program entirely. If one simply flunked the exams, one could always take them again in the spring. But a terminal master's was the end.

It was a great relief to learn that I had done quite well on the examinations. Having passed them, I began to work on the prospectus for my dissertation, and became a teaching assistant in the Philosophy Department, a further requirement for the Ph.D. About half of each week I spent researching and teaching in La Jolla and the other half I devoted to my political work in Los Angeles.

I was glad to be in a position to resume attending the weekly Che-Lumumba meetings. It was an extremely important period for us. In June, Charlene Mitchell, our founding chairperson, had been selected by the national convention to be our Party's candidate for President, thus becoming the first Black woman ever to run for that office. We were immensely proud that the first Black woman presidential candidate was also a Communist. Because it had been twenty-eight years since the Communist Party had participated in the presidential elections, her candidacy marked the beginning of a new era for the Party. The vestiges of McCarthyism were being repudiated, and more and more people were realizing that they had to be defeated once and for all.

During September and October, Charlene was constantly

on the road, speaking in some twenty-one states and Puerto Rico as well. (No other candidate even bothered to go to Puerto Rico.) In Southern California, we campaigned for Charlene outside factory gates, at union meetings, in churches, on campuses, in the streets and everywhere else our message might fall on a receptive ear. Naturally we harbored no illusions about the outcome of the elections. Therefore we weren't so much interested in the number of votes she would pull, as in her ability to reach people who otherwise would never have been inspired to consider political alternatives outside the Republican and Democratic parties, and economic alternatives outside monopoly capitalism. Charlene's candidacy gave us the opportunity to speak about socialism as a real solution to the problems confronting the working class, and especially Black and Brown people.

Around this time Charlene's brother, Deacon, and I entered into discussions with leaders of the L. A. Black Panther Party, who had approached us about working with their Party. They were considering opening an office on the West Side of the city and wanted Deacon to lead that section. I was asked to participate in the political education program. In view of the fact that all the other members of the club were already deeply involved in mass movements of one kind or another, we both gave serious thought to this idea. Some of our comrades were active in the antiwar movement, pushing for an approach among antiwar activists which recognized the relation between aggression in Vietnam and racism and repression at home. Others, including Kendra and Franklin, were working with students, primarily at Southwest Junior College. I felt that it would be important for some of us to assist in the work of the Black Panther Party which, at that time, was like a magnet drawing large numbers of young Black people, all over the country, into its ranks.

After a series of meetings with the Panthers to air problems and explain and set aside past hostilities, and following discussion of the proposal in the Che-Lumumba Club, Deacon and I both agreed to go into the Panther Party. We found a building for the West Side office on Seventh Avenue and Venice Boulevard, and within a few days young sisters and brothers from the surrounding community began to stream in. No sooner were programs organized than they were bulging with eager young people. From three-thirty in the afternoon, when the junior high school students came in, until ten at night, the office was the scene of meetings, classes and discussions on such topics as the Black Liberation Struggle in the United States, the Movement in the Los Angeles Area, Strategy and Tactics in Community Organizing, and Marxist-Leninist Theory of Revolution.

If I still retained any of the elitism which almost inevitably insinuates itself into the minds of college students, I lost it all in the course of the Panther political education sessions. When we read Lenin's *State and Revolution*, there were sisters and brothers in the class whose public school education had not even allowed them to learn how to read. Some of them told me how they had stayed with the book for many painful hours, often using the dictionary to discover the meaning of scores of words on one page, until finally they could grasp the significance of what Lenin was saying. When they explained, for the benefit of the other members of the class, what they had gotten out of their reading, it was clear that they knew it all—they had understood Lenin on a far more elemental level than any professor of social science.

Not long after the office opened, we learned about a brutal killing which had occurred in the neighborhood. This was the account given us: One evening when a young brother had tried to buy some beer in a liquor store nearby, the owner refused to accept his money in the absence of identification proving him to be of age. Angry about not being able to get his beer, he said a few strong words to the owner and stormed out of the store. Apparently for no other reason than sheer frustration, the brother kicked over a garbage can standing on the corner. The owner grabbed his weapon, hidden under the counter, and fired through the glass door, instantly killing this brother who had done nothing more than vent his anger on a garbage can outside. When later questioned about the incident, the owner claimed he had a right to protect his property. The irony of this tragedy was that we had just been reading about the function of the state as providing protection for the propertied classes. It was clear that if people did not make their protests heard, this shell of an excuse would be accepted without question by the courts. That is to say, they would accept the owner's claim that the life of this young Black man was worth less than a five-dollar garbage can.

We assumed responsibility for organizing the community to see to it that this man was brought to justice. This meant marches through the streets of the surrounding neighborhood, door-to-door leafletting, street rallies, particularly on the parking lot of the store, and a constant picket line urging people to withdraw their patronage from this man we considered a murderer. As a result, the store's business dwindled down to a mere fraction of what it had been, and criminal charges of manslaughter were filed against the owner. As usual, however, he did not even spend a night in jail, since his bail was so low that it was tantamount to no bail at all. Still, we were determined that he be prosecuted for—and convicted of—murder.

This movement gathered momentum. Classes and meetings at the office had reached a total attendance of over two hundred. We were having to deal with much more concentrated police harassment. Suddenly, in the midst of all this, crisis struck at the Black Panther Party. Nationally, numbers of police agents had been discovered to be infiltrators inside the Party. A purge began. Once it was initiated, it began to engulf many sisters and brothers who were as innocent as any of those advocating the purge. It was my opinion that some of the enemy sympathizers who themselves should have been purged had made their way into the decision-making process, where it was determined who would be expelled and who would remain in the Party. The West Side office was practically decimated. Deacon was called up on the question of his membership in the Communist Party— in very much the same way he might have been called before the Subversive Activities Control

Board. Obviously, there was something more behind this than simply the fact that he was a Communist—this had certainly been known by all at the time he was approached to join the intermediate leadership of the Black Panther Party. Moreover, they did not even confront me with the ultimatum given Deacon—namely, to choose one of the two parties—Black Panther or Communist. (This had been discussed before we entered the Panther Party, and it had been agreed on both sides that the two parties were not in competition with each other and that thus there existed no problem of conflict of loyalties.)

Needless to say, this was the perfect moment for the enemy to move in and take advantage of the disarray and confusion. Sure enough, around this time, a leading member of the BPP—one who had helped a great deal with the building of the West Side section—was found one morning in an alley with a bullet through his brain. Shortly thereafter, around the middle of January, before we had had a chance to recuperate from the shock of Franco's death, Deacon and I heard a flash on the radio: two leaders of the BPP, Bunchy Carter and Jon Huggins, had been shot to death during a meeting of the Black Student Union on the campus of UCLA. That very day I had planned to visit Jon and his wife Ericka to continue the dialogue about the problems within the Party. With a few sisters and brothers from the West Side office, we rushed over to the apartment to make sure nothing had happened to Ericka and her newborn child. By the time we arrived, the police were just completing their raid. Justifying their arrests of the sisters and brothers in the apartment, including Ericka and the baby, they said they had word that the Panthers might try to retaliate for the killings of their people. This was absurd, because at that point, no one was fully aware of the circumstances surrounding the murders. It was only later that we learned that two members of Ron Karenga's US-Organization were the ones who actually pulled the trigger.

Many times before, movement leaders and activists had been felled by the bullets of police, conscious agents or crazy, confused brothers who let themselves be used. We had cried before, we had attended funerals before, and we had felt and expressed rage at seeing the life of a brother, a comrade, so cruelly blown out of him. We knew that for the moment our commitment meant that we were chained to a vicious circle of violence—in this way our enemies were trying to force us to retreat in fear. In a sense, therefore, we always expected the violence, we knew it was coming, though we could never predict the next target. Yet each time it struck, it was equally devastating to us. No matter how many times it was repeated, there was no getting used to it.

For me personally, the death of Jon Huggins was especially painful—of all the Panther leaders, he and Ericka were among the ones to whom I felt closest. Despite all the problems which had recently arisen, I had an enormous respect and admiration for him and felt he was in good faith in his determination to find a solution to the crisis within the Party. I was convinced then, as I remain today, the police were involved in some way in his murder because they feared his strength and his will to always do what was best for his people.

Ericka and the other sisters and brothers were released late that night. When she walked through the gates of Sybil Brand Institute for Women into the hard rain cutting through the night outside, she seemed as strong as ever. Seeing our sadness, our empathy with the pain she was surely suffering, she said, "What's wrong with you all? We can't stop now. We've got to keep on struggling." That was a moment I shall never forget. The sisters who had been with her inside the jail said that she was the one who had kept everyone's spirits high. She was the one who had most resolutely continued to carry the banner of struggle.

Amid all the speculation about the motives behind the killing and the verbal attacks on US-Organization, we attended Bunchy's funeral, and Ericka left for Connecticut to bury her husband and to find a safe place for her young daughter Maya. We learned that she had immediately begun to organize a chapter of the Black Panther Party in New Haven where, a few months later, police arrested her on a charge of conspiracy to murder.

Meanwhile, things quieted down around the BPP in Los Angeles, and because the problems surrounding Deacon's membership in the CP were never resolved, I felt it would be unprincipled of me to continue to work with the Panthers. I decided to spend the rest of the school year on the campus in La Jolla, where I worked again on a day-to-day basis with the Black Student Council. At the beginning of the second quarter, the sisters and brothers in the leadership of the organization all agreed that something was needed to set our membership in motion once more. We needed an issue around which to struggle. But what was the right issue? What was the most magnetic and most dramatic issue? Each of us thought seriously and intensely; our individual proposals were argued out in meetings that seemed never to end.

Finally, we reached unanimous agreement. Since the San Diego Campus of the university was to consist, ultimately, of a series of separate colleges, we decided that it would be just and appropriate to demand that the next college—the third college—be expressly devoted to the needs of students from oppressed social groups. Specifically, it should serve the needs of Black students, Chicano students and white students of working-class origin. While tightening our already close relationship with the Chicano students in the Mexican-American Youth Association, we drew up plans for our college. In order to project the radical character of our demands, we decided to call it Lumumba-Zapata College—after the assassinated Congolese revolutionary leader, Patrice Lumumba, and the Mexican revolutionary, Emiliano Zapata. We wanted our goals to be transparent: Lumumba-Zapata College, in our theoretical formulation, was to be a place where our peoples could acquire the knowledge and skills we needed in order to more effectively wage our liberation struggles.

After a brief period of strategy planning sessions, we decided that the time was right to confront the university administration. One afternoon the members of our two organizations streamed into the chancellor's office, insisting that he listen to our demands. I had been designated by the sisters and brothers to read the statement collectively drawn up by the BSC and MAYA. Along with our demands for Lumumba-Zapata College, we issued a very serious warning: in the event that the chancellor refused to negotiate, we would not guarantee that the university would continue to function undisturbed.

As could have been predicted, the chancellor did indeed refuse. His refusal was our signal for an all-out offensive: more rallies, demonstrations and confrontations. We knew that in order to be effective we needed the support of a significant number of students and faculty. Our actions, therefore, were designed to attract as many of the white students and professors as possible. Some white students were involved from the outset, since one very important aspect of our demands was the integration into the college of white students from working-class backgrounds. But we needed many more; we aimed to draw hundreds into the movement for Lumumba-Zapata and hoped to eventually bring the majority of the students over to our side. Only in this way could we isolate the administration, and thus force it to accept our demands.

Our actions were climaxed first by an appearance of our organizations in an Academic Senate meeting. With the aid of sympathetic professors—including Herbert Marcuse and others in the Philosophy Department—we began to win over a sizeable number of faculty members to our position. The next dramatic demonstration of our demands was a takeover of the registrar's office. As a result of our occupation of one of the central nerves of the university, the administration and those professors who were not already convinced were made to understand the seriousness of our position.

We had put up a fierce struggle. Large numbers of UCSD students had experienced the radicalization that was occurring on campuses throughout the country. The university hierarchy decided, apparently, that it was best to make the concessions we were demanding, rather than risk a prolonged disruption of campus activities. To tell the truth, we had not really expected them to agree so readily to our notion of the third college. And when they did, those of us leading the movement knew that despite our victory—of which all of us were proud— Lumumba-Zapata College would never become the revolutionary institution we had originally projected. Concessions were going to be inevitable, however the creation of the college would bring large numbers of Black, Brown and working-class white students into the university. And it would be a real breakthrough to have a college in which students would exercise more control over the education they received.

At the end of the school year, as I prepared to leave for a conference in Oakland, and go from there to Cuba, students selected by our organizations were settling down to a summer of drawing up concrete curriculum, faculty and administrative proposals for the college. The fight was not over. On the contrary, it had just begun. The most important responsibility resting with us was to ensure that whoever became involved in the college—students and faculty alike, carried on the legacy of struggle out of which the idea of Lumumba-Zapata was born.

The era of massive national conferences was still in full force. In July 1969, movement activists, Black, Brown and white, from throughout the country, converged in Oakland, California, to attend a conference called by the Black Panther Party to found a United Front Against Fascism.

The organizational theory behind the conference was excellent: people with various ideologies—the broadest possible representation of people—joined together to forge a United Front to combat the increasingly ferocious repression. But there were problems with the conference, and I was perhaps overly sensitive, since I had just recently been forced to break my relatively close ties with the Panthers. The basic difficulty, I thought, was that we were being asked to believe that the monster of fascism had already broken loose and that we were living in a country not essentially different from Nazi Germany. Certainly, we had to fight the mounting threat of fascism, but it was incorrect and misleading to inform people that we were already living under fascism. Moreover, the resistance dictated by such an analysis would surely lead us in the wrong direction. First, in seeking to include absolutely everyone who had an interest in overthrowing that fascism, we might be pushed into the arms of the liberals. Our revolutionary thrust would thus be blunted. And if we were not led in that direction, we would be pressed toward the opposite end of the political spectrum. For, if we believed we were living under genuine fascism, it would mean that virtually all democratic channels of struggle were closed and we should immediately and desperately rush into the armed struggle.

In many of the speeches, the word "fascism" was used interchangeably with the word "racism." Certainly, there was a definite relationship between racism and fascism. If a full-blown fascism ever erupted in the United States, it would certainly ride on the back of racism in much the same way that anti-Semitism provided the handle for German fascism in the thirties. But to think that racism was fascism and fascism was racism was to cloud the vision of those who were attracted to the struggle. It was to hamper their own political development and to impede the *organized mass* fight against racism, against political repression—and especially in defense of the embattled Panthers.

In the midst of the confusion, Herbert Aptheker, the Communist historian, made an excellent presentation, laying out the relationship between racism today and the potential of fascism tomorrow. For me, it confirmed the correctness of my decision to join the Communist Party almost a year ago to that date.

With all its obvious flaws, the conference was nevertheless one of the most important political events of the season. It established the basis for breaking out of the narrow nationalism so prevalent in the Black Liberation Movement and pointed the way for alliances between people of color and white people around issues which involved us all.

As soon as the conference had adjourned, Kendra and I

boarded a plane for Mexico City, where we joined the remaining members of a delegation of Communists invited by the Cubans to spend a month in the "first free territory of America." I was nervous and depressed during the flight to Mexico: my purse had been stolen while I slept in a Haight-Ashbury park, and I had no money and no passport. Kendra had lent me enough for the ticket to Mexico City, but I was less than certain of being able to secure a passport before the others took off for Cuba. My only hope was that the Cubans would let me enter the country without my traveling papers.

Not only did the passport present problems insofar as the trip was concerned, we all had to worry about concealing our intentions from the Mexicans, who, on several occasions, have deported activists from the United States trying to get to Cuba. During the student demonstrations of 1968, when the police had massacred crowds of people, a group of activists, among whom were Bobbie Hodges and Babu (with whom I had worked in SNCC) were in Mexico City attempting to get a plane for Cuba. They had all been detained by the police, interrogated about the purpose of their trip (were they going to receive guerrilla training?) and asked about their participation in the student rebellion in Mexico City. The outcome of the whole affair was deportation for them all. They had been randomly and separately placed on planes leaving Mexico— Bobbie, for instance, had ended up in Paris.

We devised a plan to elude the Mexican police. As soon as we landed, we would look up the address of the Cuban Embassy, where our visas were supposed to be waiting, and check into a hotel somewhere in the vicinity. After we had deposited our luggage, we would go out on foot to locate the Embassy. The next morning, we would make a dash for it. We knew that if the police discovered us before we got inside the Embassy, we might be detained before we could even obtain our visas. After receiving the visas, we would remain in the Embassy and at the last moment we would rush for the airport, stopping off for our luggage on the way.

That night we walked for hours, but in vain, for we could

not find the Cuban Embassy anywhere in the neighborhood. Only after much wandering the next day did we discover on the other side of town another street with exactly the same name. The Cuban Embassy was located there. Reaching the Embassy finally without incident (although we noticed men outside who appeared to be U.S. agents), we were told that our visas had not yet arrived and that unfortunately it would not be possible for us to leave for Havana that evening. It was Monday and if everything could be arranged in time, we could take the Friday plane to Cuba.

And then came the coup de grâce. Explaining that my passport had been stolen two days before, I asked whether I could board the plane without it. Trying to console me, the Cuban comrade told me that they were not the ones who required the passports; it was the Mexican immigration department. No one could leave Mexico for Cuba without first presenting their papers to the Mexican authorities. The comrade suggested that I go to the U.S. Embassy there in Mexico City and attempt to get a new passport as quickly as possible.

I was not at all optimistic about being able to get my passport replaced. The State Department still kept lists of Communists and often refused to deliver passports to our comrades until a lawyer challenged them in the courts. Kendra, for instance, thinking she had lost her passport, had put in an application some six weeks before the trip. Normally a passport is ready within a week after one applies, but each time Kendra inquired, they told her that there was no information concerning the date her passport would be ready. Luckily she found her misplaced passport before we left the country, because the new one had still not arrived. Another member of our delegation had also waited for weeks for his passport and at that moment in Mexico City was awaiting word from his lawyer, who was dealing with the State Department. I was still willing to try any scheme we could concoct in order to acquire a passport by Friday. I returned to the hotel, picked out the nicest clothes I had—the ones which would identify me as an innocuous tourist whose passport and money had just been stolen. At the U.S. Embassy, I tearfully explained that I had been planning this trip through Mexico, Central America and South America for over a year, and my vacation plans had been ruined by some thief. A friend was waiting for me in Nicaragua and I had no way of reaching her. Wasn't it possible to get a passport on some kind of emergency basis? The Embassy official took pity on me and by the next afternoon, there was a new passport waiting for me. The ploy had been pulled off; I had obviously aroused no suspicions, so they had issued the passport without first checking with the State Department in Washington.

We had almost given up when the visas finally came through. With the exception of Jim—whose passport was still in the hands of some bureaucrat in the State Department—we all prepared to take the Friday flight to Havana. Whoever was about to board the Cuban plane had to agree to be photographed by the Mexican immigration officials. No one, not even the nun on her way to Cuba, douhted that these photos would soon end up in the files of the CIA. We were not completely cured of our paranoia until we had actually lifted off the ground.

As we were flying over the lush Havana Green Belt, studded with tall, graceful palm trees, the pilot announced over the loudspeaker, "You are about to land on the first free territory of America." Several minutes later, when the plane touched the runway, everyone on the plane spontaneously burst into applause.

It was the day before Cuba's most important national holiday—the 26th of July. On this date in 1953, Fidel led an assault on the Moncada Garrison, a central base for the dictator Batista's army and a well-known symbol of his power. Though Fidel and his comrades were all either killed or arrested, people viewed their courageous act as the first great challenge to Batista's dictatorship. After the ultimate triumph of the revolution, July 26th, the Day of the National Rebellion, continued to be celebrated as the anniversary of the first armed attack of the revolution.

Ordinarily there would have been a mass rally at the Plaza de la Revolución at which Fidel and other leaders would have spoken to the hundreds of thousands in attendance. This year July 26 would mark the beginning of an agricultural campaign to process more sugar cane than ever before in the history of their economy. To be exact, they wanted to produce ten million tons of sugar. Instead of going to the Plaza on July 26, everyone was going to the fields to work. While it would be an honor to participate in the Campaign of the Ten Millions, I must confess that I was disappointed that there would be no rally at the Plaza. This was the first time since the triumph of the revolution that the traditional celebration would not take place.

Colorful billboard posters lined the road from the airport to the hotel: posters about the Campaña de los Diez Milliones; posters of El Che; posters praising the people of Vietnam. Many of these billboards had been used in the past to advertise U.S. products, bearing slogans such as "Drink Coca-Cola," and "The Pause that Refreshes." I felt a great satisfaction knowing that the Cubans had ripped down these trademarks of global exploitation and had replaced them with warm and stirring symbols that had real meaning for the people. The sense of human dignity was palpable.

Our bus carried us across the grounds of the Havana University, reserved for two hundred years for the sons and daughters of the wealthy. Now the students were the children of workers and peasants—Black and Brown as well as white.

The bus stopped in front of the Havana Libre, formerly the Havana Hilton, now freed from the veined fingers of decadent old capitalists. This was the first time I had stayed in such a fancy hotel. Its elaborateness, however, was quieted by the guests: workers on vacation, young couples on their honeymoons and by the *compañeros* who staffed the hotel— men and women with none of the servility usually associated with bellboys, chambermaids and waiters, people who would never accept the tip that natives of capitalist countries are accustomed to giving.

In the early morning hours of July 26, we drove to the fields. Buses, vans, trucks and automobiles were packed with young and old, proudly dressed in work clothes, singing as they made their way to the country. It seemed as if every able-bodied resident of Havana was rushing to the fields as though to a joyous carnival. On these faces reigned the serenity of meaningful work—the passion of commitment. They were finished with the politics of class and race, done with the acid bile of outdoing one's neighbor for the sake of materially rising above him.

The sugar cane campaign was closely connected with work in other realms of agriculture. The higher the rate of productivity in preparing and harvesting tobacco, citrus fruit, coffee, etc., the more the workers would be able to devote their energies to cane-cutting. Our first trip to the countryside was to the coffee fields in the Havana Green Belt. On July 26, we spent the day hoeing away the weeds and breaking up the soil around the coffee plants to permit them to grow unhindered.

It was a hard day. In the white-hot sunlight sweat drenched my clothes before I had hardly gotten started. I was in fairly good condition but the hoeing was difficult work for me. The Cubans, on the other hand, did it with ease. I was determined to ignore the sun and to keep the same pace as the hundreds of *compañeros* around me. Even when a spell of vertigo threatened to overcome me, I said nothing and refused to stop.

Being North Americans, we all felt we had to constantly demonstrate our worth. At the precise moment when I was certain I was going to faint, Kendra chopped her foot with the hoe and I had to accompany her to the first aid station. It was a convenient "out," but I returned to the fields still determined to survive the day. Besides, I had to build up my endurance for the coming week, which we were going to spend cutting cane in the province of Oriente on the eastern end of the island.

After a shower, a change of clothes and a few moments'

rest in the air-conditioned comfort of the Havana Libre, I left the hotel with one of the comrades from our delegation to explore the streets of Havana. The old Spanish architecture in some parts of the center made me think back to the War of Independence, the Black General Antonio Maceo, wounded some eighty times before he finally fell. Down on the Malecon, we saw the statue erected by the United States. The eagle at its tip was missing. The revolutionaries tore it down after their march on Havana.

We saw a young militia woman wielding a machine gun on guard duty in front of her work center. Wearing the light-blue shirt with epaulets, olive-green pants, military boots, she defended her assigned territory. With the archenemy so near—Florida was a mere ninety miles away—one of the most noticeable aspects of everyday life in Cuba was bound to be defense.

People were still talking about the Bay of Pigs invasion as if it had happened only yesterday. Eight years had passed since the burial ceremony for the seven who were killed when airplanes from the United States and its bases in Guatemala and Nicaragua had bombed the airports in three Cuban cities. On April 16, 1961, Fidel had proclaimed the socialist character of the Cuban Revolution and called upon his people to mobilize themselves lest the "puppets of imperialism expand their acts of aggression." Sure enough, the very next day, Cuban exiles—trained by the CIA with participation by the Kennedy administration—landed with U.S. ships and planes on Playa Giron.

Eight years was indeed a short span of time, considering that the Cubans were trying to build a new world and would fight to the death for their right to build it.

U.S. aggression had expressed itself in other ways as well. Using the presence of Soviet missiles on Cuban soil as an excuse, the Kennedy administration openly declared its intention to annihilate the Cuban Revolution even if it meant a thermonuclear catastrophe. And during the days of the October crisis, the world tottered above the abyss. Moreover, there was the U.S.-imposed economic blockade; there were U.S. troops on Guantanamo Base in Oriente, and news had leaked out that Kennedy had actually discussed the issue of whether to assassinate the Prime Minister, Fidel Castro.

One of the mass organizations very much in evidence from one end of the island to the other was the Committee to Defend the Revolution. During our first walk through the streets of Havana, we had noticed that on at least one house door in every block there was a poster in red, white and blue, with the words "Comité de Defensa de la Revolución."

The origin of this organization had been spontaneous. On September 28, 1960, during a rally at which Fidel was reporting on his trip to the United Nations, two bombs were set off by someone in the crowd. Fidel's response was swift:

> We are going to establish a system of collective vigilance and then we're going to see if the lackeys of Imperialism will be able to operate, because we live all over the city; there is not a single apartment building in this city, nor is there any block, any square block, that is not widely represented here. . . . We are going to establish a Committee of Revolutionary Vigilance in every square block, so that the people stand vigilance, so that the people see everything, so that the enemy understands that when the masses of people are organized, there is no imperialist nor lackey of the imperialists, nor sell-out to the imperialists, nor instruments of the imperialists that will be able to operate again.*

By 1969, there were CDR's in literally every block on the island. It was amusing to recall some of the propaganda which was floating around in the United States about the Cuban Revolution—particularly the lies about the Committee for the Defense of the Revolution. According to the government propagandists, this was a spy organization, something like the FBI, that snooped around gathering intelligence on the people and communicating it to the government. This was obviously absurd, since the majority of the Cuban population

* Discursos de Fidel en los Aniversarios de los CDR, 1960–1967. (p. 17)

belonged to the CDR's; they had joined because they wanted to help root out the saboteurs and enemy agents who were trying to subvert the Cuban Revolution.

Another widely accepted falsehood about Cuba had to do with the role of Fidel Castro. According to the propaganda, he was not only a "tyrannical dictator," imposing an iron will upon his people; he was projected as an infallible charismatic figure, whom the people were expected to worship. After seeing all the spectacular posters of Che Guevara and other leaders of the revolution, I looked hard for pictures and posters of Fidel. The only ones I could find were historical in character—in which he was shown with guerrillas in a typical scene of battle. But there were no portraits of the Prime Minister anywhere to be seen. When I asked some of the *compañeros* why there were many portraits of Che to be seen but absolutely none of Fidel, they told me that he himself had prohibited people from mounting pictures of him in their offices or work centers. This upset people sometimes, I learned, for they thought he was more self-effacing than was necessary.

Talking to almost any Cuban about Fidel, it soon became clear that they did not see him as being anything more than extraordinarily intelligent, exceptionally committed, and an extremely warm human being endowed with great leadership talents. He made mistakes, human errors, and people loved him in large part because of his honesty with them. Fidel was their leader, but most important he was also their brother, in the largest sense of the word.

We spent a week in the small village of Santa Maria II, located in the sugar center, Antonio Guiterras, living in log cabins with cement floors in an encampment which normally served as a Party retreat camp for political education. Our eating place was an open area with a roof to shade it from the sometimes unbearably hot Oriente sun. The toilet was a regular outhouse, until plumbing was installed toward the end of our stay. The shower was a cement stall into which we took large buckets of cold water fetched from the one faucet on the grounds.

We were roughing it, even by Cuban standards. We followed the regular routine: up at five, breakfast and out to the fields with our machetes. Back in the camp by eleven; lunch and rest during the noon hours when the sweltering tropical heat would be dangerous even for those accustomed to it. Back in the fields by three, and by six it was time to lay down the machetes for the day.

Cane-cutting was far more difficult and fatiguing than the work in the coffee fields. But again, I was determined to do at least my share, and I meticulously followed the system: A powerful stroke at the root of the plant; careful strokes down the side of the stalk to shave off the leaves; then the last motion of slicing the stalks into pieces the right size for processing. It was hard, and the heat was even more intolerable because our clothes were blue jeans, heavy long-sleeved work shirts, high-top boots, and gloves. All this was for protection from the liquid that seeped out of the cane leaves and could cause a severe skin rash. It didn't take me long to accept the fact that during the working hours of each day I was going to be soaking wet with sweat. In two days I was able to get into the swing of it; I had recovered my energy, it seemed, and could work alongside a Cuban *compañero*—though I did suspect that he was slowing his pace to remain with me.

One day I remarked to a Cuban how I admired his skill in cutting cane—it was almost like an art, the way he did it. He thanked me for the compliment, but quickly added that his skill was a skill that needed to become obsolete. Cane-cutting was inhuman toil, he said. Before the revolution thousands had had to depend for their survival on working like animals during the cane season. Many of them would end up having to cut off a finger with the machete for a little insurance money to make ends meet a little while longer.

The job of cutting cane had become qualitatively different since the revolution. No one was a cane-cutter *by trade* any longer; during the cane season everyone pitched in. Also profits for others were not being squeezed from their sweat and toil. They knew that the returns from sugar sales abroad would be used to raise the living standards of the Cuban people as a whole—new schools would be built, more hospitals constructed; child care centers would multiply, better housing would be available to those who had the greatest need.

Even so, this Cuban said, the business of cutting cane was work not fit for human beings; it made you old before your time. He continued to do it because he knew that he was working for the day when his sons and their children would not have to toil under the sweltering sun. Mechanization of the entire industry was on the agenda, but the rapidity with which it could be put into operation depended on the sacrifices they were all willing to make.

In this way he subtly criticized me for having romanticized something which was really nothing more than terribly hard work. It was then that I began to realize the true meaning of underdevelopment: it is nothing to be utopianized. Romanticizing the plight of oppressed people is dangerous and misleading.

As the time went by, Kendra and I and the rest of us began to feel as if we had taken root in this small village in Oriente. We had met almost every resident; we knew the Communist Party headquarters well and we knew all the children in the barrio. Despite the language barrier, the children accepted us as members of the family. They helped me with my Spanish lessons each day. I was extremely embarrassed that I had not learned a little Spanish before the trip, for it is an affront to a people to visit them before having attempted to learn their language. Because I spoke Spanish so poorly, never having studied it, I felt less inhibited with the children. They were patient, corrected me and helped me find words when no dictionary was available.

It was a sad day indeed when we had to pack up our things and board the bus, ready to move on to the next stage of our journey. All of us cried—men and women alike, in our delegation as well as on the Cuban side. The hardest part for me was saying good-bye to the children. A young boy of about nine or ten, who had always been the toughest one of his group, seemed reluctant to come up and say good-bye. I thought that it was his natural shyness. Just before I got into the bus, I went over to him and gave him a kiss on the cheek. He tore away from me and ran as fast as he could. But once in the bus, I saw him standing behind a tree, trying to conceal himself as his body shook with sobs. The tears that had been flooding my own eyes slid down my face.

We had an unusually rugged schedule over the next weeks: schools, hospitals, child care centers, historical spots, a workers' resort center, the University of Santiago, a dam, a rice-producing center.

Wherever we went, we were immensely impressed by the results of the fierce struggle that had been waged against racism after the triumph of the revolution. The first executive decrees of the new government had been to abolish segregation in the cities, brought to Cuba by corrupt capitalists from the United States. Now it was simply a crime to discriminate against Black people in any way, including the use of racist language. What was more important, of course, was the destruction of the material base of racism—weeding it out of the economy. During our trip, we saw Black people in leadership in factories, schools, hospitals and wherever else we went. It was clear to us—and Kendra, Carlos and I, the three Black members, incessantly discussed it—that only under socialism could this fight against racism have been so successfully executed.

Around the end of August, our delegation, together with a larger Puerto Rican delegation, boarded a Cuban freighter which would take us on the first leg of our trip back home as it transported cement to the French Antilles. The freighter steered out of the Santiago Bay that evening. By the time we had cleared the island, the moonless night made it impossible to see land or sea. We were settling down, finding our way around the ship, and along with the large Puerto Rican delegation returning via this route, we were trying to get acquainted with the crew. The captain was a twenty-six-year-old ex-philosophy student, with whom I was eager to discuss philosophy. This was his first voyage manning this ship and, like us, he was having to familiarize himself with the ship and the crew as well.

As we sailed farther into the darkness, a plane suddenly flew low over the ship at lightning speed. Before I could collect my thoughts, it crossed above us once more. As Kendra and I rushed toward the captain's bridge to find out what was going on, one of the crew members told us calmly that this was an exhibition of aggression by a U.S. aircraft carrier enforcing the economic blockade.

By means of lights, the U.S. carrier began signaling to our ship to identify itself and its mission. Of course, they could see the Cuban flag; this whole episode was the routine harassment which Cuban ships confronted whenever they sailed out of their own waters. We signaled back that before we identified ourselves, we wanted the name and mission of the party desiring the information.

Amusement mingled with tension during these moments of our encounter with the U.S. aircraft carrier. Suddenly in the near distance, a bizarre, soundless explosion-effect lit up the darkness. At first, it looked like a miniature mushroom cloud. A second later, it seemed to be heading directly toward us. I was too frightened to ask what was going on; if this was lethal gas, there was no way for us to escape. Finally, it engulfed the ship with its bright light, illuminating the whole area as if it were high noon. A crew member then remarked that it must be a new flare, and that the United States was using the blockade to test it.

We finally shook off the North American military men and enjoyed for a few days the legendary beauty of the Caribbean. We passed the politically not so beautiful countries of Haiti and Santo Domingo, and at last received instructions that the ship was to dock in Guadeloupe.

I did not like the idea of being responsible for communications with the Guadeloupeans, but I was the only one on board who knew French, so I had no other choice.

Our delegation had very little luggage. But the Puerto Rican delegation had boxes of books which the Cubans had given them for their bookstore in San Juan. I was careful to ask the customs people whether or not they wanted to inspect all the packages. We wished to avoid any kind of incident on the island, and the Puerto Ricans wanted to make sure they would be able to mail the packages to San Juan from Basse-Terre, the port where we had docked. The Frenchman told me not to worry about a thing; all they wanted to see was our passports. After they were stamped, we would be completely clear.

The Cuban captain had the name of a women who would allow us to eat at her restaurant-hotel and would let us leave our belongings there while we made arrangements for a flight to Puerto Rico. After depositing our things, I went to an agency to buy plane tickets for the twenty-five of us. Some of the Puerto Rican brothers began to cart their packages to the post office.

I was negotiating with the travel agent when one of the Puerto Rican comrades broke into the office, frantically explaining that all the packages had been confiscated. The police had confiscated the passports of several members of their delegation, and it seemed that they had been charged with a crime. Because of the language barrier, they did not fully understand what was happening. They needed me as an interpreter.

As I walked through the streets of Basse-Terre, I was certain that this was a minor misunderstanding which could be instantly cleared up. The passports would be returned and we would be on our way to Puerto Rico later that night. The comrades led me down a broken-down street, through a dark driveway into a dingy garage which was being used as a storage area, apparently by the French Customs Department. In the dim light of this cellar, about ten members of the Puerto Rican Delegation were standing in a circle around an old French colonialist who was waving their passports in the air while he ranted about communism infiltrating the "free

French world" of Guadeloupe. The faces of the Puerto Rican brothers were distorted in incomprehension.

Calmly, but quite firmly, I asked him what it was that disturbed him so much. My cool-headed posture did not sober him, as I had hoped. but rather set him off on a tirade that was even more vitriolic than the first. He was accusing us all of being agents of Cuban communism, bringing communist propaganda to foment revolution on this tranquil island where the "natives" loved their French governors and had peacefully coexisted with them for so many decades. I thought to myself that it would have indeed been a good thing if in such a short time we could have fomented an insurrection there. Unfortunately, our presence on the island had nothing to do with revolutionary activity.

When he quieted down, I began to tell him the simple truth: Some of us were Communists—I, for example—and some of us were not. We were returning from a trip to Cuba and hoped to leave Guadeloupe on the next plane to Puerto Rico. As for the books and literature, we had no intention of leaving a single one of them in Guadeloupe. Their destination was a bookstore in Puerto Rico. Besides, they were written in Spanish and as far as I knew, French, not Spanish, was the language spoken in Guadeloupe. Moreover, the majority of the books were not political in character, but rather were classical and contemporary Spanish-language literature of all sorts.

When I tried to catch my breath to move on to the next part of my speech in French, the man made a wild sweeping gesture, moved from one side of the room to the other and pointed an accusing finger at me: "*Mademoiselle, vous êtes communiste!*" he screamed, a horrified look crumpling his face. My casual reference to myself as a Communist had apparently confirmed his worst suspicions.

I knew that I was carrying on a dialogue with a raving lunatic. But despite the bizarre circumstances, in this dingy cellar on the terrain of French Imperialism, I felt called upon to defend my Party, Cuba, the Socialist Countries, the World Communist Movement and the cause of oppressed people across the globe. *"Oui, Monsieur, je suis communiste et je le considère un des plus grands honneurs humains, parce que nous luttons pour la libération totale de la race humaine."* Yes, I am a Communist and I consider it one of the greatest honors, because we are struggling for the total liberation of the human race.

In the heat of this quarrel, I had not bothered to ask the comrades standing around what kind of approach they wanted to take to the situation. With my speech I had gotten them even more deeply involved. The Frenchman's face had turned bright-red, and he furiously threatened to lock us all up for five years and throw the books into the sea. Obviously it was time to bring this dialogue to a different level. After all, they were in power on this island and if we didn't watch out, we could really find ourselves locked away in a dungeon with no one knowing our whereabouts.

I repeated my original statement: we had not come to Guadeloupe on any political mission. We simply found this to be the most convenient way of returning to our own countries. But the man wouldn't be appeased. He began to tear open some of the boxes which were piled up on the floor. When he discovered a box of *Tri-Continentals*, a revolutionary periodical published in Cuba, he asked me where all that classical Spanish literature was supposed to be. He ripped open another box, discovering this time something that sent him soaring to new heights of rage: posters depicting Jesus Christ, with haloed head, wielding a carbine on his shoulder. For him, this was the straw that broke the camel's back. He completely lost control, and literally fell on the floor waving his arms and legs, bellowing inarticulate sounds. I stared incredulously at this desperate creature and decided to wait quietly until his fit had subsided.

Uniformed men entered the room, as though they were going to arrest us. As it turned out, they wanted all the passports that they had not yet confiscated. I told them that they had no right to seize our passports—we weren't even formally charged with a crime. One of the colonialists announced that we were to appear before a judge the following morning for the reading of the charges and the trial. If we did not want to give up our passports, then detention in jail was the alternative. Imagining what the dungeons must have been like, and realizing that we would be without any kind of movement to back us, hidden away on this island in the Caribbean, we all decided that we would turn over our passports and take advantage of our freedom to make some plans for escape.

Using some of the captain's connections with sympathetic Cubans living on the island, we made contact with a Black woman, a respected lawyer and a leading member of the Communist Party of Guadeloupe.

Maître Archimede was a big woman with very dark skin, penetrating eyes, and unassailable confidence. I will never forget the first meeting we had with her. I felt as if I were in the presence of a very great woman. As for our predicament, there was never any doubt in my mind that she would rescue us. But I was so impressed by her personality, by the respect that she clearly commanded as a Communist, even from the colonialists, that for a while our problem became a secondary concern for me. If I had surrendered to my desires, I would have remained on the island to learn from this woman.

Over the next days, she worked tenaciously at negotiating with the customs officials, the police, the judges. We learned that there was indeed a law which could be legitimately invoked—insofar as colonial laws could be legitimate—to put us behind bars for a substantial period of time. The only way out was a compromise: the colonialists would let us leave the island only under the condition that the Puerto Ricans leave the literature behind. We fought this, of course, but at least we had won the first stage of our battle. Our final decision was to take our passports, leave Guadeloupe and leave the question of the books in the hands of Maître Archimede, who promised to do everything possible to retrieve them.

In an informal ceremony, we thanked Maître Archimede

for her invaluable assistance. With affection, we took leave of her, the woman who had allowed us to stay at her hotel, the Cuban captain and the ship crew. Then we headed for the other side of the island, Point-à-Pitre, where we caught a plane the next morning for Puerto Rico. From there, we North Americans took off for New York.

The Cuban trip had been a great climax in my life. Politically I felt infinitely more mature, and it seemed that the Cubans' limitless revolutionary enthusiasm had left a permanent mark on my existence. I had expected to spend a few days in New York, then go directly to my place in Cardiff-by-the-Sea, where I could quietly reflect on my Cuban experiences before I began the year teaching at UCLA.

I did not discover until I returned to the coast that an FBI agent had published an article in the campus newspaper about a Communist who had recently been hired by the Philosophy Department. William Divale revealed in his article that he had been instructed by the FBI to infiltrate the Communist Party. Undoubtedly he had also been instructed to publish the article about my membership in the Party.

Another article had appeared in the *San Francisco Examiner*, under the by-line of Ed Montgomery, one of the most reactionary reporters in the state. According to him, I was not only a member of the Communist Party, U.S.A., but (despite the contradiction) I was a Maoist as well. The article alleged that I also belonged to the Students for a Democratic Society and the Black Panther Party. Moreover, he said he had information that I was a gun runner for the Black Panther Party, and that he knew for a fact that I had been under surveillance for some time by the San Diego Police Department.

When I read this nonsense, I laughed. But at the same time, I sensed that I was in the midst of a serious situation. My suspicions were confirmed when I learned that the governing body of the university—under the leadership of Governor

Ronald Reagan—had instructed the chancellor of the Los Angeles campus to formally ask me whether I was a member of the Communist Party.

I was somewhat shocked, I admit, by this march of events. Not that I had expected the issue of my membership in the Communist Party to be totally ignored. What shocked me was the ceremonious character of the confrontation and what seemed the beginning of an inquisition à la McCarthy.

When I accepted the job at UCLA, I was unaware of the regulation in the Regents' handbook—dating back to 1949—prohibiting the hiring of Communists. This clearly unconstitutional statute was pulled out of the closet, and invoked by Ronald Reagan and company in order to prevent me from teaching at UCLA.

As this whole affair was brewing, I realized that the personal goals I had set for myself were about to collide head-on with the political requirements of my life. Originally I had not intended to begin working that year. I had not yet completed my Ph.D. dissertation and wanted to get that out of the way before I went out job-seeking. Later I had decided to accept the position at UCLA because its light teaching load would leave me the time and flexibility I needed to finish writing the thesis. I wanted desperately to get that part of my academic life behind me. But now, I had been challenged. To accept the challenge meant that I would have to abandon the idea of receiving my degree before the end of that school year.

My comrades in the Che-Lumumba Club immediately committed themselves to building a campaign within the Black community in Los Angeles around my right to teach at UCLA. White comrades were active as well. On the campus, the Black Student Union and the Black Professors' organization took up the banner. Large numbers of students and professors began to understand the need to fight the Regents' political encroachments on the autonomy of the university.

The unanimous position of the Philosophy Department was to condemn the Regents for interrogating me about my political beliefs and affiliations. None of them had been asked, as a condition of their employment, whether they were members of the Democratic, Republican, or any other party. The chairman of the Philosophy Department, Donald Kalish, had assumed a principled, unyielding position from the outset. It was largely because of his work, and the efforts of the few Black professors, that the movement to support my right to teach expanded throughout the faculty.

The stage was set for the battle. The first step was to answer the chancellor's letter asking me whether I was a member of the Communist Party. Only my lawyer—John McTernan—and a few close friends and comrades were aware of the way I was going to reply to the question. Most people assumed that I would invoke the Fifth Amendment to the Constitution, declining to answer on the grounds that I might incriminate myself. During the McCarthy era, this had been the strategy of most Communists, for at that time, if it could be established that a person was a Communist, he or she could be sentenced, under the Smith Act, to many years in prison. Gus Hall and Henry Winston, the General Secretary and the Chairman of our Party, had spent almost ten years of their lives behind walls.

Since there was going to be a fight in any event, I preferred to pick the combat area, and to determine myself the terms of the struggle. The Regents had moved in with an attack on me. Now I would assume the offensive and would move in with an attack on them.

I answered the chancellor's letter with an unequivocal affirmation of my membership in the Communist Party. I strongly protested the posing of the question in the first place, but made it clear to them that I was prepared to fight openly, as a communist.

My reply caught the Regents unawares, and some of them considered my announcement of my membership in the Communist Party a personal affront. I am sure that they had taken for granted that I would call upon the Fifth Amendment. Their strategy, in turn, would have been to publicly ransack my immediate past in order to prove that I was in fact a Communist.

They countered my move with an impetuous, angry response: they announced their intention to fire me.

The racists and anti-Communists throughout the state responded with furor. Threatening calls and letters poured into the Philosophy Department and into the offices of the Communist Party. A man broke into the Philosophy Department offices and physically attacked Don Kalish. A special telephone line had to be installed in my office, so that all my calls could be screened before they reached me. The campus police had to be placed on alert at all times. Several times they had to check out my car because of bomb threats I had received.

For security purposes, a brother was assigned by my comrades in Che-Lumumba to stay with me at all times, and I had to change many of my personal habits and remold them for the requirements of security. Things which I had taken for granted for so long were now completely out of the question. If, for instance, I got bogged down on some work I was doing, I could no longer go out alone for a walk or a drive at two o'clock in the morning. If I needed cigarettes at an hour when most people were sleeping, I would have to wake Josef and ask him to go with me.

It was difficult for me to accept the necessity of someone's being with me practically all the time, and I was constantly criticized by members of the Che-Lumumba Club for taking security so lightly. Kendra and Franklin Alexander kept reminding me that if anything ever happened to me they would be the ones to be blamed. Whenever I made light of the need for security, they reminded me of all the incidents that had already occurred. There had been the time when I was pursued by the police while driving home alone at night. They had followed me for some distance and as I slowed down to turn into my driveway, the cops aimed their spotlight into the car and kept it trained on me until I reached the door. I had assumed that this was just one more of their attempts to har-

ass me, so I ignored them. But afterward, a comrade remarked I underestimated them—they could have been setting
me up for an assassination.

It wasn't just a question of police either. The comrades
would often remind me that out of the thousands of threats
that had been made on my life, there might be one person
crazy enough to actually try to kill me. Just one person, one
crazy person.

After our first victory in court—an injunction prohibiting
the Regents from firing me for political reasons—the hate letters and threats multiplied in number and ferocity. Bomb
threats were so frequent that after a while the campus police
stopped checking under the hood of my car for explosives. Of
necessity, I had to learn the procedure myself. One afternoon,
a Black plainclothesman interrupted my class to tell me that
serious threats had been received and that the campus police
had instructed him to guard me until I was ready to go home.
That day several calls had been received at various points on
the campus warning that I would not get off the grounds alive.
Apparently the same person had made calls all over Los Angeles, to friends and acquaintances of mine and people involved in the movement. When I walked out of the classroom,
Franklin, Gregory and several other comrades from Che-
Lumumba were waiting to take me home, their long coats not
quite concealing the shotguns and rifles they had brought
along. We all remembered that barely a year ago John Huggins and Bunchy Carter, two members of the Black Panther
Party, had been shot to death on that campus—not far from
where I was holding my class.

If the need for constant security made life unwieldy for
me, it was only one facet of the larger problem of getting used
to the fact that I had been transformed into a public figure
overnight. I hated being the center of such excessive attention.
The snooping, often parasitic news reporters jarred my nerves.
And I loathed being stared at like a curiosity object. I had
never aspired to be a "public revolutionary"; my concept of

my revolutionary vocation had been vastly different. Still, I had accepted the challenge which the state initiated and if that meant I had to become a public personality, then I would have to be that personality—despite my own discomfort.

But there were the enormously moving moments which more than compensated for the unpleasant aspects of my public life. Once I was grocery shopping in the supermarket near my house. I could tell that the middle-aged Black woman behind a nearby cart thought she recognized me. When our eyes met, hers lit up. She rushed over and asked, "Are you Angela Davis?" When I smiled and said yes, tears came into her eyes. I wanted to hug her, but she was faster than I. With a firm, warm embrace, she told me in a motherly way, "Don't worry, child. We're behind you. We're not going to let them take your job. Just keep on fighting."

If this one moment had been the only fruit of the many seasons I had devoted to the movement, it would have made all the sacrifices worthwhile.

There was never a doubt in my mind that my mother and father, in their own gentle way, would stand with me. I knew they would not bend under the terrible pressures to denounce their "Communist daughter." At the same time I realized that the more strongly they defended me, the more their own safety would be placed in jeopardy; I worried a great deal about them.

As I thought of their being exposed to the most virulent Southern racism and anti-communism, my apprehension mingled with fears I had experienced during my childhood in Birmingham. I remembered how terrified I had felt when I heard the bombs explode, ripping to pieces the houses across the street. I remembered how my father's weapons had always been waiting in his top drawer in anticipation of an attack. I thought about the time when the slightest sound was enough to send my father or my brothers searching for a hidden explosive device outside. One night after the publicity broke, I spoke to my youngest brother, Reginald, who was attending college in Ohio. He, too, was very much afraid that our parents might come under attack and he wanted to go back to Birmingham to protect them.

Whenever I talked to our mother and father, they assured me that things were going well. Perhaps there had been no physical assault, but I could detect in their voices that they were being hurt in other ways. Maybe someone who was supposed to be a friend had been frightened away because he did not want to be associated with the parents of a Communist.

The psychological impact of anti-communism on ordinary people in this country runs very deep. There is something about the word "communism" that, for the unenlightened, evokes not only the enemy, but also something immoral, something dirty.

Among the many reasons for my decision to publicly talk about my membership in the Communist Party, was my belief that I could help explode some of the myths on which anti-communism thrives. If only oppressed people could see that Communists are profoundly concerned about them, they would be forced to reevaluate their irrational fear of "the Communist Conspiracy."

I soon discovered that in the ghetto, among poor and working-class Black people, anti-Communist reactions were often not deeply ingrained. To relate only one example: A brother who lived across the street from me came over one day and asked me what communism was. "There must be something good about it," he said, "because the man is always trying to convince us that it's bad."

But in Birmingham, the image most people had of me was doubtlessly abstract and irrational. Many people who had known me as a child, people who still wanted to love me, probably assumed very simply that I had been captured, led astray and brainwashed by the Communists. I could imagine them using every euphemism they could think of in order to avoid calling me such a dirty name as Communist.

While I was home during the Christmas break, my mother admitted that people who had counted themselves among her friends had broken down under the pressure. Some, she said, had abruptly stopped calling or coming around to visit. Some of my father's customers at the service station had suddenly disappeared.

Yet at the same time, she insisted, many of her friends had taken forthright positions in my defense. If someone even implied that I had been innocently lured into the Communist Party, they would firmly declare that I had made up my own mind about my political affiliations.

My mother and father had always encouraged my sister, my brothers and me to be independent. From the time we were very small, they repeatedly counseled us to forget about what other people said and to do what we felt was right. I was proud that both my parents were determined to defend my right to seek an independent, revolutionary answer to the oppression of our people.

I kept in close touch with my brother Ben, who is a football player with the Cleveland Browns. If there were any repercussions on his job because I was a Communist, I wanted to be prepared to defend him immediately. Although nothing overt happened at that time—the problems were still to come —he was very much conscious of the conspicuous silence which surrounded him. No one had even asked him whether he was with me or against me.

My sister, Fania, was living only a hundred miles away in the San Diego area at the time. She and her husband, Sam, were attending the University of California in San Diego. There was a greater than average concern about the UCLA affair there because I had attended the university for two years and was officially still a philosophy graduate student, studying for my doctorate under Professor Herbert Marcuse.

I had kept my little apartment near the university in Cardiff-by-the-Sea, thinking that it would be a perfect refuge when I wanted to get away from the hectic pace of Los Angeles. Since the rent was forty dollars a month and my place in Los Angeles was only eighty dollars, I had decided I could afford to keep the two places. Fania and Sam had stayed there before they moved into a place of their own. Afterward, they continued to use it whenever they felt like it.

After the Regents fired me, and my membership in the Communist Party was thoroughly publicized and attacked in the press throughout the state, I could not help worrying about Fania and Sam. The San Diego area was home territory for the Minutemen, Southern California's version of the Ku Klux Klan. The police were not much better. With recent memories of being followed by the police for being in the leadership of the Black Student Council at UCSD, I warned them to be on their guard.

My fears were not unfounded. One morning in the fall the telephone beside my bed rang so early that I knew something was wrong. My heart was beating fast when I said hello.

"Angela," whispered a voice which I immediately recognized as my sister's, "Sam's been shot." She sounded like she was talking in her sleep. Her words were so unreal.

"What do you mean?" I asked unbelievingly.

"The pigs shot Sam," was all she said.

She didn't say whether he was still alive, and fearing the worst, I didn't want to ask. Instead, trying to sound calm, I asked her to tell me exactly what had happened.

Two sheriff's deputies had broken into their house and fired on Sam, hitting him in the shoulder. He had grabbed the shotgun they kept in the house, fired back and run them out of the house. When she said that he was in the hospital, I felt tremendous relief; now I could ask her how he was doing.

The bullet had lodged a mere quarter of an inch from his spine. But it had already been removed, and she thought he was going to be all right. The biggest problem at that moment was that they had placed him under arrest. As soon as he was released from the hospital, they were going to put him in jail.

She said she was calling from Evelyn and Barry's—the upstairs section of the house in Cardiff where my apartment was. I told her to hold on, and that I'd drive down as soon as I could.

After I woke Josef and told him, I called Kendra and Franklin to have them alert the other comrades. Kendra said she was going with me. Franklin volunteered to go to Riverside, where I was scheduled to speak at the university that day. After apologizing for my absence and delivering a speech himself, he said he would head for San Diego.

When we arrived in Cardiff, we found Evelyn and Barry in a state of panic. Shortly after Fania called me, several sheriff's cars had pulled up in front of the house. With their weapons drawn, they had rushed in announcing that they had a warrant for the arrest of Fania Davis Jordon. They had handcuffed her and led her away to a patrol car. Some police had ransacked both my apartment and Evelyn and Barry's place upstairs. Evelyn was in a state of rage because one of the cops had aimed his rifle at her baby. Hearing the infant squirming in his bed behind a closed door, the cop had broken into the room, pointing his weapon at the bed.

Both Fania and Sam were subsequently charged with "attempted murder of a peace officer." It took two days to raise the money for their bail—and it would have taken much longer were it not for the fact that Herbert and Inge Marcuse contributed a substantial sum.

The story of their arrest was splashed across newspapers up and down the state. ANGELA DAVIS KIN ARRESTED FOR ATTEMPTED MURDER was a typical headline. In all the papers I saw, with the exception of the *People's World* and a few underground weeklies, the fact most emphasized was that Fania and Sam Jordon were the sister and brother-in-law of the "self-avowed Communist," Angela Davis.

Later Fania told us that the cops and matrons had continually called her "Angela" and had tried to rile her with their vulgar, anti-Communist remarks.

I publicly accused the San Diego Sheriff's Department of collaborating, in the basest way, with the most reactionary forces of the state. In particular, I charged them with carrying Ronald Reagan's racist, anti-Communist policies to the extremes of premeditated murder. In the scuffle in their house,

Sam would certainly have been killed if Fania had not been as bold as she was. After the cop had fired on Sam and hit him once, she grabbed his gun arm, deflecting the rest of the bullets into a nearby wall.

Fania and Sam were indicted twice by the Grand Jury. Both times, the judge assigned to the case realized how futile it was to try to prosecute them and dropped the charges. But their case dragged on for well over a year.

At the turn of the year, with one academic quarter behind me, my job was temporarily secure. The courts had declared unconstitutional the rule prohibiting the hiring of Communists. Everyone knew that although the Regents had been immobilized for the time being, they were seeking other ways of eliminating me before the beginning of the next school year. They had devised a system of provocation and espionage carried out by people posing as students in my classes; I was struggling with them daily.

As time went by, it became clear that the assault on my job was only a tiny part of a systematic plan to disarm and destroy the Black Liberation struggle and the entire radical movement. The fight for my job had to be interwoven with a larger fight for the survival of the movement.

Repression was on the rise throughout the country. The worst victims of judicial frame-ups and police violence were members of the Black Panther Party. Bobby Seale and Ericka Huggins had been indicted in New Haven. Fred Hampton and Mark Clark were murdered by Chicago policemen as they slept in their beds. And in Los Angeles, the Black Panther Party headquarters was raided by the Los Angeles Police Department and their special tactical squad, with the National Guard and the Army on alert.

I witnessed this raid firsthand and, along with my comrades, helped to organize resistance within the Black community. Our success in pulling together a grass-roots challenge to this repression put the city and state government on the defensive for a short time. It also doubtlessly increased their desire to eliminate all of us.

Early one morning—toward five A.M.—I received a telephone call about an emergency situation at the Panther headquarters on Central Avenue. The police had tried to break into
the office, but the sisters and brothers inside had held them off
and were still fighting back, guns in hand. I woke Josef and
told him to get dressed as quickly as he could—I would explain the rest in the car.

The area surrounding the office had been cordoned off;
each station of the blockade was at least three blocks away
from the shooting. Circling the area, we caught sight of a
figure spread out against a wall, being frisked by a policeman.
When I looked more closely I saw it was Franklin. Kendra
and a few other comrades were standing some twenty-five
yards down the street. We jumped out of the car to ask them
what was going on.

They said they had been trying to get as close as possible
to the scene of the battle when a policeman had come up and
aimed his shotgun at Franklin, ordering him up against the
wall. Kendra, Taboo and the others had been told that if they
didn't get out of the way their heads would be blown off. It
was Franklin who interested them. When they found a piece
of Party literature on him, they said something like "You dirty
Communist" and led him away to a patrol car.

All the while gunshots could be heard in the background.
As we walked down Central Avenue toward the police cordon,
dawn was just beginning to break. In the new day's light,
armed figures, dressed in black jumpsuits, were creeping
snakelike along the ground or hiding behind telephone poles
and cars parked along the avenue. From time to time, they
discharged their weapons.

More black-clad figures were stationed on roofs along the
entire block where the office was located. A helicopter hovered
overhead. A bomb had just been dropped on the roof of the
Panther office. Regular Los Angeles patrolmen were swarming
throughout the entire area.

None of these cops were talking to one another. Their
concentration on the attack had a hypnotic, even insane qual-

ity about it. They were like robots. The assault was too efficient to have been spontaneous. It appeared to have been
planned well in advance, perhaps even down to the position of
each cop.

The silence was almost total, broken only by the sound of
gunshots. If shots were still being fired from the office, this
was the only evidence that at least some of the Panthers were
still alive.

A few people were standing around in the area. One
woman looked extremely pained each time she heard a burst
of shots. Her daughter, I learned, was inside. From our obser-
vation point—through the binoculars we had secured—the
situation looked dismal. Between the guns and the dynamite,
the office had been practically destroyed. The woman said
nothing. No words could have expressed the terrible anguish
that stood so clearly in her eyes.

I walked over to her and, as gently as possible, told her
not to worry. I told her about the chains of telephone calls
that had been started, carrying the message to people
throughout the city to rush down to the Panther office immediately. There would soon be hundreds of people out in the
streets. Their presence alone would force the police to retreat.
Her daughter Tommie was going to be all right.

By seven A.M. people from the neighborhood and from
throughout the city had crowded into the area. But the cordon
had been extended. Only those of us who had come down
early were close enough to see what was happening. We
found ourselves inside the cordon.

Kendra and I and the other members of our club were
extremely worried about Franklin. We were torn between the
need to stand vigilance over the battle and our desire to find
out what the police had done with him. I volunteered to try to
get out of the cordon, survey the situation outside, determine
whether Franklin was around and try to return. Josef was
going with me.

We discovered an alley which we thought would take us
safely through the cordon, but just as we thought we were on

the other side, we caught sight of some policemen and had to turn around. Looking for another alley, we noticed a group of children from the neighborhood. Realizing that they probably knew the area better than anyone, we asked them whether they could get us through the blockade. They eagerly agreed and proceeded to lead us through labyrinthine walkways, backyards and alleys which could not be seen from the streets. If someone sighted the police, a sign was given, and we quickly retreated and tried another route.

Finally we made it to the other side. There were crowds of people with anger written all over their faces. As we searched the area for Franklin, we met scores of movement sisters and brothers we knew. We reached the block where Jefferson High School is located. The police motorcycle corps was parading in front of the school, trying to pull off a grand show of force. Over a hundred cops, all trying to look tough, and managing only to look racist, were speeding through the streets. They gunned the motors of their cycles, thinking the roar was the sound of their own power. At that moment, I saw in this scene historical traces of Hitler's troops trying to terrorize the Jews into submission.

One young sister, moved by righteous indignation, picked up a bottle and threw it into the procession. The motorcycle parade came to a halt. There was an extraordinary moment of tension. Many of us were certain that a full-scale confrontation was about to explode. But this peacock parade of force was only for show. The cops had not been ordered to go into combat. The procession started up again and the pigs continued to flaunt their presence through the ghetto.

Rumors were sprouting in the crowd and spreading at full speed. Peaches was dead, someone said. Bunchy and Yvonne Carter's baby was in the office, according to someone else, and had been killed by the pigs. The crowd's anger was mounting. Its size was greater than the visible police force. The students from Jefferson High School were angry. People who lived in the community were angry.

One woman who had just gotten off work was telling a

small group that she couldn't even get to her own house because the police had blocked off that area. "These pigs think
they can come into our community and take over." Some
wanted to fight. Others counseled caution for the moment,
because those inside the Panther office were still in danger.

Josef and I continued to search for Franklin. Finally, we
saw him walking in our direction on the other side of the
street. We were about to run over to him when we noticed him
subtly motioning us away. He returned shortly, telling us that
he had thought he was being followed and didn't want to
jeopardize us.

He had been working with the students at Jefferson High
School, helping them to prepare the conditions for a community rally inside the school. Totally absorbed by the immediate problems of the rally, he had almost forgotten the incident of earlier that morning. The police had locked him in the
patrol car and had parked it close to the Panther headquarters. He had literally been able to see the bullets flying. After
an hour or so, they had driven him off and had pushed him
out of the car some ten blocks away in a typical act of police
harassment.

The location of the LAPD Command Post had been discovered, so Franklin told us. Someone returned to Central
Avenue to get Kendra and the other comrades while we
headed for the house which the chief of police had taken over
as his headquarters. It was surrounded by cops, and reporters
were swarming all over the place. Some of them recognized
me and immediately wanted to know whether I had come to
act as an "intermediary" between the police and the Panthers.
I told them in so many words that I had nothing but contempt
for the LAPD. My loyalties were with the sisters and brothers
under attack.

The woman who lived across from the house which had
been commandeered by the LAPD was indignant about the
police invasion of the community. She offered us—sisters and
brothers from the Panthers, the Black Student Alliance and

Che-Lumumba—the use of her house as headquarters for the resistance. A call went through to the Panther office. The sisters and brothers inside were all still alive, although most of them had been shot up and hurt in the explosion.

They said they were prepared to leave the building, but only if community people and the press could observe them coming out. They realized that if they had not defended themselves from the beginning, they might have all been shot down in cold blood. They had tried to hold out until we could gather enough people to witness the aggression, as well as to stand watch as they lay down their weapons and left the building.

A piece of white fabric was thrown out of the window. Everyone was silent. When the sisters and brothers walked out, eleven of them altogether, they were all standing strong. They were bleeding, their clothes were torn, and they were dirty from the debris of the explosion. But they were still standing strong. I found out later that Peaches had been shot in both legs. Yet she had marched proudly out of the building.

When the last of the eleven had come out, a huge roar of applause and cheers surged up from the crowd. Slogans were triumphantly shouted: "Power to the People." "No more pigs in our community." This was indeed a victory. The police had crept into the community in the early hours of the morning and launched a murderous attack on the Panthers. Without a doubt, they had planned to kill as many as they could and capture the rest, thus destroying the Panther chapter in Los Angeles. But with the support of the people outside, the Panthers had emerged victorious.

With the sisters and brothers out of the building, the crowd grew bolder. One sister actually jumped out and hit one of the cops from behind. Before he realized what had hit him, she was back under the cover of the crowd.

The students Franklin had talked to earlier had made preparations for a rally. They had informed their administration that they were going to use the gym for a community meeting to protest the unwarranted police raid on the Panther headquarters. The word was passed in the crowd to move over to Jefferson for the rally.

Emotions were high. The speeches were passionate. All carried the theme of the need to protect and defend the Panthers and the need to protect and defend the community. Some of the students gave speeches, as did a brother from the Black Student Alliance, Franklin and myself. By the time the rally was over, the students had called for a walkout so that they could spread the news of the attack throughout the Los Angeles Black community. They committed themselves to help mobilize the community for the coming fight, and we all walked out of the hall singing, "I want to be a Mau Mau. Just like Malcolm X. I want to be a Mau Mau. Just like Martin Luther King."

In order to organize the resistance, a coalition was established between the Black Panther Party, the Black Student Alliance and our Che-Lumumba Club. On the basis of this coalition of the Black Left, we felt we could call for a broad united resistance emanating from all sectors of the Black community.

That night we sponsored a meeting, attended by delegates from Black organizations throughout the city. This body approved a call for a general strike two days later in the Black community. On that day, we would hold a massive protest rally on the steps of City Hall. We had about thirty-six hours to put the rally together. It was no time at all, but the quicker the community reacted in an organized way, the more effective our protest would be.

That very night, thousands of leaflets were printed. The next morning, teams saturated the community with literature about the attack and the need to resist. The local Black radio station and an underground FM station gave us free time to issue the strike call and to publicize the rally. Others announced the rally as a part of the news.

I personally recorded spot announcements and held press

conferences, since my name was known in the community. Yet I also felt the need to involve myself on a grass-roots level. I needed to acquire a sense of the mood of the community—and that could not be done from behind a microphone.

A team was on its way to Jordon Down Projects in Watts to distribute leaflets. I decided to go along. In all my experience of door-to-door community work, never had I seen such unanimous acceptance of our appeal. Literally no one was abrupt, no one tried to shut us out, and all agreed that we had to resist the attack on the Panthers. Many of the people recognized me, and I was surprised that they also volunteered their support for me in the fight for my job. Virtually every person with whom I spoke made a firm promise to observe the general strike and to attend the rally the next morning.

There were problems back at the Panther office. The woman who lived in the house behind the office had reported that early in the morning the police had returned and shot tear-gas cartridges into the office. The fumes were stronger now than shortly after the attack had halted. It was impossible to remain inside for any length of time without becoming sick.

It was decided, as a result, to hold a vigil in front of the office at all times. Participants in the vigil would form themselves into shifts in order to clean out all the debris. When the sun went down, there were still more than a hundred people taking part in the vigil. The tear-gas fumes had not abated and most of the group was clustered at the end of the block so no one would be overcome by the gas. The plans were to keep the vigil going throughout the night. Franklin led the group in freedom songs.

While the singers were warming up, I noticed some strange movements in the area: police cars creeping by—unmarked, but unmistakably police cars with agents peering out at us. I assumed that this was the normal surveillance. It seemed unlikely that they would try anything on a group which included not only the usual young movement people, but ministers, professors, politicians as well.

The singing broke into full blast. Perhaps the police felt affronted by the words of "Freedom Is a Constant Struggle" and "I Woke Up This Morning with My Mind Staid On Freedom" because they abruptly interrupted with a voice projected through a loudspeaker. "The Los Angeles Police Department has declared this an illegal assembly. If you do not move out, you will be subject to arrest. You have exactly three minutes to disperse."

Even if we had tried, we could not have dispersed in three minutes. We decided immediately not to disperse, but rather to form ourselves into a moving picket line. As long as we kept moving, we would not be an "assembly" and would theoretically have the right to remain. Senator Mervyn Dymally, a Black state senator, decided that he was going to speak to the policeman in charge, thinking he could calm them down.

The line stretched from the corner where the group had been singing, well past the office, which was near the next corner.

I moved toward the end nearest the Panther office. It was dark and difficult to determine exactly what was happening at the other corner. Suddenly there was a dash of the crowd. Thinking that this had been precipitated by nothing more serious than a show of force at the other end, I turned to calm everybody and tell them not to run. But at that moment, I saw a swarm of the black-suited cops who had executed the attack on the office the day before. They were already beating people further down, and some of them were about to converge on us.

I had been facing the crowd. I turned quickly, but before I could break into a run, I was knocked to the ground. I hit my head on the pavement and was momentarily stunned. During those seconds of semiconsciousness, I felt feet trampling on my head and body and it flashed through my mind that this was a terrible way to die.

A brother screamed, "Hey, that's Angela down there." Immediately, hands were pulling me up. I could see the billy clubs smashing into these brothers' heads. Someone told me later that as soon as the police realized who I was, they had come after me with their sticks.

Once on my feet, I ran as fast as I could.

This was insane. Clearly, the police had no intention of arresting us. They only wanted to beat us. Even Senator Dymally hadn't been immune. After his futile conversation with the chief of police, I learned later, he had been the first to be hit.

We raced through the neighborhood, across lawns, through alleys, wherever it seemed we could find temporary refuge. As I ran across a front yard with some sisters and brothers I didn't even know, I heard a voice coming from the dark porch, telling us to come in. We ran into the house, lay down on the floor and tried to catch our breath. It was a middle-aged Black woman who had opened her doors to us. When I tried to thank her, she said that after what had happened the day before, this was the very least she could do.

We were on a side street, off Central Avenue. I looked through the draperies in the front room and could see nothing except a police car cruising by. Then I noticed some of our people on a porch across the street and decided I would try to get over to that house.

In all the excitement, I hadn't noticed how badly I had been bruised by the fall. Blood was streaming down my leg and my knee was throbbing with pain. But there was no time to think about that now. I thanked the woman, said good-bye and ran toward the house across the street as fast as I could.

The family who lived there had allowed a comrade from our Party to organize a first-aid station in the house. People with blood all over their faces were already waiting to be tended, and a squad had gone out searching for others who were wounded. Apparently, people throughout the neighborhood had opened their doors. Their spontaneous show of solidarity had saved us from a real massacre.

I was worried about Kendra, Franklin, Tamu, Taboo and the rest of my Che-Lumumba comrades whom I had not yet seen. The Panther leaders not under arrest as a result of the original assault were also missing, as were key members of the Black Student Alliance. A brother from the BSA said he would accompany me around the neighborhood in order to determine what had happened to our friends. People were crowded in the storefronts along Central Avenue. By hiding in the shadows along the way, we were able to reach one of the storefronts without incident. The people we were worried about were among the crowds in the storefronts. One person had been arrested.

On Central Avenue, a squadron of cops in black jumpsuits was marching in formation. When they saw one of our people in the street, several of them would jump out of line, swing at the person with their billy clubs and then calmly fall back into the march. It appeared they were determined to hold us prisoner indefinitely in these houses and storefronts.

Later, we learned that the police in the black jumpsuits were members of the Los Angeles Police Department's counterinsurgency force—the Special Weapons and Tactical Squad. Subsequent research determined that the SWAT Squad was composed primarily of Vietnam veterans. For over a year, they had been in training, learning how to wage counterurban guerrilla warfare, learning how to "quell" riots, and obviously also how to provoke them. They had made their public debut with the attack on the Panther office. Their offensive against our vigil was their second official appearance.

The attack on us had begun around six o'clock in the evening. It wasn't until ten-thirty or eleven that it appeared we might be able to leave the houses and storefronts. Around that time, one of Senator Dymally's aides got word to us that the police were prepared to retreat if we all left the area immediately. Whether or not this guarantee was good was a matter for speculation.

Even in this moment of crisis, our most important concern was making the rally a success. Most of the organizers and speakers for the meeting were down on Central Avenue. There was only one logical explanation for this ruthless siege: the police were trying to sabotage our rally. We had to take the chance of trying to get people out of the area so that we could go on with preparations for the mass meeting.

The exit took place without incident. After almost everyone had left, Kendra and I, together with other comrades, headed for a house to hold an emergency Che-Lumumba meeting. Everyone was cautioned to shake off all police tails before arriving.

There we discussed a proposal we were going to present to other members of the coalition the next morning: a march, at the conclusion of the rally, to the county jail where the Panthers were being held. The march would culminate in a demonstration raising the demand for their immediate freedom.

In the middle of our discussions, the brother on security out front rushed into the room to tell us that the police were cruising by in unusual numbers. They had discovered our meeting place, and we had no idea what they would try to do. Our uncertainty, our firm belief based on previous experience that the Los Angeles Police would stop at nothing to crush their adversaries meant that we would have to prepare for the worst.

Weapons were checked out, loaded and distributed. In the formidable silence, in the tension-laden room, we waited in readiness. Fortunately, the attack did not materialize. Despite the excitement and the threat of an assault looming over us, we managed to get through our meeting early enough to catch a few hours' sleep before the rally. Everyone else was going home. But it was too dangerous to go to my house on Raymond Street. I had to resign myself to sleeping on Kendra and Franklin's floor.

I woke up the next morning with a terrible feeling of apprehension that only a few hundred people might show up. If the rally were poorly attended, then L.A. ruling circles, particularly the LAPD, might take it as a sign that the Black community was accepting the repression without resisting it. The police could therefore claim a mandate to escalate their aggression. They would attempt to totally obliterate the Black

Panther Party and would move on to other militant Black organizations. The arbitrary police violence in the ghetto would mount.

With these fears digging at my stomach, I drove down to City Hall with Kendra, Franklin and other members of the club. It was about an hour and a half before the meeting was scheduled to begin. We arrived early to see that equipment was set up and raise the question of the march with the others.

What we saw when we arrived made us all feel euphoric. At least a thousand people were already on the steps—and four-fifths of them were Black. People were still steadily streaming into the area.

By the time the first speaker took the microphone, the crowd had swelled to eight or ten thousand strong. It was a magnificent multitude, studded with signs and banners demanding an end to police repression, demanding a halt to the offensive against the Panthers, demanding immediate release of the captured Panthers.

The speeches were powerful. As we had previously agreed, the theme of the rally—the theme of all the speeches —was genocide. The aggression against the Panthers embodied the racist policy of the U.S. government toward Black People. Carried to its logical conclusion, this policy was a policy of genocide.

The Panthers had been charged with conspiracy to assault police officers. In my speech, I turned the idea of conspiracy around and charged Ed Davis, the Chief of Police, and Sam Yorty, the mayor of L.A., with conspiring with U.S. Attorney General John Mitchell and J. Edgar Hoover to decimate and destroy the Black Panther Party.

Months later, the existence of just such a plan was revealed to the public. The government had decided to wipe out the BPP throughout the entire country. J. Edgar Hoover had called the Panthers "the greatest threat to the internal security of the country," and police forces in most of the major cities had moved on local Panther chapters.

As I emphasized in my speech, our defense of the Pan-

thers had to be a defense of ourselves as well. If the government could carry out its racist aggression against them without
fearing resistance, then it would soon be directed against other
organizations and would finally engulf the entire community.

We needed more than a one-day stand. Papers circulated
in the crowd to be signed by those who wanted to play an
active role in organizing the mass movement we needed. By
the time the speeches were over, the people were in a fighting
mood. Franklin took the microphone and called for the march
and demonstration. It was instantly approved with unanimous
and roaring applause. We set out for the jail.

When we reached the County Courthouse where the jail
was located, the collective anger was so great that the people
could not be contained. Defiant throngs pressed forward
through the doors of the building. So great was their rage that
they began to destroy everything in sight. As they attacked the
coin machines in the lobby, they were probably fantasizing
about ripping down the iron bars of the jail upstairs.

There were only two ways out of the lobby—one exit on
each side. If the police decided to attack, it would be a blood-
bath, without a doubt. They only had to lock off the exits and
we would be bottled in the building, with no place to run, no
room for maneuvering.

But the crowd was ungovernable. I tried to get their attention. But my voice does not carry well without the aid of a
microphone and it was drowned out in the clamor. It was
Franklin who eventually assumed the role he always seems to
excel in: he stood at the top of the lobby steps and with his
voice blasting forth like a trumpet, he elicited complete silence
from the raging demonstrators. He explained our immediate
tactical disadvantages. The police had already sealed off one
of the entrances. They were stationed throughout the area and
could fall upon us in just a matter of minutes.

It was not enough to explain the dangers of the moment.
What had to be emphasized was that the Panther prisoners
would be freed by the actions of a *mass movement*. The militant protests of a movement of masses, the determined thrust

of thousands of people, could force our enemy to release the sisters and brothers upstairs. Rather than waste our energies giving vent to our frustrations, we should be trying to organize ourselves into a permanent movement to defend our fighters and to defend ourselves.

The people left the courthouse and the demonstration continued outside in full force and with unabated enthusiasm. Thousands marched around the jailhouse chanting slogans of resistance.

Later, the street in front of the Panther office was over-flowing with people who came down to assist in the ongoing work of this movement. In all respects, this had been an extra-ordinarily triumphant day. The rally had more than served its purpose. But in order to realize the potential of what we had just witnessed, much day-to-day organizing was needed. Sisters and brothers would have to commit themselves to work that might not be as visible or dramatic as what we had just done, but which, in the final analysis, would be infinitely more effective.

In the aftermath of the rally, its immediate effects could already be seen. For a while, at least, there was a noticeable let-up of police violence in the community. If you were stopped, you could see that the L.A. police were not as self-confident and certainly not as arrogant as they had been before. By the same token, the collective confidence, pride and courage of the community was definitely on the rise. I felt deeply gratified each time someone in the community expressed his satisfaction to me that something was finally being done about the brutality and insanity of the police.

Around the time of the attack on the Panther office, a strange series of events drove me out of my apartment on Raymond Street. The day the police besieged the Panthers, Che-Lumumba comrades and members of the BSA had come over to the apartment to discuss strategy. The meeting had hardly gotten started when the manager of the apartment house burst into my living room frantically raving about my harboring Panthers. If we didn't leave the premises immediately, he said, he would call the police. Apparently, he was afraid that the cops were going to shoot up the house just as they had shot up the office and homes of the Panthers.

At first, I argued with the man, telling him that he had allowed the police to do exactly what they wanted to do to the Black community—namely to inflict terror on everyone. But he could not be calmed down. So we finally decided that since we already had enough trouble on our hands and didn't want to land in jail because of the stupidity of a house manager, we would leave for another comrade's house.

It was only the beginning. His conduct became increasingly eccentric. Frequently, when he heard me descending the stairs (my apartment was just over his), he would come out on the porch and, as I locked my door downstairs, he silently stared at me with the most peculiar kind of hostility. He would stand there, following me with his eyes until I had driven off in my car. (This, incidentally, happened to be at a time when there was no security person living at the house. Josef had to move out and we hadn't found anyone to replace him. I was happy though at the thought of being liberated from the stringent security precautions.)

I didn't let the man's odd behavior bother me—I figured that as long as I paid the eighty dollars rent each month, he could hold nothing against me. I did think that one of two things was wrong with him: either he was a little psychotic or took drugs from time to time. The latter possibility was quite realistic, because my neighborhood was saturated with drugs.

One day, I found the man again waiting for me on the front porch. As soon as I appeared, he started to babble incoherently about my holding him prisoner in his own house. He was saying something about hearing my voice coming from upstairs, hypnotizing him and forcing him to stay in the house the whole weekend. He kept asking me what I was doing to him. And he mumbled something about communism —about Communists being able to brainwash people.

I was in a hurry that day and could not be bothered with his madness, so I told him that he was crazy or had been drinking too much or taking too much dope and went on about my business. The next morning, on my way to UCLA, I was stopped by the police, who told me they had received a complaint about me from a man in the neighborhood. According to their story, the man had told them that I was out to kill him and through hypnosis had already forced him to put a gun to his head. The cop was arrogant as he told me that unfortunately they couldn't take me in because the man had refused to sign a complaint. I told the cop that he knew as well as I did that the man was crazy and that there was no basis whatever for their leveling any charges against me. Trying to conclude this little encounter on a note of victory, the cop added that the man had officially informed the police that if anything happened to him, they should come for me. His tone implied that he almost hoped that something would happen to this man so that they could arrest me for the crime.

By now, I was used to the police stopping me on the slightest pretext—or for no reason at all—so this incident was quickly shoved to the back of my mind. But later on that week, this whole insane sequence of events came to a climax. It was on the day I finally got around to buying a decent secondhand dining room table. One of the comrades from Che-Lumumba helped me transport it from the store to the house. When we arrived, the man came out on the porch and, as he had done many times before, stared at us with antagonism written all over his face as we struggled to get the table up the stairs. The job accomplished, we came downstairs and noticed with some astonishment that the man was lying on the back seat of his car, which was parked out in front of the house. As we got into my car, he raised himself up to watch us driving off. I casually remarked to Gregory that my manager had been behaving very strangely over the last weeks.

After I dropped Gregory off and ran some errands, I returned to the house alone to do some work. It was dusk and when I drove up, I noticed a figure rising up on the back seat of the man's car. I couldn't believe that he was still there. He must have been sinking deeper and deeper into his psychosis, I thought. Yet I didn't feel that his sickness was any great menace to me. Pushing him out of my mind, I went on upstairs to get into my work.

When some time had passed and I noticed that it had gotten completely dark, I got up from my desk to close the curtains in my front room. As I closed the curtains and was looking at nothing in particular outside, my eyes fell upon the house manager's car, which was now in the middle of the street. He was at the steering wheel and was intently staring up at my apartment. Noticing that I had discovered him, he drove off. For the first time, I began to think that this man just might be crazy enough to try something. The car drove up in front of the house again. Closing the curtain and peering through a small opening so he would not see me, I stood there for some fifteen minutes until I could determine that he was systematically circling the block, stopping each time, apparently to make sure I was still upstairs.

If it had been the cops or the FBI, I would not have been so worried—for they did this all the time. Obviously my house manager was mad and it was impossible to predict his next moves. Having decided that the most reasonable thing was to go for help, I left the house, just as the man had pulled off to circle the block once again. Or at least I thought he was going to circle the block. I drove the half-block down Raymond to Jefferson and as I turned, I realized that he had been waiting for me at the corner.

He fell right in behind me, tailing me with his front fender less than a foot from my back fender. I accelerated, trying to shake him off and found myself driving fifty miles an hour down Jefferson Boulevard. But his '69 model car was in far better shape than my '59 Rambler, so he had no trouble staying right on my back fender.

On the corner of Jefferson and Western there was a newly opened supermarket where I had just recently begun to shop. The manager of the store, a Black man in his early forties, was always especially friendly to me whenever I came in—surely he would help me shake off this madman.

I made a sharp right turn into the driveway of the market's parking lot—and the man turned in right behind me. I pulled into the first parking space I saw, rushed out of the car and was about to run into the store when I noticed that the man had waited for me in the driveway. To get to the store, I had to cross in front of his car. Taking a deep breath, I decided to run for it. But the man was quick—almost quick enough to run me over. Fortunately I jumped back in time to escape, and was only brushed by the car's fender. I ran into the store.

What I hadn't wanted to admit to myself since I first sensed I was in a potentially dangerous situation, I had to admit now: He was actually trying to kill me. Although I hadn't the faintest idea what his motive might be, there was no doubt in my mind about his intentions—he had tried to run me down.

My friend the store manager was more than willing to help; he sent his security personnel out to look for the man while I called Franklin and Kendra to tell them what had happened. That evening after I had made it to their house, the first thing on the agenda was criticism and self-criticism. It had been foolish for me to move around without some kind of security. After all, I might well become a target because this man had evidently been severely influenced by all the propaganda about communism. Thinking that Communists could "brainwash" people, and confusing brainwashing with hypnosis, he had convinced himself that I was able to hypnotize him into doing things against his own will.

The collective decision was that I should not stay at my Raymond Street apartment alone again and that I should move as soon as possible. I hated to give up my eighty-dollar-a-month six-room apartment. It had really grown on me over the last seven months, and I was sure I wouldn't be able to find such a good deal again. Nonetheless, I had to agree—the house manager was a dangerous man and we knew for a fact that he had a weapon downstairs.

The pieces of this fantastic story did not completely fall together until I was in the process of moving out. In one of his moments of lucidity, the man came upstairs and wanted to talk. After making sure that he didn't have a weapon and confirming that my gun was within reach, my sister and I decided to let him in. He began by apologizing profusely about what had happened, explaining that he had heard voices that night instructing him to kill me before I killed him. Fania began to put him through the third degree: Did he realize what he was saying? Why had the voices told him to kill me? All he knew was what had happened that weekend when I kept him locked up in the house and made him do all kinds of things, including holding a gun up to his own head before a mirror. Fania asked how he knew it was I who was behind all that. The voice was coming from my apartment, he replied—and besides, he could recognize my voice. The night he tried to kill me, other voices had possessed him, convincing him that it was my life or his. When he failed to run me down, he had gone to the house of an acquaintance and had all but destroyed their garage—he had simply gone wild.

The strangest thing about his whole confession was an account he gave of what he had done that weekend when I was supposedly holding him prisoner. He had written poems about himself and me. By this time, Fania was thoroughly fascinated with his story, and persuaded, for the moment at least, that he was harmless, she asked him to go and get the poems. He returned with a huge sheaf of papers that looked like the manuscript for a book. With great curiosity, Fania and I leafed through these papers with dialogues carefully printed in pencil in a childlike writing. We both knew that the man was semiliterate and could imagine the incredible effort that must have gone into the creation of those poems. A constant theme broke through the poems: the man felt some kind of attraction toward me. But it was couched in the ambivalence that stemmed from his socially inflicted fear of communism. I was a Communist, a monster, yet at the same time educated and, in his eyes at least, somewhat physically attractive. The poems brought into play a constant conflict between those two poles.

It was clear that this man's writings were the work of someone stumbling into madness. I suggested very strongly that he see a doctor and explained to him that I was preparing to move, since it was impossible to predict when he might go into one of his trances again. He halfway agreed, but at the same time was manifestly disturbed by the fact that I would no longer be living above him.

I was angered by the fact that I had to move, but at the same time, felt sorry for this man and wondered just how much of his illness was the product of his being Black in a racist, anti-Communist world.

With these thoughts, I left the neighborhood, the man and his sickness, and moved into an apartment on 45th Street with Tamu Ushindi and her baby. Tamu had been a member of the club for some years; her husband, also a comrade, was about to go to jail for a number of months in connection with a high school demonstration in 1968. We had found a place large enough to hold the three of us; it was conveniently located some five blocks from Franklin and Kendra's, and we knew that the neighbors were friendly and would shield us in the event of a police attack.

One afternoon as I sat working in my office at UCLA, I heard a knock at the door. Without looking up, I said, "Come in." A moment later, a white man in uniform, with guns swinging from his hips and a sheaf of papers in his hand, was standing in front of my desk. The brother on security immediately stood up beside him. Startled and expecting the worst, I asked him who he was and what he wanted.

"County marshal," he said. "You have been subpoenaed to appear in court." He dropped the papers on my desk.

I picked them up and asked what it was about. His job, he said, was only to deliver the subpoena; he had no idea what was in it. The marshal turned and walked out.

The papers did not reveal anything more than the date for the court appearance, a courtroom number and a name which was entirely unfamiliar to me. Someone who called himself Hekima had subpoenaed me to appear as a witness on his behalf.

Confused and full of apprehension, I telephoned my attorney. John's advice was to wait until the court date and try to determine at that time what the story was. He said that a lawyer in his firm would accompany me.

On the date designated in the subpoena, Wendell Holmes —a young Black attorney in the firm—went with me down to the County Courthouse. Inside the courtroom, a trial was under way. A white man and a Black man were arguing. The white man was the district attorney. The Black man, articulately conducting the defense, seemed to be the defendant as well.

So this is the mysterious Hekima, I thought. When he saw me, he nodded and smiled warmly. His face was just as unfamiliar as his name and I still could not imagine why I had been called to testify on his behalf.

Wendell approached the dock and, explaining to the bailiff that I was a witness in the case, asked him to arrange a conference with the defendant during the next recess. At the break, I walked up to Hekima and extended my hand. We went through the four movements of the solidarity handshake. As I took a seat at the defense table, he told me that he was very happy that I had responded. "You want me to testify in your defense?" I asked him. He nodded his head and went on to explain why he had subpoenaed me.

Some years ago, Hekima had been convicted of murder. The charges stemmed from an incident during which a white man had been robbed by several Black men. In the course of the scuffle, the white man fell, hit his head on the cement sidewalk and died shortly thereafter. Though it was an open question whether Hekima had personally struck the man, it was clear that he had been with the group. His conviction of first-degree murder had been recently overturned by an appellate court. This time, he said, he was conducting his own defense. This time he was going to present a "political defense." He was going to try to demonstrate before the jury how racism and poverty could drive Black men and women to desperate solutions.

He did not want to justify the killing of the white man—even though it had been clearly accidental. Nor did he wish to say that it was all right to rob people. What he wanted to do was to point the finger at the real criminal: a society which keeps Black people imprisoned in such atrocious conditions of oppression that too often it is a question of stealing or going under.

Having read about my fight for my job at UCLA, he felt that I could assist him in constructing his defense. He wanted to call me to the stand as an expert on the socioeconomic function of racism. I would testify about such things as the incidence of unemployment in our communities; that most of the time at least 30 percent of the young people in black ghettos across the country are unable to find work. He wanted me to talk about the things that white people generally try to ignore—about the starvation and severe malnutrition which Black people still suffer.

"What is a Black man to do," he asked, "when he has applied for jobs day in and day out, when his unemployment insurance is running out, when he can't pay his exorbitant rent for his rundown apartment, when his wife is desperate, when his children are hungry? What is he to do?" He spoke in a voice haunted by personal tragedies.

The more Hekima talked, the more compelled I felt to do whatever I could to help him.

I would not be called to the stand that day, he said. The prosecutor had not yet rested his case. Moreover, it was going to require a struggle to convince the judge to allow him to present a defense of that kind.

As the trial unfolded over the coming days, the judge openly displayed his favoritism for the prosecutor and his disdain for Hekima. He had no intention of allowing me to testify. Eventually Hekima was denied the right to present the defense he had so carefully worked out. The judge did not want the Black Liberation Movement to be brought into his courtroom.

Since I was on Hekima's witness list, I could meet with him in the attorney's visiting room at the county jail. There we would not be separated by a glass wall and could talk directly to each other, rather than over the telephone as in the regular visiting room.

During our visits, Hekima always spoke very softly—perhaps as a result of his many years in confinement—but knowing that he had much more to say than could be said during the short time we spent together, he also spoke rapidly. He was incisive and intense. He never looked down while he spoke. His eyes were always fixed on mine.

I was fascinated by the hours I spent with him, and began to learn, for the first time, about the transformation prisoners were undergoing. A new consciousness had taken root. It was not simply the consciousness of those who were in prison for political reasons. This was a mass phenomenon. Prisoners—particularly Black prisoners—were beginning to think about how they got there—what forced them into prison. They were beginning to understand the nature of racism and class bias. They were beginning to recognize that regardless of the specific details of their individual cases, most of them were in prison because they were Black, Brown and poor.

The jailers placed a limit on my visits: after two three-hour meetings in the attorney's room, I had to see Hekima in the visiting room during regular visiting hours.

When he was convicted the second time, he did not allow himself the luxury of depression. He immediately began to work feverishly on his appeal. I agreed to become his legal runner, which meant that I would deliver legal papers to and from the jail and run errands relating to his case on the outside. With that relationship we could resume our meetings in the attorney's room, which continued throughout the next months—throughout the period of my involvement with the Soledad Brothers Defense Committee. There, under the hostile glares of jail guards, I became convinced that there were impending explosions behind the walls, and that if we did not begin to build a support movement for our sisters and brothers in prison, we were no revolutionaries at all.

Around the middle of February, I picked up the Los Angeles *Times* and noticed on the front page a large photograph of three very striking Black men. Their faces were serene and strong, but their waists were draped in chains. Chains bound their arms to their sides and chains shackled their legs. "They are still trying to impress upon us that we have not yet escaped from bondage," I thought. Angry and frustrated, I began to read the story. It was about Soledad Prison.

Soledad Prison was a household word in the Black community. During my last two years in Los Angeles, I must have heard it a million times. There was San Quentin, there was Folsom—and there was Soledad.

Soledad is the Spanish word for solitude. Solitude Prison —this name seemed to expose what the prison was trying to hide. When Josef was living in my apartment, he told me how they had kept him in solitary confinement during most of his imprisonment. He still bore the stamp of Soledad. He still preferred solitude. For hours and often days he would stay on the sunporch which was his bedroom, reading, thinking, alone. And when he talked, it was always in a soft whisper of a voice—as if not to disturb the massive silence that had so long surrounded him.

The L.A. *Times* article reported the indictment of George Jackson, John Clutchette and Fleeta Drumgo for the murder of a guard at Soledad Prison. An entire month had elapsed since the killing took place. Why had it taken so long to return the indictments? I wondered why the author had not commented on this time lag. The article reeked of deception and evasiveness. It seemed that the *Times* was trying to turn public opinion against the accused men even before the trial got started. If one accepted the article on its face, one would have come away with the assumption that the three men were guilty.

During the next days, I kept thinking of the faces of those brothers. Three beautiful virile faces pulled out of the horrible anonymity of prison life.

A few weeks later, the Che-Lumumba Club was contacted about a meeting on the Soledad situation. It was being arranged by the Los Angeles "Committee to Defend the Bill of Rights," which wanted to discuss the mounting of a mass campaign to free the three from Soledad.

I was drowning in work, but I simply couldn't stop thinking about those three haunting faces in the newspaper. I had to attend the meeting; even if I only became involved in a minimal way, at least I would be doing something.

The night of the meeting, Tamu, Patrice Neal—another club member—and I went down to the run-down old Victoria Hall. (It had been famous once for its swinging Saturday night dances. Now, in this hall, people were no longer having fun. They were talking about a very serious thing, about liberation.)

About a hundred people answered the call. Though they were predominantly Black, a sizeable number of white people had turned up as well. There were young people, older people and people who were obviously attending their first political meeting. There were those who had come because they had sons, husbands and brothers in Soledad Prison.

Seated behind the long tables stretched across the front of the hall were Fay Stender, lawyer for George Jackson, George's mother and sisters—Georgia, Penny and Frances Jackson—Inez Williams, Fleeta's mother, and Doris Maxwell, the mother of John Clutchette.

Speaking of Soledad, Fay Stender explained that from the warden down to the guards, the prison hierarchy had a long history of promoting racial enmity in the prison population. As long as the Black, Chicano and white prisoners were at each other's necks, the prison administration knew they would not have to worry about serious challenges to their authority.

As in an old Southern town, segregation in Soledad Prison was almost total. All activities were arranged so that racial mingling would not occur—or so that when it did occur, the prisoners would be in a posture of battle. With the collaboration of some of the white prisoners, Soledad had developed its own counterpart to the Ku Klux Klan—a group called the "Aryan Brotherhood." Tension in the prison was so thick that even the most innocuous meeting between the races was bound to set off an explosion.

Before January 13, 1970, exercise periods, like everything else, were segregated. On that day, with no explanation, the guards sent Black, Chicano and white prisoners to exercise together in the newly constructed yard. Not a single guard was assigned to accompany them. The explosion was inevitable. A fight erupted between a Black prisoner and a white prisoner, and within a few minutes, there was havoc.

O. G. Miller had the reputation of being a hard-line racist, and was known to be an expert marksman. He was stationed in the gun tower that day. He carefully aimed his carbine and fired several times. Three men fell: W. L. Nolen, Cleveland Edwards, Alvin Miller. They were all Black. A few days later the Monterey County Grand Jury was convened to hear the case of O. G. Miller. As could have been predicted, he was absolved of all responsibility for the deaths of the three brothers. The Grand Jury ruled that he had done nothing more serious than commit "justifiable homicide."

There was a brutal familiarity about this story. As I listened to Fay Stender's narration, the specter of Leonard Deadwilder invaded my thoughts. As he was rushing his pregnant wife to the hospital in Los Angeles, a white handkerchief attached to the antenna to indicate an emergency, the cops stopped him for speeding and without even seeking an explanation, they shot him to death. It was called justifiable homicide by the courts. I remembered Gregory Clark, the eighteen-year-old Black child who was stopped by the police because "he didn't look like he fit the Mustang he was driving." Though Gregory Clark was himself unarmed, the cop said he moved in self-defense. As the brother lay defenseless, face down on a hot ghetto sidewalk, his hands cuffed behind him, he was shot in the back of the head. Later the courts ruled that the cop had committed "justifiable homicide."

"Justifiable Homicide"—these innocuously official words conjured up the untold numbers of unavenged murders of my people.

Fay Stender's story recaptured my attention. She was talking about the Soledad prisoners' proud attempts to challenge this judicial endorsement of a clearly racist assassination. Spontaneously and with the intense desperation of men in chains, the Black prisoners had shouted unexecutable threats meant for the assassin O. G. Miller, and banged angrily at the bars of their cells. Soledad Prison pulsated with resistance. A guard inadvertently stumbled into the brothers' fierce but chaotic rebellion and was engulfed by their collective desire for revenge. No one knew who pushed the guard over the railing.

This was the beginning of the story of George Jackson, John Clutchette and Fleeta Drumgo. There was no evidence that they had killed the guard. But there was evidence that George, John and Fleeta were "militants"; they had been talking with their fellow captives about the theory and practice of liberation. The prison bureaucracy was going to hold them symbolically responsible for the spontaneous rebellion enacted by the prisoners. They were charged with the murder of the guard. The prison hierarchy wanted to throw them into San Quentin's death chamber and triumphantly parade their gassed bodies before thousands of California prisoners, as examples of what the prison and the State did to those who refused to observe the silence of acceptance.

Fay Stender's legal analysis left us to suffer in the privacy of our individual emotions. But when Georgia Jackson began to speak, her voice brought a new dimension to our meeting, her words expressed her unashamed maternal pain. Georgia Jackson, Black, woman, mother; her infinite strength under-girded her plaintive words about her son.

When she began to talk about George, a throbbing si-lence came over the hall. "They took George away from us when he was only eighteen. That was ten years ago." In a voice trembling with emotion, she went on to describe the incident which had robbed him of the little freedom he pos-sessed as a young boy struggling to become a man. He was in a car when its owner—a casual acquaintance of his—had taken seventy dollars from a service station. Mrs. Jackson in-sisted that he had been totally oblivious of his friend's designs. Nevertheless, thanks to an inept, insensitive public defender, thanks to a system which had long ago stacked the cards against young Black defendants like George, he was pro-nounced guilty of robbery. The matter of his sentencing was routinely handed over to the Youth Authority.

With angry astonishment I listened to Mrs. Jackson de-scribe the sentence her son had received: one year to life in prison. One to life. And George had already done ten times the minimum. I was paralyzed by the thought of the absolute irreversibility of his last decade. And I was afraid to let my imagination trace out the formidable reality of those ten years in prison. A determination began to swell in me to do every-thing within the limits of the possible to save George from the gas chamber.

Fleeta Drumgo was his mother's only son. She spoke about her pain quietly but intensely, and appealed to us to rescue her son from his enemies. The mother of John Clutch-ette told us how she had received a note bearing the single word "Help." This was the first sign that the three brothers were being set up by the prison bureaucracy. Alone she could do nothing to help John, Fleeta or George. Only we, the peo-ple, could hope to stop the legal lynching which was planned for them.

By the time these women had finished, the prosecution appeared to have the logic and coherence of a conspiracy against the brothers—against them, their politics, their principles, their commitment. There was only one question: What were we prepared to do to prevent the consummation of the conspiracy? We addressed ourselves to the details of building a mass movement to fight for our brothers' freedom. The chairperson asked for volunteers to participate in the various subcommittees which needed to be set up—fund-raising, publicity, research, etc.

Although I already felt totally committed to George, John and Fleeta, I knew that I had too many responsibilities to assume a major role in the defense committee. The fight for my job raged on and was sending me up and down the California coast, exposing and challenging Ronald Reagan, and seeking support for our side. I was active in the Che-Lumumba Club, working in the area of political education. And, of course, I had to prepare for the two sets of lectures I was giving at UCLA. I was already killing myself trying to fulfill all these responsibilities. How could I possibly find time to be active on a day-to-day basis in the Soledad Brothers Defense Committee?

Even though these were my thoughts as the subcommittees were being constituted, my arm shot up when they asked for volunteers for the subcommittee on campus involvement. Something more elemental than timetables and prior commitments had seized me and made me agree to coordinate the committee's efforts in the local colleges and universities.

The decision had been made. How to find time was a secondary question. I thought about my initial reluctance to take on a substantial role. How presumptuous it had been to weigh the outcome of the fight for my job against the outcome of the fight for the lives of these men. At UCLA I was fighting for my right as a Black woman, as a Communist, as a revolutionary, to hold on to my job. In Soledad Prison, George Jackson, John Clutchette, Fleeta Drumgo were fighting for their rights as Black men, as revolutionaries, to hold on to their *lives*. Same struggle. Same enemies.

The majority of the students and professors—except on

the very reactionary campuses—agreed at least in principle with my academic freedom to teach, regardless of the fact that I was a Communist. I could utilize the widespread interest in the struggle around my job and the natural curiosity of people who wanted to see "a real, live, self-avowed Communist" to get onto the campuses and to call for support of the Soledad Brothers.

At the end of the meeting at Victoria Hall, the members of the campus subcommittee got together and decided to hold the first meeting the following week. I volunteered Kendra and Franklin's place on 50th Street. In the meantime we would try to recruit sympathetic students and professors from schools in the area to attend the meeting. We would try to devise proposals for the organizing efforts we were going to carry out in the Los Angeles academic community.

I left the meeting with a new sense of direction. I thought about George, John and Fleeta. We had to find some way to let them know that they were no longer alone. That soon there would be thousands of combative voices shouting "Free the Soledad Brothers" and thousands willing to fight for them.

I was still busy working out an agenda for the meeting when Kendra ran into the bedroom, excitedly describing what was going on in the living room. "You won't believe how many people are out there. It's not even eight o'clock, and the place is already so crowded that they're sitting on the floor."

Kendra and Franklin's eighty-dollar-a-month duplex was located in an area on the East Side which had seen a lot of action during the 1965 Watts Rebellion. Their place on 50th Street wasn't too far from the apartment on 45th which Tamu and I had recently moved to. From their front porch you could see South Park, which had a long history of militant mass rallies. Since the Che-Lumumba Club hadn't yet acquired a headquarters, Kendra and Franklin's one-bedroom place had become something of a center. We held our meetings in their living room, and whenever a club member who couldn't afford to rent an apartment needed a place to stay, the living room floor was always available.

If we had wanted to hold a mass meeting, it would have been a simple matter to do a door-to-door leafleting in the surrounding community. But we had not distributed any literature about this meeting because it was only to be a gathering of the subcommittee on campus activities. Consequently it was with tremendous astonishment that I greeted the fifty-odd sisters and brothers who had assembled in the living room. The word had gotten around that a meeting about George, John and Fleeta was going to take place. So they came—unaware that it was originally planned as a special meeting to talk about building support on the campuses. In fact the majority of the people who came were not even students or professors, but rather workers or ex-prisoners or people who had experienced some personal clash with the California prison system. Some of the brothers there had even done time with George, John or Fleeta; others had known them when they were on the streets in Los Angeles. Mrs. Jackson was there with her daughter Frances. Inez Williams and Doris Maxwell were also present.

Those of us who had organized the meeting were extremely moved to see how deeply these sisters and brothers had been affected when they heard the news of the frame-up. We could feel the enthusiasm which agitated the meeting. All these people—Black, some young, some old, workers, students, ex-prisoners—all of them were ready to defend and liberate the three brothers at Soledad.

With so many people at the meeting, we couldn't confine the discussion to campus activities alone. We simply could not tell the people that they were at the wrong meeting; this enormous excitement had to be seized at that moment and channeled into active protest. People eagerly volunteered to write and mimeograph literature about the case, and others volunteered to organize community leafleting teams. We talked about a mass rally to be held in a few weeks. The picnic which had been discussed in the Victoria Hall meeting was brought up again and volunteers agreed to immediately begin work on it.

Things were in motion. People were caught up in the immense and passionate desire to get their teeth into something—something that would shake the judges from their benches; that would tear down the indifference of greedy public defenders and peel the cruelty from the eyes of prison guards. They wanted for once to fight the machine that had ground them—their fathers, their brothers, their sons—into the dirt. Many of them knew George, John or Fleeta—but their anger, like mine, was for every Black mother's son whose life had been frozen or destroyed in the Soledads of this country. They didn't need to be educated or informed—they knew. The gray walls, the sound of chains had touched not only their lives, but the lives of all Black people in the country. Somewhere, at some time, they knew or knew of someone who wore those chains. They had moved from ancient and individual despair, resignation, and savage fury to a Hydra-headed unit that said with one voice: "No more. It stops here." It was natural and right that this group become the nucleus toward which the permanent Soledad Committee gravitated. And the position I had initially accepted—coordinator of campus activities—was soon transformed into the leadership position of the entire Los Angeles committee. Though I knew that I would have to push myself to the very limits of my capabilities, it did not even enter my mind to step down. The exhilaration I felt in experiencing all this energy and enthusiasm could have persuaded me to drop everything else.

Within a few short weeks, the campaign to free the Soledad Brothers was being talked about all over the Black community, the college campuses and Left political circles throughout the city. Our "Free the Soledad Brothers" buttons were being worn by many people. A brother in the BSU at UCLA had donated some silk-screen posters of the brothers, and a printing operation had produced masses of them at no cost to the committee. Wherever movement activities were going on—meetings, rallies, conferences—and at concerts and other events in the Black community, there were always committee activists, armed with literature, posters and buttons, inviting people to attend our weekly meetings at the 50th Street house.

At the rally downtown, Penny Jackson and I spoke on behalf of the brothers and were joined by other Black community leaders: Masai, then Minister of Education of the Black Panther Party, spoke about the frame-up of the Soledad Brothers as part of the same trend of repression manifested in the police attacks on his party.

At UCLA, we moved to build a Soledad Brothers–Bobby Seale–Ericka Huggins Defense Committee, and organized a rally which attracted thousands of students. The members of the committee who worked at the L.A. County Hospital invited me to speak about the case at a meeting of hospital workers. Frances Jackson and I accepted an invitation to speak at San Diego State College. It was a good rally, but we had to make a quick exit to make sure that the prominently and abundantly posted Minutemen did not carry out the threats of violence they had made against us. After that rally, I went over to the university in La Jolla to give another speech on the Brothers, after which I helped to pull a committee together down there. Even though Fania and Sam were still very much entangled in their own case, they were eager to build the Soledad Brothers Defense Committee in La Jolla.

Our work was gaining momentum, and its impact on the community was growing stronger. The committee's numbers were increasing each week, reflecting the growth in strength of the broader defense campaign. I stepped up my own personal involvement. No requests for speaking engagements were turned down—but I made it clear that any speech I gave would be on the Soledad Brothers case, and whatever honorarium I received would be donated to the Soledad Brothers Defense Fund. Loyola College in L.A. Pasadena City College. University of San Francisco. University of the Pacific. Monterey Junior College. University of California at Santa Cruz. Palisades High School. There were also the churches and the social groups, including sororities and fraternities that were being stimulated by the growing political involvement of the sisters and brothers around them.

I had become so totally immersed in traveling and speaking engagements that when a pretrial hearing took place in Monterey County on May 8, I could not join the delegation from our committee. I had never seen the Soledad Brothers and had been looking forward to attending the hearing, if only to catch a glimpse of them. A few days earlier, I had received a message from George, saying that they were all eager to see us.

Kendra, Tamu and a few committee members made the seven-hour drive to Salinas, along with the families of the brothers. Having discovered that John Clutchette was the same John she had known in high school, Kendra was especially excited about seeing him after so many years. Reluctantly, I stayed home and worked on my course lectures.

Everyone who had attended the hearing came back to L.A. recharged by their contact with the Brothers and angered by what they had seen and heard in the courtroom.

At the conclusion of the hearing, Frances, Penny and Mrs. Jackson had been able to visit with George. He wanted me to know, they said, how grateful he and the other Brothers were —but that they had all been disappointed that I had not come.

The next hearing was a week off. I planned my schedule in order to take the day off for the trip to Salinas. In addition to the families, three of us were going up this time. Cheryl Dearmon, from UCLA, and Carl X, from the Che-Lumumba Club, were going to ride with me. Dearmon, as her friends called her, was active in the BSU at the university and had been one of the first to join the campaign around my job. Because she was tall, light-skinned and wore a full natural, she was constantly being mistaken for me—even, sometimes, by the police who were assigned to keep me under surveillance.

I had planned to take my trusty old 1959 Rambler, but no

one else shared my confidence that the car would make it along the steep winding route leading to Salinas. Overruled, I agreed to drive Kendra and Franklin's station wagon.

When we left the highway on the Salinas turnoff, we still had a few minutes to spare. As I drove through the streets of this city, my eyes instinctively searched for Black faces in the cars and among the little groups of sidewalk strollers. There was not one Black person in sight. There was a laziness about Salinas and a small-town atmosphere which reminded me of the South. The white people looked Southern. Their faces seemed to convey that familiar combination of inanity and a desperate striving to feel superior to something. I wondered whether the many Chicanos whom I saw walking the streets had heard about the Soledad Brothers case. This was where Cesar Chavez and the Farm Workers Union had been conducting an organizing campaign. Perhaps, I thought, we could solicit support from them, should the trial take place in Monterey County.

We had no trouble finding the courthouse. As in most small Southern towns, it dominated the downtown area. White and massive, its architecture in neoclassical design, the courthouse was surrounded by little parking lots filled with sheriff's patrol cars and a whole array of official vehicles with Monterey County stamped on their sides. This was the famous Monterey County—scenic, luxurious—where thousands of people converged each year to relax to the sound of their favorite jazz musicians. The Monterey Jazz Festival, Big Sur, Carmel Valley—it all sounded so soothing and idyllic. It was such a perfect cover for the Soledad persecution of prisoners, the repression of Chicano farm workers, the Aryan Brotherhood, and Judge Campbell, who had made no secret of his intention to deliver George, John and Fleeta into the hands of their executioner. Being in Salinas was like having ventured into enemy territory.

Trying to be inconspicuous as we looked for a parking space, we ran into the Jackson family as they were arriving.

After following them to the lot behind the courthouse, we all walked into the building. Like most courthouses I had seen, this one had a plastic, shiny veneer. Its sparkling marble walls and antiseptically clean floor almost seemed designed to hide the dirty racist business being conducted there. It was as if the sheer weight of the marble, the inhuman tidiness of the halls alone spelled justice. Could there be bribery behind pink-veined Vienna marble? Could the sound of footsteps on those glistening floors be that of any other than the most righteous? How could those massive doors open onto any but the most fair and compassionate litigation?

Here as elsewhere Justice was an image—heavy, slick and wholly deceptive.

The Bay Area Soledad Committee had done an excellent job of mobilizing people to attend the hearing. The line outside Judge Campbell's courtroom stretched down the other end of the corridor. While it was good to see so many people already involved in the campaign, I was distressed by the fact that so few Black people were there. (Later, I discovered that the problem was the composition of the committee—it was active and had attracted numbers of enthusiastic members, but the Black people on the committee could be counted on one hand.)

When Georgia saw all the people, she told me that it didn't make sense for us to stand in this long line; the courtroom couldn't even seat all those already waiting. I had never felt so crushed. After all the shifting of schedules to make time for the hearing; after all the feverish running around to make sure we arrived on time; after all this, I wasn't going to get in. Full of rage, I saw myself standing outside the doors while the hearing took place, waiting breathlessly for some news of the proceedings.

Georgia tried to cheer me up by saying that there was still a chance that something could be arranged. Dearmon and I took the hint, and when the bailiffs opened the doors for the families, we both slipped inconspicuously into the chambers.

Inside the crowded courtroom, the silence palpitated with

the frustration of people powerfully stimulated by the tangible presence of the enemy. The red-faced bailiffs stationed along the walls stared at us with the hostility they had learned for their role. We waited. I hoped that something would soon happen to break this incredible tension before it exploded of its own accord.

Despite, or because of, this intense waiting, the sudden appearance of a fat, hard-looking uniformed white man startled us all. As he waddled through the door behind the bench, he epitomized the fascist atmosphere of this hearing. We knew already that Judge Campbell would try to tighten the knots of the conspiracy. He would try to lock the Brothers more securely into a fate leading unwaveringly to the death chamber. The presence of this Soledad guard was supposed to instill awe and fear in us. We were supposed to feel impotent before the apparatus he represented. We were supposed to already smell the odor of cyanide.

But we did not feel afraid, we did not feel impotent. And we vigorously applauded the heroes of our struggle as they strode proudly, courageously, powerfully into the courtroom. The chains draping their bodies did not threaten us; they were there to be broken, destroyed, smashed. The sight of those shackles designed to alarm us, to make the prisoners appear "dangerous," "mad," only made us itch to tear the metal from their wrists, their ankles. I knew that my own anger was shared by all. The bile rose in my throat. But more powerful than the taste of outrage was the dominating presence of the Brothers, for the Brothers were beautiful. Chained and shackled, they were standing tall and they were beautiful.

George looked even more vibrant than I had imagined. I had thought that the scars of the last decade would be immediately apparent. But there was not a trace of resignation, not the least stamp of the bondage in which he spent all the years of his adult life. He walked tall, with more confidence than I had ever seen before. His shoulders were broad and muscular, his tremendous arms sculptures of an ancient strength, and his face revealed the depth of his understanding of our collective condition and his own refusal to be overwhelmed by this oppression. I could hardly believe the refreshing beauty of his smile.

John was the tallest of the three. Dark, with handsome, well-wrought features, there was an appealing earthiness about the way he walked into the courtroom. And Fleeta, so visibly full of hope. He greeted us with his beautiful, unrestrained smile.

It was so wrong that they should be the ones to wear these clanging chains. Whatever the time it took, whatever the energy, these chains would be broken.

The hearing itself was a series of formal denials of every motion the defense lawyers tried to argue. Predictably, it was punctuated with the little racist quips for which Judge Campbell was already notorious—such as telling the spectators to remember that they were not sitting at a barbeque table. Amid all the screaming back and forth between prosecution lawyers, defense lawyers and the bench, the Brothers were calm and self-contained. During the proceedings, George read through a huge sheaf of papers. Wearing his black-rimmed glasses and reading with intense concentration, he looked very studious, like the teacher he had become for so many brothers in prisons up and down the state.

At the end of the morning session, I approached the defense table, hoping to exchange a few words with them. The guards said nothing when George walked over to the rail to speak to me. There was no time for formal introductions, and there was none of the stiffness that usually characterizes first meetings. George spoke as if our friendship already had a long, full history behind it.

"Angela, did you get my letter?" he asked.

"The note you sent to the house last week?" I referred to a short letter on prison stationery mailed through official channels, in which he asked me to apply for regular correspondence with him.

"No, I'm talking about a long letter on yellow legal paper. You didn't get it yet?"

"No, I haven't seen it."

"Damn it. I wanted you to read it before you came in today."

Obviously, there was something quite important about the letter. I wondered what it was.

"H. probably has the letter. Do you know her?" He spoke rapidly, now that our time was running out.

I shook my head.

"She's around here somewhere. She shouldn't be too hard to find. But make sure you get the letter before you leave."

"Don't worry, George," I assured him, "if it's around, I'll find it."

There was so much more I wanted to say. But from the beginning of the conversation, the bailiffs had been screaming for the courtroom to be cleared. The Soledad guards were growing restless and seemed to be looking for a superior to order them to move in on the little crowd around the Brothers. Reluctantly, we said our good-byes.

I didn't find the letter that day, but I did manage to find out who H. was. She did have the letter, but not with her. We made arrangements for it to reach me over the next days.

The first time I saw Jonathan Jackson, he reminded me of my youngest brother, Reginald. Like Reggie, he was tall, light-skinned, with a full head of sandy-colored hair. I had been invited to speak at the annual conference of the L.A. Committee to Defend the Bill of Rights. The organizers of the conference had selected the prison struggle as its major theme and had asked the families of the three Soledad Brothers to attend. Mrs. Jackson, Penny and Jonathan, together with Inez Williams and some of John Clutchette's relatives, participated in the workshop on prisons and political prisoners.

Sometime after the May 16 hearing, Georgia and Penny Jackson asked me to attend a meeting of the Democratic Club in Pasadena, which was headed by Don Wheeldin, a Black man who had a long history of involvement in progressive causes. He wanted to raise the issue of the Soledad Brothers case before this meeting in order to appeal to the membership for financial and political support. A sister named Fannie, who was a student at UCLA and one of the leading activists in the Soledad Committee, had driven us there. Since we had to drop Georgia and Penny off when the meeting was over, they invited us to stop by the house for coffee.

It was late when we arrived, and everyone in the Jackson home had already gone to bed. The four of us were sitting around the dining-room table discussing the meeting we had just left and waiting for the coffee to brew, when Jonathan appeared in the doorway, in his bathrobe and rubbing the sleep from his eyes. With a faint smile, he mumbled, "What's all the noise about? Can't anyone get some sleep around here?" And he walked on in, took a seat at the table and joined in the conversation.

This was the first time I had exchanged more than a few words of greeting with Jonathan. George had mentioned him in the letter, praising him for his intelligence and especially for his unshakable commitment to him. He had said that Jon was somewhat withdrawn and had asked me to try to get him interested in attending the Soledad meetings at Kendra and Franklin's. I decided to talk to him about the committee right then.

Jonathan only wanted to talk about George. All of his interests, all of his activities were bound up in some way with his brother in Soledad. At sixteen, Jonathan was carrying a burden which most adults would refuse. The last time he had seen George on the "free" side of the walls, he was a seven-year-old. From that time to this, there had been the visits overseen by armed guards in Chino, Folsom, San Quentin, Soledad. And the letters. The letters in which they had developed the relationship which should have unfolded at home, in the streets, in the gym, on the baseball field. But because it had been cramped into prison visitors' cubicles, into two-page, censored letters, the whole relationship revolved around a single aim—how to get George out here, on this side of the walls.

Jonathan was extremely proud of the relationship he had with his brother, proud of its maturity and of the trust George had in him. In the course of our conversation, he brought out a thick sheaf of letters he had received from the various prisons his brother had inhabited over the last ten years. He wanted us to read George's descriptions of the brutal treatment he and the other brothers had received at the hands of the prison guards.

Without ever having been involved in mass movements, he instinctively understood the need to get large numbers of people pushing for the freedom of his brother. As he talked about his experiences at Pasadena High School, where he was finishing his third year, he bitterly complained about the apathy of most of his classmates. They didn't know what struggle was all about, he said—particularly the white students, who were in the majority at the school. He showed Fannie and me an article which he had written in the school newspaper, running down the facts of the Soledad Brothers case and criticizing the students for not being involved in issues such as this.

The article was brilliantly written. Like George, he expressed himself in powerful and compelling language. Recalling that George had said in his letter that we should try to attract Jonathan to the work of the defense committee, I told him that we were sorely in need of good writers to get the literature of the committee together. As Fannie and I were leaving, I said we were expecting to see him at the next meeting.

Jon was present at the next meeting on 50th Street and after that he rarely missed a session. He never said much during the meetings, but when it came to producing material and distributing it, he was a dedicated worker.

As the Soledad Committee gained in influence, and as its work became more complicated and demanding, I began to spend a great deal of time with the Jackson family. Frances, Penny or Georgia and I frequently had joint speaking engagements in order to publicize the activities of the committee. More often than not, Jonathan accompanied us. We grew closer, and I came to look upon him not only as a brother in struggle, but as something like a blood brother as well.

My communications with George became more regular. We too grew closer. As we agreed and disagreed with each other on political questions, a personal intimacy also began to develop between us. In his letters, which dealt for the most part with subjects such as the need to popularize communist ideas among the Black masses, the need to develop the prison movement, the role of women in the movement, etc., George also talked about himself, his past life, his own personal desires and aspirations, his fantasies about women, his feelings about me. "I've been thinking about women a lot lately," he once wrote. "Is there anything sentimental or otherwise wrong with that? That couldn't be. It's never bothered me too much before, the sex thing. I would do my exercise and the hundreds of katas, stay busy with something . . ."

I came to know George not only through the letters we exchanged, but also through the people who were close to him—through Jon and the rest of the Jackson family, through John Thorne, who, as his lawyer, saw him regularly. The closer I felt to George, the more I found myself revealing to those who knew George a side of me I usually kept hidden except from the most intimate of friends. In the letters I managed to get to him I responded not only to the political questions he posed; I also told him that my feelings for him had grown deeper than a political commitment to struggle for his freedom; I felt a personal commitment as well.

George knew about the tons of hate mail which poured into my office at UCLA demanding that I be expelled from the university. He knew about the many threats which had been made on my life and was concerned for my safety. George was aware that whenever I appeared in a public situation, sisters and brothers from the Che-Lumumba Club did security duty. Yet, he didn't think this was enough. From his own experience—behind walls—he was convinced one could never be too vigilant. Besides, the sisters and brothers from Che-Lumumba were necessarily abstract for him. He had never seen them and knew them only through my letters. He knew and trusted Jonathan much more than anyone else on this side of the walls. He wrote me that he wanted Jon to stay with me as much as possible. Jon also received a message from his brother asking him to make sure that I was secure from the racists and reactionaries who might try to make me a martyr.

When George's book *Soledad Brother* was being prepared for publication, he asked me to read over the manuscript and make suggestions for improvements. The evening I received it, I thought I would skim through a few of the letters, saving the bulk of the book for another time. But once I got started, it was impossible to put the manuscript down until I had seen every word—from the first letter to the last. I was astounded. The formidable magnetism of the letters came not only from their content, not only from the way they traced George's personal and political evolution over the last five years—but even more from the way they articulated so clearly, so vividly, the condition of our people inside prison walls and outside. And in several passages George stated so precisely, so naturally, the reasons our liberation could only be achieved through socialism.

On June 15, one of the most important of all the pretrial motions in the Soledad case was scheduled to be heard in Salinas. The lawyers were going to move for a change of venue. I drove up with Mrs. Jackson, Frances and Jonathan. Two other carloads of our committee members had also been mobilized to attend the hearing. Fannie Haughton, my sister Fania, Mitsuo Takahashi, Jamala and several others were there to represent the L.A. movement.

We had expected a fierce courtroom battle, but we had not expected the judge to be so audacious as to ban the Brothers themselves from the scene of the hearing. Apparently the Salinas officials had been frightened by the sight of large numbers of people from all parts of the state who had come to attend the hearing. The judge had issued an order prohibiting the Soledad guards from bringing the Brothers to the courthouse.

When the lawyers and the spectators learned about this ploy, pandemonium broke loose. The lawyers were screaming at the judge and the audience joined in. In the midst of all this, Fay Stender shouted that we were all there only to assure that the trial was moved to a place where the Brothers would stand a better chance of being fairly judged. By now, the judge was in a state of total confusion. He simply did not know how to cope with the supporters in the courtroom. Answering Fay, he screamed something like "All right, you can have your change of venue. Where do you want the trial to take place?"

"San Francisco," she immediately responded, thinking, as she later told us, that there was not the slightest possibility that he would accept her suggestion.

"All right," the judge said now, almost in a state of panic, "I am ordering that the trial be moved to San Francisco." With this, and without even formally adjourning court, he left the bench and headed for his chambers.

We rejoiced over our victory. We had won the change of venue, which we expected would be denied, as all the other motions had been. The victory was important: a trial in San Francisco would be far more public, it would require far less effort to fill the courtroom, and it would be far easier to mobilize demonstrators to stand vigilance each day.

For the Soledad Brothers Defense Committee, the months of June and July were filled with spirited activity. All of us worked assiduously to publicize and expand the movement for the freedom of George, John and Fleeta.

On June 19, our L.A. group sponsored a demonstration and rally outside the State Building, which houses the Department of Corrections and the Parole Board. Quite coincidentally, this happened to be the day when the Regents were meeting to deliberate on the question of my position at UCLA. This was both a boon and a disadvantage. On the one hand, it meant that we would receive far more publicity than we had hoped for, since all the reporters seeking my response to the Regents' decision would find their way to the demonstration. But on the other hand, it could prove fatal to the goal of our demonstration if it overshadowed the cause of the Soledad Brothers.

Before we went down to the State Building that morning, I decided that whatever the decision of the Regents, and regardless of the number of reporters around, I would forestall all comment on that situation until we had completed our actions around the Soledad Brothers.

At the rally, Masai Hewitt, Minister of Education of the Black Panther Party, spoke on behalf of his imprisoned comrades, Bobby and Ericka, Huey and the scores of others so that the Soledad case would be seen as one of the crests of a mounting wave of repression. Since Josef had done time in Soledad, we asked him to describe his experiences behind the walls in order to give people an understanding of the forces which had led to the frame-up of the Soledad Brothers. Jane Fonda, who had eagerly agreed to participate in the rally, was on hand to make the appeal for funds. I spoke of the work of our committee in organizing for the freedom of the Brothers. I told how we had come to the conclusion that it was not enough to fight around individual cases. We had to do that and much more. A movement was burgeoning behind the walls, and sisters and brothers needed our support and solidarity. The demands we were going to present to the Adult Authority reflected our resolve to expand our movement; they were demands on behalf of all prisoners.

With my speech, the rally was over. We fell into formation and marched across the street to the building housing the California Adult Authority—the Prison Parole Board. There were hundreds in our ranks as we poured into the building, into the elevators, and streamed several flights up the stairs until we reached the offices of the Adult Authority. For the occasion we had printed posters demanding the freedom of the Soledad Brothers, Bobby and Ericka, and all political prisoners and listing our demands to the Department of Corrections and the Adult Authority. All along our route, we had pasted the posters on the walls.

The crowd was beautiful in its varied composition: Black, Chicano, Asian and white. There were young people, many over thirty and some much older. Workers, students, and professionals were in our ranks. A fairly good representation from UCLA included the chairman of the Philosophy Department, Donald Kalish, who could always be called upon to lend his support to progressive causes. I was extremely happy to see that the two young Black women who were clerical workers in the department—Connie and Betty—had come out to participate. Some passers-by had also joined in the demonstration.

A small-scale confrontation took place between us and the Adult Authority people when we demanded a meeting with the members of the board. Surrounded by hundreds of chanting demonstrators, they were searching for some way out. They insisted that the board members were not in Los Angeles, but rather were meeting in some other part of the state. When they had learned of our intentions to stage this demonstration on the date of their monthly meeting in L.A., they had probably moved the meeting elsewhere. We were not so much interested in pushing the confrontation further. We had served notice on them of our intentions.

Not long after the demonstration had come alive, several reporters informed me that the Regents were done with their meeting and had already released their decision: I was not going to be rehired for the coming year. Now that our demonstration had been successfully concluded, we prepared to hold a press conference on the sidewalk outside the State Building. It seemed that the news media had been following a conscious policy of minimal or no coverage of the Soledad Brothers movement. I was determined that they not get away with it this time. Thus I made a point of phrasing all my responses in such a way that each sentence said something about the relationship between my firing and the repression of the Soledad Brothers and other political prisoners.

The Regents could no longer invoke the statute prohibiting the employment of Communists at the university; the court injunction against the Regents on this issue was still in effect. Moreover, they had been unable to produce any evidence that I had been delinquent in the performance of my academic duties. Not even the secret ad hoc committee of professors appointed by the Regents to investigate my classroom activity had come up with anything the Regents considered useful.

Thus the Board of Regents was left only with the notion that my political speeches outside the classroom were "unbefitting a university professor." Interestingly, this decision was announced on the very day of one of these speeches in which I had "unbefittingly" charged high government officials, including Ronald Reagan himself, with participating in and condoning a conspiracy to suppress all radical political activists, particularly those in prison.

Members of our Defense Committee were all pleased to learn that the photograph accompanying the story about my firing had been snapped while we were walking the picket line. It carried the message of our fight through the international wire services to people all over the world: I was carrying a sign reading SAVE THE SOLEDAD BROTHERS FROM LEGAL LYNCHING and Jonathan, walking close behind me, carried a sign reading END POLITICAL REPRESSION IN PRISONS.

A few days after our June 19 demonstration, a statewide meeting of the Soledad Defense Committee took place in San Jose at the home of Joan and Betsy Hammer. On the agenda was the question of strategy for the upcoming San Francisco trial. The committee in San Francisco was not nearly as strong as it should have been, especially in the Black community. It was obvious that there had to be more grass-roots work in San Francisco and Oakland in order to lay the groundwork for the large-scale participation in the events around the trial. I was asked whether I would consider spending some time in San Francisco during the summer to help with these tasks. I said I had to think it over very carefully.

Back in Los Angeles, our committee held cocktail parties to raise funds. We sponsored a showing of a film on Vietnam, *The Year of the Pig*; there was quite a successful mass rally at the Unitarian Church on Eighth Street. One of the Soledad Committee's most outstanding fund-raisers was the art auction we pulled together. A number of artists, Black and white, professional and amateur, agreed to donate their works. Two brothers who operated an art gallery in the Crenshaw area of L.A. (and who, incidentally, had attended nursery school with me in Birmingham) readily agreed to let us use their place for the showing. We planned many more such events for the remainder of the summer and the fall.

As all these activities unfolded, the academic part of my life was also demanding attention. Knowing that under ordinary circumstances—that is, if the UCLA affair had not exploded into an all-consuming aspect of my life—the dissertation would have already been done, I now wanted to get it behind me as quickly as possible. By the end of the summer, it absolutely had to be finished. This was the goal I set for myself. My work was going to be facilitated by the research grant I had received from the university for the months of July, August and September.

While there was no question of my ceasing to be active in the Soledad Committee, I did want to pare down my political involvements to a minimum. I began to make certain practical changes. In the apartment, I tried to reestablish my study, which had been taken over by the work of the committee. I moved the mimeograph machine and the other materials being used by the committee from my study into our adjacent dining room. I had thought that I would then be able to develop a work routine involving at least eight hours of study a day. But by the summer our apartment on 45th had become a real center, an office and a "crash pad." People constantly dropped by to inform themselves about the work of the committee—and this was good, because it meant that we had created a movement which was attracting many people in the community. Tamu's husband, Malcolm, had been released from prison and was now living at the house, and a friend of theirs from Canada was sleeping on the couch. Baby Kendra had reached the age where she required a great deal of attention. Whenever she was around, I simply could not resist the temptation to play with her. All this added up to the fact that the only time I could accomplish serious work on my dissertation was after everyone in the house was asleep. Sometimes I worked from one or two A.M. until six or seven. But since I never slept during the day, it became impossible for me to keep up this pace.

Feeling very frustrated about my work, I decided to look for a small, inexpensive apartment where I could hide away during the hours I wanted to work. The place I finally found was located on 35th Street, just ten blocks away from the other apartment. The rent was only seventy-five dollars, which meant I could still pay half the rent at the other place and continue to stay there when I needed to. Remembering the experience of the phone on 45th ringing at all hours of the day and night, I decided to keep this apartment free of its incursions, receiving all my calls on 45th.

Since I couldn't move in until the first of July, Georgia Jackson invited me to spend the intervening time out at their house in Pasadena so I'd have a quiet place to work. On the first, I moved my books and papers, my desk and typewriter and a bed into the new place. Over the next month, I allowed nothing to interrupt my studying, with the one exception of the Soledad Committee.

Around the middle of July, I made a short trip to the Bay Area to speak about the Soledad Brothers at a meeting of activists from various organizations in San Francisco, Berkeley and Oakland. Since the venue of the trial had been changed, the Brothers had been transferred from Soledad to San Quentin. Jonathan and his father were driving up to see George around the time of the meeting, so we all went up together.

The meeting was being held at the office of the National Lawyers Guild. Together with Fay Stender and other members of the Bay Area Soledad Committee, I spoke of the importance of broadening the movement around the Brothers, especially in the months and weeks preceding the trial. The Left throughout the Bay Area had to be mobilized, and there had to be a concentrated organizing effort focused on the Black community. A brother from the Black Panther Party assured us that they would assume a large part of the responsibility of getting masses of Black people involved in the attempt to save the Brothers' lives.

Present at the meeting were representatives of the Defense Committee, which was doing a highly successful job developing support for a group of Chicano activists on trial at that time—Los Siete de la Raza. We agreed upon a loose coalition between our groups and decided that we would launch the new era of our work to free political prisoners with a mass rally in San Francisco on August 12. Charles Garry, attorney for Los Siete, eagerly agreed to speak at the rally, and I said I would speak as well.

George's lawyer, John Thorne, had filed a motion with a San Francisco judge requesting that I be recognized as George's legal investigator—which was essentially the same thing I had done for Hekima. Since I was there, we both went to the courthouse in order to argue the motion that day. On the same floor where John was arguing the motion, the trial of Los Siete was in session. I sat in for a while, made the sign of solidarity to the brothers and talked for a few minutes with Charles Garry about the coordination of the work of the committees around the two groups of political prisoners.

While I was in the Bay Area, the Soledad Committee activists once again raised the question of my spending a little time up there to help with the organizing of the committee. Having just found the apartment where I could devote most of my days to my dissertation, I was hesitant to seriously entertain the possibility of dismantling everything again. But the Bay Area Committee was not in the best of shape and could no doubt benefit from the experiences we had accumulated in Los Angeles. I told them that I would think about it, but in the event that I could not come, I would try to persuade one of the more experienced Black members of our group to come up instead. I was thinking about my roommate Tamu.

Around the beginning of August, I had decided that it might be possible for me to spend a few weeks in the Bay Area, particularly since the library on the Berkeley campus was far more complete in works relating to the topic of my thesis than the UCLA library, and I was going to have to do the last part of my research there anyway. I thought it might be possible to spend some time in the Bay Area, dividing my days between the University and the Soledad Brothers Defense Committee. Around the beginning of August I went up to see about a place and check out the library.

AUGUST 7, 1970

Courtroom number one, presided over by Judge Harold Haley, was in session. On trial was James McClain, a prisoner from San Quentin who had been charged with assault in connection with a recent incident at the prison. Acting as his own attorney, he had already begun to present his defense. When Jonathan entered the courtroom and took a seat in the spectator section, Ruchell Magee, another San Quentin prisoner and a witness for the defense, was being examined by McClain. Jonathan sat there for a while. Then he stood up, a carbine in his hand, and directed everyone in the courtroom to freeze. McClain and Ruchell joined Jonathan, as did William Christmas, who was waiting to testify in a nearby holding cell.

Some of the sheriff's people later testified that the brothers shouted out, "Free the Soledad Brothers!" Others claimed they heard "Free Our brothers at Folsom!" and yet others,

"Free All Political Prisoners!" The prosecutor maintained that the purpose of the revolt was to have the Soledad Brothers released from prison.

The judge, a shotgun taped to his neck, the district attorney prosecuting the case and several jurors were led by the brothers into a van parked in the lot outside. A San Quentin guard fired on the van. Then a barrage of shots tore into the van and when the smoke had cleared, all except one inside had either been killed or wounded. Judge Haley was dead. D.A. Garry Thomas was wounded. A woman juror was wounded. McClain and Christmas were dead. Ruchell was wounded. And Jon . . .

When I learned about the revolt later that evening, when I saw the Marin County scene on television, I kept repeating out loud, "There must be some mistake. That can't be Jonathan, not our Jon. It can't be. He was so alive, so strong."

Jonathan had just turned seventeen. A few months earlier, George had written me:

> Jon is a young brother and he is just a little withdrawn, but he is intelligent and loyal. . . . He is at that dangerous age where confusion sets in and sends brothers either to the undertaker or to prison. He is a little better off than I was and than most brothers his age. He learns fast and can distinguish the real from the apparent, provided someone takes the time to present it. Tell the brothers never to mention his green eyes and his skin tone. He is very sensitive about it and he will either fight or withdraw. Do you understand? You know that some of us don't bother to be righteous with each other. He has had a great deal of trouble these last few years behind that issue. It isn't right. He is a loyal and beautiful black man-child. I love him.

And Jon's feelings for George had overshadowed everything else in his life. Jon was still so young, yet I don't think he had ever really been a child. He had been robbed of his childhood by a society that had kept his brother behind bars for almost as long as he could remember.

Seven is the age when most boys play with bright-red plastic water guns. But at seven, Jon knew that guns were big and gray and that when they were drawn from a prison guard's holster and the trigger was pulled they did not eject a fresh stream of water. They shot bullets that brought streams of blood and death. Death. From the age of seven on, Jonathan saw George only during prison visits. He saw his brother living with the reality of death, every day, every hour, every moment.

During the few months of our friendship, I don't think I realized how wracked he must have been by that decade of accumulated frustrations, by that terrible sense of impotence before the walls, the bars, the guns, and those tidy courtrooms presided over by fastidious white judges.

Now the enemy had closed in on Jon, who had tried to make some dent in the formidable prison system which was turning his brother—all his brothers and sisters—around and around, faster and faster in a vicious orbit of misery and brutality, frame-ups and assassinations.

In those days following the revolt in the courthouse, I tried to dispel my blind rage over Jonathan's death in order for my anger to become constructive. I knew that there was only one way to avenge Jon's death—through struggle, political struggle, through people in motion, fighting for all those behind the walls.

Not to fight in this way was to leave Jonathan forever lying on the asphalt—lying there in his own blood as though that was where he belonged. Not to fight would be to forever deny him—all the young and unborn Jonathans—the beauty of lush green mountains instead of cold gray bars, the freshness of a trip to the seaside, instead of a dismal journey into a Soledad Prison visiting room. A childhood full of smiles and nice toys and older brothers who are beautiful, strong and free . . .

The hand between the candle and the wall
Grows large on the wall. . . .

It must be that the hand
Has a will to grow larger on the wall,
To grow larger and heavier than
the wall . . .

WALLACE STEVENS

PART FIVE

Walls

*W*hen the plane landed in California after the twelve-hour extradition trip across country, there were as many armed men waiting outside as there had been on the East Coast airfield to oversee my departure. The sheriff's deputies and policemen seemed to be lost among the hundreds of men wearing the uniforms of the United States Air Force. They were stationed throughout the area and lined both sides of the route taken by the caravan as it sped through the base.

The trip lasted ten or fifteen minutes. Then the caravan turned into the Marin County Civic Center, which I recognized from newspaper photographs taken since the August 7 revolt. The car in which I was riding drove into a garage, and a steel gate immediately banged down. On the other side of the gate, a crowd had gathered, and when I got out of the car, they let out a clamorous "Free Angela Davis and all political prisoners!" Still handcuffed, I made the sign of solidarity with a double fist.

Although I hadn't recognized any of the people, their presence rejuvenated me, like the roars of support in New York on the day of my arrest. A few seconds after I had raised my fists, I was pushed into an elevator that opened into the booking area of the jail upstairs. And for the third time since I was arrested, I went through the same ritual: the forms, mug shots and fingerprints.

The difference between the Marin County Jail and the Women's House of Detention in New York was stark. Seeing the House of D. for the first time, I had been repelled by its consummate filth. The Marin County Jail, on the other hand, was strikingly, antiseptically clean. There were no mice scurrying about the shiny floors. There were no graffiti on the newly painted walls. Whereas the House of D. had been dingy, dim and dungeon-like, this jail was painfully bright. I was used to the sixty-watt bulb in my New York cell; my eyes burned from the bright fluorescent lights here.

During the booking I noticed a set system of small television screens behind the desk. The entire jail was obviously subject to the surveillance of closed-circuit TV. I wondered whether I would find a camera in my cell.

Once the booking process was over, and I had made sure they gave me receipts for everything I had brought from New York, the matron signaled for the door at the end of the corridor to be opened. A button was pressed; the metal door slid heavily into the wall. This mechanical perfection was much more frightening than the archaic fixtures of the House of D.

With an entourage of female guards, I walked down a corridor lined with iron doors, windowless except for small square peepholes. At the end of the corridor we turned right and faced two single cells separated by a tiny shower cubicle which opened directly onto the corridor. A TV camera, mounted on the ceiling, pointed in the direction of the cells.

The head matron unlocked the last of the two cells. As I walked in, my feelings were ambivalent: anger at being subjected to the will of racist jailers again; slight relief at finally being alone with time to think.

Once the gates were locked behind me and the matrons had left me alone (although they were probably watching me on TV), I examined my surroundings. Larger than my cell in the House of D., this one was about seven feet square. Extending from one wall was a metal slab with a three-inch mattress on top. On the opposite wall was a pale-gray combined toilet-and-sink fixture—the water from the basin drained down into the toilet bowl. To brush your teeth or wash your face, it was necessary to stand over the open toilet bowl. The only other furnishings in the cell were a twelve-inch shelf with two clothes hooks underneath and a small metal table attached to a round wooden stool.

I stretched out on the little mattress and tried to imagine what was happening on the other side of the walls. I hadn't had a chance to speak to either Margaret or John after the Supreme Court ruled that I was to be returned to California. I was certain that they would both come out immediately, but as yet there was no word. No word from them or from anyone else.

I was still lying there, staring at the ceiling, trying to sort out my thoughts, when a matron came to say that a lawyer was waiting to see me. Expecting to see Margaret or John, I followed the matron into the lawyers' visiting booth. On the other side of the metal screen was Terrence Kayo Hallinan, a Bay Area lawyer who had been involved in the defense committee, and Carolyn Craven, whom I had known from Los Angeles, who was at that time a reporter for the local educational television network. Carolyn had been able to get in as Kayo's legal assistant. When the jailers learned afterward that she was also a news reporter, they announced that only "attorneys of record" would be allowed in the jail. That meant that until Margaret or John arrived from New York, I would literally be held incommunicado.

With nothing to keep me occupied but the thoughts racing through my head, I wondered about my brothers in San Quentin. I knew that not far from this jail was that medieval fortress, surrounded by water, where they were holding

George captive. Did he know that I was now in California? Perhaps I would soon receive a message from him and the brothers with him in the Adjustment Center, the very worst section of the prison. Thinking about them, reflecting upon our common predicament, I was able to rise above the depressing and threatening solitude.

I did not sleep that night—and I did not even try to shut out the speculations about my future, about George's, John's, Fleeta's, Ruchell's. I knew the gas chamber was waiting for us all. Then, like an omen from hell sent to verify my wildest fears, a woman's screams shattered the silence. I could feel my heart beating like a frightened caged bird. In between her bloodcurdling screams she seemed to be pleading: "Let me out of here! Let me out of here!" Her shrieks were made more terrifying and disorienting because I was unfamiliar with my surroundings. Except for my cell, the one next door, and the visitor's booth down the hall, I had no idea of where things were. The screaming continued. The cries were so close and I felt so powerless. Darkness lay on me like a coffin lid, closing my first day at Marin County Jail.

Early the next morning Margaret and John came in to see me. Shortly afterward I was led down the maze of underground corridors through which prisoners were taken from their cells to their court appearances. My arraignment on the charges of murder, kidnapping and conspiracy was scheduled for that morning. Margaret and John requested a continuance for the arraignment, explaining that the legal team was just in the process of being formed. After the presiding judge of Marin County granted our request, he officially announced that he, as well as all the other judges in the county, had disqualified himself because his relationship to Judge Haley would probably prevent him from presiding fairly over the case. He then handed down a gag order designed to prohibit me, the lawyers, and anyone directly or tangentially connected with the case from making public statements about evidence which might come up during the course of the suit.

Everything was modern and spotless in this courtroom.

The lights, shining much brighter than daylight, accentuated the newness. In this neat, pretty room, I thought, men and women are sent to dirty cells, some to the death chamber just across the way at San Quentin. As I had learned from press accounts, the courtrooms—and the entire Marin County Civic Center—had been designed by Frank Lloyd Wright. For the courtrooms, he had used a motif of circles. In the one where my first court appearance took place, the ceiling had a large round panel with lights encircling it. The fixtures of the room were arranged to correspond with the circle above—the judge's bench, the jury box, and the tables for the prosecution and defense—all were strategically placed to form a circle.

Later I discovered that in designing the courtrooms, Wright had had something very definite in mind. He wanted to depict the nature of justice in the United States. The participants in a trial, he believed, should not be seen as struggling against one another. On the contrary, judge, jury, prosecutor and defendant are holding hands around a circle in the common pursuit of justice.

When I learned about Wright's hand-holding message, I thought about the game we used to play as children—"Ring around the rosie, Pocket full of posies . . . Ashes, Ashes . . ." —and the way the game itself picked certain children to be "out." There was absolutely nothing I had in common with the men sitting around the courtroom circle. My comrades, my friends and I—we all saw these men as the manipulators of a judicial game that was rigged against me. We therefore had to continually strengthen the people's movement that was our only hope of beating the odds. Two days later, in fact, the National United Committee to Free Angela Davis (NUCFAD), led by my sister Fania and my comrade Franklin, held a Christmas day vigil outside the Civic Center. The walls of my windowless cell were far too thick for their chants to penetrate. But I could feel them and I felt happy and strong because of them.

❊ ❊ ❊

Now that I was in Marin County, I had to prepare to face my accusers on their ground. A legal team had to be formed. John was planning to go back to the East Coast once the question of the lawyers was squared away, but Margaret was going to stay. I would have to have complete and total confidence in my lawyers; in a very literal sense, I was entrusting my life to them. Margaret and I already had established that deep trust, for we loved each other as sisters.

There were many criteria which I hoped the other members of the legal team would satisfy. Naturally I wanted lawyers who would be compatible with me and with each other. We would be spending many months working together. However, there was one criterion that outweighed all the others. I had to have lawyers who agreed that the case was a political one. They had to be sensitive to the fact that the trial would be political in every respect. Moreover, the courtroom battle would be interwoven with a battle conducted by a mass movement. The lawyers would have to understand from the outset that what happened in the courtroom would of necessity be related to and coordinated with the campaign in the streets.

Hayward Burns, the president of the National Conference of Black Lawyers, had put me in touch with Howard Moore. On the day I was extradited from New York, I had talked with Howard, who had flown in from Atlanta at my request. It was clear during our first conversation in the New York jail that in trying civil rights cases in the South, he saw his lawyer role as part of a larger effort to defend oppressed people who were fighting for their freedom. When Howard talked about the struggle, there was an intensity about him that convinced me that the most important thing in his life was the liberation of Black people. He understood immediately why I thought it was important for me to participate directly in the defense. The evidence being mounted against me was political evidence: my speeches at rallies, my leadership in the mass movement to free the Soledad Brothers, my membership in the Communist Party. My politics were at stake and it was up to me to defend them. Howard had agreed that one of the first motions we filed should call for my participation in the legal team.

Aside from Howard's strong political commitment and his expertise as a lawyer, he was also a warm human being. I liked him. The decision was made. Margaret called his office to ask whether he would be willing to take on the major responsibility of the case. He agreed at once and Franklin left for Atlanta to finalize the agreement. The first hurdle had been surmounted. I felt tremendously relieved.

Although Howard had agreed to shoulder the main burden of the trial, previous commitments in his Atlanta law practice prevented his coming to California permanently before the beginning of April. During the three intervening months, we needed lawyers to work on the pretrial motions. And for the team that would eventually try the case, we needed one or two lawyers who had been admitted to practice, on a regular basis, before the California Bar.

We asked three lawyers to join the team for purposes of filing and arguing the pretrial motions: Al Brotsky, who was a partner in Charles Garry's firm and whose office he put at the disposal of the other lawyers; Michael Tigar, whom I had known while he taught in the law school at UCLA; and Dennis Roberts, a friend and colleague of Michael's. Later, Sheldon Otis, a well-known trial lawyer from Detroit, also joined the team.

The physical arrangement of the jail seemed to be designed to utilize the minimum amount of space for everything. The little lawyers' booth in the women's section could accommodate one lawyer uncomfortably; two could squeeze in if they weren't too large, one sitting and the other standing behind the chair. My side of the metal screen was equally small—whenever I was forced to sit in the booth for any length of time, it took me some time to conquer the claustrophobia I had developed in jail.

At first I was thoroughly confused by the legal jargon with which the lawyers discussed the case. When I was sealed in the tiny booth, these mysterious terms would whirl around in my head. "One of our first motions has to be the 'Nine ninety-five,'" someone said. What did a "Nine ninety-five" have to do with my life and the attempt to rescue it from the death chamber? I hadn't the slightest idea what it meant.

The lack of space for lawyers' meetings was the cause of the first major skirmish with the jailers. The issue was as clear as the legitimacy of our complaint. If they did not furnish us with some opportunity to meet as a group, they would be denying me a basic, constitutional right—the right to counsel of my own choice. But the overseers of the jail made it clear that they did not feel compelled to respect my rights, and they were not going to yield an inch without a fierce struggle.

Jails are thoughtless places. Thoughtless in the sense that no thinking is done by their administrations; no problem-solving or rational evaluation of any situation slightly different from the norm. The void created by this absence of thought is filled by rules and the fear of establishing a precedent (meaning a rule they had not yet digested). Before we could even approach the major battle for my life—to create weapons to slay the monster, as it were, we had to spend endless energy fighting minnows. Because of the rules by which prisons survive, the only wellspring of passion left to their administrators is the proximity of pain and death. Those quickest to kill were always those most outraged by the infraction of a rule.

After they agreed to provide us with a place for a lawyers' conference, they made arrangements for a heavily "secured" meeting in what turned out to be the sheriff's staff room. It was the captain who came to fetch me, surrounded by uniformed and armed guards. Grim-faced guards were stationed along the way. It seemed to me that they had mobilized half their police force. Who could believe that they seriously regarded me as such an enormous threat? It was much more likely that they were trying to make me appear to be so dangerous that scores of guards were needed to hold me down. It was part of the conspiracy to find me guilty before I even had a chance to be tried. The closer we got to the staff room, where there were windows and doors to the outside world, the greater the number of guards and the smaller the space between them. Just before entering the meeting room, I had to walk down a narrow aisle created by two shoulder-to-shoulder rows of deputies. Did they think I was going to run for it? It was McGuire Air Force Base all over again. But then it struck me that these men were probably even more dangerous than the ones at the base in New Jersey: they were the same men who had been disarmed and held at bay by Jonathan—by a seventeen-year-old man-child. No doubt they were thinking about the August 7 revolt. No doubt their behavior was motivated by a combination of shame and embarrassment and an obsessive yearning for vengeance.

JANUARY 5, 1971

At the push of a button, the iron door closing off the women's section slid open. I was on my way to the courtroom where I would be formally charged by the state of California with murder, kidnapping and conspiracy. After the long walk through the underground prisoners' corridors, I was directed into a holding cell just outside the courtroom. A few minutes later, Captain Teague, the chief of the detail, pulled out his keys from his gun belt, opened the door with a commanding gesture and said, "Miss Davis, you may enter now."

When I walked into the courtroom, there was thunderous applause and my eyes were momentarily blinded by flash bulbs and bright lights. Looking straight into the spectator section, straining to see familiar faces, I raised my fist to acknowledge their reception.

Some days later, looking at a photograph of that moment, I was struck by the glaring incongruity of the scene. There I was, my face adorned with a glowing smile; my unencumbered arm raised high. At the table a few feet to my right, there sat Ruchell Magee, whom I had not yet seen. He was tangled up in a mess of chains, a trace of a grimace on his face, as if he were trying to find a more comfortable way of coping with the chains. Had I seen Ruchell sooner, my first gesture would have been to reach out to him, to affirm the bond between us. Then I would have turned to show my gratitude to the supporters. Ruchell and I should have been able to acknowledge, together, their presence. Only when I sat down in the seat which faced the door I had just entered, did I see the chained Black man who was my codefendant. When I did see him, I smiled as warmly as I could, trying to tell him that I loved him and that we were together. Ruchell smiled back.

The arrangement seemed all wrong. We were so far away from each other. The judge's bench was closer to me than Ruchell's chair. So was the prosecutor's. Ruchell was all the way on the other side of the courtroom. This "justice in the round" seemed intent on breaking up the natural alliance between my brother and me. I was furious and upset. It even looked as if I were there on my side of the circle with five good movement lawyers, while Ruchell sat with his court-appointed attorney, Leonard Bjorkland.

When I read the San Francisco *Chronicle* the following day, I could detect the beginnings of a campaign to publicly pit me against Ruchell. The article on the arraignment began: "Angela Davis, accused of murder and kidnapping, strode confidently into a Marin County courtroom, raised a clenched fist, and later told the judge, 'I am innocent of all charges.'" About fifteen paragraphs into the article was the sentence: "There was a gasp from courtroom spectators when Ruchell Magee, a San Quentin convict charged as a co-conspirator with Miss Davis, was brought into the circular room from an adjoining holding cell."

That was on January 6. On January 18, the same reporter wrote an article which began: "They call Ruchell Magee 'the other defendant' in the Angela Davis case . . . overshadowed by the newly acclaimed heroine of black revolutionaries." And then: "If Magee is a revolutionary it is the prison environment—not a course of intellectual endeavor—that has made him one."

That was the way the press tried to push Ruchell and me as far from each other as possible in the eyes of the public. Even in the autobiographical sketch of Ruchell, I was made the point of comparison: "Magee's prison life began when he was 16, at about the same age Miss Davis, the daughter of a middle class family, earned a scholarship to Brandeis University. . . . In the years that Miss Davis followed a college career that took her through Europe and finally to the University of California at San Diego to study for her Ph.D. under Herbert Marcuse, Magee studied law books in his cell."

It seemed that the intent of the article was to burn away all semblance of solidarity between us—to turn those who supported me against Ruchell and to turn those who supported Ruchell against me. They wanted disunity and division; for divided, we would both be most vulnerable. Unity was the only sure way to carry us both to victory.

When the superficies of our two lives were set aside, what they had in common could easily be seen. It all boiled down to the fact that we were Black and in our own ways had tried to fight the forces that were strangling our people.

I had always thought it was fortuitous that I was among those who had escaped the worst. One small twist of fate and I might have drowned in the muck of poverty and disease and illiteracy. That is why I never felt I had the right to look upon myself as being any different from my sisters and brothers who did *all* the suffering, for *all* of us. When I later learned how Ruchell had spent his thirty-two years, it became so clear that he was among them.

Born in Louisiana, he had been convicted as a boy of thirteen of the "attempted rape" of a white girl and had been locked up in Angola State Penitentiary. He grew to adulthood behind those walls, where just to live out another day was a constant fight. Eight years later, the authorities told him he could leave the prison—that is, if his mother agreed to take him to another state. They left for California. Ruchell was on the streets for just a little more than a year when the Los Angeles police picked him up for being involved in a trivial fight with another brother. With such a heavy record behind him, they did not bother to give him even the appearance of a fair trial. The system was poised against him, even to the extent that his court-appointed lawyer entered, over Ruchell's objection, a plea of "not guilty for reasons of insanity." When the trial was over, Ruchell had been sentenced to life in prison, having been convicted of kidnapping. (The allegation had simply been that he drove the brother in question a few blocks in a car.)

Ruchell was all of us, not only in the way he was made a scapegoat of racism, but also in his resiliency, in his refusal to concede defeat. The schools in Louisiana had not taught him to read and write. Behind walls in California, by using the Constitution of the United States as his reader he conquered his illiteracy. He read law books and became sufficiently conversant with the law to write briefs on his own case, which he filed with the appropriate courts. With nothing to fall back on but his own sheer determination, he became such an efficient lawyer that an appellate court reversed his conviction on the basis of an argument he had made.

But the second time around, his trial also led to a conviction, for they refused to recognize his right to defend himself. Again, he was sold out by a court-appointed lawyer. But even in face of this second conviction, Ruchell did not give up. He continued to file briefs with the courts—and not only for himself, but for other brothers as well. At the same time, he wrote to everyone on the outside whom he felt could assist him in exposing the injustice done to him.

Ironically, I did not realize that I, too, had received one of those letters from Ruchell until it was presented in court, having been taken from my apartment by the FBI. It was one of the hundreds of letters I received each week during the affair at UCLA. Because I had no one to help me with my mail, it had remained buried under all the other unanswered letters. If I had only known then.

The Women's Section of the Marin County Jail was obviously designed under the assumption that few female arrests would be made in this county, which ranks among the wealthiest in the country. The very small percentage of Black, Chicano and poor people bore a direct relationship to what the authorities felt their female jail needs would be. Counting the sick bay, the isolation cells and the juvenile tank, there were a mere seventeen beds on the women's side.

One would have thought that this small-scale jail would produce matrons with less impersonal, less brutal responses. And, in fact, my first impression of the female jailers was that they were amateurs groping around for the role they felt matrons should play. But precisely because they were straining to be good jailers, they frequently chose to assume the most extreme posture they could manage.

Shortly after I arrived, I had a run-in with one of the matrons, the first of an unending series of such conflicts. It happened on a Sunday in January. I had spent part of the morning reading the least boring sections of the San Francisco *Examiner*. During the late morning, I was called out for a visit, but I had hardly gotten past the formalities of the introduction when a raving matron broke into the visiting cubicle.

"Where's the razor blade? Just give it up! If you don't hand over the razor blade, you'll see what we can do . . ."

I didn't know what she was talking about. The last time I had even seen a razor blade was before my arrest. I didn't respond.

She continued her cryptic demands. "Unless you produce the razor blade immediately, you won't be able to finish this visit."

I stared her straight in the eye for a few seconds and finally asked her what she was talking about.

"What happened to the razor blade in your newspaper?" she asked frantically.

"What razor blade? What newspaper?" I asked.

I finally gathered from her sometimes incoherent remarks that the Sunday paper had carried an advertisement for some brand of razor blades and that a sample had been included.

"I don't read the advertisements," I said. "If there was a razor blade in the paper, it must still be there."

I told her that if she'd stop being so hysterical, she could have the ridiculous razor blade. And I walked down the corridor to my cell. The bulky paper was stacked up on the bed. Not about to help her with her searching business, I told her to get the razor blade herself. Still frantic, she tore through the paper until she found the advertisement. When she pulled it out and, with a vicious scowl on her face, showed me that the razor blade was missing, I was certain that I was being set up by someone.

"Obviously," I said, "someone has removed the razor blade. But that's your problem, not mine. I haven't the slightest idea what happened to it . . ."

As I expected, she spat loud, bold threats at me. "You won't have another visit until you give up the razor blade. We're going to cut out your commissary privileges. And if you think that you're going to call or see your lawyers before you produce the razor blade, you're wrong. You're wrong."

I tried to keep myself from blowing up. I had to show them that they weren't going to provoke me with such pettiness. "I have said all I'm going to say," I answered. "It's clear that I couldn't have a rational discussion with you, even if I wanted to. One thing, though. I do know something about my rights. I know full well that you cannot prevent me from seeing my attorney. Just try—and you'll have a real fight on your hands."

I turned around abruptly and sat on my bed. "You may leave now," I said. Still flustered, she whirled around and rushed out, almost forgetting to lock the gate behind her.

Alone in my cell, I thought about the dilemma. If they dared, they could hold me incommunicado indefinitely. But I kept reassuring myself that if they really tried to prevent my lawyers from seeing me, the lawyers would find some way to get in.

Late that afternoon, shortly before the matron's shift was up, she came back to my cell looking embarrassed. "I guess I have to apologize to you, Miss Davis," she said hesitatingly. "A deputy at the booking desk took the razor blades out of all the papers before they were sent in."

"They aren't going to get off so easily," I thought to myself.

The next day I went into the matron's office to put through the daily telephone call which all prisoners were allowed to make. In a loud and disdainful voice, I related to Brotsky every detail of the razor-blade incident. I wanted the matrons to know that whenever they challenged me, I was ready for a fight.

The lawyers' protests, addressed to various levels of the jail hierarchy, put them on the defensive. The National United Committee to Free Angela Davis joined in. I could see that they were beginning to fear the rapidly developing mass movement. They knew that any unjustified attack on me could be exposed.

Very early in my stay at the Marin County Jail, I was introduced to the jailers' racist bias. The same matron involved in the razor-blade incident unlocked my cell one day and brusquely told me to come with her. Dressed in full uniform and carrying a shoulder bag, she was apparently about to leave the jail.

"I'm not going anywhere until I find out what's going on," I said.

"Just come on," she said.

When I refused, she conceded that there was an emergency in the building. Still not satisfied, I demanded that she explain further and finally got her to admit that a bomb threat had been called in, and the entire complex was being evacuated. The women prisoners would be taken to a bomb shelter downstairs.

I was accustomed to being handcuffed with my arms behind me—it had become a part of the routine. When the three other women prisoners were brought out into the corridor (and this was for months the only direct contact I had with other prisoners), the manner in which we were handcuffed revealed the blatant racism of the matrons. There was a Black woman and a Chicana woman. They were cuffed to each other, the right arm of one locked to the left arm of the other. The one remaining prisoner was a white woman. The matrons had done nothing to restrain her movements. So there we were, me with both arms manacled behind me, the Black woman chained to the Chicana woman, and the white woman with both hands free.

The Marin County jailers were determined to hold me in solitary confinement, so we began to press for relief from the court. The pretense was the same as in New York. That is to say, it wasn't that I was so dangerous. On the contrary, it was my life they were trying to safeguard. They were afraid, they said, that some fanatic anti-Communist or someone who was excessively affected by the death of Judge Haley might try to do me some harm. And how easy it was to get arrested in Marin County, they said. Someone might actually commit a petty crime to get into the jail—and get me. The jailers had to consider these things, they said.

The judge refused therefore to issue an order permitting me to go into the main population—he wanted a detailed, documented motion from us, specifying precisely the conditions of my incarceration and setting forth in legal terms the reasons we felt I should not be kept in solitary. This was a typical way of reversing the process of justice. Whenever my rights were violated—it was up to us to show why they should not be violated.

Doubtlessly the judge knew what he was doing because he ultimately went along with a compromise solution. He did not allow me to "mingle" with the other women; instead he ordered the jailers to provide permanent facilities for meetings with the team of lawyers, a request we had made in the same motion.

These permanent meeting facilities were established "within the security area," i.e., behind a series of electrically operated, heavy iron doors, and within the range of the closed circuit TV monitor system. Inside one of those rooms, behind the iron door with the little peephole window, was what they called the juvenile cell. It was adjacent to the matron's office. All they had to do was pull down a metal flap on their side and they could spy on me through a porthole-type window. This cell was slightly larger than mine. The walls were painted the same drab gray, the concrete floors the same institutional rust-color. It contained bunk beds—i.e., metal slabs extending from the wall, with a thin mattress like the one I slept on every night. There were a few other superficial differences between it and my cell—the toilet bowl was not attached to the sink, and there was a shower inside. But the only difference that mattered to me was the skylight above. By this time I was so starved for a bit of natural light that I rejoiced when I discovered that on occasion I would be able to tell whether it was light or dark outside. The skylight was translucent, rather than transparent, so I could not really see the sky, but I could hear airplanes passing above and on rainy days the monotony of my surroundings would be broken by the sound of raindrops. In my nighttime dream fantasies, I climbed through this skylight to freedom.

At first, when the attorneys came, I was escorted to and from my cell to the meeting room. Later, though, we managed to convince the judge that if he did not intend to relax the solitary conditions any time soon, I should have access to this conference room even when the lawyers were not present. Emphasizing for his benefit the fact that I had already announced my intention to file a motion to act as one of the counsels in my case, we made the point that it was the responsibility of the jail to furnish adequate access to legal materials as well as facilities where they could be studied. He agreed, then, that I could use the conference room—the juvenile cell—as a work area between the hours of eight in the morning and ten in the evening.

We had won a minor skirmish, which was the signal for the jailers to retaliate. Since they knew that they couldn't violate the judge's order to allow me access to the working quarters, they contrived as many annoying trivial rules as their little minds could discover. First, they declared that it was against the rules for me to take my meals in the work cell. The two-second trip around the corner and a few yards down the corridor could only take place after they had brought breakfast to my sleeping quarters. Come lunchtime, they opened the door of the work cell and directed me back to my sleeping cell. After lunch—the trip back; dinner, the same. The only time this routine could be broken was if one of the lawyers happened to be visiting me in the work area—then I could take my meals there.

The fact that this cell was to be the area where I worked on my case, they pushed to absurdity: because I was supposed to be working there, I could not also eat there; I could not do my daily exercises there. But they could do nothing to prevent me from doing calisthenics, katas, or headstands when I felt like it in the work cell. Often I exercised precisely at the moment when I knew they were peeping in on me.

The work I managed to do in jail required far more than normal powers of concentration. In that state of almost continuous solitude, getting totally involved in my work was a fundamental condition of survival and sanity. The jailers knew this and were willing to resort to the paltriest acts, hoping to obstruct me in some small way. The head matron was especially good at this.

I can't say I was able to dismiss everything they did. There were things which I found merely exasperating, and there were other things which really angered and frustrated me. Often lunch or dinner time would find me deeply immersed in work—reading or writing a statement, letter or something I simply wanted to write for my own benefit. A matron would open the door for me to return to the sleeping/eating cell to take my meal. During my unsavory, solitary meal—it hardly ever took me more than ten minutes either to consume it or to decide that I wasn't going to eat it—I continued to think about the work I had been doing. Naturally, as soon as I was done with the food, I was eager to return to my work. A half-hour would pass without my cell gate having been opened. Forty-five minutes, an hour. At these times I simply could not contain my frustration and would scream as loud as I could for them to come and unlock the gate. Inevitably the more I screamed, the longer they would wait before they came with the key. Sometimes they tried to justify the delay by saying, for example, that a prisoner was being booked and fingerprinted in the corridor—no prisoner, at that point, was allowed to lay eyes on me. Other times, they snidely said that they were sorry that they could not eat as fast as I—and they weren't going to let me disturb their leisurely meal. This situation became so unbearable that rather than put up with it I decided to skip meals when my work might be disrupted.

For months, this work cell was the center of a constantly raging battle between the head matron and me. She noticed, for instance, through her spy window that I would sometimes lie down on the bottom bunk in the work cell and read in that position. Within a short time, the mattresses were removed from the cell. Afterward, to show her that she had not disturbed my routine, I would lie down on the metal slab—the thin mattresses hadn't made the bed much more comfortable anyway. This matron and the others were particularly incensed when we got the news that David Poindexter had been acquitted on the federal charges of harboring a fugitive. (They could not prove that David knew that the FBI, as well as the California Police, was looking for me.)

I wondered, at times, just how much I was allowing myself to be diverted by these inane episodes. Realizing how easy it is to lose perspective when you are imprisoned—particularly if you cannot communicate with others who share your condition—I wondered whether I was reacting to trivial incidents as if they were a matter of survival. I feared becoming obsessively wound up in these small things, because if I did, this in itself could be a way for the jailers to control my mind. There was a pill-taking ritual, for example, which seemed to hold a special importance for one particular matron. Her obnoxious personality was surpassed only by her stupidity. She actually believed that if she gave me an aspirin for a headache or for cramps that I was going to follow her instructions and lift my tongue up so she could see whether I had swallowed it or whether I was hiding it until she left the cell. It was this same matron, in fact, who once tried to prohibit Margaret from bringing books in to me. One Saturday morning Margaret had brought me some hardcover books and one paperback anthology on fascism. This matron believed all paperback books were novels. She allowed Margaret to bring in the hardbacks, but not the "storybook," as she called the book on fascism. According to this dull-witted woman, I was not allowed to have "storybooks," that is, fiction, in my work cell—and *The Nature of Fascism* was such a book.

The Marin County Jail doctor misdiagnosed a rash I had contracted, and while he was treating me with antihistamines for what he said was an allergy, the rash spread over my entire body. This gave us the leverage we needed to demand that a doctor from the outside be able to visit me. Bert Small, a young Black movement doctor who ran the Panthers' Free Health Center, immediately recognized my rash as a jail fungus that had progressed so far it was going to be difficult to cure. Bert began to come in at least once a week to examine me. During his visits a matron always stood outside the cell, peering at us through the bars. Once we discovered that a second matron was hiding with a note pad in the shower adjacent to the cell and was obviously taking down everything we said.

After a few weeks, Bert was told not to hug me (he always greeted me with a big hug). Soon afterward, they told him that all nonmedical conversation was forbidden. Since the matrons were not very smart, we developed without too much trouble a code language in which we could discuss just about anything without their understanding.

Of all the matrons, there was only one who went out of her way to be kind. Timid and soft-spoken, she was young and obviously inexperienced in police work. I imagine she was one of the women they hired when they used my presence in the jail as an excuse to increase the number of female deputies. One night when this deputy was on duty alone, a sister in the main tank screamed out, just before lights went out, "Good night, Angela." As loudly as I could, I screamed back, "Good night." (The main tank was two hundred feet down the corridor, around the corner and at the end of the next corridor.)

For several months this deputy continued to be silent while I carried on conversations and developed friendships with women prisoners whom I had never seen and whom I could never hope to see. On the day Ericka Huggins and Bobby Seale were acquitted of murder charges in New Haven, we held a regular celebration. Once this matron handed me two bars of candy which the sisters in the main tank had sent as presents. When I opened them, I discovered long letters—kites—concealed under the wrappers.

Thursdays and Sundays were women's visiting days in Marin County Jail. During the first six months, I received my visits only after all the other women had finished, since no contact between us was allowed. As long as the person had identification, anyone could come in to see me. NUCFAD arranged visits, more often than not, with people I had not yet met. Often the visits were strained, introductions rendered difficult by the glass and telephones separating me from the visitor. And usually by the time we got settled into a conversation, it was time for the visit to end.

After voluminous, well-documented motions were filed, the judge finally issued an order that legal investigators of our designation be admitted into the jail during certain hours of the day. I could visit them in the regular lawyers' booth when they came alone; when an attorney of record was present, they were let into the work cell. Legal investigators, at various times during the year, were Franklin and Kendra, Fania, Charlene, Cassandra Davis, and Bettina Aptheker.

I had first met Bettina in New York when we were both high school age. She was among the friends introduced to me by Claudia and Margaret Burnham. At that time, Bettina was in the leadership of Advance, the youth organization I joined, which had fraternal ties with the Communist Party. What subsequently remained most vividly in my mind about Bettina was the way she had described a trip she made to the Soviet Union. I had been enormously impressed by the egalitarianism she said she witnessed. She had visited the apartment of a worker and the apartment of a doctor; the doctor's she said, was no more luxurious than the worker's. Bettina's father, Herbert Aptheker, was the director of the Institute for Marxist Studies, and I felt excited and enlightened by the lectures I heard him deliver.

In 1964, some years later, Bettina emerged as one of the key leaders of the Berkeley Free Speech Movement, which prepared the way for the campus rebellion of the sixties. When she visited me in Los Angeles at the time of the struggle around my job, it had been about ten years since I had seen her. Writing for the *World Magazine* (the magazine section of our Party's daily newspaper), she interviewed me about the fight to keep my position at UCLA. When we saw each other after that, it was always only for a short time and in the midst of some political urgency. I had felt frustrated that we weren't able to find the time to sit down and talk in relaxed surroundings.

At the time I was extradited to California, she was living in San Jose with her husband, Jack Kurzweil, who was a professor at California State University in San Jose. Their child

Joshua was around four years old. Bettina was just finishing the manuscript of her book *The Academic Rebellion: A Marxist Critique*. She had decided to devote a large part of her time to working on the National United Committee. I was happy to learn that she could also spare the time to act as one of the legal investigators on the case, for this meant that she could visit me for longer periods and outside the regular visiting hours.

During one of her earliest visits, Bettina mentioned that the Defense Committee in England wanted to publish a book of writings by and about me and the movement for my freedom. They asked us to put together a packet of materials out of which they could select the literature for the book.

After some discussion, Bettina and I decided that a more accurate and complete representation of the movement could be included in the book if it were compiled by the Committee here. Moreover, if it were done here, it could also be used as an organizing tool for the campaign in this country. Immediately after this discussion, Bettina and I began to work on the project ourselves.

From the inception of the idea, we saw the book as an instrument through which people could deepen their knowledge of repression, through which people could become acquainted with cases of political prisoners, and could learn what was really happening behind the walls in general. I insisted that the content of the book should not only revolve around my case, but had to relate to other political prisoners as well—George, John, Fleeta, Ruchell and the many incarcerated sisters and brothers throughout the country. One of the central theses of the book would be the need to reevaluate the traditional definition of "political prisoner," as a result of the intensification of racism. Aside from the scores of men and women in prison because of their political beliefs and activities, there were many thousands more who had been framed or had received disproportionately long sentences for the sole reason that they were Black or Brown. The book had to provide a voice not only for the political prisoners in the strict sense of the term, but also for those who were victimized in one way or another by the racism of the police-court-prison apparatus.

Bettina and I both wrote articles concerning prisons and political prisoners. During long meetings in jail, rendered difficult by the glass and telephones or the mesh of metal between us, we made our decisions about the other materials to be included. The jailers would not allow the investigators to bring anything into the jail except a pad of blank paper and a pencil. Therefore all the materials had to be given to me by one of the attorneys. And the things Bettina wanted to discuss, she had to try to memorize before she came.

Finally, after several months of intensive work, the book was practically done. George, Jon, Fleeta and Ruchell, as well as Bobby and Ericka had contributed writings. Howard and Margaret had written about essential legal aspects of the case, and Fania, Franklin and Kendra had written about the mass movement. Out of the innumerable appeals which had been made on my behalf, we selected a representative number both from the United States and abroad. To begin the book, we used James Baldwin's moving letter to me. "Some of us, white and black," he wrote, "know how great a price has already been paid to bring into existence a new consciousness, a new people, an unprecedented nation. If we know, and do nothing, we are worse than the murderers hired in our name. If we know, then we must fight for your life as though it were our own—which it is—and render impassable with our bodies the corridor to the gas chamber. For, if they take you in the morning, they will be coming for us that night." It struck us that the title of the anthology should be *If They Come in the Morning*.

Originally, it had been our intention to have the book published by a movement company. After all, we did not see it as destined for mass commercial distribution—it was to be an organizing weapon. But it had to come out immediately, if it was to have any impact on the campaign for my freedom and the freedom of other political prisoners. At that time, no movement publishing operation had the resources to bring it out so quickly. As a result, we gave the book to a Black company, The Third Press. Unfortunately we did not realize that the overriding interest of this company was to push the book commercially—even at the expense of misrepresenting it as a book authored (rather than edited) by me.

But despite the problems, the publication of the book was an important event for all of us behind walls. One of the most moving things Ruchell said to me was that *If They Come in the Morning*, which contained a large section on his life and his case, had done more to expose the state's persecution of him than anything else.

At the same time arrangements had been made for legal investigators to visit me, the judge had ordered the jailers to allow potential defense witnesses to come back to the work cell in the presence of an attorney of record. My parents and Benny and Reggie were able to see me in this way.

When my mother and father came out on March 16 for the opening of the pretrial motions and the big rally outside the Civic Center, we had spoken to each other in the booth, through glass, on telephones. It was good, finally, to be able to embrace them. Herbert Marcuse and his wife Inge came up several times. And our Party leaders, Henry Winston, Jim Jackson and William Paterson, came in together from New York.

I anxiously awaited the visits of George's lawyer John Thorne because it was one of the ways I kept up with what was happening with George and the other brothers in San Quentin. Margaret, Howard and Sheldon visited George, John, Fleeta and Ruchell as often as they could manage.

In the month of June, Howard argued the bail motion before the new judge in the case, Richard Arnason, who had been brought in from Sonoma County. Everyone's hopes were high—everyone's except mine, that is—that Arnason would rule in our favor. The issue was simple; persons accused of capital crimes were not to be released on bail when the "proof of guilt is evident and the presumption thereof great." The corollary was that the lack of sufficient evidence meant that the accused person should be let out pending trial. Howard and Kendra were as certain that I would be released as they were of their own lives and were both trying to cheer me up with promises of freedom tomorrow.

During the bail hearing, Albert Harris felt so confident that Arnason would deny our motion that he said into the record: "When she checks out of the Marin County Jail, if she is released on bail, she might as well be given an air travel credit card along with her belongings, because we will never see her again."

When Arnason said no, I felt the vise closing once more, but I did not feel terribly shocked, having expected him to take the easiest way out anyway. Kendra cried and Howard was more depressed than I had ever known him to be.

It appeared that the motions the judge did grant were an attempt to compensate for the terrible blow he had delivered in denying bail. Arnason said yes to our contention that I should be allowed to act as co-counsel in the case. And because bail had been denied, he agreed to order that more favorable conditions (especially for the preparation of the case) be established at once within my jail cell.

He ordered that I be given access to a typewriter and that, like the other women, I be allowed to have a radio. He even ordered the matron to allow me to spend brief periods of time with the women in the main section. I discovered that things in the main tank in the corridor around the corner were not very different from what I had seen in the House of Detention in New York. I rediscovered how vitally important it was to resist every destructive current of prison life . . .

For jails and prisons are deadly places. There was the mesmerizing inanity of television; a few boring high school texts, some mysteries and a lot of unbelievably bad fiction. The women could write if they wished, but the small notepaper, which was seldom available, discouraged serious writing in favor of casual notes which would be censored anyway before they were mailed. Even getting hold of a pencil could be an extensive and complex undertaking. There were the well-worn cards and games, indispensable props for every jail—

things to coat the fact of imprisonment with sugary innocu-
ousness, fostering an imperceptible regression back to childhood. As I had noticed from the parlance at the House of D.,
in the jailers' eyes, whether we are sixteen or seventy, we are
"girls." They loved to watch over their child-prisoners happily
engrossed in harmless games. Any pastime that was intellectu-
ally demanding seemed suspect. The jailers in Marin County
were extremely hostile to allowing a chess game in, and
agreed to it only if it fit silly specifications. The one finally
admitted to the day room was toylike, a child's version of chess.

One other jail "outlet" was overwhelmingly sexist. It was
the stubborn presence of the washing machine, clothes dryer
and ironing paraphernalia which, discounting the metal tables
and backless stools, were the sole furnishings of the day room.
The "reasoning" behind this was presumably that women, because they are women, lack an essential part of their existence
if they are separated from their domestic chores. The men's
linens and jail clothes were sent elsewhere for laundering; the
women were expected to tend to their own. If they did not
volunteer to do the washing and ironing, a work schedule was
imposed. This work system also proved to be racist. When, out
of boredom, many women volunteered to do the washing,
black women were consistently rejected. But when no one
volunteered, black women were ordered to do it.

In the midst of all this, sleep emerges as a kind of luxury.
Just because it involves unconsciousness, the complete nega-
tion of an already empty existence, it becomes the least monotonous way to pass the time. The matrons encouraged us to
think of sleep as a privilege by making the availability of a
bed during the day a reward for "good conduct." If, for instance, a woman was not up, fully dressed, with her blankets
tidily tucked under the mattress, when breakfast arrived at
6:30 A.M., then all the women in that cell would lose their
"bed privileges" for that day. They were all locked in the
adjacent day room, where the only resting places were stools.

They are serious people, jailers, thoroughly caught up in
the glitter of their badges. When challenged, this seriousness

shows its true face. A young Black woman prisoner was told that since she was occasionally let out of the jail on a work-furlough program, she could not join the other prisoners in the television day room. TV was not very important to her, but this reprisal made her furious. She told the matron that her badge didn't give her the right to punish her so. In response, the matron called upon a power greater than her badge—her racism. She told the Black woman that she had "overstepped her color." This incident stirred a terrific battle among the women, and interestingly enough the battle lines defied racial demarcation: though all of the Black women supported the sister, some white women did too.

This badge-seriousness extends into areas that are truly deadly. Many times when I rode in the elevator with armed guards on my way to a court appearance, the men would unsnap their gun holsters—all a show for my eyes alone.

JULY 8, 1971

Howard, John Thorne and I followed the jailers through the brightly lit prisoners' corridors into a holding cell in the courtroom area. A seatless toilet stood in the corner and two wooden benches lined opposite walls of the narrow cell. The upper half of one of the walls was made of transparent plexi-glass. It was just a little smaller than the one where Ruchell and I waited for our court appearances.

Although I should have known what to expect, the heavy metallic rattling which precipitously dissipated our silence startled me. The chains, locks, shackles, handcuffs, whose rumblings I had first heard in the courtroom in Salinas, now sounded very familiar. On the other side of the glass wall, George was descending the stairs for an all-day meeting between him and his lawyers and me and my lawyers.

Since I was now officially recognized as co-counsel for myself, the judge had agreed to issue an order for a meeting between me and each of the Soledad Brothers and my codefendant, Ruchell. A few days later, I wrote George about my impressions of that first moment.

"A scene frozen in my mind: I am standing in the little glass cubicle downstairs, standing waiting, loving, desiring and then hot cold rage when the chains begin to rattle as you slowly descend the stairs ... I'm supposed to rip off the chains. I'm supposed to fight your enemies with my body, but I am helpless, powerless. I contain the rage inside, I do nothing. I stand there watching, forced to assume the posture of a disinterested spectator, the whole scene perceived through glass, laboratory-like, mad at them for thrusting this upon me, mad at myself for doing nothing. Mad at myself too because I could not fail to see how much counter force you were exerting upon yourself, each step, long, hard, unwilling to be restrained by chains and pigs, your entire body with each foot movement in a hard sway ..."

As soon as he came into the cell and saw that we were there, the disdain on his face immediately dissolved into the smile I remembered so well from Salinas. Instinctively, his first gesture was to try to reach out. An embrace. He had forgotten that his wrists were chained to his waist and that he could only move them a few inches. With my free hands—they had not cuffed me this time—I tried to make up for his chains.

Eight hours was not long enough. We talked about everything, but there was not enough time. We discussed our strategy for the defense and talked about the possibility of George's testifying during the trial. He was certain that we would beat the case. I told him that our victory would have to be a victory together. All of us.

Subsequently there was an all-day meeting with Ruchell. It came at a critical time. Though we were both solidly united on our political approach to the case, we did not entirely agree on the way it should be attacked from a legal standpoint. Ruchell wanted the trial transferred from the jurisdiction of the State of California to the federal court system. Based on his years of experience with the California courts, he was convinced that they wanted his life. He felt that the chances of minimizing the repressive and racist treatment both of us were receiving would be greater if we could agree upon this strategy of removal. I had studied this strategy, I had reflected upon it, and had held long discussions with Margaret and Howard about the viability of Ruchell's position. Finally, I had decided that it would be best for us to fight it out on the state court level.

Among the many reasons for my decision, one pertained in a very practical way to our ability to get the best possible jury. In federal court, it was the judge who questioned potential jurors and made all decisions concerning the presence or lack of biases in them. In state court, on the other hand, we, the defense, could demand the right to conduct an extensive voir dire of potential jurors, probing into areas such as racism and anti-communism. Huey Newton's case had already established the precedent as the result of Charles Garry's work in picking the jury. It would not be possible to conduct this kind of courtroom investigation into the jurors' backgrounds if we litigated the case in federal court.

During the many months of the pretrial period, Ruchell and I held brief discussions about this in the holding cell where we waited in the mornings for court to be convened and during recesses. We corresponded with each other about our differences. Margaret, Sheldon and Howard visited Ruchell in San Quentin, arguing out all the pros and cons of removal. It was important to me that we reach agreement on this, because my position from the very beginning had been that he and I should go to trial together. There had been much pressure, from many quarters, including from the judge himself, to sever the cases. But the position of our defense team had always been that all such efforts to separate us had to be resisted.

So long as the situation regarding removal was in abeyance, we had not been able to proceed with many of our pretrial motions. Proceedings at the state court level might possibly jeopardize Ruchell's fight for removal. It was a difficult predicament. When the time came to throw aside all indecisiveness in order to begin serious litigation of the case, Ruchell and I were still at odds on our respective legal positions.

This is where we were, at the beginning of the eight-hour jail meeting. Lawyers—mine and Ruchell's—were present, as were members of our committees. At times, the arguments became rather heated. But even with all this, there was no breach of the solidarity which bound us together. Ruchell made a point of letting it be understood that this was a technical disagreement on legal strategy and not a fundamental rupture between us.

When it appeared that this gap between our legal positions was not going to close before the end of the meeting, I felt compelled, for the sake of unity, to make a concession: I proposed that in conjunction with Ruchell's efforts, I file a motion for removal, but only under the condition that if the motion were denied in federal court, Ruchell would agree to jointly fight the case in state court. He gave his approval to my proposal.

Later, I could see that our agreement was defective from the outset, more a result of our desperation than a real attempt to solve our differences. For Ruchell was certain beyond a doubt that the judge would grant the removal motion, and didn't earnestly consider the possibility of a denial. I was equally certain—beyond a doubt—that the motion would in fact be denied, so I never earnestly considered the possibility of fighting the case in federal court.

The motion was denied. Rather than begin litigation in state court, Ruchell decided he wanted to pursue the removal strategy further. I knew how passionately he was committed to his position, so I could not really blame him for what he did. But, now, the impasse we had hoped we would elude subbornly imposed itself. If we wanted to get on with our respective defenses, there was only one way to confront the impasse—and both of us understood this. Severance now was the only way out. Severance was a word I hadn't wanted to hear, but since we were both wedded with equal conviction to our own particular strategies, we had to move for the separation. Immediately afterward, our Committee issued a statement to the press:

> On Monday, July 19, Judge Richard Arnason granted a motion to sever the case brought against Angela Davis and Ruchell Magee by the State of California. . . .
>
> From the inception of the frame-up the general mass media, joined in by dubious "left friends" have attempted to drive a wedge between Angela and Ruchell. The devices have ranged from phoney and racist comparisons between Angela and Ruchell all the way to the establishment of a hierarchy of political prisoners.
>
> Angela and Ruchell have devoted many hours to the co-ordination of legal strategies. During the first seven months of pretrial hearings they made continuous attempts at developing complementary legal strategies. However, unable to coordinate their strategies, the final result was a severance motion agreed upon by both defendants.
>
> . . . It should be clear that the decision to sever was not reflective of political divergencies. Nor did it bear upon sub-stantive issues of the legal defense. Rather differences were procedural in nature . . .
>
> Ruchell will attempt to take [the] battle to Federal court, and Angela will attempt to fight the same battle in a state court. But both believe that without a massive, Black-led movement which uses the courtroom as only one forum of struggle, this battle will not be won. And we *will* win.
>
> For those of us around the country who are actually struggling to build a mass movement capable of freeing all political prisoners, our responsibilities are doubled. The cases of Ruchell Magee and Angela Davis must be taken before the people with the idea of providing masses of people with a close insight into the oppression of the penal system . . .
>
> The first anniversary of the insurrection which was seized upon to frame Angela and Ruchell is soon approaching. Committees in California and throughout the country are com-memorating August 7 through various activities, ranging from rallies and teach-ins to memorial services. In Pasadena, California, a park is being dedicated to the memory of Jonathan

Jackson. It is through these kinds of activities that people will come to understand the conditions against which Ruchell and our slain brothers were fighting on August 7, 1970.

AUGUST 21, 1971

In the little lawyers' booth in the visiting area, Bettina and I were trying hard to finish the manuscript of *If They Come in the Morning*. When Howard arrived, bringing Barbara Ratliff, who was doing the research for one of our legal motions, all three of them were able to come back to the work cell. We had hardly gotten settled when the big key turned in the lock, the door swung open and, addressing Howard, the woman deputy announced, "Mr. Moore, you'll have to leave. There's an emergency in the building."

It had been months since the last bomb scare. Nevertheless, the procedure was not unfamiliar to us.

"We'll be back when it's over," Howard said. And the three of them left the cell. I assumed that the woman deputy would return shortly to direct me and the other prisoners to the bomb shelter downstairs, as had been done the last time, but a half-hour, then an hour, passed, and no one had appeared at the door. She finally came back to the cell and told me she had instructions to take me to the sleeping cell. When I asked what was going on, she refused to say anything more than that she was simply following the orders she had received.

I don't know how many hours I lay on my cot, staring at the ceiling, letting my imagination run wild. I waited. I waited for some word from one of them, from Howard, Margaret, someone. It was very late when the deputy came back to my cell and told me, "Mr. Moore is waiting for you." She unlocked the gate and I walked a few steps behind her. Turning the corridor corner, I saw Margaret and Howard standing in front of the work-cell door.

Margaret's eyes were red and swollen, and the only time I

had seen that expression of utter desperation on her face before was the morning about ten years ago when her mother came into the bedroom where we were sleeping to tell her and the other children that their father had died of a heart attack that night. Howard was sweating heavily, his forehead was all wrinkled, his eyes were squinted, and he was breathing hard as if from exhaustion.

I looked at them, feeling something giving way inside me. We were alone, in the cell, the door closed behind us, and no one had yet broken the silence. During the last interminable hours of waiting I had fought back broken pictures of an explosion at San Quentin that kept trying to insinuate themselves into my thoughts. How many times had George said that the war declared on him by his jailers could break out into open combat at the slightest provocation? I was screaming inside. "Don't let it be that something has happened to George." But the louder I screamed, the more their faces told me that something *had* happened—that the worst had happened.

"George?" I asked, leaving his name hanging there. I didn't want to make my question more concrete.

Howard nodded.

"He's not . . . ?"

Howard bowed his head, and I was aching with hope that I had not really heard that little, almost inaudible "yes."

I reached out to Margaret, who broke into huge sobs, and we stood there, holding on to each other. I felt frozen, unable to move, unable to bring words out of my mouth, unable to bring tears to my eyes. As if someone had encased me in ice.

"The pigs killed him, Angela." Howard's voice penetrated my consciousness from the distance. "They murdered him. Shot him in the back."

Already the key was turning and the deputy was telling them they had to leave.

Back in the cell, I woke up from the frozen nightmare to face the reality of George's death. It was then, alone in the darkness, that I began to cry.

I thought about Georgia, Robert, Penny, Frances, Delora, and George's nephews and nieces. It was in this way they had to observe the first anniversary of Jonathan's death.

George was a symbol of the will of all of us behind bars, and of that strength which oppressed people always seem to be able to pull together. Even when we think the enemy has stripped us of everything, left us bereft even of our souls. The strength that comes out of an almost biological need to feel that we have something to say about the direction of our lives. That need had gnawed at George, behind bars all of his adult life—and, what was most important, he had known how to give the clearest, most universal expression to that need, and his writings had aroused people all over the world.

The sisters in the House of Detention in New York had learned something important about themselves when they read *Soledad Brother*. When my message reached George in San Quentin that the women were exhilarated by the book, but disturbed by his earlier uncomplimentary remarks about Black women, he apologized and wanted them all to understand his misjudgment.

Tonight men and women in every prison in the country were probably awake, like me, mourning and trying to channel their anger constructively. People all over the world must be talking about vengeance—constructive organized mass retaliation.

The next day it seemed as if the whole world were inside my cell. Every seat around the work table was occupied. At first, it was difficult to get the words moving in conversation—no one knew quite where to begin. When I looked at Charlene, Kendra, Franklin, Margaret, Howard . . . I couldn't keep back the tears. Then Franklin broke into sobs.

It was Charlene or Kendra who said that the Committee had begun to organize a vigil outside San Quentin—the lives of the other brothers had to be safeguarded, and the conditions of George's murder had to be investigated immediately. They said that reports were seeping out of the prison about brutal beatings and horrifying torture sessions. Already our

Committee had contacted Rep. Ron Dellums, Assemblyman Willie Brown, Dr. Carleton Goodlett and many other concerned public people, asking them to demand that they be allowed to tour San Quentin, interview the prisoners about the events that had led to George's death, and examine the wounds inflicted upon the brothers by guards.

After they had left, to rush back to the work of organizing the counterattack, I tried to compose a statement to be released to the press.

"George knew," I wrote, "that the price of his intense revolutionary commitment was having to live each day fighting off potential death blows.

"George's example of courage in the face of the spectre of summary execution; his insights honed in the torment of seven years of solitary confinement; his perseverance in the face of overwhelming odds will continue to be a source of inspiration to all our sisters and brothers inside prison walls and outside."

I wrote about the Jackson family: "Their grief is deep. In little more than a year, two of their sons, George and Jonathan, were felled by fascist bullets. I express my love to Georgia and Robert Jackson, Penny, Frances and Delora.

"For me, George's death has meant the loss of a comrade and revolutionary leader, but also the loss of an irretrievable love . . . I can only say that in continuing to love him, I will try to express that love in the way he would have wanted—by re-affirming my determination to fight for the cause George died defending. With his example before me, my tears and grief are rage at the system responsible for his murder. He wrote his epitaph when he said:

'Hurl me into the next existence, the descent into hell won't turn me. I'll crawl back to dog his trail forever. They won't defeat my revenge, never, never. I'm part of a righteous people who anger slowly but rage undamned. We'll gather at his door in such a number that the rumbling of our feet will make the earth tremble.' "

Then I was left with the radio.

All day long one station broadcast readings from George's book, and the all-news station began to develop the preposterous story that George had smuggled a bulky pistol, hidden under a wig, from the visiting area to the Adjustment Center, the most heavily guarded section of San Quentin. I listened to the radio talk shows. The majority of the people who called in to the shows suspected that something was very wrong inside San Quentin; that whatever was askew was not the fault of the prisoners, but of the prison hierarchy. The most consistent aspect of these responses was the belief that the prison administration had taken them for fools. Over and over again, people commented on the contempt the administration had shown by not even constructing a sensible story. Who on earth would believe that the tale about the wig justified all the violence unleashed on the prisoners?

George was dead, and the deeply personal pain I felt would have strangled me had I not turned it into a proper and properly placed rage. I could not dwell on my own loss. Any individual gnashing of teeth would bring me to my knees. Personal sadness in that still gray cell under the hateful eyes of my jailers might break the cords of will that held me together. George's death would be like a lodestone, a disc of steel deep inside me, magnetically drawing toward it the elements I needed to stay strong and fight all the harder. It would refine my hatred of jailers, position my contempt for the penal system, and cement my bonds with other prisoners. It would give me the courage and energy I needed for a sustained war against the malevolent racism that had killed him. He was gone, but I was here. His dreams were mine now.

AUGUST 3, 1971

Judge Keating takes the stand. He looks pitifully thin, and the deep wrinkles in his face make him look older than his years. Something about him reminds me of the racists who peopled my childhood. I feel confident and eager as I rise to question him about his judgment in selecting the Marin County Grand Jury. This time I am launching the attack.

Our position was that the indictment against me had been returned by a Grand Jury (that needed only eight minutes and no extended discussion to indict me) that was racist and nonrepresentative. A hearing was granted us to determine whether the judges' selection of the Grand Jury was based on their own race and class prejudices. We believed that the judges were unacquainted with the black community, the working class community, and the youth community, and therefore could not have picked representative jurors.

We were well into the examination when I produced a photograph which Margaret had given me. Approaching the witness stand, I handed him the picture and asked him whether it was a true representation of his house (and by implication of his wealth). Surprised and annoyed by the fact that we had photographed his home, he mumbled, under his breath, but loud enough for the court reporter to hear, "Judges don't have any civil rights or privacy, huh? The people that enforce the civil rights don't have any. Yes, that's my house. I might say it might be dangerous to do that again. . . . We don't take kindly to burglars up there."

When I asked Keating whether he would consider recommending a member of the Black Panther Party to serve on the Grand Jury, he said: "They are the blatant racists outside Adolph Hitler." And he went on to insist that "they are advocates of hatred, violence and murder. . . . They spew hatred and violence and murder all over." He added that this also held true for the Communist Party.

I was speechless, shocked not so much that these were his sentiments as by the fact that a Superior Court judge had shouted these statements into a permanent court record.

A survey we conducted confirmed the deep-seated racist and anti-Communist prejudices of the average resident of the county. Judge Keating was a typical Marin County resident. How could my trial take place in the Civic Center, next door to Judge Haley's courtroom? We prepared to argue our motion for a change in the venue of the trial. For, a trial here would be a ceremonial slaughter, a sure prelude to San Quentin's gas chamber. All the Superior Court judges in the county had confessed that they could not fairly preside over my trial. That grand gesture disengaging themselves was to me another way of saying that they were hopelessly convinced of my guilt.

Our survey demonstrated that the majority of the people in Marin County, who were both white and wealthy, believed me guilty of kidnapping, murder and conspiracy. But even more telling, they believed that I was guilty of something worse—of being a Communist, of being a Black woman. Many of them felt outraged that I had been allowed to teach the children of decent white Californians. If they could vote on the matter, they would banish me forever from the universities in California.

Since that survey had been conducted George had been murdered by San Quentin guards. The hysteria whipped up around these events—designed to turn the victims into the criminals—was pervasive. Public opinion in this wealthy white county considered anyone who spoke out on behalf of San Quentin prisoners as guilty as they presumed the prisoners to be.

Our motion for a change of venue was thorough and well-documented. Judge Arnason, the presiding judge called in from another county, had no choice but to grant it. But we didn't want just any change of location for the trial. Any Black person knows that there are only a few places in the state of California where even the semblance of a fair trial could take place. If there was to be a trial, we wanted it to take place in San Francisco, where we could hope to pull some Black people from the jury panel. But those who determined the locality of the trial didn't want to go to San Francisco, sprawled on the other side of the bridge, with its multicolored people of many social opinions and political persuasions. San Francisco was too unpredictable; the potential of a large local movement rising up to be vigilant over the trial was much too strong.

They wanted a more tranquil place, a place where controversies were smothered by soft-spoken civilities. A place where Black people did not live in large numbers, but where there were enough leading Black figures in the community to veil the existence of racism. They wanted a place with substantial geographical stature, but without political color, and especially without a tradition of progressive political struggles.

That place, we discovered, was to be San Jose. Marin County jailers and sheriffs accepted this change of venue as a personal defeat. Their faces wore expressions of deep regret—regret that they could not preside over the slaughter themselves. With undisguised pleasure, they refused to give us the smallest hint about the date or hour of the move. Howard and Margaret warned me that I should be prepared to leave at a moment's notice, and had brought me cardboard boxes to pack my things: books, papers, letters that I had accumulated over the last year in that jail.

Their warnings served me well. One morning around three or four A.M. the chief matron woke me, screeching that I had better be ready in a few minutes. I was prepared. There was nothing to do but wash and brush my teeth.

DECEMBER 2, 1971

The trip to San Jose was much longer than I had expected. Even though I didn't know much about the geography of Northern California, I could tell that they were taking a roundabout route for what they called "security reasons." I had been hoping to see San Francisco or Berkeley, or some place with normal (but for me extraordinary) scenes of human activity. But when I arrived at the jail in Palo Alto, I had no pleasant memories to bring in with me. The trip had been freeway all the way, the caravan traveling far above the speed limit. And until we began the approach to Palo Alto, it had been pitch-dark.

A slight, pale man was riding in the car with me. At the

time I didn't know that he was the undersheriff of Santa Clara County. He did not have the usual manner of a law enforcement officer. He seemed unsure of himself. He tried to console me, to assure me that the stint I was going to do in the jail there would be much more tolerable than the year of horrors I had just left in Marin County. But jail was jail. Unless you had resigned yourself to the fact of being locked up, there were no degrees of better or worse.

As with the FBI, as with the New York House of D., as with the Marin County Jail, now with the Santa Clara Jail, the ritual: Name . . . Address . . . Age . . . Birthplace . . . Previous arrests . . . etc., etc., etc. Mug shots . . . fingerprints . . . Would there ever come a time when I would finally be booked out?

I had learned that each time a prisoner is booked she has a right to two phone calls. I called my lawyers first so they would know I had arrived, and then my parents. I hardly ever had the chance to talk to them on the phone except when I was being booked into a new jail. They were overjoyed to hear my voice, yet at the same time frustrated and tense about what this new situation might bring. Mother said she was coming out before Christmas. My younger brother, Reggie, on work leave from his college, was also going to come to the West Coast. My mother was trying to concentrate on things that would let her escape the reality of my predicament. Although she remained strong until the end, I think the whole ordeal was harder on her than on anyone. I asked whether she had started eating regularly again, and whether she had managed to gain back some of the weight she had lost. Each time we saw each other or talked, we ended up admonishing each other for the same reasons. She reminded me this time to eat more and try to gain my own weight back. I asked her not to worry so much and reluctantly said good-bye.

As soon as I hung up the receiver, a shaded door to the left of the booking area was unlocked. We walked into a short and narrow hall and as I glanced to my right, I saw the most frightening jail cell I had yet seen. The area was walled off in glass. On the other side of the glass was a twelve-by-two-foot corridor, off of which were two cells. Each cell was about six feet by eight feet. One contained the metal slab bed, a thin mattress, toilet and sink; the other was a padded cell completely lined with a heavy tufted fabric painted a silvery gray. The padding was broken by a single hole in the floor which served as a toilet.

"You have to take off your clothes," the matron said.

She handed me a dress, some pajamas, a sweater, and a pair of underpants, a bra, some socks and rubber thonged slippers. I told her I would put on the clothes but not the underwear. She insisted that I had to give up my own underwear and put on the county's. I was serious about not wearing jail underwear. In New York, wearing unsterilized underwear, I had contracted a terrible fungus which had spread all over my body and had taken months to finally cure. I told the matron she could have my underwear but nothing she said or did was going to make me put on those jail panties.

Female jailers must have something of the voyeuse in them—even those who are not homosexual inevitably stand and watch you with deep interest while you strip down to the nude. This matron must have been unconscious of the intensity with which she was looking at me, because when I asked her what she found so interesting, she looked terribly embarrassed, and left abruptly.

The faded, smock-like dress was too tight and too short. The drab gray sweater would not reach my waist, and its sleeves came halfway up my arms. I could not pull the white children's socks over my heels nor fit into the rubber slippers. I threw the slippers and socks through the open door into the corridor.

Then I realized how cold it was in that cell. Not only was it cold, the toilet was leaking and water was running all over the floor. I stepped out into the cell corridor to shout a complaint, but no one was in sight, and the door to the larger corridor was locked. I told myself that Margaret and Howard would be there soon, and we could begin to fight these subhuman conditions. In the tight childish smock, without under-wear, and barefoot, I was freezing, so I put the pajama bottoms on under the dress, the tiny sweater over it, and the pajama top over the sweater. I imagine I looked absurd.

Since there was no place to sit, I climbed up on the bunk, pulled the army blanket over my shoulders and tried to concentrate on the book I had brought along. I had hardly gotten through one page when a matron with long, flaming-red hair came through the door into the corridor outside. She unlocked the door and, sounding somewhat kindly, I thought, asked whether I cared for breakfast. I said yes. Five minutes later she came back, saying that I wasn't "eligible" for breakfast. She had checked with the Marin County people and they had told her that I had had tea—tea!—before my trip down. Since that was the case, I didn't have anything coming until lunchtime.

"You people just don't know what it means to behave like humans, do you?" I blurted out.

Quickly but silently she darted out of the cell. I scolded myself for having said yes in the first place to her nice offer and tried to get back into my book.

Later, when Margaret came, and saw me all huddled up in the blanket, freezing above a water-logged floor, her mouth fell open. "They must be kidding!" she said. "I've been inside a lot of jails, but this beats them all."

Her outrage made me feel a little better. For a while, I had been wondering whether I was overreacting. And then I thought of the descriptions George had given of the many dungeons they had thrown him into over the last decade. This place couldn't be as bad as O Wing in Soledad or the Adjustment Center in San Quentin or solitary in Folsom or any of the other cells where they had tried to squeeze the will and determination out of George.

"This place isn't even a jail," I told Margaret. "It's what they call a 'holding facility'—a place to keep prisoners for a few hours or maybe overnight. But they want to keep me here for months. I can't believe it," I went on, "there isn't enough room in here to do exercises, even the ones where you stand in place."

We decided to draw a scale sketch of the cell, with an accompanying description. We wanted the Committee to use it in their press release and propaganda about the conditions of my confinement.

Margaret left to give the drawing to the Committee. "Hold on," she said, "there will be some big changes around here very soon!"

I smiled at her. "Margaret, you know I'll be O.K."

A little later the matron led a young, very desolate-looking white woman past my cell. I heard a gate being unlocked next door. She must be in on a drug bust, I figured. Not feeling like talking to someone I couldn't see, I said nothing to her but went back to the inner cell, got back on the top bunk and continued to read *The Female Eunuch* until Margaret and Howard came.

They brought news that the Committee was already putting wheels into motion. All over the country and even in other countries people were receiving communications about the conditions under which I was being held. In a matter of hours telegrams and telephone calls began to pour into the sheriff's office. Sheriff James Geary, who regarded himself as a man of liberal persuasions, responded to this massive protest and ordered some changes. In an interview that appeared in the San Jose *Mercury*, he lamented the fact that people all over the country thought he had shoved me into the most wretched of dungeons. One woman, he said, had protested my being kept in a "heatless hole, barefoot, wading in water up to her ankles."

Not only were there physical changes such as heat, clothing, and shoes, but the manner of the jailers changed. Some of them had become almost kind: "Miss Davis, is there anything you need?" "Are you sure everything is all right?" "How was your dinner?" "Do you have any complaints?" "Would you like anything in particular tomorrow?"

Before the downpour of protests, meals were tasteless TV dinners, justified by the jailers by the fact that prisoners were rarely there longer than a day or so. After the protests, a cook was brought in and the jailers suggested to the lawyers that I could have a television in my cell, and could keep the radio and electric typewriter I had acquired in Marin.

With these innovations the cell became cluttered. Magnanimously the jailers opened the door to the padded cell for my use. Thus I came to have what, in the prosecutor's propaganda, became a "two-room suite." A two-room suite consisting of a six-by-eight cell and an even smaller padded cell, the toilet hole of which backed up one day and covered my books and the floor with liquid excrement.

Just as the "two-room suite" was a farce, so was "my own private television" of which the prosecutor constantly spoke. My television was "private" only because they insisted on keeping me in solitary confinement. The prosecutor never mentioned that in the regular women's jail a color television was available for the prisoners. Nor that when I got mine I insisted on one for the prisoner next door and that when the jailers refused, the Committee purchased a TV for her as well.

During those days, as the conditions of my imprisonment improved, I felt a profound sadness welling up within me. What had been done for me had, so far, been done only for me. But I was haunted by the specters of all those sisters and brothers whose lives were eroding in other jails. Ruchell, Fleeta, John, Luis, Johnnie Spain, David Johnson, Hugo Pinell, Willie Tate, Earl Gibson, Larry Justice, Lee Otis Johnson, Martin Sostre, Marie Hill, the Attica Brothers . . . The names kept tolling in my ears. My head was bursting with jumbled images of their dungeons, their keepers—terror-ridden images that made the improvement of my own physical circumstances extremely painful for me. The tremendous energy of the movement which had so swiftly transformed my jail situation was energy my sisters and brothers had a more than equal right to. I tried to assuage some of my pain by establishing contact with sisters and brothers in prisons all over the country. Compulsively almost, for hours at a time, I answered letter after letter from prisoners—letters which had piled up over the months in Marin when the jailers refused to give me all of my mail. More than ever before I felt a need to cement my links to every other prisoner. My very existence, it seemed, was dependent on my ability to reach out to them. I decided then and there that if I was ever free, I would use my life to uphold the cause of my sisters and brothers behind walls.

Shortly before the change of venue, Sheldon had had to leave the case for personal reasons. And with the pretrial motions at an end, the original legal team had been disbanded. Around this time, we asked Doris Walker, a lawyer with a long history of involvement in progressive causes, to join the team. We welcomed her participation not only because of her qualifications as an attorney and her unquestionable commitment to the struggle, but also because we felt it was politically important for women to assume visible roles in the defense.

Once the transfer to Santa Clara County took place, we had to move quickly to make the last addition to the legal team. There were Howard, Margaret and Dobby. We wanted one additional lawyer. During the original discussion about lawyers in the House of D. in New York, the name of Leo Branton came up along with Howard's as one of the first lawyers we wanted to speak to about taking the case. I was particularly interested in Leo Branton because he had been one of the few lawyers courageous enough to defend Communists during the Smith Act Trials. Recently, he had come out of retirement to take the case of the L.A. Panthers which stemmed from the January 1970 police attack on their office.

When we first approached him about the defense team, he was all tied up in the Panther case and could not therefore assume another major responsibility. As a result of a misunderstanding—our impression was that he had left the country after his involvement in the Panther case terminated—we had not contacted him since the fall of 1970. When Dobby told me that he had appeared extremely receptive about the idea of joining the team now, I was absolutely delighted. Shortly afterward, he made a trip from L.A. to San Jose to discuss his entrance into the case.

I had seen Leo once before—very briefly during one of the pretrial hearings of the L.A. Panthers. At that time he wore a mustache. Because everyone was talking about this tremendous Black lawyer who felt so strongly about the Panthers that he had come out of retirement to defend them, I retained an impression that he was well up in the years. On the day his visit was scheduled, I saw a young-looking man with a well-developed physique, dressed very sharply. It did not enter my mind that this could be the Leo Branton who had come out of retirement to take the Panther case—but who was he?

I was so shocked that after Howard introduced him, one of the first things I asked him was how old he was. As it turned out, he had retired at the age of forty-five and had gone with his wife Geri to live in Mexico for a while. Leo's background was fascinating. He had tried the Smith Act cases, had gone to the South in the early sixties to defend Civil Rights workers and eventually had become one of the few Black lawyers to represent people in the entertainment field. He had been, for example, the attorney for Nat King Cole, and at the time we asked him to come into the case, he was handling the Jimi Hendrix's estate in England, on behalf of his family.

The outcome of our discussion was that Leo would become an attorney of record as soon as he completed the litigation in England. His decision was a source of pleasure and pride for us all. With Margaret, Howard, Dobby and Leo, our legal team was now the best we could hope for. This was an indisputable step in the direction of victory!

Soon after the move, I began to attend court regularly on pretrial matters. The jailers insisted on making the ten-minute trip to downtown San Jose some three hours before court was scheduled to begin. The caravan of armed men would leave between five-thirty and five forty-five in the morning. Some cars drove ahead of the unmarked car I rode in; some were behind, and there was always a car moving alongside. If their intention was to make the trip inconspicuously, they were hardly successful. Each morning a whole series of machinations and manipulations was necessary to keep this formation in shape as it sped at over seventy miles an hour to San Jose. Early one morning, as I was dressing for one of these predawn trips, I turned on the radio as I always did upon waking. There was a news flash: "Yesterday evening the Supreme Court of the State of California voted to abolish the death penalty on the grounds that it is cruel and unusual and thus unconstitutional." I was convinced at first that I had misheard the announcement. I had talked many times with Anthony Amsterdam, the attorney who prepared the papers and argued the death penalty case before the high court. He had visited me in jail while preparing our appeal of the bail denial before the federal court. At no time did he seem optimistic about the outcome of his case. But there it was. The death penalty annulled.

My thoughts at that moment flew to the brothers in San Quentin with pending cases carrying the death penalty. No longer could Ruchell be condemned to die in the gas chamber so near his cell. John Cluchette could not now be killed by the state. Fleeta, my brother, as much like a blood brother as Benny or Reggie; my dear Fleeta would not lose his life to the cyanide tablets dropped in the acid beneath the death chair. Johnnie Spain, Luis Talamante, Hugo Pinell, David Johnson, Willie Tate—the state could not take any more of their lives than prison had done already. Earl Gibson and Larry Justice would escape the official death that is often the lot of those who refuse to be obsequious before their keepers.

I laughed out loud. If I had been anywhere else I would have shouted, but there in the solitude of that jail I held my joy.

Margaret came in. I could tell that she had already heard the news: she was almost dancing with excitement. We hugged each other. I told her that this was one day I wouldn't mind being in San Quentin's Adjustment Center on Death

Row. "There must be a carnival going on now over there," I said.

Margaret was animatedly saying something about Howard preparing for a bail hearing that morning.

"Bail hearing?" I asked. "What kind of bail hearing?"

Margaret looked at me as if I were a little crazy.

"Angela," she said, "the death penalty has been abolished. Don't you realize that this undercuts the whole legal basis for Judge Arnason's denial of bail? He has nowhere to turn now. He has to let you out!"

Of course! In his original decision denying me bail, Arnason had emphatically stated that if not for the fact that I was accused of a *capital* crime, he would be more than willing to set me free on bail. Now there were no capital crimes. Arnason's words were on the record. The argument he had invoked when he rejected our bail motion no longer held water. According to the judge's own argument, I was now "legally" eligible for bail.

In my joy that Fleeta, the other brothers, and I could not be condemned to death, I had forgotten all about bail. We howled then. It was the first time I had laughed freely and deeply in sixteen months.

"We called Judge Arnason early this morning," Margaret said, "and he's already agreed to hold a bail hearing today. Howard and Dobby are trying to get copies of the Supreme Court decision now. They should be here in a few minutes. And Franklin, Kendra and the rest of the Committee are frantically trying to raise the bail money."

I had been close to euphoria when Margaret said that I would certainly be out on bail soon. But the more concrete she became, the more she began to talk about the facts and specifics, the more my euphoria dwindled away into an overwhelming pessimism.

"This judge isn't going to let me out on bail," I said, "not after all these months, not now, right on the eve of the trial. Just wait. He'll find a loophole somehow."

I didn't want to dampen Margaret's enthusiasm, but I

remembered only too vividly our experience when the bail motion had been argued the last time. Virtually everyone in the Committee had been positive that we would win. I think that I was the only one—the lawyers included—who had profound reservations about the possibility of being released. So when Arnason announced that he could not "legally" release me, it was such a terrible letdown for everyone, creating such an all-pervasive climate of gloom that it was hard to pick up the pieces and start the movement rolling again. I felt that another enormous defeat would be disastrous for the movement. There was also the psychological damage such a defeat would have on me; I had to husband my strength in order to survive. I could not allow myself to build up my hopes for release, which would only be shattered by the arbitrary words of a white man in the black robes of the judiciary. Certainly, there was a remote possibility that I might be released on bail, but in the opinion I was forming now, it was precisely that, a remote possibility. Moreover I was certain that Arnason would not make the decision alone. The real decision, I thought, would be made on levels of government much higher than that of a Superior Court judge.

We entered chambers for the preliminary bail hearing. I had already plotted out the scenario in my mind. Arnason, in his efforts to be the fairest judge possible, would agree to reconsider his ruling and, in fact, would hold a new bail hearing. But between now and the time he held the substantive hearing, he would have pried into each one of his law books, read the Supreme Court decision a thousand times for a loophole, and would announce on the day of the hearing that he was terribly distressed, but the law prohibited him from releasing me on bail.

When the three lawyers and I moved into the judicial chambers, we came face to face with a despondent-looking prosecutor, Albert Harris. Howard presented our extremely simple argument for bail: 1) The previous denial of bail was based entirely on the capital nature of the charges against me;

2) Only hours ago, the Supreme Court had abolished the death penalty—there was no such thing as a capital crime; 3) Ergo, I should be granted bail immediately.

So convinced were Howard and Dobby of the infallibility of their argument that they had a bondsman waiting at the back door of the court. But my pessimistic appraisal was correct. The judge set a date for yet another hearing. He said he needed time to review the Supreme Court decision, and that the prosecutor needed time to prepare his answer to our argument.

FEBRUARY 23

The bail hearing was set for Wednesday—in chambers. The judge responded to Howard's vigorous resistance to a closed hearing by saying that if we wanted to have the proceedings in open court, he would be only too happy to accommodate us—but he would have to postpone the date of the hearing for quite a while. We well understood the significance of this. In my state of mind I regarded it as a very broad hint that the motion would once more be denied. If not, why would he shy away from holding the hearing before the public?

Kendra, Franklin and Margaret kept trying to persuade me that this time the judge had no way out. In Margaret's "professional opinion," she kept reminding me, the law could not supply him with a loophole. Not this time. All of us, however, understood Howard's reticence on the subject. The last time he had been so sure—and had suffered so much for me when the denial came down. Almost everyone else was telling me to pack everything, to be on the alert so that when the decision was rendered, I could walk through the gates without a second's delay.

But I refused to pack, to make any gesture that might lead someone—particularly the jailers—to believe that I really thought I was going to get out. I recalled only too vividly, and with a great deal of depression, the arrogant deportment of the Marin County matrons and sheriff's deputies after the judge had said "denied" to our bail motion in June the year before.

Finally, quivering with nervousness, I had to submit to the handcuffs and be led through the steel doors for the court appearance. I was hyperconscious of every gesture I had to make: how to hold my manacled hands outward, turn my back to the car, sit down on the edge of the seat and slide myself to the middle. I never accepted the help of a jailer, no matter how difficult it was to get into the car. So many times before, I had strained to absorb every little detail along the route from the jail to the courthouse. On some of these trips I had enjoyed the sight of children playing in the street; on others I examined with sadness the faces of Black maids on their way to work for the Palo Alto rich. But always there was the stark and obscene Moffett Airfield, the coven from which planes were sent to kill Laotians, Vietnamese and Cambodians.

Now I might be seeing these scenes through the window of a police car for the last time—yet I could not persuade myself that there was even a remote possibility that it might be true. I felt as though I were walking a tightrope. If I continued to reject the possibility of receiving bail, my pessimism could send me plummeting into an abyss of depression. But if, on the other hand, I succeeded in convincing myself that today would be the day, I ran the risk of the fall from euphoria into an even deeper abyss. During the next few minutes, I tried desperately to maintain my balance. I kept looking for that medium between total pessimism and unrestrained optimism. Just to walk the rope a little longer.

There we were, arranging ourselves in the judge's chambers for the pronouncement of the verdict: Margaret, Howard, Dobby and myself on one side of the room; Albert Harris and Clifford Thompson on the other, and the judge in his great thronelike chair in the center.

Arnason's nonchalance must have been deliberate. Because of the casual way he announced his decision, we had no opportunity to let loose our screams of triumph. Sixteen months of imprisonment were coming to a close. Just like that.

The lawyers discussed conditions of bail with the judge. Without yet feeling the impact of my impending freedom, I wondered why he had finally decided to set me free. It was certainly not because he personally wanted to release me before trial. If that had been the case, he could have let me out months ago. He would not have had to wait for the abolition of the death penalty. Neither was it only because of the new court decision that Arnason had granted our motion. He could have very easily accepted the prosecutor's proposition that the Supreme Court decision would not be final for ninety days yet; therefore, he should wait out those three months and release me then—assuming no revisions were made in the decision. (Later I discovered that every judge in the state of California who had heard a bail motion on the basis of the abolition of the death penalty had followed the prosecutor's suggestion and waited out the ninety days.)

It was not the judge.

It was not the law.

Only one other explanation remained. That very morning, the judge himself had given me a glimpse into what had motivated him to grant bail.

He spoke about ". . . the mail I've received in the last two days and the telephone calls, none of which I have personally taken, but which my staff has taken, from . . . a tremendous number of states and telegrams from foreign countries. It is a case of amazing interest."

The real reason he felt compelled to hand down a decision in our favor had to do with the mushrooming defense campaign. Arnason did not mean to imply that he was "yielding to public pressure." Yet it was clear that the tremendous agitation of millions of people had affected him.

This realization brought to mind the many heated arguments we had had around the bail movement—arguments which usually found me alone on one side and Fania, Kendra, Franklin and the other Committee leaders on the other. It had been about a year since the bail campaign was launched. I had profound reservations about devoting so much of the energy of the campaign to the single question of bail. In the first place, I had been certain that there would not be the flimsiest chance of victory. In the second place I thought the political content of the bail issue too weak. It did not permit people to express their resistance to the *system* of repression, which was not only behind my own imprisonment but was why so many others were languishing in prison.

Only after many months had passed did I begin to understand my own misjudgment. True, the demand for bail was not a revolutionary demand. True, it did not of itself expose the rotten core of the capitalist system. But precisely because a bail demand was something which could appeal to anyone who wanted to side with justice, it allowed the campaign to reach out to many thousands of people who at that time could not have been stimulated to call for my complete freedom. They would not go on record demanding my freedom, but they would go on record demanding that I be released pending the determination of my innocence—or guilt—by a court of law.

The participation of so many people had been in itself phenomenal, but what impressed me most and what convinced me of the correctness of the bail fight was the way in which the people who waged the fight began to evolve politically. Many of them began to involve themselves in other areas of the campaign. Once they had been exposed to the realities of the prison and judicial systems, they were forced to give serious consideration to the political repression we spoke about. In learning about my case they learned about the Soledad Brothers, about the subhuman conditions of the jails, about the indeterminate-sentence law, under which George had been given a term of from one year to life for something which, had he been white and well-off, would have resulted in probation at worst. They learned about racism and how it pervaded every corner of the prison system. And they learned about the dynamic which makes racism an essential ingredient of the political persecution of revolutionaries and progressives. Many who began, reluctantly, demanding bail, ended up as strong and effective leaders of the campaign.

Arnason told us that the defense and the prosecution had to agree on the conditions of bail before he could formally set the bond, which he said would be $102,500—of which $2,500 had to be paid directly to the court in cash. The prosecution, of course, tried to see that, once on the outside, I would be imprisoned within so many restrictions that I might as well be in jail.

The battle raged on. Harris used the opportunity to lash out against the Committee (whose presence always seemed to offend him personally). He insisted I was not to attend or participate in anything that was organized by or had anything whatever to do with the National United Committee to Free Angela Davis. If he had had his way, I would not have been able to associate with my own sister, because she was one of the national coordinators of the defense campaign. Harris seemed to see as his main enemy not me, but rather this multitudinous movement which had risen up to jam his apparatus of persecution.

It seemed as if many hours had gone by when we had finally reached the point of agreement—or rather of truce. Outside, a large assembly of sisters and brothers had gathered to wait out the hearing and receive news of the decision firsthand. What we knew from the opening moments of the hearing, they knew not at all. When Howard and Dobby had to get legal papers from the office, the judge instructed them to keep silent about his decision, to speak to no newsperson, to go directly to the office and come directly back. Margaret and I went into the jury deliberation room to wait. We hoped that Howard would ignore—just a little—the judge's instructions.

Suddenly a huge roar was heard in the courthouse. Cheers, screams, laughter. The message had gotten to the people. And it was their own victory they were claiming. It was at that moment that the emotions I had had to contain during that long hearing were suddenly unleashed. It was right that it should be so; that my own happiness should emerge and merge with the emotions of those who had created it.

Howard and Dobby returned shortly. I told Howard that I knew he would not be able to keep the bail a secret when he went out.

"But I didn't say anything," Howard insisted. "I walked out with as straight a face as possible. I could see how tense and upset Franklin and Kendra and the others were. Still, I kept walking. Then Franklin ran up to me, and all I did was smile. I was smiling all over—I couldn't help it. Franklin didn't need anything else. He hugged me, Kendra, and then all pandemonium broke loose."

Now we had to get down to the concrete. Where was the money and property for the bond coming from? There were problems with the bondsman, Howard said. The one they had expected to use (a so-called "movement" bondsman) had apparently gotten cold feet at the last moment and begun talking about the way Eldridge Cleaver had split the country. This bondsman had proved himself such a racist, Howard said, that even if he changed his mind, we couldn't use him on principle.

In situations where bad news had to be broken, Howard had a way of assuming a fatherly air. There in the jury room, he told me very tenderly that I should expect to have to hole up for a few days while the bond was raised and a bondsman was found.

There had been Aretha Franklin's public promise some months before to put up the money for the bond. Now she was out of the country, but when my mother reached her, she said she was still willing to go bail for me. The problem was that she had to remain abroad for a while longer, and the money could not be released without her personal signature.

The Committee kept on looking. They quickly raised $2,500 to be handed over to the court and $10,000 to be kept on hand for the 10 percent bail bondsman's fee when the $100,000 in property was found. This time, when I rode back to jail, my hands cuffed, in the caravan of armed men, I felt strong. What had just unfolded was incontrovertible proof of the power of the people.

Back in my cell, I lay down feeling a profound sadness. Why me and not the others? I could not get rid of a sense of guilt. But I knew that my freedom would be significant only if I used it to push on for the freedom of those whose condition I had shared.

All of a sudden people were coming back to my cell. Franklin said that I would be getting out right away. What did he mean? Stephanie came in with this same cryptic news. Then Howard explained that they had found someone who was willing to put up his property as bond. Someone who had simply appeared, attracted to us by the magnetism of the movement. A white farmer from Fresno County, who had inherited a large stretch of land from his father, and who was a sympathizer with our movement. Soon there was news of another possibility. The bondsman whose office was downstairs from our legal offices in San Jose had decided to take over the operation. Negotiations were being conducted right outside the jail. Finally Howard came in with the joltingly exciting news: the bond had definitely been raised; all that remained was the paper work! I wanted to scream with joy. But the sluggish jail bureaucracy hindered the natural flow of my emotions. Every second of waiting now was like the months and seasons I had spent waiting behind bars. I could not shed the ugly jail clothes fast enough and pull on the purple pants Kendra had brought—pants too small for her and certainly too tight for me. My hands were trembling so I could hardly dress. Yet, seconds later, I was out front at the booking desk waiting for the jailers (who were silently burning with rage) to push the buttons which would fling open the gates.

The first gate was sliding open at its own maddeningly slow pace. One step and that threshold was crossed. My heart pounded as I waited for the gate behind me to slam shut with the hateful banging sound that had seared my nerves so many times before. This was the last time. I stepped through the next gate that was opening before me and was greeted by a tumultuous roar.

I threw my arms around the first person I saw outside, Refu, a brother I had known in L.A. I wanted to embrace every sister and brother in the crowd. Jail, imprisonment, sheriffs, chains—all that was far behind. For security reasons we had to leave the jail grounds quickly. Refu gently reminded me that I would have time to see all the people in safer surroundings. Margaret and I got into Victoria Mercado's yellow Mustang and plowed through the supporters and reporters who had converged on the car. Speeding down the freeway, we screamed, laughed and kissed each other. I was out there; no guards, no police car, no handcuffs. "Everyone's meeting over at Bettina and Jack's," someone said.

When we walked into the house, my face was hurting from smiling and laughing so much. Margaret's six-year-old son, Hollis, and Bettina and Jack's four-year-old, Joshua, were both there. With the special tenderness that young children can show, Joshua asked me, "Angela, are you really free?" And Hollis was so ecstatic he flung his arms around my neck.

There were the members of the national staff, the leaders and activists from the San Jose Committee, and committees from throughout the Bay Area, all gathered under one roof. I thought back on all the difficulties we had confronted trying to organize the Soledad Brothers Defense Committee. My admiration for the leaders of my committee was limitless. I was meeting many of them for the first time, all these beautiful sisters and brothers who had snatched my life from the pale hands of racist persecution.

I met in a back room with the leaders of the Chicano Defense Organization. El Comité Para la Defensa de los Presos Políticos had given special attention to my case. Their support was critical in Santa Clara County, where the Chicano population outnumbered the Blacks. Victoria Mercado, a Chicana sister who had joined the national staff of the Committee very early, had spent many months working in San Jose with El Comité.

Throughout the evening an unbroken stream of people came in. In the midst of all that, I picked up the telephone and dialed Birmingham. Mother and Daddy. Knowing the deep personal pain they had suffered, and their complete devotion to the fight, I felt happier for their sake than I did for my own. Our emotions were so high that the telephone seemed more a barrier than a medium of communication. Then I had to call my brother Benny and his wife Sylvia. Their commitment was both personal and political, and we had come to love each other even more. Then the New York calls. I had to reach Charlene, who had tackled the formidable job of handling the national campaign. Afterward I called Winnie. Henry Winston, chairman of our Party, and Gus Hall, our General Secretary, had together carried the message of the campaign to the world.

Then a problem insinuated itself. Franklin ran it down. Hundreds had assembled at Solidarity Center—the office of the San Jose Committee—to celebrate. They were waiting impatiently for me to drop by. Since the bail order included a prohibition on my speaking to or being present at any large gathering organized by the Committee, the suggestion was that I not go. What should I do? The first violation of my bail condition could be seized upon as a reason for putting me back in jail. Should I play it safe and follow the judge's order to the *t*? For some selfish concern for this little bit of freedom, should I ignore the sisters and brothers who had given so much? Court order or no court order, I was accountable only to those who had fought with and for me. If in fulfilling my obligations to them, I was risking my freedom, then so be it. If I stayed with the people, I would never be alone.

As we entered the Solidarity Center the crowd broke into a long, thunderous ovation—an ovation that almost made up for my last eighteen months in clandestinity and prison.

* * *

We had already decided that I would move in with Margaret. Bob and Barbara Lindsay, friends of ours in San Jose, had lent her a house for the duration of the case. For sixteen months Margaret had visited me in jails—New York, Marin County, Santa Clara; now it was strange to know that we could go to sleep and wake up under the same roof. Like many years ago, when she spent the summer in our house in Birmingham, or when I stayed with her family in New York.

It was futile to even try to fall asleep, so I spent these first hours of silence and darkness in thought. It was frightening to think about the profound impact jail had had on me. My responses were still geared to the sparseness of jail surroundings, to the thick hostility pervading the whole environment. Being accustomed to sleeping on a slab only slightly wider than my body, it felt peculiar to be able to roll over in Margaret's big bed.

There was something else about this house that saddened me and broke the spell of celebration. The house had belonged to Barbara Lindsay's mother, a beautiful woman named Emma Stern. I had come to know her as the white-haired old lady, lines deeply etched in her face, who had written the first pamphlet on the Soledad Brothers. Over seventy years old, she had been one of the most active leaders of the Soledad Defense Committee. In the summer of 1971 she fell ill. For a while she was in and out of the hospital and seemed to be recovering. When George was killed, the forces keeping her alive must have been consumed by sorrow. Shortly after George's funeral, Emma Stern died.

FEBRUARY 24

There was not enough time to savor the first morning of sun shining on the lush backyard. I wanted to abandon myself to primitive sensations: stretching out on the grass, soaking up the solar warmth and energy I had missed so much in my succession of cells. But I had to restrain this compulsion to touch trees, watch clouds and listen to the sound of children's voices. In a little while I had to face the press and confront the media and the millions they reach.

Just then the bell announced Fania's arrival. She had worked so hard on the campaign, traveling throughout the world, that she was not even there when I was released. She had had a speaking engagement that night in Idaho. We embraced each other, full to bursting with the deferred joy of the last eighteen months. Sisters, we had become comrades.

After the press conference, we made our way to Bettina and Jack's, where Gus Hall was waiting to see me. Gus understood better than anyone what I was feeling. He had spent some eight years in Leavenworth Federal Penitentiary. He described the moment when they first learned that the judge had granted him bail. The news arrived in the midst of a session of the Party Congress. They were torn, he said, between the impulse to make the announcement immediately and the knowledge that the news would hopelessly disrupt the remainder of the meeting. They risked disruption, and the rest of the day's business gave way.

Accompanying Gus on this trip was Luis Figueroa, a leader of the Communist Party and Senator from Chile. Short, with a huge mustache falling over his lips, he was like a benevolent uncle. In his warm, down-to-earth manner, Gus asked me whether I'd like to have dinner with a few comrades from the area. I accepted, and someone reminded me that we must hurry to meet my mother's plane.

I had suffered through such painful prison visits with my mother. She was such a sensitive person, especially about her children, I could only begin to sense the anguish my imprisonment caused her. If there was a single overriding personal reason why I wanted to be free, it was for my mother's sake.

As she stepped off the jet that afternoon, there was a radiance about her which I had never seen before. Eisa, my young niece, was in her arms. In an instant, we were entangled in hugs. No jailers to sully the privacy of this meeting.

After dinner, when I had finished one glass of champagne —all I dared to drink—I toasted practically everyone who was present. Spontaneously we began to sing "The Internationale": "Arise ye prisoners of starvation . . ." and immediately afterward "The Negro National Anthem." My mother's voice sang loud and clear: "Lift every voice and sing till earth and heaven ring . . ." Even the Black waiters joined in.

FEBRUARY 25

The burly white policeman in charge was evidently jarred by my appearance. His voice quivered with rage as he told me to step behind the white line over there. How many mug shots did this make?

Like the other cops lining the walls, he was wearing a dark-blue jumpsuit with a matching baseball cap. One could have easily mistaken him for a parking-lot attendant, a television repairman or an auto mechanic. But there was that heavy pistol swinging from his waist, and the two-foot truncheon his right hand was so tightly gripping.

When the photographer was done, the same fury-laden voice directed me to another white line—this one reserved for the women. My steps heavy with hesitation, I moved from the line to the other side of the screen. I held my breath while they frisked my body, dug their fingers in my hair, and asked me to lower my underpants.

Kendra, Victoria, Franklin and Rodney were already acquainted with the special routine in the San Francisco County Courthouse for those attending the Soledad Brothers' trial. But Mother, Sylvia and Benny were incredulous, outraged and horrified by this degrading prelude to the court session.

It was frightening to realize the regular trial-goers had to submit themselves to these humiliating searches day after day. Undoubtedly, the repetition conferred a dangerous aura of normality on this manifestly fascist routine. Undoubtedly, it had already created a dangerous precedent for political trials in the future.

Names were recorded, special seats assigned, photos taken for the San Francisco Police and the FBI. And inside, we in the spectator section were separated from the scene of the trial by a bulletproof shield extending the entire width of the courtroom.

Behind the plexiglass, things took on a staged appearance. Ritualistically, it seemed, the figures marched in to assume their habitual places: defense, prosecution, the twelve jurors and four alternates; finally, John and Fleeta, whose strength and beauty seemed to split the bulletproof glass. We reached out for one another.

It was difficult to concentrate on the facts at hand, so thoroughly was I haunted by the thought that I was free and they were still in chains. The circle had closed. As a free woman before, I had vowed to fight relentlessly for their freedom. John, Fleeta and George . . . This new freedom must be no different.

This is what I had planned to tell John during the meeting the lawyers had arranged for the lunch break. But I should have realized that things were moving along too smoothly. Upstairs in the holding area, the Chicano guard gave us the news. Unfortunately, he said, Judge Vauvaris had changed his mind. No meeting with John Clutchette.

My immense disappointment subsided slightly when I realized that John's cell was visible from the counter where I stood. The guard did not object when I called out to him, telling him to hold tight and keep strong; it was only a matter of time.

Downstairs a huge throng of people had gathered, and the press had been alerted to my presence. Conceivably, because of this the judge could construe my attendance at the Soledad Brothers' trial as a violation of the bail order. But at this point, that didn't matter very much. What mattered was that I reaffirm my commitment to the fight to free all political prisoners—first and foremost, the Soledad Brothers. It was important not only because it put me where I wanted to be—back in the struggle—but also because of the meaning it would have for all the sisters and brothers who had fought for my freedom. If I could not be satisfied with my freedom alone, they could not be satisfied either.

Walls turned sideways
are bridges

PART SIX

Bridges

*E*arly one Saturday morning during my first year at Brandeis, my friend Lani and I decided to hitchhike up north to see the fishing boats in Gloucester, Massachusetts. We had plans to stay the night. But since we knew no "adults" in Gloucester, we had to engage in a small transgression of the ridiculously puritanical rules governing the conduct of female students. Signing out of our dormitory, we indicated that we had permission from our parents to visit a family in New York, whose name and address we gave. (They were people who would know how to act if any checking was done.)

Gloucester was magnificent, with its multicolored autumnal trees, the massive beauty of its seaside boulders, its throng of ships and fishermen. For hours we walked along the coast, then we toured the little streets dating from the eighteenth century. Though we were practically moneyless, a nice man in a little restaurant gave us as much food as we could eat and wouldn't hear of letting us work off our meal.

When the sun's warmth began to fade away, we had to reconsider our original intention to sleep out on the beach. With no money, we could hardly think about checking into a motel, so we said good-bye to the friends we had made in the town and headed back down the highway with our thumbs as our only means of transportation.

It was late by the time we reached the campus in Waltham, later than the curfew hour for first-year female students. If we risked crossing the campus to Hamilton quadrangle, where our dorm was situated, we would probably be picked up by the security men and charged with curfew violation. Even if we weren't picked up during the run for it, it was very probable that we'd be caught as we tried to get into the dorm unnoticed.

Ridgewood—the men's dorms—were on the edge of the campus, right off the highway where our ride had dropped us. There wouldn't be much security around those dorms, so we decided to ask a friend to give up his room for the night. When we woke him, he was quite willing to find another bed and give us the two beds in his room for the night. The next morning we got up early and made it back to our rooms without incident.

Somehow—we never found out exactly how—word got back to the Dean of Women that we had "spent the night in the men's dorms." She called us in to say that we were going to have to stand trial before the women's tribunal. Lani and I were incredulous. This whole thing was absurd—stand trial before a group of upper-class women brainwashed into believing that because we were young women, what we had done was immoral. We had to appear before this tribunal or be expelled from the university—because we had simply wanted to enjoy the beauty of an autumn day, and had not allowed the rules to inhibit us.

In the bare, windowless room, Lani and I sat on one side of the long table. The members of the tribunal sat on the other side.

"Don't you know that you have marred the reputation of this university by accepting rides from strangers?"

We both looked with disgust at the student who pronounced these words. "Brandeis' reputation must really be marred," I retorted, "with all the hitchhiking that's done around here."

"Decent students do their hitchhiking on the campus, and not on strange roads."

A long contest followed, with the tribunal women hurling their invective at us, and Lani and me treating their words with the derision they merited.

As we knew when we walked into the room, the verdict was guilty, and the sentence was the maximum. For thirty days we were "dormed," meaning that we had to be in our rooms every day after dinner and remain there or give proof that we were studying in the library for the evening.

I never forgot the self-righteous condemnation of that tribunal. They were convinced they had a right to play God, master and mother. Since we refused to accept their way of life, we were "moral criminals" and they wanted to see us punished.

FEBRUARY 28

As the first potential jurors were brought into the courtroom, I thought back on that little mock trial which had unfolded more than a decade ago. I felt the same sense of unreality, the feeling that the same sort of game was being played, the contestants with the dangerously obsolete ideas having an unfair advantage.

But this was another game—more deadly. And the risks were far higher than thirty days in my bedroom.

On the desk directly in front of our table, a brown wooden raffle box is spun around. When it comes to a stop, the clerk reaches inside and pulls out a slip of paper. He reads the name carefully, pronouncing each syllable distinctly. People upstairs are watching and listening on a television monitor. Downstairs in the courtroom we are keenly conscious of the cameras and microphones transmitting our actions to that roomful of strange people corresponding to the names and numbers on our jury list.

Shortly after her name was called, Mrs. Marjorie Morgan appeared and took her seat in the witness box. Mrs. Marjorie Morgan, who described herself as the wife of a retired tractor shop owner. Mrs. Marjorie Morgan ... provincial and biased ... Mrs. Marjorie Morgan, who didn't hesitate to tell Leo, who was examining her, that she thought I was "probably guilty" of murder, kidnapping and conspiracy, and that I never should have been allowed to teach at UCLA. It was illegal and improper, she insisted, for Communists to teach at a university. The only decent trait she exhibited was her honesty about her inability to judge me fairly. The judge was thus forced to eliminate her from the panel.

The questioning of potential jurors—the voir dire—was divided into two parts. First the potential juror was asked about his or her exposure to publicity about me and the case. If the judge was satisfied that pretrial publicity had not created irreversible prejudice against me, then that person was temporarily seated in one of the twelve jury seats. When the jury box was full, the second stage of the voir dire began, during which we intensively questioned the potential jurors on a whole range of subjects. We attempted to draw out any hidden racist, pro-police or other biases which might surface as a result of evidence produced during the trial.

The next day an even bolder anti-Communist was examined. William Waugh, when asked about his attitude toward Communists, said that "if anyone wants to be a Communist, it seems they could go back where they come from." That, he admitted, included me as well—if I wanted to be a Communist, I should go back to where Communists are in power. But because he would not agree that this position would affect his ability to give me a fair trial if I were tried for something unrelated to communism, he was not unseated. For the time being, he remained on the panel.

But this was also the day when Mrs. Janie Hemphill was called in. Mrs. Hemphill was the only Black woman in the entire pool of potential jurors. A robust woman in her early forties, she pleasantly insisted that she could give me a fair trial. But before she even uttered a word, we were certain that Albert Harris, the prosecutor, would strike her from the panel at the earliest possible moment.

A few days later, when she was voir dired in depth, she poignantly described her background. I was so moved by what she said that I almost forgot that this was a part of the process of selecting a jury that might send me back to the other side of the walls. When Howard asked her about the jobs she had held, she took us back to Arizona, where she had picked cotton and cut onions at the age of twelve. "Later," she said, "I was a short-order cook. I went to Los Angeles and I worked as a short-order cook . . . And I also worked in a sandwich factory for those trucks that pass by . . . When I first came to San Jose, I did domestic work and I worked at Spivey's as a dish-washer."

As she spoke, she reminded me of my mother—her fight to get out of Good Water, Alabama, to get herself through high school and college doing all the odd jobs she could find. All this in order to finally get a job teaching in a little school.

Mrs. Hemphill's story was the universal story of the Black woman in a world that wants to see her crushed. Mrs. Hemphill had overcome. My mother had overcome. But many others had not. The system was poised against us. That was what had come through so powerfully in Mrs. Hemphill's words. My own present predicament was, on a different level, evidence of that same politically, economically, socially hostile world which almost every Black woman must contend with every day of her life.

On March 13, fifteen days after the jury selection had opened, Mrs. Hemphill was eliminated by one of the prosecution's peremptory challenges. She was the only Black person to have been questioned in the witness box. Court was adjourned.

The next day, March 14, we accepted the jury as constituted. It was not because we were satisfied with the people who sat in the box. By no means—after all, the only Black person had been eliminated by Harris. Yet, from our cursory investigation of the remainder of the jury venire, we were convinced that the combination of jurors we had on March 14 was probably better than anything else we could hope for. If we had continued to challenge those whom we felt were most prejudiced, then it was certain that Harris would challenge those whom we felt had the greatest inclinations toward fairness. They would be picked off one by one, as he had already picked off Janie Hemphill and the few others who did not seem totally prosecution-prone.

We were hoping that our instincts were correct about Mrs. Mary Timothy, whose son had been a conscientious objector to the Vietnam war. During the voir dire, she had come across as a fiercely independent person who, we thought, would know how to hold her own. If only she, and the few others we had been vaguely pleased with, would look at the evidence objectively and with intelligence, and would refuse to be swayed by the demagogic tricks of the prosecution, we could hope for a hung jury at least.

When the jury was sworn in on March 14, it included a woman whose presence on the panel had worried us from the very beginning. When Howard had examined her on the question of communism, she had said that Communists seek to obtain their goals "kind of by force."

"And when you say 'force,'" Howard asked, "what are you referring to? What do you mean?"

"Subversive," the woman answered, ". . . this type of thing. I really don't know . . ."

"Now, you say a 'subversive' type of thing. Could you tell us what a subversive type of thing is, in your opinion?"

"I can reduce it," she said, "to terms of my eleven-year-old, and that would be 'sneaky.'"

When Howard asked her how she would define "sneaky," she tried to explain her use of that word by saying, "I kind of reduced it to an oversimplification. I am just not that well educated. You read and hear about their activities, that they try to promote riots. I don't know this to be a fact. This is what we read in the paper."

Howard was convinced that she was putting on a show every time she tried to appear naïvely unaware of things and thus capable of being a fair juror. After all, she was the daughter of a retired sheriff's captain—a man who had spent over twenty-five years of his life in what Mrs. Titcomb termed "police work."

During the voir dire, Howard had asked her whether she had Black friends. She answered, "Oh, we had some very dear Black friends many years ago that moved away from this area. There is a family behind us that we are friends with."

Asked when she last had Blacks in her home as social guests, she responded, "Blacks in my home as social guests . . . My children have them in almost daily."

On March 14, she was sworn in, along with eleven other jurors. But, a few days after the swearing of the jury, she was relieved of her responsibilities. The spectators and the press were told that she was leaving because of "personal reasons." Few people ever heard the real story. Perhaps if the transcript had not been kept sealed, the media would not have been so quick to praise the U.S. court system for its guaranteed fairness to everyone.

It all started when the sketch and description of the jury appeared in the papers on the day following our acceptance of it. Judge Arnason's clerk said that a call came into his office that day from a person who identified herself as the juror's daughter. The clerk described her voice as hysterical—all she could say was "If my mother remains on the jury, God help Angela Davis."

The defense team and the prosecution had been urgently called into the judge's chambers to hear the account of this incident. What did we suggest be done? We insisted that the daughter be brought into chambers so that she could elaborate on her fears that her mother was out to get me.

She was pale, of slight build and appeared to be much younger than her eighteen years. It was apparent that she was not accustomed to such official surroundings. She seemed timid and a bit frightened. I wanted to ask her what it was that impelled her to take this great risk. Had she been reached in some way by the movement for my freedom? It could only have been this movement that had compelled her to become aware of her own individual political responsibility, even if it entailed an attack on her mother.

I could not help feeling sorry for her as she stared apprehensively at all the strange people sitting around the walls of the judge's chambers. Even the judge felt moved, and in a fatherly gesture, he walked over to her, placed his arm around her shoulder and told her gently that there was nothing to be frightened about.

When some of the terrible tension subsided, we were able to get down to the business of the session. Yes, she was certain that her mother would vote for a conviction, regardless of the evidence that was presented. Her mother had never liked Black people, and had told her daughter not to make friends with Black children. The one Black girl friend the daughter had had as a child could not visit her at her house—not only because her mother would not allow it, but also because the girl's parents would not let her be subjected to a woman who was known in the community for her anti-Black feelings. The daughter had cried on one of her birthdays because her friend could not attend.

After we had waded our way through the facts of this episode, the daughter began to relate, with not a small amount of confusion, a story about a Black boyfriend of hers, on whom her mother had spewed her vitriolic racism.

The second stage of this encounter involved a meeting with the juror where we confronted her with the accusations her daughter had made. Of course, she insisted that everything her daughter had said was a lie. She said that she and the daughter had never been able to get along—of all her children, this was the one she liked least.

What about the little Black girl friend her daughter had not been allowed to bring home as a child? The story was a fabrication, she insisted. Then, what about the Black boyfriend? Her daughter had told her she had been raped, according to the woman.

No, she had not lied during the voir dire. No, she would not voluntarily step down. She felt she had a right to serve on this jury, and she was determined to carry out her civic responsibilities.

This woman seemed ready to risk almost anything to stay on that jury and convict me. We threatened to bring her daughter back in to confront her face to face with the charges of racism. But she was more than willing to face up to her daughter. We had to go further. Was she prepared to listen to her daughter and all the other witnesses we could uncover make these accusations on the witness stand, before the court, the spectators, the press and the world? She reflected for a moment, and then decided that she would back out altogether. The world was a little more than she was willing to take on.

MARCH 27

When court recessed for lunch, Kendra and I were the last to leave. Suddenly Leo came rushing back into the courtroom shouting, "The Soledad Brothers were acquitted." We screamed, we hugged each other, we jumped up and down. "The Soledad Brothers are free." Our loud, unrestrained, joyous cries pealed through the empty courtroom.

I was laughing and crying with joy, but thinking also, Why not George? If only they had let him live a little while longer.

Relaxing in his chambers, Judge Arnason had heard our wild yells and had come rushing to the door. Looking somewhat frightened and probably fearing the worst, he asked in a soft voice whether something had happened. The three of us could only repeat what we had been screaming: "The Soledad Brothers were acquitted."

This was the opening day of the trial. Two autumns, two winters, two springs had already been consumed by the preliminary skirmishes. Now, at last, we had moved into the final, decisive contest. And the exoneration of John and Fleeta was like an omen portending our future victory.

This victory would confirm one of the fundamental elements of my defense: the political character of my involvement in the movement to defend the Soledad Brothers and the strategy of developing mass protests and mass resistance to the persecution of the Brothers.

Harris had attempted to work up the jury with an absurd theory of my having been impelled to commit murder, kidnapping and conspiracy by my "boundless and all-consuming passion" for George. By purging his case of the original political accusations, the prosecutor thought he was being shrewd. In the indictment, the first "overt act" of the "conspiracy" had been my participation in a rally on June 19, 1970, for the immediate freedom of the Soledad Brothers. Policemen had testified before the Grand Jury that I had advocated the release of the Soledad Brothers, at this rally, as well as in other meetings and assemblies. Now, because so many people accepted the idea that I was a political prisoner, the prosecution was on the defensive. Harris was undoubtedly afraid to use the key evidence he had initially relied upon. This was the impact of the mass campaign, the central theme of which was the repressive, political character of the prosecution.

"There will be no evidence offered by the prosecution over the next few weeks," he insisted before the jury, "of the exercise by the defendant of her right of free speech and assembly under the First Amendment, except for certain letters that she wrote. You will be satisfied that the case of the prosecution does not rest in any degree whatever upon the nature of the political views of the defendant, whatever they may be.

"The evidence will show that the claim of political persecution, the claim that the defendant is a political prisoner, the claim that the defendant is the subject of prosecution because of her political beliefs—all of these claims are false and without foundation."

But if he weeded out the "political evidence," the prosecutor had to build another framework for the case. This new framework was based on the motive of passion. I simply wanted to liberate, he said, a man whom I loved.

Throughout his opening statement, although he was diligently trying to make political considerations seem totally irrelevant to the case, politics kept creeping back in. "This morning," he said, "you heard of evidence through her books that this teacher of philosophy is a student of violence. [He was referring to two books, *The Politics of Violence* and *Violence and Social Change*.] Other evidence that we will present will show the defendant does not live only in the world of books and ideas, but that she is committed to action, that she is committed to violence."

But then, he tried to backtrack: "Her own words will reveal that beneath the cool academic veneer is a woman fully capable of being moved to violence by passion. The evidence will show that her basic motive was not to free political prisoners, but to free the one prisoner that she loved. The basic motive for the crime was the same motive underlying hundreds of criminal cases across the United States every day. That motive was not abstract. It was not founded basically on any need, real or imagined, for prison reform. It was not founded on a desire for social justice. It was founded simply on the passion that she felt for George Jackson. . . ."

On the second day of the trial we had our chance to attack the prosecution's case. Since we had decided a few days before that I would deliver the opening statement to the jury, I had spent every moment of the last days discussing it with the lawyers and preparing my notes. Now I felt certain that we could tear the prosecution's case to pieces.

Our weapons were together. Our legal team was in good

shape—Howard, Margaret, Leo, Dobby and myself. The mass movement had unprecedented global strength. Fania, Franklin, Charlene, Kendra, Rob, Victoria, Phyllis, Stephanie, Bettina and the others on the staff were accomplished organizers. They were preparing to steer the movement across the finish line. Besides, this new twist, this new theory of passion that Harris had propounded, left the state's case even shoddier, if that were possible, than it had been in the beginning. This was a last-ditch approach to the trial, developed and elaborated when it became clear that the political case would simply not be accepted.

On this second day of the trial, as Victoria and Rodney Barnett, who were in charge of my personal security, drove with me through the unfamiliar San Jose streets, my thoughts were totally absorbed by the task I thought I would soon be carrying out.

As we neared the Santa Clara Civic Center, we noticed an unusually large crowd milling around the building. Armed sheriff's deputies were running around the yard. Others were posted atop the roofs of the Civic Center buildings.

Ignorant of what the commotion was all about, I thought that whatever it was that was going down, it must be a part of the larger conspiracy to send me to prison for life. Every day, people entering the courtroom—spectators, press people, we ourselves, and even the jurors—had to submit to metal detectors, humiliating frisks, and for the audience and the press, cameras which took mug shots of them. Now the whole area was occupied by deputies toting shotguns, rifles and machine guns.

Looking around the yard, I saw some of the jurors sitting on the municipal court steps, and others on the benches on the opposite side of the yard. Someone said there was an escape attempt in progress, involving prisoners in the men's county jail located in the same complex of buildings as the courthouse.

The sheriff's deputy guarding the back entrance, where the lawyers entered the courtroom, refused to let me through.

The building was under emergency security measures, he said, and no one could leave or enter. We discovered later that the press people had been locked in the pressroom, the spectators had been locked in the corridor outside the courtroom, and a few jurors who had already entered the building were locked up in the jury room.

When the judge rescinded the security measures for the participants in the trial, and we all gathered in the courtroom, he announced that the trial would be adjourned until the next morning and immediately dismissed the jurors for the day.

Apparently three men being held in the county jail while they waited to be transferred to various prison facilities had decided to make a run for freedom. They had taken hostages and had attempted to negotiate their release. But, as if they were following the example of the San Quentin guards, the sheriff's deputies moved at the first clear moment to shoot their way out of the negotiations. The person who had been considered the leader of the effort was killed, and the other two were captured.

The evening papers carried headlines like JAIL ESCAPE TRY AT ANGELA TRIAL SITE. And a number of articles contained lengthy comparisons between this incident and the August 7 revolt. Whether it was planned this way or not, the suggestion planted in the minds of many who read the accounts was that we had something to do with the escape attempt.

This episode, which came before we had even had a chance to present our case to the jury, raised some very difficult questions for us. On the one hand, the only way to ensure that I would not be judged by a jury with prejudices grown sharper from their experience of the escape attempt would be to move at once for a mistrial. But on the other hand, if we did move for and were granted a mistrial, then the jury selection process would start from scratch again. Since we felt we had already picked the very best jury Santa Clara could offer, a new jury could only be worse.

The defense team and the campaign organizers met throughout the evening before we finally agreed upon a definitive position: a brief voir dire of the jurors to determine whether they had become more biased against me as a result of the escape attempt they had witnessed.

The next day, at the conclusion of the individual examinations of the jurors, we decided that the damage was not irreparable. We would move on with the trial.

The podium was behind the prosecutor's table and slightly to the left. Arranging my notes, preparing to begin our statement, I could see Harris squirming in his seat.

"The prosecutor," I said to them, "has introduced you to a very long and complicated path down which he hopes his evidence will lead you in the course of this trial. He says that this path will point squarely in the direction of my guilt. He says that his evidence is so conclusive that it will eliminate every doubt in your minds with respect to my guilt, and that you will have no choice but to convict me of these very serious crimes of murder, kidnapping and conspiracy.

"But we say to you, members of the jury, that the prosecutor's evidence itself will demonstrate to you that this case is no case at all. The evidence will show that I am totally innocent of all the charges against me. It will reveal that the prosecutor's case is entirely without substance. It will reveal that his case is based on conjecture, guesswork, speculation . . .

"The prosecutor began on Monday by telling you that this case against me, basically, is a case involving the crime of passion. He said that my passion for George Jackson was so great that it knew no bounds, that it had no respect for human life.

"He went on to say later in the statement that I was not concerned with the struggle to free political prisoners, that I was not concerned with the movement to improve the character of prison life in this country. He told you that he intends to prove that I was exclusively interested in the freedom of one man, of George Jackson, and that that interest was motivated by pure passion.

"Members of the jury . . . the evidence will show that when I was indicted, the Grand Jury of Marin County considered evidence of my participation in the movement to free the Soledad Brothers, not only George Jackson, but also Fleeta Drumgo and John Clutchette.

"The evidence will show that the first overt act of the conspiracy count consists of a description of a rally in which I participated, around the freedom of the Soledad Brothers. On June 19, 1970, I was exercising constitutionally guaranteed rights—rights guaranteed to me by the First Amendment—when I participated in this rally which dealt with the persecution of the Soledad Brothers, with other political prisoners, and prison conditions in general. Yet, this was supposed to be the first overt act of a conspiracy to free the Soledad Brothers, through the events of August seventh.

"The evidence will show, members of the jury, that this indictment provoked widespread concern, concern throughout the world, that I was a victim of political repression. I ask you whether or not it would not be reasonable to infer that the prosecutor is aware that no fair-minded juror would convict me on the basis of such evidence. Therefore, he has said to you that he will present no evidence of my participation in the struggle to free the Soledad Brothers. What he has done is that he has transformed the character of this case.

"Now he will have you believe that I am a person who would commit the crimes of murder, kidnapping and conspiracy, having been motivated by pure passion. He would have you believe that lurking behind my external appearance are sinister and selfish emotions and passions which, in his words, know no bounds.

"Members of the jury, this is utterly fantastic. It is utterly absurd. Yet it is understandable that Mr. Harris would like to take advantage of the fact that I am a woman, for in this society women are supposed to act only in accordance with the dictates of their emotions and passions. I might say that this is clearly a symptom of the male chauvinism which prevails in our society."

I had not realized that these remarks would strike such a responsive chord in a number of the women jurors. I tried throughout my statement to watch the jury closely for its responses. As I spoke about the male supremacist character of Harris' case, heads nodded and receptive expressions broke out on some of the female faces. They too had known the experience of being accused because they were women of acting irrationally and according to emotions rather than logic.

"The evidence will show," I continued, "that my involvement in the movement to free the Soledad Brothers began long before I had any personal contact with George Jackson. You will learn that shortly after Fleeta Drumgo, John Clutchette and George Jackson were indicted by a Monterey County Grand Jury . . . I began to attend public meetings designed to lay the basis for a movement to publicly defend them from the unfounded charges that they had killed a guard behind the walls of Soledad Prison . . .

"The evidence will show that my own efforts to free George Jackson always expressed themselves within the context of a movement to free all the Soledad Brothers and to free all men and women who are unjustly imprisoned."

Describing the Soledad Brothers Defense Committee, I told the jury that ". . . our meetings were open to anyone who wanted to participate in them . . . We organized demonstrations, rallies, leafleting campaigns and various other informational and educational activities. . . .

"Members of the jury, you will see when testimony is adduced to this effect, that we sought out those kinds of activities which permitted us to involve ever greater numbers of people in the public defense of the Soledad Brothers."

And emphasizing what we felt would be the critical element of our defense, I told them that "testimony will make it clear that we felt that the influence of large numbers of people would help win them an acquittal and that they would be freed in that way from an unjust prosecution.

"Members of the jury, we were correct in our understanding of the Soledad Brothers' case, for Monday morning as you sat here listening to the prosecution's opening statement, and as you heard that I was not interested in furthering the movement to free the Soledad Brothers, the ultimate fruits of our labor were attained. The twelve men and women who, for a period of many, many months had listened to all the evidence that the prosecution could muster against the Soledad Brothers, ended up, in the courtroom in San Francisco, by pronouncing the two surviving Soledad Brothers not guilty. And if George Jackson had not been struck down by a San Quentin Prison guard in August of last year, he too would have been freed in that way from that unjust prosecution."

I continued the statement by describing in detail the activities of the Soledad Defense Committee, and placing them in the framework of my experiences in the struggle for Black Liberation and for the rights of all working people—Chicano, Puerto Rican, Indian, Asian and white. I spoke about my experiences in the Black Student Council at the university in San Diego, the Black Student Alliance, the Black Congress, SNCC, the California Teachers Federation, the Black Panther Party, the Che-Lumumba Club and the antiwar movement.

I tried to show the jury how my activities around the defense of the Soledad Brothers were part of a history of involvement in the movement to defend and free political prisoners such as Huey Newton, the New York Panther 21, Bobby Seale and Ericka Huggins, the Los Angeles Panther 18 and the seven other brothers from Soledad Prison also charged with killing a guard.

"The evidence will show," I told them, "that I corresponded with the Soledad 7, and that I expressed to them my love and my compassion and my solidarity with their struggle. . . .

"The prosecutor has said that this trial has nothing to do with a political frame-up, but, members of the jury, during the entire time I was involved in the movement to free the Soledad Brothers, I was the object of an extensive spy campaign. The prosecutor himself is in possession of numerous reports made to various police agencies throughout the state of California about my activities on behalf of the Soledad Brothers. He has police reports on rallies where I spoke. He has films of demonstrations where I and others proclaimed our support for the Soledad Brothers.

"The prosecutor contends that I was not interested in bringing about prison reform, but he has in his possession police reports made specifically for the administration at Soledad Prison concerning my activities.

"The prosecutor contends that, during the period prior to August 7, I was a mere creature of passion, that I was not genuinely striving toward the elimination of repression in the prisons, but he has evidence that will refute his own contentions, evidence gathered by an entire network of police spies and spies from the Department of Corrections on the content of my political efforts to free George Jackson, Fleeta Drumgo and John Clutchette.

"But, members of the jury, he has told you that you will not see this evidence. He will present no evidence of that sort. He will present no such evidence because, if he did, it would show you the process whereby an innocent person can be set up and accused of outrageous crimes. No, he will not bring this evidence to you. He will continue to tell you that I am not the person you see standing before you, but rather an evil, sinister creature pushed to the brink of disaster by ungovernable emotions and passions."

When the time came to deal with my relationship with Jonathan, I placed it within the context of the relationships I had developed with the families of all three Brothers. Referring to the Soledad Brothers Defense Committee, I told the jury that "Jonathan Jackson was a unique part of our group, for he brought with him the angry frustrations and concerns of a young man who had no memories of his older brother except those which had been obscured by prison bars. Jonathan was a child of seven when his brother was first taken to prison, and for ten long years he accompanied various members of his family to various prisons throughout the state of California to visit with his brother.

"These visits must have left an indelible impression on him about what a prisoner's life was like, and I know, though he was only seventeen years old, he must have been extremely and intimately sensitive to the plight, the frustrations, the feelings of depression and futility that men like James McClain, Ruchell Magee and William Christmas must have felt. And I might say that now, in retrospect, I understand the frustration, the very deep frustration and the very deep desperation that Jonathan must have been experiencing."

Next I moved on to the question of the guns and the other physical evidence which Harris was using to try to prove that I was guilty. I touched upon the facts which we did not contest:

"This is a sick kind of game which the prosecutor has been playing. He has invented a scheme, a diagram, a conspiracy, and then he fits his conspirator, his criminal into that picture. There is a crime scene, a plan. And he seeks ways of pulling me into it so that it still appears plausible. But since I committed no crimes and since all my activities were open and above board, the prosecutor is left with only one alternative. He must shape his circumstantial case out of the ordinary circumstances of everyday life. And he leaves it to you, members of the jury, to supply the missing link which converts ordinary activity into criminal conduct."

After two hours of explaining the outlines of our defense to the jury, I felt confident enough to tell them:

". . . We have reached the conclusion of our opening statement, and we ask you to think toward the conclusion of this trial, when you will have sat patiently, almost to the point of exhaustion, and will have heard all sides of the heated contest which is to unfold in this courtroom, when you will have sat in calm reflection and deliberation. We have the utmost confidence that your verdict will be a just verdict. We have the utmost confidence that your verdict will be the only verdict that the evidence and justice demand in this case. We are confident that the case will terminate with your pronouncement of two words—'*Not Guilty.*'"

Of course, we were not nearly so certain as I had made it appear, for we knew that some of the jurors were probably more prosecution-prone than objective judges of fact. The legal team had observed them meticulously during both the state's presentation and our own. A couple of them seemed far more engrossed in the story the prosecution had concocted than in the defense I had presented. Yet at the same time, we thought that a number of them, such as Ralph Delange, the maintenance electrician, and Mary Timothy, had listened very carefully to the analysis I had proposed.

At the end of my statement, I was exhausted and kept wondering whether I had said the right things in the right way. The outline I had given them was going to have to serve as the background against which they would judge months of prosecution testimony. (Harris said, at first, that his case would last six months.) Had I put it forcefully enough for them to retain our analysis of the facts—or would they remember only the neat little scheme the prosecutor had provided? There would be no more argument until the very end of the trial and the conclusion was so far away.

Coolly and calmly, Judge Arnason assumed control over the courtroom. "Thank you, Miss Davis. Before we proceed with the calling of the first witness, we will take a recess at this time, and this will hopefully be the regular recess of the afternoon, so we will give you a little break time. Thank you."

Testimony began. The prosecution called to the stand several women who, on August 7, 1970, had been listening to Ruchell Magee testify on behalf of James McClain when Jonathan came into the courtroom. Harris was visibly stunned when one of the women described McClain's manner as "almost gentle."

Harris presented to the jury horrifying, bloody photographs, in poster-sized enlargements. It was only because of Judge Arnason's sense of propriety that the prosecutor did not succeed in entering into evidence the pictures of Judge Haley with half his head blown off by a shotgun blast.

I had to close my eyes and keep my anguish and rage to myself when he brought out the photographs of Jonathan lying dead inside the van, and on the cement where he had been dragged with a rope.

During the first phase of the testimony, the prosecutor had strategically decided to avoid all mention of my name. He simply wanted to establish what had happened at each instant as the rebellion had unfolded.

We used our cross-examination to defend Jonathan, Ruchell, McClain and Christmas, to refute Harris' allegations that they were brutal terrorists. Already this early in the trial, his theories began to erode, both because of their internal defectiveness and as a result of our attacks during cross-examination.

He could not prove, for example, definitively—"beyond a reasonable doubt," in judicial parlance—that there had been a demand advanced to "free the Soledad Brothers." We pursued this because Ruchell had written in a publicized letter to me that the plan had been totally different—it had not been to hold hostages until the Soledad Brothers, or any other prisoners, were freed. It had not even been to guarantee their own escape. They wanted simply to reach a radio station, Ruchell said, where they could expose to the world the railroads so many of them had received instead of trials, the incredibly wretched conditions of their existence behind walls and, in particular, the recent murder by San Quentin guards of a prisoner named Fred Billingslea.

Many of the witnesses who had been on the scene in the courtroom had not heard "Free the Soledad Brothers." Others heard no demand at all. Some had heard "Free the brothers at Folsom." Captain Teague—the same Captain Teague who had overseen all the operations around me when I was in the Marin jail—was certain he had heard "Free all political prisoners," but he admitted that this was a slogan widely used at rallies and demonstrations of the Left, and could have very well been an exclamation as opposed to a ransom demand. Sheriff Montanas of Marin County, according to the theory of the prosecution, had received a telephone call from McClain from the courtroom. It was during this phone conversation that McClain is supposed to have demanded the freedom of the Soledad Brothers in exchange for the hostages. Naturally, everyone was expecting the sheriff to relate this conversation to the jury from the witness stand. Yet Montanas never testified for the prosecution.

This is not to say that plenty of his coworkers did not take the stand—and not only sheriff's deputies from Marin County (many of whom had been assigned to guard me in the Marin jail), but also cops from all the cities in the area—San Rafael, Novota—not to mention the San Quentin guards.

Harris tried to recreate with mathematical precision every single instant of the incident. He became so involved in minutiae—who was standing at what point when, and for how many seconds—that he did not even realize that his interminable procession of witnesses grew tedious and began visibly to bore some of the jurors.

When Sergeant Murphy from San Quentin testified, Leo cross-examined him on the policy of the prison regarding escapes.

"And to be certain I understand the significance of that policy, sir, does that policy mean that if people are attempting to escape, and if they have hostages, and if the guards are able to prevent that escape, that they are to prevent that escape even if it means that every hostage is killed?"

Sergeant Murphy's emotionless answer: "That is correct."

"And that means, whether they are holding one judge or five judges, or one woman or twenty women or one child or twenty children, that the policy of the San Quentin guards is that, at all costs, they must prevent the escape. Is that right?"

"That also includes the officers that work in the institution, sir."

"All right. Even if they are holding other officers who work at the institution, that should not deter the San Quentin correctional officers from preventing an escape at all costs. Is that right?"

"That is correct."

"In other words, it is more important to prevent the escape than to save human life. Is that correct?"

"Yes, sir."

The courtroom was on tenterhooks. Jurors, press and spectators waited anxiously, intensely, for the prosecutor to reach the critical passage in my letter to George. But he went on and on, his monotonic words falling flatly on the otherwise unbroken silence of the hall.

" 'To choose between various paths of survival means the objective availability of alternatives. I hope you don't take this as an apologetic stance. I'm only trying to understand the forces that have led us, Black women, to where we are now. Why did your mother offer you reprimands instead of the flaming sword? Which is equivalent to posing the same question about every other Black woman—and not only with respect to the sons, but the daughters, too (this is really crucial). In Cuba last summer I saw some very beautiful Vietnamese warriors—all female. And we know that the Algerian war for national liberation would have been doomed to defeat from the very beginning without the active participation of Algerian women. In Cuba, I saw women patrolling the streets with rifles on their backs—defending the revolution. But also young *compañeras* educating their husbands and lovers—demythologizing *machismo*. After all, if women can fight, manage factories, then men ought to be able to help with the house, children . . .

" 'But returning to the question: We have learned from our revolutionary ancestors that no individual act or response can seize the scepter of the enemy. The slave lashes out against his immediate master, subdues him, escapes, but he has done nothing more than take the first step in the long spiral upwards towards liberation.

I could see the beads of perspiration rolling down Albert Harris' face as he struggled to read my letter to George before the jury. Often, his reading reminded me of that of a child who knows how to pronounce the syllables, but is unaware of the sense of what he is reading.

" 'And often that individual escape is an evasion of the real problem.' "

Harris read the last sentence as if he were noticing it for the first time. As if he were realizing that my words offered no proof whatever of my participation in the August 7 rebellion; that, on the contrary, they tended to exonerate me from the crimes he had charged me with. Although it appeared as if he wanted to be done with it and throw the whole bunch of letters away, he could not stop. He continued, monotonously, falteringly.

" 'It is only when all the slaves are aroused from their slumber, articulate their goals, choose their leaders, make an unwavering commitment to destroy every single obstacle which might prevent them from transcribing their visions of a new world onto the soil of the earth, into the flesh and blood of men . . .

" 'A mother cannot help but cry out for the survival of her own flesh and blood.' "

Harris read this as if he were a foreign student of English repeating a sentence uttered by the teacher. I looked into the jury box. A few of the women, particularly Mrs. Timothy, seemed to be straining to understand his motive in reading these passages.

" 'We have been forbidden to reach out for the truth about survival—that it is a collective enterprise and must be offensive, rather than defensive—for us, the principle of survival dictates the annihilation of all that compels us to order our lives around that principle.' "

He pronounced "annihilation" with extra emphasis, as

was the case with every word which he thought had something to do with violence.

" 'Anxieties, frustrations engendered by the specter of a child dead of starvation focus our minds and bodies on the most immediate necessities of life. The "job" harangue, the "make yourself something" harangue. Exhortations grounded in fear, a fear brought into being and sustained by a system which could not subsist without the poor, the reserve army of unemployed, the scapegoat.

" 'Survival instincts perverted and misdirected by a structure which coerces me to kick my jobless man out of the house so the social worker doesn't stop those welfare checks which I need to feed my hungry child.' "

He rushed through this sentence in order to make it as unobtrusive as possible.

" 'A labyrinthine network of murderous institutions in order to allow my man no flexibility, no room, lets me receive the checks, lets me in the back door to scrub floors (so the reserve labor force remains alive) and has the audacity to consider that a favor in return for which I must submit to the white rapist and/or subjugate my Black man. The principle of (un)Just Exchange is omnipotent.' "

Harris pulled out his wrinkled white handkerchief and wiped the sweat from his face. This pause was obviously deliberate. He was about to read the section he felt was most incriminating of all. It was as if by setting this passage off with a pause, he could make the jury forget all the other ideas expressed in the letter and focus their attention and their memories exclusively on these things.

" 'Frustrations, aggressions cannot be repressed indefinitely. Eventual explosion must be expected. But if the revolutionary path is buried beneath an avalanche of containment mechanisms, we, Black women, aim our bullets in the wrong direction and moreover, we don't even understand the weapon.

" 'For the Black female, the solution is not to become less aggressive, not to lay down the gun, but to learn how to set the sights correctly, aim accurately, squeeze rather than jerk and not be overcome by the damage. We have to learn how to rejoice when pigs' blood is spilled.'"

Harris had spoken slowly, with all the determination and drama he could muster.

I hoped that the jury was not as unintelligent as he counted on their being. Some of them must have heard of metaphor.

Harris reverted to his previous monotone.

"'But all this presupposes that the Black male will have purged himself of the myth that his mother, his woman, must be subdued before *he* can wage war on the enemy. Liberation is a dialectical movement—the Black man cannot free himself as a Black man unless the Black woman can liberate herself from all this muck—and it works the other way around. And this is *only* the beginning.

"'Is it coincidental that Leroi Jones and Ron Karenga and the whole lot of cowardly cultural nationalists demand the total submission of the Black female as rectification for the "century-long wrongs she has done the Black Male." Like you said, George, there are certain obvious criteria for measuring the extent to which counter-revolution is being nourished by those who call themselves our companions in struggle. Their attitude toward whites is one criterion. Their attitude toward women, another.'"

I thought that Harris wanted to steer the jury's attention away from my criticism of the indiscriminately anti-white nationalists in the movement. He was depending on them to instinctively associate me with the anti-white wing of the Black Liberation Movement, and thus to be reinforced in their already existing political biases.

"'Women's liberation in the revolution is inseparable from the liberation of the male.'"

He read this last sentence as if it had no apparent meaning.

"'I have rambled. I hope I have not been talking in tautologies.'"

Here, he had recourse to the same intentional pause as

before. The last part of the letter was what he wanted to read most dramatically, most emphatically. This is what he wanted them to retain.

" 'Jon and I have made a truce. As long as I try to combat my tendencies to remind him of his youth, he will try to combat his male chauvinism. Don't come down on me before you understand—I never said Jon was too young for anything, I just mentioned how incredible it is that in spite of Catholic school, etc., he refused to allow society to entrap him in adolescence. But still, he doesn't dig any mention of age.' "

The words had rung out strangely when Harris had tried to project his voice: " 'I never said Jon was too young for *anything* . . .' " This phrase, which I had casually scratched down on paper, this phrase, with which I meant to tell George that I knew how much he loved and respected his brother, this phrase, Harris wanted to utilize as a virtual confirmation of his conspiracy theory. But he had just started; there was still more:

" 'The night after I saw you in court, for the first time in months, I dreamt (or at least the dream was significant enough to work its way into my consciousness) we were together, fighting pigs, winning. We were learning to know each other.' "

It was as if Harris wanted the jury to think that I was so wrapped up in this so-called conspiracy that I conspired even in my dreams.

" 'I love you. Revolutionary Greetings from Che-Lumumba and the Soledad Brothers Defense Committee. Angela.' "

When Harris reached the end of the letter, he inhaled deeply and allowed a tremendous sigh to escape. He did not display the confidence which one would have expected from a prosecutor who has just presented critical portions of his evidence. On the contrary, his demeanor seemed to bespeak a profound sense of defeat. And his sigh was a sigh of relief—as if he never thought he would reach the end of this letter he had been forced to recite like a schoolboy.

The ambivalence I felt was disarming. On the one hand,

seeing the letter as evidence, I had the impulse to proclaim once more the utter bankruptcy of the state's case—it was with this kind of evidence that they had kept me in jail for those sixteen months. But on the other hand, I felt depressed at having to see my most intimate feelings hurled out into the public like that through the calculating and cold presentation of the prosecutor. And the unmitigated grief was revived, the grief at Jon's death, the grief at George's death, and the burning anger at their murderers. I couldn't cry, I couldn't scream. I had to sit there at the counsel table, waiting for the next piece of evidence which the prosecutor was going to use to try to convince the jury of my guilt.

One of the next witnesses to take the stand was Mrs. Otelia Young. A Black woman, about sixty years of age, she was rather short, and her back was bent as if from decades of hard labor. But she approached the stand with firm, determined steps. Her face, although not quite in a frown, revealed an almost angry seriousness. I wondered whether people were interpreting this determination, this seriousness, as being directed against me; the jurors looked puzzled.

Mrs. Young had lived in the flat downstairs from me in the house on 35th Place. We had exchanged greetings numerous times, and I had used the telephone in her apartment on several occasions. I had liked her a lot—there was a vitality about her that was obviously the secret of her survival. The sparkle in her eyes and her pleasantly caustic sense of humor had made me want to pursue a more than casual friendship with her. But there had been no time.

She had seen Jonathan at the house a few times, and they had hit it off quite well, both of them enjoying the subdued game of dozens they played. With unmistakable affection, Jon would say, "How are you doing, you old hag?" And before he had a chance to catch his breath, she would retaliate with "What have you been up to, you crazy yellow-haired brat?" And they would go on.

Now she was being asked by the state to testify against me.

Harris was trying to set the stage for his conspiracy theory. By his usual method of trying to convert everything I had done in the period prior to the Marin rebellion into conspiratorial activity, he was going to attempt to prove—so he said in his opening remarks—that I had obtained the 35th Place flat expressly for the purpose of conspiring with Jonathan, who, he said, had also moved into the place. He was calling Mrs. Otelia Young to prove his hypothesis.

Yes, she said, she had seen Jonathan Jackson at the house on 35th Place. Had he been there often? No, not often, just a few times. Had she seen me moving into the flat, bringing my things in a white station wagon? Yes, she said, she had seen the station wagon. Was Jonathan with me when I moved in— had he moved the things upstairs? No, the station wagon was full of books, and I carried them all up alone.

Bewildered expressions were all over the courtroom. We could tell that the jurors were wondering why Harris had bothered to call Mrs. Young to the stand at all. We had already figured that he would call all the Black people he could muster—almost regardless of what they would say. A racist ploy—based on the idea that jurors would think twice about my innocence if Black people were acting as state's witnesses. But obviously Mrs. Young's testimony had backfired.

One thing that stood out particularly was her answer to Harris' question regarding her employment status.

"Do you spend a good deal of time at work?"

"Yes, I work—I work from seven o'clock in the morning to eight o'clock, eight-thirty at night." She spoke angrily and from deep down in her throat, sending her words thundering across the courtroom. Everyone understood immediately that she was a domestic worker in some white family's household, doing its drudgery every day from breakfast time to dinner time. I wondered whether some of the jurors thought back to what I had written George about Black women. Did they realize that I had been writing about Otelia Young and all her sisters in the struggle for survival?

It was apparent that Harris had interrupted the examination without having brought it to a conclusion. He had been the aggressor in this duel, but he could not summon up the courage to fight it out to the end.

There was no need for us to cross-examine, so Mrs. Young stepped down from the stand as proudly as she had walked up to it. Her eyes were aimed directly in front of her—toward the door in the back of the courtroom. It was therefore startling to us all when she reached the railing and abruptly turned in my direction to give me an immense, almost extravagant, smile. With the old sparkle back in her eyes, she greeted me with an affectionate, prolonged "Hi," and waved her hand the way one waves at little children.

March had been rapidly consumed by our efforts to pick a jury that would penetrate the smoke screen of the scores of witnesses the state was calling. (Their original list had included over four hundred.) Now there was nothing left of April.

I had long since forgotten how to relax; though I could never become really settled in the mode of existence imposed upon us, there was something very frightening about the way the trial developed a life of its own—a life that was devouring our lives. Monday through Thursday, Margaret and I would rush out of the house for our nine-fifteen appointment with the judge, jury and prosecutor, as if we were running off to a job or trying to make it to classes. On Fridays, I had to report to the Santa Clara County Probation Department so that they could be sure that I had not jumped bail.

Saturdays and Sundays were our meeting days—days on which we evaluated our legal positions, days of criticism, self-criticism, arguments, and finally collective agreement on what was to be our courtroom posture for the coming week. Then there were meetings with the staff of the Defense Committee, where ideas for mass dissemination of trial literature were aired and formulated, where demonstrations and rallies were planned, where the global defense effort was coordinated with the events unfolding inside the courtroom.

But it was not only my life that had been appropriated by

this case. Margaret, Howard, Leo, Dobby—they worked incessantly. Charlene, Kendra, Franklin, Fania, Bettina, Stephanie, Rob, Victoria, Rodney, and all the other leaders of the mass campaign had ordered their lives entirely around building the movement. Even on the day Fania's baby was born, she had spent a few hours at the jail discussing the campaign with me. Several months later, she asked Mother to keep Eisa with her in Birmingham so that all her time could be devoted to organizing. When Mother traveled around the country and through Canada, appealing to people to support me and all political prisoners, she carried Eisa around with her in her arms.

On May 4, one of the prosecution's star witnesses told the story the prosecution hoped would convince the jury, definitively, of my guilt. Alden Flemming, a plump, pink-complexioned man whose clothes sort of hung off him, was the owner of a service station situated at the foot of one of the entrances to the Marin County Civic Center. He testified that he had seen me with Jonathan at his service station on August 6, the day before the revolt. Cross-examination revealed that he had originally identified me from a group of photographs so carefully selected as to leave him no other choice. The group included several mug shots of straight-haired Black women with their names written across the photos. There was a picture each of Fania, Penny Jackson, Georgia Jackson, and about six or seven shots of me, all taken during the highly publicized June 19 Soledad rally, which was also the day I was fired from my UCLA position. In some of the photos I am speaking into a microphone, and one of them even showed Jonathan walking at my side. No one could have failed to miss the point—Flemming was being asked to identify Angela Davis.

In court, he not only identified all of my pictures in the group, he pointed to my sister Fania as well and said he wasn't quite sure, but he thought that the picture of Penny Jackson might also be me. When Leo asked him about his experiences in relating to Black people, he hastily informed us that 20 percent of his customers were Black—which seemed incredible in a county whose population was barely 3 percent Black.

"Do you have any experience in having seen Black women with Afro hair styles?" Leo asked.

"Yes."

"Have you seen them many times in your life?"

"Since it has been popular."

"All right, and how long would you say that the Afro hair style has been a popular hair style for Black women?"

"Oh, maybe seven years."

"And I take it that during that period of time you have seen many Black women wearing Afro hair styles? Would that be a fair statement?"

"Twenty percent of the people that come into my station."

"You mean all of the people that come into your station wear Afro hair styles?"

"I would say fifteen of the twenty percent."

"So you have seen an awful lot of Black women with Afro hair styles?"

"Right."

Then Leo pursued another line.

"How many light-complexioned Black people have you had the experience of seeing in your lifetime?"

"As fair as this lady is, I would say not more than ten."

(Any Black person or anyone who has spent any time around Black people would know that if 20 percent of his customers were really Black, he would have seen a great number of people with skin as light as mine, and many with much lighter skin.)

"Is that one of the things that helped you identify her?"

"Yes."

"Anything else?"

"Her features."

And when Leo asked him to be more specific in describing what it was that was outstanding about my features, he said:

"Well, she has, I would say, large eyes. The cheek bones are higher. I wouldn't say she has as strong a face, as heavy a face as what colored people have."

Then Leo asked the inevitable question, mockingly, pronouncing "colored people" with Flemming's own accent.

"Is there a certain kind of face that 'colored people,' in your opinion, usually have?"

After stammering a bit, Flemming finally said, "Well, I would say the ones I have dealt with, their faces are flatter, and that is about it."

"Faces are flatter?"

"Yes."

"And Miss Davis' face was not flat, and that made her unusual. Is that right?"

"Well, I—I don't think she has a flat face."

Leo looked Flemming in the eye, allowed a noticeable pause to intervene, then said, "Mr. Flemming, don't you think that all colored people look alike?"

And, as if he were definitively proving his veracity before the jury, he answered without hesitation, "Not in Miss Davis' case."

It was clear that this man's attitudes were so permeated with racism that he would be unable to make an honest identification of a Black person even if his life depended on it. The results of our cross-examination were never published in the established press—what received all the publicity was the direct examination by Harris, the scenario of which, we believed, had been perfected and rehearsed beforehand.

The jury appeared to be impressed by a bit of Perry Mason dramatics that Howard came up with. Unbeknownst to me, he had asked Kendra a week before to drive him out to Marin, where they stopped in the Flemming Service Station. As he was permitted to do with any of the prosecutor's witnesses, he questioned Flemming about the content of the statement he had given the attorney general. Before they left, however, Kendra got out of the car, asked Flemming to check the oil, and, making herself as obvious as she could, she engaged him in a bit of casual conversation.

It came as a surprise to me when Leo asked Flemming whether he had ever seen the Black woman sitting next to me behind the counsel table. I assumed he was merely trying to confuse the witness. Flemming answered that although he had never seen her in person, he thought he remembered seeing a news story in which her picture appeared. As it turned out, although he had insisted that he had seen no more than ten Black women as light-skinned as I, he had absolutely no recollection of having talked to Kendra in his service station.

While the lawyers were hammering away at the most important evidence of the prosecution, the sisters and brothers on the Committee stoked the fires in the streets, among the people. The more the movement for my freedom increased in numbers, strength and confidence, the more imperative it became for everyone to see it not as something exceptional but as a small part of a great fight against injustice, one bough in a solidly rooted tree of resistance. It was not only political repression, but racism, poverty, police brutality, drugs, and all the myriad ways Black, Brown, Red, Yellow and white working people are kept chained to misery and despair. And it was not only within the United States of America, but in countries like Vietnam, with the bombs falling like rain from U.S. B52's, burning and dismembering innocent children.

We wanted the culminating mass demonstration of the campaign to bring all these struggles together in a single, unified dramatization of our power. All our separate movements—political prisoners, welfare rights, national liberation, labor, women, antiwar—might generate storms here and there. But only a mighty union of them all could beget the great hurricane to topple the whole edifice of injustice.

Many other organizations joined our Committee in issuing a call for a Rally against Racism, Repression and the War, to be held at the site of my trial—San Jose, California—on the twenty-sixth of May. The bail conditions prohibited me from being present at the rally. However, I was fortunate that the people who lived across the street from the park, directly behind the podium, put their house fully at our disposal. I watched and listened to the rally from a room in their attic.

The crowd was not only impressive in its numbers—thousands came from throughout the state—but, more important, because of its composition, which was evenly divided between Black, Chicano and white. And it wasn't the usual crowd of demonstration-going politicos, particularly since so many of them came from San Jose, which knew no long tradition of radical political protest. One could sense the pulsating freshness and enthusiasm of those who felt impelled, for the first time in their lives, to add their voices to this united demand for justice.

The speakers included Richard Hatcher, the Black mayor of Gary, Indiana; Sister Mary McAllister, one of the defendants in the Harrisburg 8 Trial; Phillip de la Cruz from the United Farmworkers; Raul Ruiz representing La Raza Unida Party; Pat Sumi, who spoke on the relation between the women's movement and repression, and Franklin Alexander, speaking on behalf of our Committee.

When the speeches were over and the multicolored crowd was hoarse from screaming its approval, no one could deny that at least a spiritual victory had been won. All that was necessary now was to carefully plot our next moves and skillfully execute them, both inside the courtroom and out in the streets.

Over the last months, the lawyers—particularly Dobby and Margaret—had put together an impressive assembly of defense witnesses. We had known from the outset that we had to worry not so much about contesting the facts of the case—since there was no clear-cut factual case against me—as about the politics implied in the prosecutor's presentation. Since the prosecutor, in a last-ditch effort, had resorted to his passion theory, we were going to have to present the true picture of my involvement with the Soledad case, especially with George, and provide, for the jury, a panoramic view of my previous political involvement, particularly as it concerned political prisoners. We were in a dilemma because, while we wanted to present our witnesses, the emptiness of the prosecutor's case was so obvious that a defense was not really necessary to crack it. Harris had not proved me guilty beyond a reasonable doubt. Thus we were under no obligation whatever to prove that I was innocent.

We had several long, rather heated meetings on what the nature of the defense should be. Among the legal team and campaign leaders close to the legal situation, some felt that the prosecution was so flimsy that to present a defense would be to confer upon it a legitimacy and credibility that it could not claim on its own. I felt, at first, that we should go on with the full-blown defense we had planned, not so much because a defense was legally necessary to my particular case as because I saw it as a tremendously effective way to expose the government's repressive methods of silencing all its opponents. Perhaps the firmness with which I defended this position also had something to do with my subjective unwillingness to throw months of preparation out the window. Margaret, Dobby and I had been working together for ages, it seemed, on my testimony and the political evidence which would be presented through other witnesses.

The advocates of the "no defense" posture reminded us that throughout the trial we had been exposing these methods of repression—and there was yet the final argument in which it would all be summed up. And redirecting our attention to the trial itself, they pointed out that we had told the jury throughout that the burden of proof lay with the prosecutor—not with the defense. If the prosecutor could not prove his case "beyond a reasonable doubt," then we were not required to utter a word of defense. If we presented a defense which spanned weeks and months, the jurors might think we were afraid of something they themselves had missed during the presentation of the state's case. But on the other hand, if there were no defense at all, the jury might think we were silent because we had nothing to say in response.

After the arguments were over and the tempers had subsided, in the end we all agreed upon a third approach to the defense—a short line of witnesses with testimony that was succinct both in the factual and the political points.

The end was near. After Leo had argued the motion for a directed verdict, which Arnason predictably denied, we put on our two-and-a-half-day defense. Several comrades, a friend and a lawyer whom I had seen in San Francisco during the days prior to the Revolt, testified about my reasons for being in the Bay Area at that time. We examined the friend whose house I was visiting when I learned about the Revolt and the death of Jonathan. My roommate Tamu took the stand to give evidence about the weapons. She explained that the guns and ammunition were used by members of the Che-Lumumba Club for target practice and that the place where they were kept—in the house on 45th—was easily accessible to a whole number of sisters and brothers. Our final witness was Dr. Robert Buckout, an expert on eyewitness testimony. He described experiments and showed slides which demonstrated that people have a natural tendency to fill in details themselves about individuals and events they cannot fully remember. One experiment which seemed to impress the jury involved a white college student who walked around on a campus with a black bag on his head. As it turned out, large numbers of those who were later questioned about him were certain they had seen a Black man.

We closed our defense, Harris put several rebuttal witnesses on the stand and then made his closing argument before the jury. His confidence had eroded considerably since the opening day of the trial, and I had the feeling he just wanted to get the whole thing over with.

Leo presented the closing argument for the defense. There were moments when I became so involved in his presentation—which was eloquent and moving—that I found myself forgetting that it was *my* life at stake. He closed the argument by referring to the defense lawyers:

"We have carried on our shoulders a great responsibility. We've tried to carry that responsibility with truth and with dignity. With these last few words of mine, we are now going to transfer that responsibility from our shoulders to yours. We hope that in so doing that when you twelve people, tried and true, write the final chapter in the case of the People vs. Angela Davis, you will be able to say that you were chosen, you served, you considered and you brought back the only verdict that could comport with justice in this case. And that is a verdict of *not guilty*. I'm sure you will."

That Friday morning shortly before noon, the jury retired to the hidden room upstairs. Courtroom spectators, movement activists, press people, gathered on the grass in front of the courthouse to participate in or observe the vigil organized by the Committee. The lawn outside the courthouse was crowded with signs, children, food, dogs and games.

Horst, a journalist from the GDR who had been with the trial from the beginning, had been asking us out to lunch for weeks. Always we had to decline because we were meeting about something during lunch breaks. With the jury out, there was nothing left to meet about, so I went along to lunch with Horst, Margaret, Stephanie, Kendra, Franklin, Victoria, Rodney, Benny and Sylvia. We were still in the bar waiting to be seated when one of the waiters called me to the phone which the bartender pulled out from behind the counter.

No one said a word as I picked up the receiver. It was Fania.

"Angela. Wait a minute. The judge wants to talk to you."

"What's going on?" I asked. "What does the judge want with me?"

"I don't know any more than you. He only asked me if I knew where you were. I have to tell him you're on the line."

"It's the judge," I said in a loud whisper to the others, with my hand over the mouthpiece. We all thought the inevitable: "A verdict already!" The intervening silence was long and made me wonder whether he was coming at all.

But he finally picked up the receiver and asked, "Miss Davis? Where are you?"

Fania knew where we were. I had a funny feeling that there might have been some reason for keeping this from Judge Arnason. But why would she have called in the first place if she didn't want him to know where we were?

"We're at the Plateau Seven," I answered. "Why?"

Ignoring my question, and with a great urgency in his voice, he said, "Don't leave. Stay there until I contact you again." He switched off the conversation as abruptly as he had begun.

Before we had time to find words for our many speculations—a verdict? jury tampering? threats?—men in plain clothes, obviously policemen, slipped into the bar and planted themselves at various points in the room.

Someone tried to reduce the tension by suggesting that we order our meals. The waiter led us through a corridor, where we noticed more plainclothesmen apparently trying to be inconspicuous, into a private dining area. The room was much too large for our small group and the table appeared to have been set for a banquet—certainly not for us. Franklin, Victoria, Rodney and Benny were quite worried about our security. What if there had been a threat—and it was about to be carried out? Franklin was going to check out the restaurant floor in order to see whether anything unusual was going on, but he was stopped by a policeman who had posted himself on the other side of the door to our room.

"I *thought* there was some reason for this room," Franklin said when he returned to the table. "They've actually locked us up in here, and policemen are guarding the doors."

A few minutes later Howard came in with Lieutenant Tamm, the public relations man for the sheriff's department. Howard was out of breath. "There's been a hijacking and they think the hijackers want you to come with them."

We were all stunned. It didn't make any sense at all.

"The judge wants a meeting. Dobby and Leo are already there. You and Margaret should come with me."

Lieutenant Tamm said nothing.

Outside the Plateau Seven, two police cars were waiting. The meeting in court was brief and shed no further light on the situation. "I'm not taking you into custody, Miss Davis," Arnason said in the presence of all the attorneys, "but for your own safety, I'm asking you to stay here in the courtroom until we get this problem solved."

It had not occurred to me before that moment that they might think that I was involved in staging the hijacking. After all, if I had really wanted to leave, there were less risky ways to do it and I needn't have waited until the deliberations began.

Leo and Dobby had ascertained a few more details. According to the FBI agent, who had stationed himself there in the courthouse, a plane had been commandeered by four Black men after taking off in Seattle. Demands had been transmitted over the plane's radio. The agent said that when they landed at the San Francisco Airport, they wanted me to be at the end of the runway with $500,000 and *five* parachutes. (There were supposed to be *four* men.) I was to wear a white dress.

Fortunately, I was dressed in red. If I had happened to put on a white dress that morning, some people undoubtedly would have been convinced that I had a part in the hijacking.

Since there was no telling how long we were going to be closed up in the courtroom, Howard arranged for the family to join us.

Lieutenant Tamm came in and announced that the hijackers had plastic explosives on board and that they were threatening, if their demands were not met, to blow up the plane with its nearly one hundred passengers.

While we sat around in the courtroom, Leo and Dobby were listening, in the judge's chambers, for more developments in the hijacking. Leo came out and informed us that under no conditions would Arnason allow me to be taken to the airport. Later Dobby came over, shaking her head and smiling wryly. "You won't believe what just happened. Apparently the plane just landed at Oakland Airport. The FBI agent was on the phone, in a panic, telling someone to get the plane back into the air—all their agents are in San Francisco dressed up as airplane attendants; there's only one agent in Oakland."

It was about seven o'clock when the real story of the hijacking finally came to light. And it had absolutely nothing to do with me, white dresses or parachutes. My name, in fact, had never once been mentioned by the hijackers. There weren't even four hijackers. All these embellishments were tacked onto the story while it moved from the radio control tower through the FBI to us. We couldn't help speculating that the FBI had tried to draw me into the hijacking in order to disrupt the jury deliberations.

The San Jose *News* was on street corners all over the city, carrying the headline story HIJACKERS DEMAND ANGELA, based on the earlier erroneous FBI reports. Although the judge had ordered all televisions removed from the jurors' motel rooms, there was still no guarantee that one of them might not catch a glimpse of a headline somewhere between the courthouse and their motel rooms. If one of the jurors did see the newspaper and was influenced by it, a mistrial could be declared. We could only hope that they knew nothing.

Out of all the chaos of the first day of deliberations, there was one undisputed cause for celebration. Ms. Mary Timothy was elected forewoman of the jury. From the very beginning we had considered her as among the most honest and most objective of the jurors. During the voir dire we had been heartened to learn that her son had refused to be inducted into the U.S. Army. During the period when the bombing of Vietnam was particularly fierce, she had come to court wearing a button bearing the three-pronged peace symbol. Throughout the trial we had directed the jury's attention to the prosecutor's efforts to exploit the prevailing stereotypes about women, persistently attacking his case for its attempt to portray me as an irrational, emotion-driven female. That Ms. Timothy had been chosen to preside over the discussions indicated that members of the jury were thinking about the question of social discrimination against women. Their first active gesture as a jury was a rejection of the notion that only men are qualified to lead.

Howard had a theory about the deliberations, which we heard him expound repeatedly during the last days of the trial. If they decided to acquit, it would be a verdict which was unanimous from the start, they would stay out not more than a few hours. If they stayed out longer than a day, they would probably be out for a very long time and, in the end, would be unable to reach a decision. Friday we were so concerned about that plane en route from Seattle to San Francisco that we hardly had time to worry about the verdict. Saturday morning, Howard was saying that they would be in before lunch. So when the clerk called Moorpark Apartments to say that the judge wanted to see one of the lawyers, we thought they might be nearing a verdict. Anxious and silent, we all went down to the courthouse. But there was no verdict at hand, only a request from the jury to have some of the evidence delivered to them. However, our spirits were lifted somewhat when we noticed that the note to the judge was signed "Mary Timothy, foreMs." We took this little bit of humor as a sign that there was no out-and-out battle in progress.

Outside on the grass, the vigil was in full force. After shooing away the reporters, Victoria, Rodney and I walked through the crowd, eating sandwiches from the big basket of food, playing with the babies and thanking people for their encouragement.

Among the vigilants was Andy Montgomery, one of the San Jose Black community's leading spokesmen and an active member of the San Jose Defense Committee. It was he who had found an office and lodgings for the members of the legal staff. He had spoken on my behalf at meetings of the Black

Caucus and had gotten members of the caucus involved in the campaign. He had successfully appealed to the members of his church to join the campaign and was generally responsible for much of the local activity around the case. Friday we had promised that, in the event the jury was still deliberating, we would have dinner at his house. As it turned out, everyone who had any connection with the case at all was either inside Andy's house or outside in the street—my family, the lawyers and their families, Bettina, Kendra and Franklin, Rodney, Victoria, and members of the San Jose Committee.

The dinner at Andy's was supposed to be a respite from our purgatory of waiting. But tensions were too agonizing for quiet relaxation. When I arrived at Andy's, a double rope was turning in the middle of the street, and Margaret was jumping to screams of "Faster! Faster!" I joined her. After getting entangled in the ropes a few times, I got it and didn't want to stop. It was the way we jumped rope when as a child I spent the summer in New York. Bettina jumped, Howard, Leo, Charlene—and we even managed to persuade my father to join in. When he got started, he didn't want to stop either. A little way down the street, Benny had gotten a football game together and we shouted at the players for disrupting our rope-jumping with misthrown passes.

When the chicken and ribs, potato salad, greens and cornbread were ready, we ate as though we were celebrating the end of a long famine. No one talked very much about the trial, but the word had begun to circulate in the neighborhood that we were over at Andy's, and for the rest of the evening there was an interminable stream of visitors.

In the end, we discovered that we had played a little too hard—Kendra was the casualty of our premature celebration. During the football game she had twisted her ankle, and Franklin had to take her to the hospital for x-rays, an Ace bandage and crutches. Perhaps we had overdone it, but the tightness in my chest had almost disappeared, and worrying about Kendra's sprained ankle made us slightly less anxious about the jury's decision.

* * *

It was Sunday morning. We assumed we were at the beginning of an all-day wait, and hadn't yet bothered to check in with one another. I had spent the night at Leo and Geri's Moorpark apartment. Leo and I had gotten absorbed in our chronic debate about the weight of the mass movement in influencing the direction of the case.

All of a sudden, Howard broke into the apartment, out of breath—he had run all the way from his apartment on the other side of the complex. He simply told us that it was time to go. For an instant, I didn't even understand what "time to go" meant. The idea that the jury would reach a verdict on Sunday morning was so unlikely that I had not even bothered to get dressed. Without telling him, I had more or less accepted Howard's theory of the deliberations.

The last moments were the most agonizing of all. We had been waiting for two days while the jury deliberated, for three months while the trial unfolded, for twenty-two months since the Marin County revolt, and now we were told that we had to wait until the press assembled before we could hear the pronouncement of the verdict. In that back room where we had waited so many times for court to convene, my lawyers kept reassuring me and themselves that there was no way the verdict could be anything but Not Guilty. Besides, with the shabbiness of the case and the mass movement pushing on, there was never any question of a guilty verdict. And, in fact, we had never considered that as an alternative—it was either acquittal or hung jury. Now a hung jury could be ruled out: they had already announced that they had reached a verdict. There was, however, one possibility we were all reluctant to discuss—a compromise verdict, which, though theoretically illegal, happened all the time in jury trials where multiple charges had been lodged against defendants. But no one had said, at least not in my presence, "The only thing we really have to worry about is an acquittal on the murder and kidnapping counts and a conviction on the conspiracy."

Leo tried to cut away some of the tension by pointing out that we would know the moment the jury entered the courtroom: the expressions on their faces—especially Ms. Timothy's and Mr. Delange's—would betray the decision they had reached. Of course, none of this helped very much. The suspense, the anxiety—all this was beyond remedy. I couldn't sit down for more than a minute without jumping up to pace off some of the strain. And when I began to pace, I had to sit down again, for the room was far too small to contain my energy. I could only clench my teeth and dig my fingernails deep into my palms. Margaret kept telling me that all we had to do was to keep cool for a few minutes more; everything would soon be behind us. Kendra was fighting hard to keep herself together.

When we went into the courtroom area, people were crowded into the corridor, but apparently members of the press still hadn't arrived; and we had to wait some more. Out in the corridor Mother insisted that she wanted to wait outside while the verdict was announced. As I tried to calm her and reassure her that I would soon be free, my own strength and my own confidence began to return.

Somewhere in the corridor crowd, a voice began to hum softly—a Negro spiritual. Someone else picked up the tune, adding the words "Woke up this morning with my mind staid on freedom." Before long everyone, including my mother, had joined in. Captain Johnson, who had been the terror of both the press and the people attending the trial, walked out, looked around, and for the first time that anyone could remember, said nothing to object.

At last we took our places in the courtroom. Howard, Dobby and Leo sat at the table, and I sat against the barrier with Margaret on one side and Kendra on the other. The bailiff announced the entrance of the judge. Within minutes the jury began to walk through the door. At the sight of the first juror, Margaret, who had been the calmest of us all, let out a muffled "Oh no," and slid down into her chair. I leaned over and gave her the same words of comfort she had given me. She sobbed softly.

I looked at the jurors filing in, searching for reassuring signs in their faces. But they were all expressionless, as if they had purged themselves of every trace of emotion. I broke out in a sweat and felt my whole body go weak. There was not a hint of the usual warmth in Ms. Timothy's face, which was cold and marble-like, and the sparkle in Delange's eyes had turned into a dull stare directed at no one in particular. Like a fragment from a broken record, Leo's words roared through my brain. "We'll know immediately what the verdict is, from the expressions on their faces."

During the judicial ritual preceding the reading of the verdict, I was searching for some explanation of this sudden transformation of the jury's posture. Their faces said "Conviction." "Guilty." But this was impossible, illogical, absurd. Unless the whole thing had been a grand hoax. Unless they had consciously tried to delude us these last months, and these glacial stares were the reality behind the masks they had finally shedded. I wanted to rush over and rescue my mother from the consequences. Born of desperation and incomprehension, these disjointed thoughts shook me so furiously that I had to strain to hear the clerk as he read the papers Ms. Timothy had turned over to the court.

The first count was murder. There was a loud, clear "Not Guilty." Heavy sobs fell into the moment of silence that followed. It was Franklin. It felt like everyone was breathing deep and hard and with the rhythm of a single being. The second count was kidnapping. "Not Guilty" rang out again. Franklin was crying louder. I did not think I could hold on much longer. But I had to hear the last verdict, the conspiracy count. My right hand tightened around Kendra's, the other around Margaret's.

When the clerk read off "Not Guilty" for the third time, we screamed, laughed, cried and embraced—completely oblivious to the banging of the judge's gavel. He wanted to close the trial with the same decorum with which he had presided. He read a rather long quote from *Twelve Men* by G. K. Chesterton, congratulated defense, prosecution and jury, dismissed the last from their duties and declared case number 52613, People of California vs. Angela Y. Davis, closed.

In her joy, my mother looked so beautiful she reminded me of the photographs of her when she was very young. I felt happier for her than for anyone else, including myself.

The last thing I felt like was a press conference—I didn't feel like structuring my thoughts and emotions in order to articulate them before cameras and microphones—yet it was the only way I could speak to and thank all the people. As we entered the pressroom, the members of the jury were just concluding their conference. Never having exchanged a word with any of them, I was not sure how to relate to them. I stood at the door. The juror to leave the platform first was the one whom we had all thought was most sympathetic to the prosecution. I wondered what her reaction would be. When she approached, I extended one hand, but she reached out with both her arms, hugged me and said, "I am so happy for you." All the other jurors followed her example.

A crowd had assembled in front of the courthouse. As soon as they heard the verdict, people had rushed down to the Civic Center. With the gag rule and the bail restrictions behind us, I could speak before a crowd for the first time in the twenty-two months since the revolt. I thanked them for coming, for all their support, and said that it was time to deploy our forces for the freedom of Ruchell, the San Quentin 6 and all other political prisoners.

From the courthouse we went over to Gloria and David's house, where my parents had been staying. Family, lawyers, friends, comrades, Committee workers, and most of the jurors —we all sat in the sun on the grass in the backyard. I sank deep into the moment, husbanding this delight, hoarding it. For I knew it would be short-lived. Work. Struggle. Confrontation lay before us like a rock-strewn road. We would walk it . . .

But first the grass, the sun . . . and the people.

Epilogue

At the victory party the evening of the verdict, our joy knew no bounds and our celebration no restraints. Yet in the echoes of our laughter and the frenzy of our dancing there was also caution. If we saw this moment of triumph as a conclusion and not as a point of departure, we would be ignoring all the others who remained draped in chains. We knew that to save their lives, we had to preserve and build upon the movement.

This was the concern of the NUCFAD staff meeting called by Charlene on Monday evening, the very day after the acquittal. Fearing that some local committees might consider their mission accomplished, we decided to send out immediately a communique requesting that they all keep their operations alive. To ensure that this message filtered down to the masses, we decided that I would go on a speaking tour. While expressing our gratitude to the people who had joined the movement which achieved my freedom, I would appeal to them to stay with us as long as racism or political repression kept Ruchell, Fleeta, the Attica brothers or any other human being behind bars.

My freedom was not yet a week old when I left with Kendra, Franklin and Rodney for Los Angeles. From there we went to Chicago and on to Detroit, where close to 10,000 people attended the rally. In New York I spoke at the fund-raising concert at Madison Square Garden, which had been organized months earlier by our Legal Defense Fund.

An enormous political responsibility had been thrust upon me—and I was more frightened than I had ever been in my life because I knew that human lives were at stake. Our ability to keep the movement alive offered the only hope to our sisters and brothers behind walls. In the mass meetings, attended by predominantly Black people, I explained that my presence before them signified nothing more and nothing less than the tremendous power of united, organized people to transform their will into reality. Many others also deserved to be the beneficiaries of their power.

I went on to Dallas and Atlanta and, after spending some time with my family in Birmingham, prepared to make a month-long tour abroad. The international campaign had not only exerted serious pressure on the government, it had also stimulated the further growth of the mass movement at home. At the center of the international movement was the socialist community of nations. It was for this reason that we decided to visit the USSR, including Central Asia, the German Democratic Republic, Bulgaria, Czechoslovakia and Cuba. The last stop was to be Chile.

We saw the trip as a natural continuation of the tour through the United States, its foremost purpose being to thank the people who had contributed to the fight for my freedom and to turn their attention to other political prisoners. In those countries rallies were attended by more people than I had ever before seen assembled in one place—hundreds of thousands, for example in the GDR, and close to three-quarters of a million in Cuba. In Havana I mentioned the case of Billy Dean Smith in my speech, a Black G.I. antiwar activist charged with the murder of two white U. S. officers in Vietnam. When the Prime Minister, Fidel Castro, delivered his speech, he vowed on behalf of the Cuban people that as they had fought for my liberation, they would raise their voices now for the freedom of Billy Dean Smith. By the next morning, as if by magic, the walls of Havana were covered with posters demanding that Billy Dean Smith be set free. As we traveled up and down the island, children who had painted pictures and composed songs about Billy Dean wanted to be sure we were going to save their *hermano*.

Here at home, work was already under way to strengthen the united front which could save Billy Dean and eventually all political prisoners. Immediately, I began another tour of campuses and communities to publicize, raise funds for and gather information about political prisoners for the organization we were building

Today, a year and a half later, we have consolidated the National Alliance Against Racist and Political Repression, which has chapters in twenty-one states. Our membership consists of Black, Chicano, Puerto Rican, Asian, Indian and white people. We are proud that we have been able to forge unity among Communists, Socialists, radical Democrats, and nationalists; between ministers and non-churchgoers; between workers and students. All of us understand that unity is the most potent weapon against racism and political persecution. As I write this epilogue, we are preparing to take thousands of people to North Carolina on July 4 for a national demonstration. For we must ensure that the Black leader Reverend Ben Chavis is not sentenced to the 262 years in prison on the charges which that state has leveled against him. We must liberate Donald Smith, sentenced at age sixteen to forty years behind bars because he participated in the movement at his high school. And we must rescue our innocent sister Marie Hill, whose death sentence, pronounced when she was sixteen, is now a sentence of living death—life without possibility of parole.

Across this country, there are hundreds and thousands more like Reverend Chavis, Donald Smith and Marie Hill. We —you and I—are their only hope for life and freedom.

June 21, 1974

ABOUT THE AUTHOR

Angela Yvonne Davis was born in Birmingham, Alabama, in 1944. She attended Birmingham public schools until she left to attend Elisabeth Irwin High School in New York. She then went to Brandeis University and spent her junior year in France. After graduating with honors from Brandeis, she went to Frankfurt, Germany, to study philosophy and then returned to UCLA in California, where she taught in the Philosophy Department. She has been politically active since then